China

Internal Market Development and Regulation

The World Bank
Washington, D.C.

World Bank Country Studies are among the many reports originally prepared for internal use as part of the continuing analysis by the Bank of the economic and related conditions of its developing member countries and of its dialogues with the governments. Some of the reports are published in this series with the least possible delay for the use of governments and the academic, business and financial, and development communities. The typescript of this paper therefore has not been prepared in accordance with the procedures appropriate to formal printed texts, and the World Bank accepts no responsibility for errors. Some sources cited in this paper may be informal documents that are not readily available.

The complete backlist of publications from the World Bank is shown in the annual *Index of Publications*, which contains an alphabetical title list (with full ordering information) and indexes of subjects, authors, and countries and regions. The latest edition is available free of charge from the Distribution Unit, Office of the Publisher, The World Bank, 1818 H Street, N.W., Washington, D.C. 20433, U.S.A., or from Publications, The World Bank, 66, avenue d'Iéna, 75116 Paris, France.

ISSN: 0-0253-2123

Library of Congress Cataloging-in-Publication Data

Kumar, Anjali.
    China : internal market development and regulation.
        p. cm. — (A World Bank country study)
    "The World Bank team consisted of Anjali Kumar (team manager and
principle author of this report)."
    Includes bibliographical references.
    ISBN 0-8213-3047-0
    1. China—Economic policy—1976- 2. Prices—Goverment policy-
-China. 3. Marketing—China. 4. Commodity exchanges—China.
5. Trade regulation—China. I. Title II. Series.
HC427.92.K8346   1994
  338.951— dc20   94-33497
                                 CIP

CONTENTS

Tables in Text

Figures in Text

Statistical Appendix

CURRENCY EQUIVALENTS

Currency Unit: Yuan (Y)

(Nominal Official Period Average Rates)

Year	Yuan (Y) per US$
1994*	8.70
1993	5.76
1992	5.52
1991	5.32
1990	4.78
1989	3.77
1988	3.72
1987	3.72
1986	3.45
1985	2.94
1984	2.32
1983	1.98
1982	1.89
1981	1.70
1980	1.50
1979	1.56
1978	1.68

* January to March

FISCAL YEAR

January 1 - December 31

WEIGHTS AND MEASURES

Metric System

ACRONYMS AND ABBREVIATIONS

ASEAN	Association of South-East Asian Nations
CASS	Chinese Academy of Social Sciences
CESRRI	China Economic Systems Reform Research Institute
CFA	Communauté Financière Africaine
CFMC	Commodities Futures Management Commission
CFTC	Commodities Futures Trading Commission
CNCC	China National Coal Corporation
CNFMGC	China Non-Ferrous Metals General Corporation
COV	Covariance
DRC	Development Research Council
EC	European Community
ECU	European Currency Unit
ETDZ	Economic and Technical Development Zones
FEAC	Foreign Exchange Adjustment Centers
FIMBRA	Financial Intermediaries', Managers' and Brokers' Regulatory Association
FSU	Former Soviet Union
FTC	Foreign Trade Corporation
GITIC	Guangdong International Trust and Investment Center
GDP	Gross Domestic Product
GNP	Gross National Product
GPAIC	Guangdong Province Administration of Industry and Commerce
GVIO	Gross Value of Industrial Output
GVO	Gross Value of Output
LAUTRO	Life Assurance and Unit Trust Regulatory Organization
LME	London Metal Exchange
MME	Ministry of Materials and Equipment
MOC	Ministry of Commerce
MOFTEC	Ministry of Foreign Trade and Economic Cooperation
NAFTA	North American Free Trade Association
NTHS	National Trunk Highway System
OEC	Office of Economic Cooperation
SAIC	State Administration of Industry and Commerce
SCETO	State Council Economic and Trade Office
SCRES	State Commission for the Restructuring of the Economic System
SEZ	Special Economic Zone
SHME	Shanghai Metals Exchange
SIB	Securities and Investments Board
SME	Shenzhen Metals Exchange
SOEs	State Owned Enterprises
SPC	State Planning Commission
SRO	Self-Regulatory Organizations
STICERD	Suntory-Toyota International Center for Economics and Related Disciplines
TVE	Township and Village Enterprises
UK	United Kingdom
USA	United States of America

CONTRIBUTORS

This report and its annexes are based on the findings of a preparatory visit to China in November 1992, followed by a full-fledged investigative study during March 1993 in China, jointly undertaken by the World Bank, the Ministry of Materials and Equipment, and the State Administration of Industry and Commerce, Government of China. In addition to discussions in Beijing, the team visited Shenyang (Liaoning Province), Shanghai Municipality, Suzhou, Wuxi (Jiangsu Province) and Shenzhen (Guangdong Province). Excellent support was provided at each location visited by the local departments of the Ministry of Materials as well as the State Administration of Industry and Commerce.

The World Bank team consisted of Anjali Kumar (team manager and principal author of this report), Wang Yuan (task coordinator from the Beijing Office of the World Bank), Mark Dutz (competition policy), James Fry (commodities and futures markets), Lawrence Wortzel (distribution systems) and Jun Ma (capital mobility, data base). Jun Ma also provided able research assistance in Washington and Cathy Song helped with document preparation. The Chinese team consisted of Wu Baozhong (task leader from the Ministry of Materials and Equipment), Zhao Jie, Wang Erling, Li Chenghuai, Qi Xiaojie and Shi Chunling and Xu Su (MME). Wang Baotong from the SAIC also accompanied the team on its field visits. Background papers for this study were prepared by a team led by Tao Fei of the Chinese Academy of Social Sciences; by the Ministry of Materials and by the Development Research Council. The team extends its gratitude and appreciation to all the officials from the various government agencies, distribution companies and enterprises with whom it met.

Executive Summary

A. An Overview

China's commitment to the creation of a market economy received new emphasis in the recent 8th National People's Congress of March 1993. The congress ratified the decision taken at the 14th Party Congress of October 1992, to develop a 'socialist market economy', shifting decisively away from central planning. The Constitution of 1982 was amended to emphasize this shift.

The development of the internal market was fostered by a series of mechanisms intended to reduce the scope of state intervention:

(1)   Progressive price decontrol was first introduced through three categories of prices (planned, guidance and market prices) and the gradual movement of goods from more regulated to less regulated categories. The 'dual track' pricing, introduced in 1985, permitted output above certain target levels to be sold on the free market. The proportion of goods in total domestic retail trade subject to planned prices fell dramatically between 1978 and 1991, in favor of 'guidance prices' and free market prices. Goods subject to planned prices have fallen considerably further, with recent announcements in early 1993 of the relaxation of controls on prices of grain and edible oils.

(2)   The allocation of goods moved progressively out of the mandatory plan. In 1980, 90 percent of industrial goods and 837 production materials were allocated under the plan system. By 1993, the proportion of industrial goods under the plan had declined to less than 10 percent and the number of production materials under the plan administered by the Ministry of Materials and Equipment was reduced to 13. At the same time, consumer goods administered by the Ministry of Commerce declined in number from 274 in 1978 to 14 in 1993.

(3)   Distribution systems and channels gradually expanded. Formerly, the system of unified purchase and sale of consumer manufactures, and the unified purchase of farm products, by designated government agencies, accounted for virtually all sales. Sales may now be made to private purchasing agencies or directly to consumers. New 'comprehensive' and 'specialized' distribution agencies have sprung up. Sales undertaken by government agencies have also diversified in form and function, and state-owned distribution agencies are providing new forms of services.

(4)   Sophisticated forms of commodities markets for many agricultural products and industrial raw materials have been established. Today there are 21 centrally sponsored commodities exchanges in China, many of which are equipped with advanced computer technology and newly constructed modern trading facilities.

(5)   In conjunction with these policy and real side adjustments, the government has drawn up a major program of legislative change for establishing a framework for a market economy.

Over the last decade, China has made remarkable strides towards the establishment of a market economy. But the progress achieved so far has been uneven. This report evaluates the extent to which China, through the adoption of the measures described above, has been able to establish well-functioning markets. Well-functioning markets imply markets which transmit accurate signals to economic agents in terms of production decisions and factor allocation. The report distinguishes between the regional or spatial aspect of market functioning, and the movement from plan to market. Following a policy evaluation, the report analyzes the new systems for allocating and distributing goods that have evolved in the aftermath of planning. The report also discusses present regulation of markets in the changing environment.

B. Main Findings

There are large potential benefits in achieving well-functioning and regionally integrated internal markets and other countries have achieved greater market integration through systematic and deliberate policies (Chapter 1, para 1.21 to 1.30). The report examines China's present industrial structure and demonstrates that **the composition of output has remained remarkably static despite shifts in the ownership of industrial output** (para 1.33). The cross-section structure of industrial output by region shows that each major industrial group is located in virtually all provinces. Firm size is also remarkably similar across provinces.

To assess the extent to which China could gain from greater integration of its domestic market, the report compares China and other large regional markets. Subject to the caveats that apply to international comparisons with the EC and the US, the findings suggest that regional differences in China appear relatively small, and there is little evidence of industrial specialization or a well-integrated structure (para 1.37 and Annex 1.1). Relative to other countries, **China is far from realizing the benefits of its potentially large internal market.** As a consequence of its relatively 'cellular'economic structure, many benefits, such as scale economies in plant size and the spreading of overheads in management, technology and learning, communications and infrastructure, associated with the development of industrial 'clusters', have yet to be exploited.

To promote regional trade and specialization, **mechanisms for the redistribution of benefits among the various regions are needed.** Today with the marked relative decline in the proportion of total revenue accruing to the central government, the scope for such redistributive mechanisms is limited. Options for such mechanisms are discussed (Chapter 1, para 1.27 and Chapter 6, para 6.21).

Using a series of measures of price behavior, an analysis shows that **there has been a significant convergence between plan and market prices** (Chapter 2, para 2.8 to 2.10). Recent price reforms in early 1993 have consolidated and extended the progress achieved with the dual track system. This shows that China has achieved notable success in replacing the allocative mechanisms of the planning regime with allocation through the market. The reduction in the proportion of goods allocated through the plan, as well as the increase in the proportion of goods subject to market prices, has been remarkable.

Progress is less evident in the regional integration of China's markets. Despite the rapid decline in the number and level of price controls, there are still persistent **regional** price differentials among both producer and consumer goods (para 2.12 to 2.16). Price convergence across regions has been slower and more erratic than convergence between plan and market prices, for specific products. Some divergence in regional prices may have emerged as a consequence of the lifting of price controls and the reflection of real costs of transport in prices. But eventual price convergence (with transport cost adjusted differentials) would still be expected. The present differentials suggest spatial segmentation of the internal market.

An analysis of domestic **interprovincial trade in goods** indicates that although this has increased in absolute terms, the share of trade flows across provinces, relative to total retail trade, has declined in many provinces, and on aggregate for the country as a whole (para 2.17 to 2.30). These declines have occurred at the same time as the shares of external trade, and inflows of external investment, have increased in most provinces. From 1985 to 1992, overseas exports and imports grew at 17 and 10 percent per year, respectively. While domestic interprovincial trade also rose in absolute terms, its rate of growth at 4.8 percent per year was low relative to foreign trade and also lower than the 9 percent annual rate of growth of total retail sales. The findings suggest that individual provinces are tending to behave like independent countries, with an increase in external (overseas) trade and a relative decline in trade flows with each other.

A part of the relative decline in internal trade could be ascribed to the reduction in the forced movement of goods under planning. Another explanation is that the partial deregulation of the output and selling price of some goods led to incentives to evade public procurement, over 1985 to 1988, in the period of the interprovincial 'trade wars'. Provincial authorities responded with the erection of export embargoes. With further relaxations in price and quantity controls, as well as the decline in the short-lived demand boom, export embargoes became less significant.

The downward trend in interprovincial trade, relative to output, continuing until the present, cannot be explained only by these considerations and requires other explanations. Some relative reduction may be due to an increase in **intra**provincial production as well as consumption, due to the rapid growth in township and village enterprises. Problems of numerous fees and fines, extracted on the road, legal as well as illegal are also an explanation. The absence of overarching regulations on interprovincial trade implies that decisions which may limit trade made at the provincial, or lower levels, cannot be easily overturned. Difficulties of transportation by road as well as by rail also hinder the domestic flow of goods. Transport facilities have not grown as fast as output. Ministerial and jurisdictional barriers have aggravated spatial segmentation. Difficulties encountered in interprovincial payments and settlement mechanisms have also segmented the internal market. Administrative market segmentation, due to sectoral barriers between departments, also remains.

Cross-provincial investment flows have declined in relative terms (compared to the share of foreign investments, and relative to provincial GDP) over 1985 to 1992 (para 2.55 to 2.60). The fiscal system, and the incentives and authority given to provincial and local governments to raise revenues, provide partial explanations. The separation of profits and taxes was accompanied by the introduction of profit retention, as well as an increase in local authorities' taxation powers. It is therefore to the advantage of local governments to retain enterprises within their jurisdictions. Incentives for interprovincial investment are also confused by the large number of special investment zones, with many authorized or unauthorized tax concessions.

Some progress is observed in **labor mobility** in terms of increased flexibility in the hiring and dismissal of labor in state enterprises, and in determining wages and bonuses. There is less progress in the regional mobility of labor, despite the recent relaxation of urban grain rationing in several locations (para 2.75 to 2.89).

Foreign exchange had been constrained in its mobility across regions, as regional differentials in swap markets indicated. Recent changes, introduced on January 1, 1994, indicate considerable improvement in the flexibility of access to foreign exchange, as well as simplification of the trade and exchange control regime. How the new system will operate in practice can only be determined after it has been in place for some months. **In conclusion, there has been considerable progress in the substitution of planned allocation by the price mechanism. Yet, markets for both goods and factors of production still show signs of regional fragmentation.**

The withdrawal of the state from allocation and pricing decisions was not accompanied by a parallel withdrawal of the state from **distribution** (Chapter 3, para 3.6 to 3.12). The share of the state sector (excluding collectives) in distribution, as measured by both the value of retail trade and the number of distribution units increased in absolute terms over the last decade. While there was a relative decline in the state's share over the early years of the reform (1978 to 1985), there was little perceptible change from 1985 to 1991.

Yet, in aggregate, retail trade grew and the level of retail trade services now available puts China above the former Soviet Union, though still below Western Europe (Table 3.3). Innovative changes have also occurred in the distribution system, in response to other changes in market mechanisms. They illustrate that the state sector has been able to respond to competitive stimuli and that changes in operation are being effected despite relatively gradual changes in ownership. The combined requirements of capital-intensive infrastructure and the need to build information networks across large regions and many entities may make it more difficult for the non-state sector to enter the business of distribution, relative to production.

While the evolution of new forms of distribution in China has been in the right direction, there is scope for better management of distribution functions of existing warehouse facilities, improved inventory management, delivery scheduling and the development of backchannels for the recycling of used materials (Annex 3.1).

In terms of the organization of the distribution of producer goods, some enterprises under the leadership of material and equipment bureaus and their sponsor, the former Ministry of Materials and Equipment (now a part of the Ministry of Internal Trade) are involved in a wide range of activities, including industry, real estate and construction. This diversification has been in part a response to poor profitability from their main task of distribution, due to price controls and allocative obligations. The structure of many materials bureaus results from the takeover of the marketing and distribution functions of some production bureaus, with agreements to maintain their structures intact. The frequently encountered grouping of ten to twelve enterprises has now developed variations in some areas and further flexbility is encouraged to adapt to local industrial needs.

Some of the warehouses owned by the materials bureaus are old, with inadequate protection against the elements, leading to spoilage and damage in storage. The location of the new facilities at the sites of existing storage centers is not optimal. Many warehouses today are located in urban areas where land is scarce and expensive in terms of its opportunity cost. The present level of mechanization of materials handling and computerization of order placement and inventory management is very limited. Due to a variety of causes, which may include internal management and administration as well as market conditions, the financial condition of some materials bureaus is reported to be precarious and should be analyzed.

Difficulties caused by trade barriers and distribution problems are compounded by real **bottlenecks in transport** (para 3.52 to 3.66). The demand for 200 million tons of freight (around 10 percent of freight capacity) was estimated to be unsatisfied in 1989. China's rate of investment in transport, at around 1.3 percent of GNP, compares unfavorably with other developing country ratios, of 2 to 3.8 percent of GNP (para 3.57). Producer goods depend largely on the **railroad system,** that suffered from underinvestment due to limited revenues resulting from low passenger and freight tariffs. Recent successive raises in tariffs are expected to improve the profitability of the system. The assignment of freight quotas to specific producers or users also distorted the prices of commodities requiring rail freight.

On **road transportation**, the regulation and administration of the trucking business is an issue of concern. Although the entry of new operators of trucking services has grown easier, and pricing has become more flexible since 1983, there is still overlap in the functions of the multiple agencies whose permits are required for licensing and registration (the local Transportation Bureaus as well as the Public Security Office). There are also constraints on the time period and permitted uses of 'own account' trucks. Deregulation of trucking tariffs has taken the form of 'decentralized regulation', with the transfer of the authority for setting tariffs to the local Departments of Communications. Consequently, there are now wide regional variations in tariffs.

The development of trucking operations is constrained by the lack of freight forwarding and consolidation centers and the limited development of intermodal transportation systems. Such systems require the development of containerized shipping, which China is now beginning to explore.

A remarkable number of **commodities exchanges** have been established in the last two to three years, in grain, non-ferrous metals, petrochemicals, and agricultural commodities such as rubber and sugar (Chapter 4). A new framework of supervision for the new exchanges was announced on November 4, 1993. The registration of exchanges remains the responsibility of the State Administration of Industry and Commerce, but the responsibility for their supervision has been assigned to the State Council Securities Commission. Day to day administration of such supervision will be entrusted to the China Security Supervision and Administration Committee. After scrutiny by this body, all exchanges will be re-registered with the SAIC. There have been wide differences in the operating rules of the various exchanges. Some regulations (concerning margin deposits and fees) have been at inappropriate levels. Essential elements of commodities market regulations (such as Fidelity funds) did not exist. It is hoped that under the new framework these difficulties will be resolved.

Continued intervention in activities related to the exchange of commodities, such as setting price ceilings or floors (as in the case of the Zhengzhou grain center), warehousing (through the provision of differential subsidies, in the metals trade) raises the risk of either undermining the price uncertainty on which such exchanges depend, or raising the pressure to continually increase government subsidies, as subsidies are transferred through arbitrage to all market participants. The recent operation of the commodity exchanges emphasizes the possibility of 'proxy markets' arising in cases where continued government intervention persists.

The most striking example provided here of the effects of controls in one market on the rest of the economy is the case of foreign exchange speculation through trade on the metals exchanges. If exporters and importers do not have free access to foreign currencies, and there are markets which deal in forward and futures contracts for internationally tradable commodities, these markets will reflect expected movements in the foreign exchange rate. Hedging or speculative transactions in foreign exchange become part of the *raison-d'etre* of such exchanges. The large and growing volume of trade on the exchanges suggests that the foreign exchange market is more constrained today than apparent, and price signals are consequently distorted (para 4.44 to 4.49).

A key issue which China must confront in its experiments with new market forms, and specifically in the area of establishing commodities markets, is that the present large numbers of such exchanges will probably diminish over time due to a number of factors; the improvement in internal communications, closer integration with the world economy and consequently closer links with exchanges outside the country. Speculative activity will fall as the 'zero-sum' nature of such trade is better understood. The establishment of independent markets, especially in foreign exchange, will hasten this process. There is a likelihood of waste in the establishment of several new exchanges, especially in view of the presently preferred capital-intensive methods of screen-trading which is an expensive option to adopt in the initial stages of an exchange.

There is room to improve the efficiency and reduce the cost of trading practices (para 4.33 to 4.40). The Metals Exchange at Shanghai is a fully computerized screen based system, where the existence of a trading floor is redundant. The Shenzhen exchange is a combination of an 'open outcry' system, with a large central screen recording bids and buys. In both cases, a simple open outcry ring dealing system may have been preferable on cost grounds. The computerized information entry requirements slow the trading process and will become a hindrance as the pace of trading accelerates. It also impedes the growth of trade by 'market makers', trading on their own account and providing essential liquidity to the system. While cultural reticence may be a factor against the adoption of 'open outcry', its cost advantages for a newly-established should also be considered. In the future, once exchanges are well-established, they could evolve towards more expensive screen-based trading.

China is aware of the **need to safeguard competition** and develop regulations for competitive markets. A law on competition was approved in September 1993, and a new law on consumer protection has also been adopted. Laws to safeguard market competition through the protection of patents and trademarks were approved earlier. The problem of monopoly in China is not pervasive, unlike many other transforming socialist countries. Consequently, the emphasis should be on market 'conduct' issues, such as the the control of unfair trading practices rather than market 'structure' issues, such as enterprise size, or mergers and acquisitions. China is today experimenting with the fostering of links between enterprises and the formation of enterprise groups and some of the experiments are likely to increase operational efficiency, and facilitate interregional investments (5.13 to 5.27).

Procedures for establishing new enterprises are still onerous (para 5.35 to 5.46). Many different agencies' permits are required and a large discretionary role is given to some agencies, such as the State Administration for Industry and Commerce (SAIC). The role of the SAIC has expanded enormously over the last few years and it may be undertaking the work entrusted to several different agencies in market economies (including licensing new establishments, safeguarding competition and registering new commodity exchanges).

A large agenda for legal reform is now under preparation as part of the Five-Year Plan for economic legislation. Many different agencies will tackle different aspects of reform, and the process could be slow, especially in view of the need for drafting assistance required by some of the agencies concerned. The World Bank has offered assistance to the Chinese government in this process of legal reform through an Economic Law Reform Project which is currently under preparation.

C. Recommendations

Key recommendations to help China accelerate its movement towards the adoption of well-functioning internal markets and an integrated domestic economy are presented below. These are grouped under four broad heads: (1) increased market integration through trade, price and factor mobility; (2) enhanced efficiency in distribution; (3) better functioning of new markets; and (4) a more appropriate regulatory framework.

Market Integration

China's authorities should **lift residual controls on prices.** So far, they have emphasized the prices, or allocation, of goods. They must now achieve further progress with the decontrol of the prices of both critical consumer goods and producer goods still subject to the Plan and then move towards price and quantity restraints on services and on factors of production.

Concerning regional trade policies and the **integration of regional markets:**

(1)   China must establish a general framework of legislation on interregional trade and prohibit trade barriers, such as internal 'export' embargoes or 'import' restraints;

(2)   The myriad fees and fines levied on interstate (and intercounty) trade must be harmonized across provinces. A nationwide standardized list of genuine charges should be prepared. The transparency of the procedure followed in each local jurisdiction can be improved through the collection and periodic publication of schedules of tariffs, taxes and other charges, at a provincial or national level;

(3)   Authorities should standardize the collection agencies for fees and publish details of persons or agencies responsible for collection; and

(4)   Once a list of genuine fees is established, authorities must stop the collection of illegal charges.

In the context of **capital mobility** and interprovincial investments, the government should:

(1)   Continue and extend the separation of profits and taxes;

(2)   Reduce the incentives to provincial or lower level authorities to restrict the transfer of enterprises to other locations through the stricter enforcement of the rule of tax accrual to the home province. Establish an appropriate monitoring system for this; and

(3)   Stop the legal and illegal circumventions of the interstate income tax regulation resulting from the establishment of special 'zones'. While many illicit zones have recently been removed, the 200-odd which have been permitted to remain are still a non-negligible number.

To ensure the equitable distribution of the benefits of the gains from increased internal trade and factor mobility, the government should consider the establishment of an appropriate **redistributive or compensation mechanism**. Alternative mechanisms include the European Community's Structural Funds, or the fund suggested in the Bank's recent Budgetary Expenditure study (see Chapter 6).

Attention should be turned towards regulations which permit an increase in the regional **mobility of labor**. One important reason for restricting labor mobility in the past was urban grain rationing. Some rations have been lifted in early 1993, and many price controls on consumer essentials such as grain and edible oils. This is an appropriate moment to begin to lift restraints on labor mobility.

In the context of the recently **unified exchange rate**, care should be taken to ensure **free access to foreign exchange by exporters and importers** through the banking system. Besides the wider implications for efficiency this should increase foreign exchange mobility and also permit the new commodities markets to fulfil their primary function.

Distribution Systems

While the evolution of new forms of distribution in China have been in the right direction, there are still shortfalls compared to best practice in market economies. A detailed study of current distribution practices should be undertaken, to investigate the scope for better management of distribution functions of existing warehouse facilities, through (i) the reduction of partly-loaded truck shipments; (ii) the reduction of the number of times goods are handled or moved; (iii) improved inventory management through more reliable shipping from producers and timely information from users; (iv) better physical management of warehouse space by arranging goods on a computerized customer order in the order in which they will be picked up from warehouse shelves; (v) the introduction of 'cross docking' practices to permit vehicles bringing in supplies to be transferred directly to delivery vehicles to purchasers, and (vi) the development of backchannels for the recycling of used materials.

Concerning the range of operations of the former MME and the organization of materials bureaus, China should:

(1)   Accord greater flexibility to the MME in their primary activities, in terms of the procurement, pricing and distribution of the goods they carry, through the accelerated lifting of price controls and allocation obligations on these activities;

(2)   Discourage the branching out of materials bureaus into unrelated activities where they are speculative in nature, such as real estate purchase or construction;

(3)   Permit the present twelve-enterprise structure to be more flexible and better adapted to the needs of local industry; and

(4)   Encourage value-adding activities at the materials bureaus, to provide additional quality or convenience for buyers. But research on products distributed may be better integrated with production enterprises than with distribution enterprises.

Actions to increase future competition through new entrants are also required. Local bureaus should be permitted and encouraged to expand into other localities, and entry into distribution by individuals and collectives could also be encouraged, for example by permitting them to lease warehouse space from government bureaus.

Detailed studies of the physical facilities of the distribution system are recommended. The costs and benefits of investing in improved facilities must be evaluated. The evaluation should examine the potential location of any proposed new facilities, as well as the relocation of existing urban warehouses to points outside major cities. The study should also appraise the costs and benefits of the mechanization of materials handling and the computerization of order placement and inventory management.

A study of the financial condition of the materials bureaus and an estimation of the extent to which the decline in profitability of the materials bureaus is due to losses made on goods which remain under planned allocation should be undertaken. The expected improvement in profitablity at materials bureaus, with recent reductions in the number of goods under planned allocation or controlled prices, should then be calculated. The examination of the profitability of the materials distribution system should also include an evaluation of cash-flow and inventory management, and should be launched as an exercise which combines marketing as well as financial expertise. Since the last major round of price decontrols has just been concluded, this is an appropriate time to begin such an undertaking.

Detailed recommendations on transport are available in other reports. This report points to some key issues affecting distributional efficiency. Regarding **railways**, the government should:

(1)   Undertake successive increases in railway tariffs, to their long run marginal cost levels, to improve profitability and ensure that decisions on industrial location are based on the right parameters; and

(2)   Phase out the assignment of freight quotas to specific producers or users, to avoid distortions in the prices of commodities requiring rail freight.

On the regulation and administration of the **trucking** business, China should:

(1)   Remove the overlap in some of the functions of the multiple agencies whose permits are required for licensing and registration (the local Transportation Bureaus as well as the Public Security Office);

(2)   Gradually remove constraints on the time period, and permitted uses, of 'own account' trucks;

(3)   Deregulate altogether the 'decentralized regulation', of trucking tariffs (which has led to the transfer of the authority for setting tariffs to the local Departments of Communications, and consequent wide regional variations in tariffs);

(4)   Develop freight forwarding and consolidation centers to encourage 'own account' truckers by serving as collection points for goods shipped in less-than-truckload quantities; and

(5)   Further promote the development of containerized shipping to facilitiate intermodal transportation systems.

New Markets

A **first** concern in this area is completion of the overall framework of supervision for the new exchanges, to be adopted by the new CFMC. The new legislation should take into consideration alternative approaches to the regulation of commodities exchanges, presented in the report (pp 109). **Second**, once the umbrella legislation is in place, the task of reconciling the differences in operating rules of different exchanges must be undertaken. Areas of the present legislation which require attention are: the nature of the supervisory Board, the regulations on participation, on transaction fees, and margin deposits. The establishment of provisions for a Fidelity Fund (for protection against default by brokers) is also recommended. **Third**, the role of the SAIC, as the body best suited to handle the registration of new exchanges, should be reevaluated. The SAIC is already considerably overextended and this is a task requiring specialized knowledge. In this context, the regulations, recently adopted by the SAIC, for traders and brokers on the exchanges, may restrict the number of participants on the new exchanges, and should therefore be reviewed. It is more desirable to have a smaller number of exchanges, but with a relatively large number of participants on each, than vice versa. **Fourth**, the likelihood of considerable waste in the establishment of several new exchanges, especially in view of the presently preferred capital-intensive methods of trading, must be recognized and more exchanges should only be established if shown to be sustainable in the medium term.

In terms of the physical organization of the new exchanges, the following improvements can be pointed out. First, the adoption of a simple open outcry ring dealing system should be considered, as an alternative to the present computerized system, not only in all new exchanges, but also in the existing ones, ast the time when the next increase in computer requirements is reviewed. Objections to 'open outcry' based on their vulnerability to fraud are exaggerated. However, if this is a major consideration, the 'Japanese Auction System' could be introduced, in which there is a single price for all buying and selling orders for a given trading session.

Meanwhile, trading costs can be reduced with the utilization of the facilities at a given trading center by more than one exchange. Since most exchanges at present do not trade every day of the week, or all hours of the day, this should be feasible.

Market Regulation

First, there is little evidence of monopoly, in the sense of industrial structure, in China. The regulatory emphasis should therefore be on market conduct issues. Care must be exercised to not snuff out early experiments with enterprise groups, with unduly restrictive regulations on mergers.

Second, entry for new enterprises should be simplified. The administration of the process of entry and exit may sometimes be as important as the law. **Third**, the functions of the SAIC and other agencies should be redefined to make them more transparent and reduce the discretionary element present today in the granting of approvals. **Fourth**, some of the functions of the SAIC (such as the monitoring of unfair practices, monitoring cases of fraud in labelling and trademarks, and taking care of enterprise entry requirements), should be delegated to more specialized agencies in the future. Finally, it should be noted that a proliferation of new laws, sometimes conflicting in scope, or in terms of agencies concerned, could be counterproductive. Care must also be taken to counter any tendencies to permit the interests of the agencies drafting the laws to dominate the new draft legislation.

1

Market Segmentation and Market Development

A. Introduction

China's commitment to the creation of a market economy, which has been the central plank of its program of economic reform, received new emphasis in the 8th National People's Congress of March 1993. The congress ratified the decision, already taken at the 14th Party Congress of October 1992, to develop a 'socialist market economy', shifting decisively away from central planning. The Constitution of 1982 was amended to emphasize this shift of policy towards the development of 'socialism with Chinese characteristics'. These decisions reflect the culmination of a series of policy shifts which began in December 1978, when the Third Plenum of the 11th Party Congress announced for the first time that planning and markets could be compatible. Over the subsequent period, further policy pronouncements steadily moved China towards the goal of an increase in the role of its markets and a decline in central planning.[1]

Shifts in administrative responsibility had been introduced in parallel to the changes in policy direction. In 1982, internal distribution functions for consumer goods were consolidated under the Ministry of Commerce, which merged the Ministry of Grains and the National Trading Corporation with the former Ministry of Commerce. In 1988, the Ministry of Materials was established, by a decision of the State Council to gradually abolish the material supply and marketing organizations of individual ministries, and consolidate the supply and marketing responsibility of producer goods at the national level though enterprises under the new Ministry. Finally, in 1993, at the 8th National People's Congress, it was decided that the erstwhile Ministries of Commerce and Materials would be merged in a single new Ministry of Internal Trade.

The development of the internal market was fostered by a series of mechanisms intended to reduce the scope of state intervention. A first key element of the strategy was progressive price decontrol, through the introduction of three categories of prices, planned prices, guidance prices and market prices and the gradual movement of goods from more regulated to less regulated categories, together with 'dual track' pricing, introduced in 1985, which permitted output above certain target levels

---

[1] Following the success of agricultural market reforms after 1979, the 12th Congress of the Party aimed to use market regulation as a supplement to planning, and in October 1984 it called for a further reduction in the scope of mandatory planning and its replacement by 'guidance planning'. The 13th Congress of 1987 adopted the goal of 'letting the state regulate the market, and letting the market guide the enterprises'. The evolution of the politics of market reform is traced in White (1993).

to be sold on the free market.[2] The proportion of goods in total domestic retail trade subject to planned prices fell dramatically between 1978 and 1991 (Figure 1.1), in favor of 'guidance prices' and free market prices. Goods subject to planned prices have fallen considerably further, with recent announcements in early 1993 of the relaxation of controls on prices of grain and edible oils.

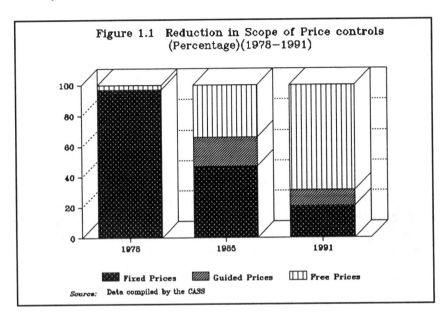

Figure 1.1 Reduction in Scope of Price controls
(Percentage)(1978–1991)

Fixed Prices Guided Prices Free Prices
Source: Data compiled by the CASS

Second, the allocation of goods was progressively moved out of the mandatory plan. In 1980, 90 percent of industrial goods, and 837 production materials were allocated under the plan system. By early 1993, the proportion of industrial goods under the plan had declined to 12 percent and the number of production materials in this category has been reduced to 11. At the same time, consumer goods whose planned allocation was administered by the Ministry of Commerce declined in number from 274 in 1978 to 14 in 1993. Third, a diversification of distribution systems and channels was gradually permitted. Formerly, the system of unified purchase and sale of consumer manufactures, as well as the unified purchase of farm products, by designated government agencies, accounted for virtually all sales.[3] Sales may now be made to private purchasing agencies, or directly to consumers. A variety of new forms of markets are evolving as a consequence, including sophisticated commodity exchanges and comprehensive as well as specialized distribution centers.

---

[2]   Explored further in Chapter 2. Descriptions of the progress of price reform in China may be traced through Byrd (1987), Wu and Zhao (1987) and World Bank (1990a&b). Sectoral details are given in World Bank (1992) 'China: The Achievements and Challenges of Price Reform', Albouy (1991) and a comparative perspective is offered in Rajaram (1991).

[3]   The Unified Purchase system dated from 1951, when it was introduced with an Implementing Decision of the State Council. Manufactured consumer goods were classified under three categories, according to whether they were deemed to be essential goods, items of mass demand, or others. The purchase and sale of goods in the first two categories were handled by the central government, while goods in the third category were handled by local governments. Agricultural goods were similarly grouped and goods in the first two categories were subject to 'monopoly purchase' and 'designated purchase', respectively, at state-determined prices. Goods in the third category were subject to purchase at negotiated prices.

At the same time as these measures to improve the functioning of the internal market were being introduced, China also adopted an 'open door' policy towards foreign trade and investment. It is clear that China has made rapid strides in the development of its external trade. In recent years, from 1985 to 1992, exports and imports grew at 17 and 10 percent per year, respectively. While domestic interprovincial trade also rose in absolute terms, its rate of growth at 4.8 percent per year was low relative to foreign trade, and also lower than the 9 percent annual rate of growth of total retail sales (Figure 1.2). As a consequence, while the share of external trade in GDP increased, the share of interprovincial trade in domestic retail sales declined.

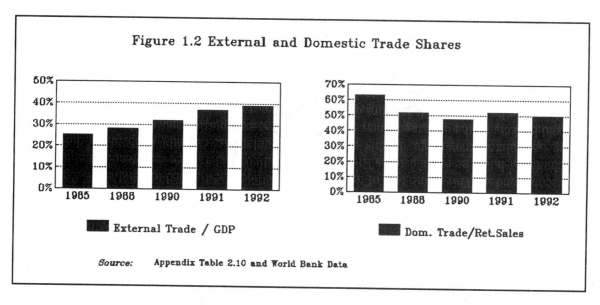

Figure 1.2 External and Domestic Trade Shares

External Trade / GDP   Dom. Trade/Ret.Sales

Source: Appendix Table 2.10 and World Bank Data

Together with the finding of the relative decline in domestic trade, there are reports of difficulties encountered in the processes of internal trade, both in terms of the difficulties of establishing new forms of markets, as well as obstacles created by authorities in some provinces, which restrict the inflow or outflow of goods and factors in their provinces. These difficulties are compounded by real bottlenecks in transport, storage and distribution. It has recently been estimated that the demand for around 200 million tons of freight, or around 10 percent of freight capacity, remained unsatisfied in 1989. China's rate of investment in transport has averaged around 1.3 percent of GNP, while other developing nations' investments in transport ranged from 2 to 3.8 percent of GNP.[4]

The limited extent to which internal trade exists has sometimes been attributed to the uniquely 'cellular' structure of the economy.[5] Though geographically vast, it has been pointed out that attempts at achieving the local self-sufficiency emphasized in the Maoist era led to a duplication of industrial pattern by province. The inefficient location of industry was compounded by dispersal resulting from the 'Third Front' policy, of moving industrial enterprises towards the interior. In later years, (as pointed out today by some government officials), with increasing dencentralization, local government officials sometimes established "repetitive and non-economic industries with a view to increasing local

---

[4]   World Bank (1992). Report No. 10592-CHA.

[5]   Commented on by Donnithorne (1972), and later by Lyons (1987). Recent evidence, particularly in the provinces around Shanghai, has been described by W. Huang (1992).

fiscal revenues, or local employment, or even to "chase achievements" during their official careers. In 1987, 80 factories in 21 provinces produced refrigerators, over a hundred factories in 26 provinces produced televisions and 300 factories in 28 provinces could produce washing machines. The pattern was reinforced by the nature of the planning mechanism and the decentralization of investment decisions in the early 1980s at the provincial level. As a consequence, industrial plant is frequently undersized. One reason why provincial and local authorities have sometimes limited the entry of goods from other provinces is to attempt to shelter these small and relatively inefficient enterprises. This protection results ultimately in higher prices for consumers and inefficient production. While there are now some signs of change, impediments to regional trade flows still exist in a variety of forms. A major potential economic advantage, the large internal market, is diminished as a consequence.

Factors Affecting Internal Markets

As the preceding paragraphs suggest, there is a wide range of factors which determine market structure and affect the functioning of markets, beginning, first, with a broad group of government policies. Most important among these are decisions regarding resource allocation and resource distribution systems, and price determination systems. Decisions to remove goods from the system of centrally-planned procurement, allocation and distribution implied by the unified purchase and sales systems represent major moves towards the creation of markets. The relaxation or removal of price controls, which permits prices to be determined by the forces of market demand and supply, is also a critical element of market creating policies.

Another key factor in the creation of efficient markets is the spatial integration of markets within an economy. The geographical size of China's internal market offers huge potential benefits from such integration, in terms of increased efficiency in industrial structure as well as in the deployment of factors and pricing of goods. The policies affecting the realization of market integration are those which relate to the mobility of goods and factors of production. The extent to which goods, or factors of production such as labor and capital, are permitted to move freely within the country depends not only on the establishment of distribution systems, but also on both national and local level policy decisions to facilitate, or at least allow, their movement. In international trade, such constraints on trade flows in goods take the form of tariff or non-tariff barriers. In internal trade, tariff barriers in the form of codified specific or ad valorem levies on goods entering or leaving provinces are rare, within a country.[6] In the case of China, there are no such formal tariffs, but there many accounts of ad hoc charges, fees and tolls on goods entering or leaving provinces, and in economic terms their equivalence to tariffs may be established. Moreover the uncertainties created by the ad hoc nature of some of these charges and the difficulties they add to interstate transactions constitute a form of non-tariff barrier to trade. Additional non-tariff barriers take the form of policies such as procurement guidelines, at the levels of provincial or lower level governments, which may restrict imports or exports.

Both central and lower level government policies also affect factor mobility. The mobility of capital refers to investment flows as well as credit flows, across provincial boundaries. Capital mobility is essential for efficient resource allocation in a market economy, if investment is to flow into its most productive uses, and in the most geographically suitable areas. Labor mobility includes the

---

[6]   In India, however, there is an interstate 'octroi', which takes the form of an ad valorem sales tax on goods crossing state boundaries. Interstate sales tax registration procedures are also cumbersome and act as a de facto constraint on internal trade.

ability of both skilled and unskilled labor to seek jobs in alternative occupations and locations, also permitting industries to have access to the labor skills they require. Policies affecting the development and functioning of markets for capital and labor are therefore integral elements of the creation of an efficient internal market.

In additional to these policies, the functioning of the internal market will increasingly be affected by the regulations of the government which monitor market behavior to safeguard competition and guard against the abuse of market power. The issues alluded to here lead to the question of the future role of the government in the support of the market economy. As the government retracts from its close involvement in market administration, its role in a more liberal market requires definition. While the government may no longer be setting prices, there may be a need for monitoring price setting in some contexts, for example, if there are possibilities of monopoly or oligopoly. This requires the creation of a legal framework which permits this to be undertaken, as well as the setting up, or reinforcement, of appropriate agencies to perform these functions. The reduction in the role of state planning also requires the proper functioning of contractual mechanisms, as well as the enactment and enforcement of mechanisms to protect consumers, for example against fraudulent trade or false advertising.

Finally, in parallel to these policies and regulations, the physical framework for transport and communication that permits the flow of goods and factors across the country will also critically determine how well the market functions. At present China does not have sufficient capacity in its transportation system to sustain its high rates of growth, and transportation is a particular impediment to the development of an internal market, leading to production stoppages due to lack of inputs, the holding of excessive inventory, and the spoilage of perishable goods, awaiting shipment.

Objectives of this Report

The overall objective of this report is to evaluate the extent to which China, in its process of transition towards a market economy, has really been able to establish well-functioning and efficient markets which transmit accurate signals to economic agents in terms of production decisions and factor allocation, and permit the efficient exchange and distribution of goods. To this end, the report examines the present efficiency of markets and evaluates policies which affect market formation. Both the regional or spatial aspect of market functioning, and the 'vertical' issue, of the movement from plan to market, are examined. Following a policy evaluation, the report analyzes 'real' aspects of market formation, in terms of the new systems for allocating and distributing goods, which have evolved in the aftermath of the diminished role of planning. The present framework of regulation for the new markets is also examined to evaluate its adequacy in the changing environment.

In the following section, the report begins by pointing out the potential benefits of well-functioning and regionally integrated internal markets and shows how greater market integration has been realized in other countries. In this context, the report examines China's present industrial structure and shows that there is little evidence, so far, of a well-integrated structure, and that, relative to other countries, China appears to be below its potential.

Next, the report aims to analyze and evaluate policy measures which affect the functioning of the internal market (Chapter 2), including, first, policies relating to the price mechanism, and second, policies directly affecting the interregional flows of goods and factors of production. The report shows that, despite some success in the integration of plan and market pricing, regional integration, in terms of the regional price convergence, has met with less success. Moreover, regional flow of goods, as well as interregional investments and capital flows, appear to have declined, at least relative to the growth of total retail sales, or provincial GDP. Issues relating to regional mobility of labor are also examined, particularly in terms of recent developments, which suggest that there has been some progress in this direction, although further gains may be realized.[7]

Third, on the real side, the report evaluates changes in the distribution system and points out its present bottlenecks (Chapter 3). It shows that the role of the state remains surprisingly large in terms of distribution, despite its withdrawal from planned allocation. However the state distribution mechanisms themselves have adapted to the new market environment. While the evolution of new forms of distribution in China has been in the right direction, there are still constraints and limitations, compared to best practice in market economies, and areas in which improvements may be achieved are pointed out. Constraints to distribution caused by transportation difficulties are also examined.

One striking development in China's evolution towards a market economy are its ambitious recent experiments at setting up new forms of markets, in particular, the commodities exchanges, some of which engage in not only spot, but also forward and futures transactions. A remarkable number of these new markets has been established in the last two to three years, notably in grain, non-ferrous metals, petrochemicals, and agricultural commodities such as rubber and sugar. The present report focuses particularly on the two non-ferrous metals exchanges as examples (Chapter 4). The report points out reasons why these markets are in many cases not functioning as intended. Areas where the efficiency and regulation of these markets could be strengthened are discussed. The report also provides a demonstration of the links between markets for commodities and the market for services and foreign exchange. One of the difficulties faced by China, in its present situation of partly regulated and partly liberated markets is that 'proxy markets' are beginning to evolve, where prices in liberated markets sometimes subsume the effects of price or quantity constraints in more controlled markets. Another difficulty is the continued government intervention in different areas of price setting.

Finally, turning to market regulation, the report aims to provide a first assessment of the elements of the legal framework which are in place already, and to point out areas where extensions to this would be required (Chapter 5). It also examines the institutions charged with the enforcement of the present system and evaluates their effectiveness, suggesting areas where reinforcement may be necessary. In the concluding chapter, the report pulls these different strands together to map out a feasible route for the integration of the internal market, in terms of appropriate policy and regulatory instruments as well as an adequate physical infrastructure. The report will discuss the specific 'real' and 'policy' variables affecting the mobility of goods and factors of production and will also describe the broader areas in the legal and regulatory framework that require attention if internal competition is to be promoted.

---

[7]   Considerable attention has already been paid to this issue in a number of works, and therefore the treatment here is largely a summary of existing work. Evidence on the extent of labor mobility is summarized in World Bank (1992) Report No. 10266-CHA, and links between poverty levels and labor mobility are discussed in World Bank (1992 October). Issues concerning the floating population of urban labor and migrants are discussed in Banister (1989); Jefferson and Rawski (1992); Rutkowski (1991); Solinger (1992 and 1992). New measures to enhance labor mobility are detailed in Ody (1991).

B. The Potential Benefits of Internal Free Markets

The benefits of market determined prices and distribution systems are now well recognized in China. The case for allowing prices to be determined by demand and supply rests upon first, the long-run allocative efficiency that this will lead to, as resources flow towards their best uses, based upon price signals which reflect relative scarcities and needs; second, on the elimination of rent-seeking and parallel markets that arise, if prices are pegged at levels which do not reflect their equilibrium values; third, a reduction in artificial losses (profits) in certain economic activities where prices are set at levels below (above) their equilibrium values, and in addition, a reduction in direct or indirect subsidies that may be paid to loss-making economic agents, if these losses are due to policy constrained prices. It is also accepted that greater flexibility in distribution systems which gives greater flexibility to producers and consumers in procurement channels can reduce costs, cut inventory requirements and shorten delivery periods.

Economic gains from regional integration and its links to market efficiency are less well understood and they are therefore the focus of this section. Regional economic integration, in its broadest sense, refers to the absence of economic discrimination and restrictions among economic agents of a region.[8] The process of integration requires the gradual elimination of economic frontiers and trade restricting instruments between territories within a region so that the mobility of goods, services and factors is not constrained. This process of 'integration from below', can be reinforced by 'integration from above', or the active promotion of economic cooperation between territories which may be encouraged through appropriate policies or institutions.[9]

Forms of Regional Integration

The core of most economic literature on regional integration refers to theories of customs unions. As a national unit, however, China is already a customs union, in the sense that it has a common external tariff. The aim in the Chinese context is to go beyond the creation of a customs union, to the formation of a common market. The creation of a common market does not necessarily automatically follow, within a customs union, as the example of Europe well illustrates. The customs union of the EEC was formed in 1957. However it was not till 1986 that the more ambitious goal of a 'market without frontiers' was adopted, together with the wider goal of economic union in other areas. An economic union, such as the EC aims to be, progresses beyond a customs union to monetary union and interlinkages in internal (for example fiscal) economic policies. In China today, there is an anomalous situation where major elements of economic union including a single currency and a common external tariff are combined with a lack of some basic features of a free trade area, such as the free movement of goods and factors.

---

[8] In this chapter, the analysis of regional integration is conducted at the level of intra-provincial trade flow statistics. It would be interesting and valuable to examine intra-provincial trade flows as well, particularly in the larger provinces, to see whether similar patterns emerge. Lack of data have prevented this from being included in the analysis.

[9] Tinbergen (1965), discussed in the Chinese context in W. Huang (1992). Huang also refers to integration from above and below as 'positive' and 'negative' regional integration, and discusses distinctions between customs unions and common markets, based on Balassa (1961).

Attempts at the regional integration of markets elsewhere have taken many forms with varying degrees of implied integration. A free trade area, for example, such as the NAFTA, does not require the free movement of factors of production (labor and capital) or a common external tariff, unlike a customs union. Free trade areas may also be created for single commodities, or single sectors of activity, and combinations of partial common markets and coordinated investment plans are also possible. Recognizing these advantages, there have been many attempts world wide at regional trade integration, among both developed and developing countries.[10]

New Moves Towards Regional Integration in Developing Countries: Central America

Recognizing the potential impact of the NAFTA for trade between the US, Canada and Mexico, the six countries of Central America have recently launched new attempts at creating free markets among themselves, and discussed an 'integration protocol' for economic union, in August 1993. Four of these countries, Guatemala, El Salvador, Nicaragua and Honduras have already begun to dismantle the barriers to movement of goods, labor and money across their borders. Trade within Central America has almost doubled (to $1.8 billion) relative to its 1986 low point. By setting up a low common external tariff, the group is also opening up to the rest of the world, unlike the previous attempt at a common market, set up in the 1960s. The four are now negotiating free trade agreements with Mexico, Columbia and Venezuela.

Business interest in the integration proposal is evident. El

Salvador's private airline, TACO, has bought shares in five other regional airlines since 1989 to face north American competition. Banco Uno, a Guatemalan bank, has recently begun to open branches in Honduras.

The proposed protocol sets out ambitious goals including monetary union and a single currency, but sets out no timetables, so far, for their achievement. A two-speed or multi-speed process may be adopted to accommodate individual countries. While Costa Rica has joined the other countries in cutting external tariffs, it is more hesitant about the idea of a single market, given its relatively more stable economy and lower current rates of unemployment. It may therefore opt out of some of these provisions for the present. Panama is similarly hesitant about the common external tariff. The importance of compromise and the need to accommodate individual requirements is well illustrated.

Source: *The Economist.* July 17 1993, p.63.

The Case for Regional Integration

The case for freer trade within a region rests upon a series of static and dynamic gains, to be achieved from production according to comparative advantage, increased competition, the benefits of scale economies, and the diffusion of technical knowledge. Traditional theories of comparative advantage point out that production costs and selling prices for different products are likely to differ between locations, due to differences in factor endowments (natural resources, skilled and unskilled labor, and capital), technical methods of production and regional differences in preferences and tastes.[11] Due to these differences in production costs and selling prices at different locations, there will be an overall economic gain to the region if locations are encouraged to engage in 'division of labor' and specialize in the production of goods and services for which they are best suited.

---

[10] Different forms of regional integration and their implications are described in Hufbauer and Schott (1992). Among developed countries the EC and recently the proposed NAFTA are examples of regional integration. Among developing countries, examples may be found in the ASEAN nations of south east Asia and among north (Maghreb) and West (CFA franc zone) African countries. A recent summary for developing countries is available in Langhammer and Hiemenz (1991).

[11] The classic Heckscher-Ohlin-Samuelson model of international trade.

The benefits of achieving scale economies in production are important in many capital intensive industries where cost-savings may be effected though the better utilization of machinery with longer production runs and fuller utilization of existing capacity. Joint management and the coordinated use of joint resources also contribute to this. Most production processes face indivisibilities at some stages, for example, large-scale handling equipment, regional infrastructure, transportation and storage costs. Scale economies are of particular significance in the group of manufactures referred to as 'process industries' (for example, cement or fertilizers) which deal mostly with the conversion of bulk industrial raw materials. In these industries, the principle of non-linearity arises due to the fact that equipment cost is a function of surface areas, whereas capacity is related to volume. In such industries, engineers estimate coefficients of the proportional increase in cost, per unit increase in volume, and the resulting coefficients are well below 1, at around 0.6 according to some estimates.[12]

Greater regional integration also permits an increase in the effective competition for all industries producing in that area. An increase in the number of firms puts pressure on each individual unit to cut costs and improve technology. Over time, there will also be a tendency towards regional price convergence, as well as a reduction in the overall number of firms, as the least cost-effective producers are forced to lower costs, or leave the market. For example, in Italy, there were 50 washing machine producers in 1960, and only 13 in 1974, as competition with other European producers increased. The Italian industry's exports to France, Germany and the UK, which by then accounted for 30 percent of its output, lowered unit costs by 8 percent.[13] Another benefit of competition is greater product diversification between producers, as different units specialize in different varieties of products.

Economic geographers also point out that there is a tendency for 'clusters' of production to develop at certain locations, and that sometimes, given a critical mass of enterprises, growth in a given region will tend to accelerate. Links between such clusters and regional growth have long been recognized by development economists.[14] There is now a growing recognition of the interrelation between the factors cited above, and its impact on industrial structure and regional development. The importance of scale economies, combined with transport costs, imply that many national economies develop 'cores' of manufacturing activities, combined with outlying agricultural peripheries.[15] The

---

[12] Balassa (1961). Economic work relating plant size to cost efficiency, by industry, has calculated the 'MEPS' or minimum economic plant size by industry for a number of industries. Examples cited, in terms of minimum annual volumes of production, are 10,000 tons of soap, between 1 and 3 million tons for steel, 160,000 units for bicycles, 90,000 units for tractors, 200,000 tons for cement, 1 million units for automobiles, and 800,000 units a year for refrigerators. See HMSO 1975, as cited in Huang (1992); Scherer and Ross (1990), as cited in Wu (1990).

[13] Similar examples are cited for the European car and truck industries. The number of automobile producers fell in Germany, Britain and France, between 1955 and 1970. Meanwhile the lowest-cost truck producer, Daimler-Benz of Germany, raised output by 7.5 percent through its increased exports to a single country, France. Owen (1983), W. Huang (1992).

[14] Hoover (1948) discussed the economics of agglomerations in the context of the US. Myrdal (1957) discussed the 'circular causation' of development and Hirschman (1958) discussed backward linkages in the context of developing economies.

[15] See particularly Krugman (1991a,b&c). Murphy, Schleifer and Vishny (1989a&b) also discuss the importance of scale economies, market size and market structure.

demand for manufactures arises not only from consumers, but also from other geographically proximate manufacturing industries. The importance of such clusters in the presence of 'growth enabling factors', such as foreign knowledge, learning, labor turnover and the diffusion of technical information is also being pointed out, both in the general context and in the specific case of its application to some of the faster-growing areas of China.[16]

Progressing towards a common market, however, requires the drawing up of a large agenda of measures, to address both physical and technical issues impeding integration. Some of these issues are multisectoral (such as border checkposts and 'customs' formalities, including delays imposed on road haulage, differences in product standards or technical regulations) while others must be examined at the level of individual subsectors (for example, variations in charges for telecommunications or other services). An illustration of the process of moving towards a 'market without frontiers' is provided by the European Community, which demonstrates that progress may be spread over long periods of time, and must be meticulously mapped out.

Regional integration which permits the free movement of not only goods but also factors of production may however have associated costs, for specific regions, in some circumstances. While the arguments in favor of integration demonstrate that there are possibilities for improved total economic welfare, the distribution of these gains among regional economies is also a consideration. One consequence of the clusters and increased polarization that may occur with greater opportunities for specialization is that, in the absence of appropriate distribution mechanisms for the total gains, some regions may be worse off with integration. The possibilities for greater polarization increase with greater factor mobility. While this is the implicit argument behind many forms of regional protection, it should be recognized that there is a potential for greater total gains, and also, that the existence of a credible redistribution mechanism during the process of integration is critical for its acceptability and success. In the case of China, the decline in the central government's budgetary expenditure as a share of GNP from 31 percent in 1978 to 20 percent in 1991 (and a parallel decline in revenue shares from 31 to 17 percent) reduces the redistributive capacity of the center. The concerns that this may justifiably arouse in the context of promoting regional integration have to be taken into account.

The economic case for regional free trade blocs also raises the question of the extent to which such a bloc creates trade, or diverts trade away from areas outside the bloc.[17] Even for the participants in the free trade area, the effects of tariff revenue losses from diverted trade may sometimes outweigh the beneficial effects of price gains. Whether this occurs in any situation is empirical and will depend on the relative attractiveness of domestic and external prices (including the effects of domestic and external tariffs or their equivalents and any premia that may be attached to export privileges) which in turn depend on the relative demand and supply conditions in these markets. It remains, however, that the likelihood of internal gain increases if current internal obstacles to trade are high. Moreover, the lower the external tariffs, the less the likelihood of trade diversion.

---

[16] Jacobs (1969), Romer (1986) and Porter (1989), as cited in Wang and Mody (1993) in the context of explanations for rapidly growing areas in China.

[17] de Melo, et. al (1992), in an extension of the classic analysis by Viner (1950). What is also pointed out (based on Kemp and Wan 1976) is that it is always possible to design a welfare improving free trade area.

The Process of Creating a Common Market: The Example of the EC

The Process of Integration

The process of integration in the European Community has taken several steps. Initially only sectoral integration was attempted, in the form of a European Coal and Steel Community, set up in 1951 with a limited duration of 50 years. In 1957 the principle of a Common External Tariff was extended to all sectors, and the EEC, set up under the Treaty of Rome, was of unlimited duration. From 1962, a Common Agricultural Policy was also adopted. But while tariffs on intra-community trade had been eliminated, many restrictions remained which limited the operation of the Community as a single market.

The 1985 policy paper of the European Commission, which paved the way for completing the internal market, attempted to identify all existing barriers to the 'four freedoms', the free movement of goods, services, capital and people. Later, competition policy, consumer protection, and the mutual compatibility of network systems was added to this list of elements essential for the smooth working of the internal market. With the adoption of the Single European Act shortly thereafter, 279 specific legislative proposals were identified to create a unified market. Several additional proposals have since been added.

Barriers were identified in three categories, physical, technical and fiscal. Frontier formalities and the associated administrative costs for business and public administration were estimated to amount to 1.8 percent of the value of goods traded in the EC (Emerson 1988), or around 9 billion ECU. Barriers due to public procurement restrictions as well as restrictions to entry, especially in service industries, were estimated to amount to another 20 billion ECU, leading to projected cost and price reductions of 10-20 percent in some industries (energy generation, transport, office equipment, financial services) where government purchases are important. By December 1992, frontier formalities were reduced through the introduction of a 'single administrative document' and modifications in statistical trade-recording. Improved transparency and new regulations for public procurement have been introduced. In transport services, there are proposals for the introduction of the rights of operators to move freight outside their member states. Bilateral quotas on road transport are to be abolished and air traffic routes to be permitted greater flexibility.

Technical barriers due to differences in product standards and licensing requirements have been reduced through the principal of mutual recognition, so that the setting of unique common standards is not essential. Fiscal barriers arose through differences in value-added and indirect tax rates, which made some locations more attractive for investment than others. These have been reduced through (i) the gradual harmonization of indirect tax rates, (ii) the adoption of rules such as the imposition of taxes by country of origin only (that is, the place of production, rather than 'ownership' of the enterprise) and (iii) the setting up of a 'clearinghouse' to divide tax receipts as appropriate between member countries.

Gains From Integration

The first phase of the establishment of the EC led to an increase in the share of exports between member countries from 34 percent in 1958 to 52.4 percent of total EC exports by 1983. Imports rose in parallel from 34 percent to 50.5 percent. Gains to be achieved from the Single Market agreement of 1986, by 1992, were assessed at between 4.3 to 6.4 percent of EC GDP, or some $270 billion, by one estimate (Ceccini 1988). The boost to capital stock, and gains from scale economies, have been estimated to add a further 1.2 to 2.6 percent to the estimated GDP gains (Baldwin 1989).

Distribution Issues and the Structural Funds

How has the EC handled the issue of the distribution of the gains from the single market? It was recognized that some regions would have structural deficits in their balances of payments with other regions in the process of growth, and also that these regions would benefit from jointly provided aid, through a series of 'structural funds'. The largest of these is the 'Regional Development Fund', which empowers the Community to finance half the cost of unemployment pay and retraining for workers made redundant because of the establishment of the Common Market. The Fund also helped finance Community programs, and national programs of community interest. Since 1985, the Regional Fund's resources have been allocated on the basis of ranges, with upper and lower limits fixed for each member state. The other principal Structural Funds are the Social Fund (to promote the geographic and occupational mobility of labor within the Community) and the Agricultural Fund (for poor farmers and rural areas), and in the Maastricht proposals, a new 'Cohesion Fund' has been suggested. Eligible regions are classified by the objective they fulfil.

The total budget of the Funds amounts to around 1.5 percent of combined GDP. With the adoption of the Single European Act, the principle of a doubling of the structural funds was adopted, in February 1989. The funds constitute a significantly larger amount in some poorer countries, such as Portugal and Greece, where they have been estimated to reach 5 percent of GDP.

Sources: European Commission DG II and DG III, European Commission (1985, 1992a,b&c), Emerson et. al. (1988), Ceccini (1988), Hufbauer (ed.) (1990), Pinder (1991), Huang (1992), Swann (ed.) (1992), Buiges (1993)

In China, the rapid rise in external trade, together with the relative fall in internal trade flows implies that trade diversion cannot be entirely ruled out. Trade expansion with the external market may well have been easier, for some provinces, than internal market penetration. However, recent moves in China to lower external tariffs make this less likely to occur. There may also have been dynamic secondary effects of external trade in some areas, which may have led to increased domestic trade as well, for example, the establishment of backward links with domestic suppliers, or increased sales to other provinces to achieve scale economies required to keep unit costs low. Estimating the real effect of this is difficult and the present report will only point out the relevant factors to be taken into account, and their behavior so far, based on available evidence.

C. Market Structure in China

It is necessary to examine the evidence of market fragmentation in China, and see how this 'cellular' character affects overall industrial structure. The extent to which market fragmentation may affect China's growth potential as a consequence must be evaluated, and this in turn depends on how China today compares, in this respect, with other large economies.

There is evidence which suggests that China has enjoyed some success in terms of reducing interprovincial income inequalities. An analysis of regional distribution of per capita income, and shifts in this over time, indicates a decline in per capita income variation.[18] Between 1983 and 1991, the coefficient of variation in regional income declined steadily from 0.77 to 0.59. There has been a similar decline in regional coefficients of variation in different measures of per capita industrial output (from 1.4 to 1.1, or 1.24 to 1.03,) and a somewhat more erratic decline in regional variations in per capita investment (0.84 to 0.75).[19] However, as explained above, greater income equality or inequality need not be associated with the structure of output. In the long run in China, the relative structural homogeneity in output may limit increases in total income for all provinces taken together.

Turning next to industrial structure and the structure of output, it is noticeable that, in China as a whole, there have been remarkable shifts in the ownership of industrial output. The proportion of gross output value accounted for by the state sector declined from 76 percent in 1980 to 65 percent in 1985, and further to 53 percent by 1990. Both the number of firms and the output contribution of collective, individual, private and other enterprises (such as joint ventures), which make up the non-state sector, have grown steadily during the last decade. Despite this, the structure of

---

[18]   However, there is also evidence that points to increasing urban-rural income differentials over the past decade. (Khan, et. al., 1992, presents carefully adjusted data from published statistics as well as a survey).

[19]   Measured as the ratio of the standard deviation to the mean. The GINI coefficient of dispersion give similar results. For per capita income, these declined over the same period, from 0.300 to 0.264 (Table A1.1, at the end of the book). There is a similar clear decline in the value of the GINI coefficients for per capita industrial output (0.5 or 0.47 to 0.43, using alternative measures, as shown in Appendix Tables A1.3 to A1.4) with a less marked decline in the GINI coefficient for per capita investment (0.36 to 0.348; Appendix Table A1.2).

industrial output over this period has remained remarkably static.[20] Looking at the structure of output, using a 15 branch classification of industry, remarkable stability over time is suggested (Table 1.1). The share of light industries, for example (industries 9-14), their share in output was 33.3 percent in 1980 and 32.8 in 1990. (More significant change had occurred earlier, from 1970, when the share of this group was 25.5 percent, to 1980).[21] It can also be shown that this is not due to offsetting changes in the composition of state and non-state output, or urban and rural output. The relative composition of each of these groups has also remained virtually unchanged. This is in spite of other considerable policy shifts which occurred over this decade, in terms of the move from plan to market allocation and pricing, ownership changes in industry, and external trade expansion.

Table 1.1 Trends in the Branch Composition of China's Industrial Output/a
(1970-1990) (percent)

	1970/b	1980	1981	1990
Metallurgy	10.5	8.6	8.8	7.3
Electricity	3.5	3.8	3.8	3.0
Coal	2.6	2.3	3.0	2.1
Petroleum	4.8	5.1	5.5	3.8
Chemicals	18.5	12.5	11.4	12.7
Machinery	30.0	25.5	20.9	28.9
Building materials	2.9	3.6	3.8	4.3
Forest products	1.7	1.7	2.0	1.3
Food processing	9.2	11.4	13.3	10.5
Textiles	15.0	14.7	16.5	14.0
Apparel	0.0	2.7	2.8	2.8
Leather goods	0.0	1.0	1.1	1.2
Paper & publishing	1.3	1.3	1.3	1.3
Cultural & craft goods	0.0	2.2	2.4	3.0
Other	0.0	3.4	3.3	3.8
Total	100.0	100.0/b	100.0	100.0

/a Excluding village level firms.
/b Adjusted to take account of adding-up inconsistency.
Source: Rawski (1993).

Looking at the cross-section structure of industrial output by region, another striking finding is that each major industrial group is located in virtually all provinces. Looking at eight principal groups of industries (coal mining, tobacco, textiles, chemicals, building materials, machinery, and electronics and telecommunication), we find that these are represented in all provinces (Appendix Tables A1.6 to A1.8). The variation across provinces, in terms of the numbers of firms or total employment

---

[20] Appendix Table A1.5 and Rawski (1993).

[21] It has been shown in greater detail (Solinger, 1991) that the proportion of the gross value of industrial output in light industry rose noticeably in 1980 and 1981, suggesting that the early policy of 'readjustment' of 1979 to 1982 did make a difference to industrial composition, albeit for a limited period. The actual numbers depend on the level of aggregation and definitions used for 'light' and 'heavy' industry.

in each sector is low, compared to what might be expected, in view of the considerable diversity of the provinces in terms of size and resource endowments. For five out of these eight sectors, the coefficients of variation for these measures are below 1 in 1991.[22] In terms of gross output value, the coefficients of variation are below 1 in six sectors in both 1990 and 1991, and the values for 1991 are lower than for 1990. The most pronounced similarity is for the average number of persons employed per enterprise, where the coefficients of variation are less than 0.5 for 5 sectors and below 0.8 for the remaining three. This suggests that firm size is also remarkably similar across provinces.

The significance of this structural similarity across provinces, especially in conjunction with a fairly static industrial structure over time, would suggest, in terms of the discussion of the previous section, that China so far has not benefited from the opportunities for regional specialization that its large internal market would permit. To assess the extent to which China may potentially gain from this, a comparison of China and other large regional markets is undertaken here. The two comparators chosen are the European Community, and the United States. The selection of the US is obvious, as another large, federal nation state. The presence of 'manufacturing belts', and sometimes highly concentrated industries in a few specific towns, is notable. The choice of the EC is due to the fact that it is increasingly approximating a single market, in the same sense as the US. Although the regions of the EC are individual countries, with huge differences between north and south, differences in size and also a high degree of linguistic and cultural diversity, advantage has been taken of relative regional specialization. Thus most manufactures are located in countries such as Britain and Germany, many agricultural products are grown mostly in Portugal and Spain, and France and Italy dominate the internal EC clothing industry.

The analysis measures the difference in the shares of individual industries between each pair of regions within the three countries (ie, for each pair of countries in the EC, and each group of provinces in China or states in the US), and then constructs an average of these differences for each of the three countries considered. The higher the value of this measure, the greater the relative regional differences in industrial structure, and the higher the degree of local specialization. Three different indices of industrial structure have been used; the shares of individual industries in output, employment and numbers of firms, in each region. Details of the analysis are provided in Annex 1.1. As shown in the Figure 1.3, regional differences in China are relatively low, suggesting that there is little industrial specialization or regional industrial concentration. The degree of differentiation is much higher in both the EC and the US, particularly in terms of the first two measures.[23]

---

[22] The coefficient of variation is the standard deviation of a distribution divided by its mean. Using coefficients of variation to measure dispersion enables 'normalized' comparisons of the dispersion of distributions, in situations where there may be widely differing ranges and mean values.

[23] As explained in Annex 1, the reason for the less pronounced difference in terms of numbers of firms is that this variable may be affected by systematic variations in firm size, across the three countries or country groups. This is one of the caveats concerning the interpretation of results of cross-country comparisons. Admittedly, the use of the EC and the US as comparators is far from ideal, since these countries are at a more advanced level of industrialization, and moreover have not undergone the process of transition from a planned to market economy. However, data on better comparators are not available at present.

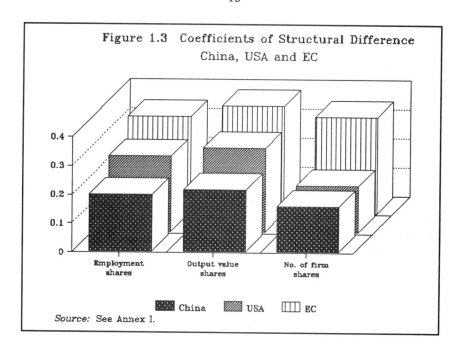

Figure 1.3 Coefficients of Structural Difference
China, USA and EC

Source: See Annex I.

To summarize the observations of this chapter, it is noted first of all that China has made many moves towards the creation of a market economy over the last decade. There have been pronounced reductions in the degree of central control over resource allocation and pricing. At the same time, there has been a remarkable opening up of the economy towards the exterior, with a rapid growth in foreign trade. Yet, there are some disturbing imbalances in this movement towards a market economy. First of all, industrial structure has remained remarkably constant over time, and moreover, the regional differences in industrial structure are very low relative to other countries or communities of comparable size. This indicates that China has taken relatively little advantage of the opportunities for regional specialization according to comparative advantage, and the potential available to it in this direction may be large. The additional finding that internal trade flows have been declining in relative terms reinforces the urgency of exploring means towards market integration, as part of the movement towards the establishment of a market economy.

ANNEX I.1 Calculation of Regional Structural Difference Coefficients[24]

Methodology

The underlying assumption is that the integration of a market can permit, and will encourage, greater regional specialization. If constraints to internal trade or factor mobility exist, regions are less likely to specialize and industrial structures across regions will tend to be more similar.

If the regions within a country have identical industrial structures, the shares of different subsectors of industry in the total for each region will be the same. These shares can be measured in terms of variables such as the numbers of firms in a given subsector, the numbers of persons employed in that subsector, or its share in output value.

If y_{ij} represents the share (in terms of number of firms, number of persons employed, output value) of subsector i in region j, and y_{ik} represents the share of subsector i in region k, then the shares of subsector i in regions j and k may be defined as:

$$d_{ij} = \frac{y_{ij}}{\sum_{i=1}^{n} y_{ij}} \ , \ \text{and} \ \ d_{ik} = \frac{y_{ik}}{\sum_{i=1}^{n} y_{ik}} \ , \ \ i = 1,2,\ldots,n, \ \ j, \ k, \ = 1,2,\ldots m$$

Then the difference in the shares of all subsectors i between regions j and k may be defined as:

$$D_{jk} = \sum_{i=1}^{n} |d_{ij} - d_{ik}| \qquad 0 \leq D_{jk} \leq 2$$

Note that the number of subsectors i in each region j and k must be equal, to permit the comparison. The upper limit of D_{jk} will be 2, because if the two regions have no industries in common, each pair of values will be counted twice. The lower limit of D_{jk} will be 0, because if the structures of the two regions are identical, each difference will be zero. For an easier understanding of the coefficient, this can be normalized, giving us

$$\overline{D}_{jk} = D_{jk}/2 \qquad 0 \leq \overline{D}_{jk} \leq 1 \qquad\qquad \text{.......(1)}$$

---

[24] This section draws upon and extends the methodology used in Krugman (1991b), 'Geography and Trade'. MIT Press, Cambridge, Massachusetts.

The greater the structural difference between these two regions, across all industries, the closer the value of this measure is to 1. If a country had three regions, we can estimate the values of this coefficient for each pair of regions within the country, and the resulting array would be a matrix of elements, such as:

$$
\begin{vmatrix}
 & j_1 & j_2 & j_3 \\
k_1 & 0 & \overline{D}_{12} & \overline{D}_{13} \\
k_2 & & 0 & \overline{D}_{23} \\
k_3 & & & 0
\end{vmatrix}
\qquad j, \; k, \; = 1, \; 2, \ldots, m
$$

By extension, an index of the 'overall structural difference', or degree of regional specialization, of all the regions of a country may be estimated as an averaged value of the elements of this matrix. Therefore, for any country with m regions, we can define:

$$
D = \sum_{k=1}^{m} \sum_{j=1}^{m} \overline{D}_{jk}
$$

D, by analogy with the above, has a lower limit of zero. The upper limit of D is determined by m, the number of regions, which is the upper limit of j and k. The limits of the measure are

$$
0 \le D \le \sum_{j=1}^{m} (m-j)
$$

For example, if m is 3, the upper limit of the value is 3, as the matrix above shows (provided the elements below the diagonal are not counted). Dividing by this upper limit, we have a 'normalized' value of D, which varies between zero and 1. Thus,

$$
\overline{D} = \frac{D}{\displaystyle\sum_{j=1}^{m} (m-j)}, \qquad 0 \le \overline{D} \le 1 \qquad \ldots\ldots(2)
$$

The advantage of this measure is that it provides a summary of the overall degree of specialization of a country, and permits comparisons to be made with other countries. For such comparisons to be valid, the number of regional groupings in each of the countries considered must also be the same.

Application to China and Comparison with Other Countries

Measures of the degree of regional specialization between different regions ($\bar{D}_{jk}$) of China were undertaken, and similar measures were also constructed for different regions within the United States (US), and the different member countries of the European Community (EC). Although China has 29 provinces, and the United States has 50 states, the provinces of China and the states of the US were grouped in 12 geographically contiguous and structurally similar units for this exercise. This was undertaken primarily to construct measures of the overall regional structural difference ($\bar{D}$) and thus enable comparisons of China and the US with each other, as well as with the EC, which has 12 member countries. The grouping also eases the interpretation of the matrix of coefficients for each country by reducing the dimensions of the array. The regional groupings adopted, as well as the data sources, are given at the end of the tables of coefficients ($\bar{D}_{jk}$) for each country, in Annex Tables AI.1a to AI.3c.

Given the 12 regional groups for each of the three areas, the overall structural difference index would be:

$$\bar{D} = \frac{D}{\displaystyle\sum_{j=1}^{12} (12-j)} \text{ , or } \quad \bar{D} = \frac{D}{66} \qquad 0 \le \bar{D} \le 1$$

The industrial classifications of the three countries were similar but not identical. A correspondence was established between the classifications, to conform as closely as possible to the International Standard Industrial Classification, at the three digit level. All manufacturing industries were included and the resulting classification has 17 groups of sectors at the three digit level.[25]

Three different measures have been used to estimate regional subsector shares, the number of firms in a given subsector and region, the number of persons employed in that subsector, and the total value of output. Of these three, the second and the third are likely to be more reliable, because the number of firms will be affected by differences in the distribution of average firm size in different regions. This is particularly likely to affect cross-country comparisons.

The results of the estimations of regional difference coefficients for regions within the three countries/ areas ($\bar{D}_{jk}$) are presented in Annex Tables AI.1a-c (number of firms), AI.2a-c (number of persons employed) and AI.3a-c (gross value of industrial output). An inspection of the matrices for the three countries suggests first, that on any of the three measures of regional shares, the differences in industrial structure across regions in China is lower than in either the EC or in the US. For example, looking at the array of coefficients for regional differences in the number of persons employed in different industries (Tables AI.2a to AI.2c, across the three selected areas), we find that in the EC, regional

---

[25] The subsectors are: Food and Beverages [311/2/3]; Tobacco [314]; Textiles [321]; Wearing Apparel [322]; Leather and Products [323]; Wood Products and Furniture [331/2]; Paper and Products [341]; Printing, Publishing [342]; Industrial Chemicals [351]; Petroleum and Coal Products [353/4]; Rubber Products [355]; Glass and Non-metal Products [362/9]; Metal Industries [371/2]; Metal Products [381]; Machinery n.e.c [382]; Electrical Machinery [383]; and Transport Equipment [384]. Details of the correspondence established across countries is available if required.

differences range from 0.79 (Portugal and Luxembourg have very little in common, industrially) to 0.15 (France and Belgium are highly similar). In the US, coefficients of difference range from a maximum of 0.46 (Florida and Texas, compared to Washington, Oregon, Alaska and Hawaii) to a minimum of 0.13. By contrast, in China, the 'maximum difference' is 0.39 (Beijing, Tianjin and Hebei, compared to Shanxi, Inner Mongolia and Henan) and the minimum is only 0.09 (Beijing, Tianjin and Hebei, compared to Shanghai, Zhejiang, Anhui and Jiangxi). Similar results are obtained by inspecting the matrices of coefficients which calculate the regional differences in terms of output value and number of firms. The contrast between China and the EC and US is more pronounced for the measures in terms of the number of persons employed and the value of output, relative to number of firms, which is not surprising, as the latter measure would also capture the effects of systematic differences in firm size across the three countries/ areas compared. As Annex Tables AI.4a and AI.4b show, there is a consistently greater degree of variance in firm size in the EC and US, relative to China, where firms tend to cluster around the average size.

Finally, the results of the findings of the individual country matrices may be compared by the calculation of the overall measures of regional differences ($\bar{D}$) for the three countries, using each of the tree measures. These results are given in Table AI.1 below.

Table AI.1 Comparison of Average Coefficients of Structural Difference ($\bar{D}$)
China, US and EC

	EC	US	China
Structure measured by number of employees	0.333	0.262	0.197
Structure measured by output value	0.371	0.292	0.214
Structure measured by number of firms	0.333	0.162	0.157

Source: Calculated from Tables AI.1a to AI.3c.

The relevance of $\bar{D}$ lies in its relative values for the three country/area groups. Thus the regional structural differences in industry in the EC, measured in terms of output value, at 0.37, are close to 75 percent larger than in China, which has a value of 0.21. The US has a value of 0.29, which is almost 40 percent larger than China.

The reasons for the relatively greater values for the EC, compared to the US, are probably due to the sharp geographic differences, as well as differences in the degree of industrialization, of its member countries, thus leading to greater regional specialization. China, however, is clearly less regionally specialized than either of the two.

It may be asked whether this measure also captures the effects of regional inequality differences, and whether, therefore, the lower results for China reflect a lower degree of regional inequality. The answer is that the focus of the present measure is on the structure and composition of output, rather than on differences in income. Structural differences in output may have no a priori implications for differences in income. If regions are producing according to their comparative advantage, specialization should help raise incomes. Second, incomes also depend critically on redistributive effects of central government investment or other expenditure. The basic aim of these measures, however, is a comparison of the degree of similarity or difference in industrial structure across regions, rather than regional income differentials.

Table AI.1a European Community: Coefficients of Structural Difference of Number of Firms, 1987

	Belgium	Denmark	France	Germany	Greece	Ireland	Italy	Luxembourg	Netherlands	Portugal	Spain	U.K.
Belgium	0.000	0.242	...	0.273	0.266	0.152	0.513	0.404	0.235	0.343	0.207	0.321
Denmark		0.000	...	0.130	0.312	0.164	0.401	0.323	0.175	0.497	0.296	0.154
France			0.000	...	...	...	...	...	...	...	...	...
Germany				0.000	0.307	0.144	0.329	0.284	0.262	0.500	0.315	0.164
Greece					0.000	0.234	0.354	0.481	0.318	0.370	0.350	0.370
Ireland						0.000	0.437	0.299	0.158	0.415	0.256	0.249
Italy							0.000	0.513	0.509	0.428	0.568	0.333
Luxembourg								0.000	0.497	0.416	0.556	0.345
Netherlands									0.000	0.460	0.280	0.209
Portugal										0.000	0.281	0.531
Spain											0.000	0.375
U.K.												0.000

Note: Data of number of firms are not available for France.

Source: Calculated from data in Industrial Statistical Yearbook (United Nations), 1991 and 1989.

Table AI.1b United States: Coefficients of Structural Difference of Number of Firms, 1987

	Region 1	Region 2	Region 3	Region 4	Region 5	Region 6	Region 7	Region 8	Region 9	Region 10	Region 11	Region 12
Region 1	0.000	0.116	0.112	0.123	0.198	0.185	0.145	0.126	0.228	0.120	0.247	0.084
Region 2		0.000	0.187	0.155	0.179	0.177	0.186	0.119	0.226	0.137	0.276	0.094
Region 3			0.000	0.148	0.252	0.231	0.159	0.151	0.257	0.160	0.277	0.149
Region 4				0.000	0.208	0.197	0.086	0.089	0.136	0.068	0.232	0.133
Region 5					0.000	0.072	0.194	0.158	0.113	0.185	0.142	0.190
Region 6						0.000	0.184	0.150	0.132	0.177	0.122	0.184
Region 7							0.000	0.091	0.152	0.106	0.201	0.148
Region 8								0.000	0.152	0.063	0.221	0.103
Region 9									0.000	0.130	0.131	0.229
Region 10										0.000	0.223	0.113
Region 11											0.000	0.248
Region 12												0.000

Note: The definition of regions are as follows:

Region 1: Maine, New Hampshire, Vermont, Massachusetts, Rhode Island, Connecticut;
Region 2: New York, New Jersey, Pennsylvania;
Region 3: Ohio, Indiana, Illinois, Michigan, Wisconsin;
Region 4: Minnesota, Iowa, Missouri, North Dakota, South Dakota, Nebraska, Kansas;
Region 5: Delaware, Maryland, Virginia, West Virginia, North Carolina,
   South Carolina, Georgia;
Region 6: Kentucky, Tennessee, Alabama, Mississippi;
Region 7: Louisiana, Oklahoma;
Region 8: Florida, Texas;
Region 9: Montana, Idaho, Wyoming, Colorado;
Region 10: New Mexico, Arizona, Utah, Nevada;
Region 11: Washington, Oregon, Alaska, Hawaii;
Region 12: California.

Source: Calculated from data United States' Census of Manufactures for 1987 (Geographic Area Series), various issues.

Table AI.1c China: Coefficients of Structural Difference of Number of Firms, 1991

	Region 1	Region 2	Region 3	Region 4	Region 5	Region 6	Region 7	Region 8	Region 9	Region 10	Region 11	Region 12
Region 1	0.000	0.155	0.125	0.131	0.109	0.159	0.149	0.219	0.225	0.216	0.169	0.232
Region 2		0.000	0.130	0.157	0.118	0.052	0.184	0.148	0.159	0.157	0.060	0.127
Region 3			0.000	0.128	0.121	0.118	0.160	0.186	0.159	0.193	0.100	0.166
Region 4				0.000	0.110	0.146	0.158	0.216	0.228	0.193	0.162	0.216
Region 5					0.000	0.129	0.181	0.220	0.238	0.204	0.136	0.205
Region 6						0.000	0.161	0.157	0.151	0.149	0.048	0.112
Region 7							0.000	0.247	0.218	0.214	0.167	0.178
Region 8								0.000	0.120	0.138	0.144	0.140
Region 9									0.000	0.119	0.132	0.127
Region 10										0.000	0.158	0.157
Region 11											0.000	0.082
Region 12												0.000

Note: The definition of regions are as follows:

Region 1: Beijing, Tianjin, Hebei;
Region 2: Shanxi, Inner Mongolia, Henan;
Region 3: Liaoning, Jilin, Heilongjiang;
Region 4: Shanghai, Zhejiang, Anhui, Jiangxi;
Region 5: Jiangsu, Shandong;
Region 6: Hubei, Hunan;
Region 7: Guangdong, Fujian;
Region 8: Sichuan;
Region 9: Guizhou, Yunnan;
Region 10: Tibet, Xinjiang, Qinghai;
Region 11: Shaanxi, Gansu, Ningxia;
Region 12: Guangxi, Hainan.

Source: Calculated from data in China Industrial Statistical Yearbook 1992.

Table AI.2a European Community: Coefficients of Structural Difference of Number of Employees, 1987

	Belgium	Denmark	France	Germany	Greece	Ireland	Italy	Luxembourg	Netherlands	Portugal	Spain	U.K.
Belgium	0.000	0.271	0.156	0.221	0.298	0.217	0.242	0.466	0.252	0.396	0.165	0.172
Denmark		0.000	0.212	0.274	0.327	0.211	0.400	0.561	0.217	0.423	0.198	0.204
France			0.000	0.183	0.327	0.232	0.255	0.551	0.231	0.402	0.137	0.064
Germany				0.000	0.463	0.349	0.204	0.500	0.270	0.538	0.297	0.185
Greece					0.000	0.277	0.436	0.649	0.409	0.217	0.232	0.326
Ireland						0.000	0.381	0.557	0.254	0.418	0.213	0.224
Italy							0.000	0.610	0.399	0.392	0.348	0.252
Luxembourg								0.000	0.491	0.791	0.550	0.570
Netherlands									0.000	0.490	0.309	0.225
Portugal										0.000	0.324	0.399
Spain											0.000	0.173
U.K.												0.000

Source: Calculated from data in Industrial Statistical Yearbook (United Nations), 1991 and 1989.

Table AI.2b United States: Coefficients of Structural Difference of Number of Employees, 1987

	Region 1	Region 2	Region 3	Region 4	Region 5	Region 6	Region 7	Region 8	Region 9	Region 10	Region 11	Region 12
Region 1	0.000	0.176	0.164	0.171	0.302	0.263	0.225	0.378	0.261	0.270	0.322	0.157
Region 2		0.000	0.200	0.179	0.186	0.192	0.215	0.316	0.229	0.299	0.269	0.189
Region 3			0.000	0.131	0.310	0.285	0.177	0.404	0.251	0.269	0.296	0.144
Region 4				0.000	0.308	0.308	0.174	0.316	0.152	0.185	0.257	0.155
Region 5					0.000	0.208	0.277	0.421	0.306	0.413	0.275	0.276
Region 6						0.000	0.279	0.369	0.315	0.420	0.229	0.268
Region 7							0.000	0.308	0.258	0.248	0.304	0.149
Region 8								0.000	0.360	0.260	0.460	0.316
Region 9									0.000	0.249	0.209	0.222
Region 10										0.000	0.363	0.170
Region 11											0.000	0.305
Region 12												0.000

Note: The definition of regions are as follows:
Region 1: Maine, New Hampshire, Vermont, Massachusetts, Rhode Island, Connecticut;
Region 2: New York, New Jersey, Pennsylvania;
Region 3: Ohio, Indiana, Illinois, Michigan, Wisconsin;
Region 4: Minnesota, Iowa, Missouri, North Dakota, South Dakota, Nebraska, Kansas;
Region 5: Delaware, Maryland, Virginia, West Virginia, North Carolina, South Carolina, Georgia;
Region 6: Kentucky, Tennessee, Alabama, Mississippi;
Region 7: Louisiana, Oklahoma;
Region 8: Florida, Texas;
Region 9: Montana, Idaho, Wyoming, Colorado;
Region 10: New Mexico, Arizona, Utah, Nevada;
Region 11: Washington, Oregon, Alaska, Hawaii;
Region 12: California.

Source: Calculated from data United States' Census of Manufactures for 1987 (Geographic Area Series), various issues.

Table AI.2c China: Coefficients of Structural Difference of Number of Employees, 1991

	Region 1	Region 2	Region 3	Region 4	Region 5	Region 6	Region 7	Region 8	Region 9	Region 10	Region 11	Region 12
Region 1	0.000											
Region 2	0.161	0.000										
Region 3	0.145	0.118	0.000									
Region 4	0.088	0.184	0.200	0.000								
Region 5	0.106	0.188	0.218	0.110	0.000							
Region 6	0.138	0.107	0.141	0.146	0.144	0.000						
Region 7	0.298	0.391	0.364	0.158	0.306	0.385	0.000					
Region 8	0.106	0.104	0.124	0.216	0.155	0.110	0.351	0.000				
Region 9	0.187	0.147	0.126	0.228	0.238	0.146	0.372	0.116	0.000			
Region 10	0.235	0.183	0.229	0.193	0.222	0.156	0.425	0.179	0.191	0.000		
Region 11	0.105	0.195	0.165	0.162	0.153	0.160	0.285	0.120	0.181	0.260	0.000	
Region 12	0.232	0.181	0.205	0.216	0.235	0.168	0.365	0.167	0.171	0.239	0.219	0.000

Note: The definition of regions are as follows:

Region 1: Beijing, Tianjin, Hebei;
Region 2: Shanxi, Inner Mongolia, Henan;
Region 3: Liaoning, Jilin, Heilongjiang;
Region 4: Shanghai, Zhejiang, Anhui, Jiangxi;
Region 5: Jiangsu, Shandong;
Region 6: Hubei, Hunan;
Region 7: Guangdong, Fujian;
Region 8: Sichuan;
Region 9: Guizhou, Yunnan;
Region 10: Tibet, Xinjiang, Qinghai:
Region 11: Shaanxi, Gansu, Ningxia;
Region 12: Guangxi, Hainan.

Source: Calculated from data in China Industrial Statistical Yearbook 1992.

Table AI.3a European Community: Coefficients of Structural Difference of Output Value, 1987

	Belgium	Denmark	France	Germany	Greece	Ireland	Italy	Luxembourg	Netherlands	Portugal	Spain	U.K.
Belgium	0.000	0.370	0.435	0.517	0.346	0.394	0.373	0.534	0.324	0.371	0.320	0.429
Denmark		0.000	0.249	0.348	0.357	0.180	0.458	0.639	0.270	0.386	0.287	0.237
France			0.000	0.177	0.307	0.341	0.266	0.599	0.293	0.357	0.175	0.069
Germany				0.000	0.439	0.315	0.265	0.546	0.328	0.431	0.291	0.152
Greece					0.000	0.427	0.422	0.650	0.396	0.216	0.277	0.357
Ireland						0.000	0.396	0.628	0.265	0.432	0.371	0.308
Italy							0.000	0.580	0.356	0.317	0.350	0.252
Luxembourg								0.000	0.596	0.749	0.619	0.589
Netherlands									0.000	0.322	0.299	0.283
Portugal										0.000	0.302	0.360
Spain											0.000	0.207
U.K.												0.000

Source: Calculated from data in Industrial Statistical Yearbook (United Nations), 1991 and 1989.

Table AI.3b   United States: Coefficients of Structural Difference of Output Value, 1987

	Region 1	Region 2	Region 3	Region 4	Region 5	Region 6	Region 7	Region 8	Region 9	Region 10	Region 11	Region 12
Region 1	0.000											
Region 2	0.249	0.000										
Region 3	0.272	0.258	0.000									
Region 4	0.283	0.279	0.221	0.000								
Region 5	0.277	0.177	0.331	0.327	0.000							
Region 6	0.212	0.161	0.223	0.284	0.157	0.000						
Region 7	0.411	0.340	0.421	0.415	0.347	0.365	0.000					
Region 8	0.413	0.268	0.364	0.363	0.285	0.295	0.252	0.000				
Region 9	0.335	0.286	0.344	0.204	0.323	0.308	0.447	0.285	0.000			
Region 10	0.199	0.241	0.218	0.167	0.303	0.254	0.404	0.343	0.240	0.000		
Region 11	0.398	0.331	0.399	0.373	0.337	0.319	0.433	0.284	0.251	0.353	0.000	
Region 12	0.200	0.234	0.208	0.185	0.287	0.225	0.374	0.279	0.213	0.103	0.324	0.000

Note: The definition of regions are as follows:

Region 1: Maine, New Hampshire, Vermont, Massachusetts, Rhode Island, Connecticut;

Region 2: New York, New Jersey, Pennsylvania;

Region 3: Ohio, Indiana, Illinois, Michigan, Wisconsin;

Region 4: Minnesota, Iowa, Missouri, North Dakota, South Dakota, Nebraska, Kansas;

Region 5: Delaware, Maryland, Virginia, West Virginia, North Carolina, South Carolina, Georgia;

Region 6: Kentucky, Tennessee, Alabama, Mississippi;

Region 7: Louisiana, Oklahoma;

Region 8: Florida, Texas;

Region 9: Montana, Idaho, Wyoming, Colorado;

Region 10: New Mexico, Arizona, Utah, Nevada;

Region 11: Washington, Oregon, Alaska, Hawaii;

Region 12: California.

Source: Calculated from data United States' Census of Manufactures for 1987 (Geographic Area Series), various issues.

Table AI.3c China: Coefficients of Structural Difference of Output Value, 1991

	Region 1	Region 2	Region 3	Region 4	Region 5	Region 6	Region 7	Region 8	Region 9	Region 10	Region 11	Region 12
Region 1	0.000	0.137	0.106	0.115	0.165	0.098	0.239	0.125	0.343	0.243	0.113	0.276
Region 2		0.000	0.169	0.164	0.172	0.127	0.230	0.096	0.304	0.240	0.116	0.209
Region 3			0.000	0.197	0.227	0.150	0.273	0.135	0.321	0.271	0.165	0.267
Region 4				0.000	0.110	0.146	0.158	0.216	0.228	0.193	0.162	0.216
Region 5					0.000	0.204	0.222	0.215	0.376	0.186	0.144	0.281
Region 6						0.000	0.227	0.150	0.293	0.245	0.109	0.222
Region 7							0.000	0.244	0.385	0.281	0.218	0.258
Region 8								0.000	0.308	0.255	0.142	0.199
Region 9									0.000	0.390	0.313	0.294
Region 10										0.000	0.245	0.293
Region 11											0.000	0.219
Region 12												0.000

Note: The definition of regions are as follows:

Region 1: Beijing, Tianjin, Hebei;
Region 2: Shanxi, Inner Mongolia, Henan;
Region 3: Liaoning, Jilin, Heilongjiang;
Region 4: Shanghai, Zhejiang, Anhui, Jiangxi;
Region 5: Jiangsu, Shandong;
Region 6: Hubei, Hunan;
Region 7: Guangdong, Fujian;
Region 8: Sichuan;
Region 9: Guizhou, Yunnan;
Region 10: Tibet, Xinjiang, Qinghai;
Region 11: Shaanxi, Gansu, Ningxia;
Region 12: Guangxi, Hainan.

Source: Calculated from data in China Industrial Statistical Yearbook 1992.

Table AI.4a EC, US and China: Coefficient of Variation of Average Employees Per Firm (Nos)

	EC/a			US/b			China/c		
	Mean	SD	COV	Mean	SD	COV	Mean	SD	COV
Total	71.44	61.92	0.87	48.48	11.85	0.24	19.43	2.97	0.15
Food and Beverage [311/2/3]/d	51.97	33.93	0.65	86.43	47.37	0.55	9.98	3.29	0.33
Tobacco [314]	318.95	217.73	0.68	n.a.	n.a.	n.a.	104.70	55.51	0.53
Textiles [321]	64.97	40.42	0.62	65.29	61.58	0.94	42.98	7.40	0.17
Wearing Apparel [322]	42.97	29.27	0.68	60.67	55.40	0.91	11.91	4.14	0.35
Leather and Products [323]	27.60	18.07	0.65	41.36	35.96	0.87	13.81	4.00	0.29
Wood Produtcs and Furniture [331/2]	24.18	16.94	0.70	26.48	9.82	0.37	7.40	3.52	0.48
Paper and Products [341]	70.83	30.76	0.43	95.23	33.77	0.35	15.36	3.57	0.23
Printing, publishing [342]	37.37	29.47	0.79	21.84	4.82	0.22	9.44	1.88	0.20
Industrial Chemicals [351]	183.36	148.25	0.81	64.26	31.01	0.48	24.67	8.61	0.35
Petroleum and Coal Products [353/4]	183.34	213.39	1.16	45.49	37.23	0.82	27.00	16.26	0.60
Rubber Products [355]	114.00	97.11	0.85	52.99	21.93	0.41	23.84	8.35	0.35
Glass and Non-metal Products [362/9]	52.75	48.52	0.92	29.71	7.48	0.25	13.78	1.65	0.12
Metal Industries [371/2]	221.29	272.50	1.23	87.69	32.00	0.36	88.89	27.68	0.31
Metal Products [381]	41.75	35.06	0.84	31.35	8.24	0.26	9.22	2.49	0.27
Machinery n.e.c [382]	70.75	58.82	0.83	34.67	7.54	0.22	24.66	5.21	0.21
Electrical Machinery [383]	105.99	73.73	0.70	97.99	30.85	0.31	53.43	23.99	0.45
Transport Equipment [384]	205.55	234.05	1.14	136.70	65.99	0.48	30.52	8.36	0.27

a/, b/   EC, US, data refer to the year 1987.
c/   China data are of 1991.
d/ Numbers in brackets are ISIC codes.

Source: Calculated from data in Industrial Statistical Yearbook 1991 (United Nations), 1987 Census of Manufactures (U.S.), and China Industrial Statistical Yearbook 1992.

Table AI.4b EC, US and China: Coefficient of Variation of Average Output Per Firm (US$ million)

	EC/a			US/b			China/c		
	Mean	SD	COV	Mean	SD	COV	Mean	SD	COV
Total	7413	6548	0.88	6522	1769	0.27	372.38	86.80	0.23
Food and Beverage [311/2/3]/d	9755	8812	0.90	14562	4598	0.32	300.67	122.43	0.41
Tobacco [314]	81747	110877	1.36	n.a.	n.a.	n.a.	14033.10	9759.63	0.70
Textiles [321]	4556	3377	0.74	5609	5579	0.99	776.26	123.08	0.16
Wearing Apparel [322]	1910	1609	0.84	2532	1561	0.62	180.24	104.02	0.58
Leather and Products [323]	2500	2017	0.81	2741	2305	0.84	217.35	115.96	0.53
Wood Produts and Furniture [331/2]	1704	1603	0.94	2709	1554	0.57	80.48	39.67	0.49
Paper and Products [341]	8342	5912	0.71	18532	10467	0.56	281.92	89.01	0.32
Printing, publishing [342]	2762	2169	0.79	1880	634	0.34	151.23	64.62	0.43
Industrial Chemicals [351]	31834	27136	0.85	18184	11795	0.65	586.96	136.52	0.23
Petroleum and Coal Products [353/4]	180538	190037	1.05	56763	58656	1.03	2142.09	1752.62	0.82
Rubber Products [355]	10681	12440	1.16	5794	3141	0.54	624.23	259.72	0.42
Glass and Non-metal Products [362/9]	6085	6186	1.02	3430	819	0.24	162.17	59.53	0.37
Metal Industries [371/2]	22217	26749	1.20	14813	6721	0.45	3107.04	1631.74	0.53
Metal Products [381]	4185	3718	0.89	2933	834	0.28	145.69	65.71	0.45
Machinery n.e.c [382]	5211	4386	0.84	4108	1075	0.26	368.76	65.15	0.18
Electrical Machinery [383]	7852	6581	0.84	11188	4981	0.45	426.84	129.32	0.30
Transport Equipment [384]	21171	28234	1.33	22628	14352	0.63	628.10	183.34	0.29

a/, b/ EC, US, data refer to the year 1987.
c/   China data are of 1991.
d/ Numbers in brackets are ISIC codes.

Source: Calculated from data in Industrial Statistical Yearbook 1991 (United Nations), 1987 Census of Manufactures (U.S.), and China Industrial Statistical Yearbook 1992.

2

Recent Evolution of China's Internal Markets

The objective of this chapter is to assess the recent evolution of China towards a market economy, in terms of key economic parameters. One important indicator of the extent to which markets are functioning, as discussed in Chapter 1, is the behavior of prices. In a market economy, the price of a good would normally be independent of the person or agent selling or buying the good, and prices in different markets would tend to equalize, subject to differentials in product quality and real costs of transportation. The first section of this chapter therefore examines price behavior, to see whether recent moves towards the lifting of price controls has brought about price convergence in different markets, both in terms of 'plan' and 'market' prices and in terms of spatial price differentials.

The following sections examine the mobility of goods and the mobility of factors of production, among alternative uses as well as in a geographic sense. Trade in goods is first analyzed, in terms of interprovincial flows of goods, and changes in these over time. The regional mobility of goods in China is compared with other countries. Next, the mobility of capital and labor is evaluated, across regional boundaries as well as, in the case of labor, flexibility of deployment between within and between occupations. Finally, since foreign exchange is also a critical scarce input in domestic production, the market for foreign exchange is also evaluated.

A. The Impact of Price Reform

The objective of this chapter is to assess the recent evolution of China towards a market economy, in terms of key economic parameters. A first extremely important indicator of the extent to which markets are functioning, as discussed in Chapter 1, is the behavior of prices. China's efforts to deregulate prices have already been noted. More specific details of the proportions of retail sales and farm produce subject to controlled, 'guidance' and free prices are available in Appendix Table A2.1. In 1978, 97 percent of domestic retail goods and 93 percent of farm produce was subject to fixed prices. During the first phase of reform, controls on prices had already diminished, particularly in agriculture. By 1985, retail goods and agricultural goods subject to fixed prices had fallen to 47 and 37 percent, respectively. After 1985, decontrol was more notable outside agriculture and by 1991, these ratios had fallen further, to 21 and 22 percent.

Although the inflationary period of 1988 to 1989 put a brake on price reforms, and in some cases, controls were reimposed on goods whose prices had been freed, by 1991, for the most part, the effects of this reversal had been allayed and for most goods, price deregulation by 1991 had surpassed the achievements of 1985. At this time, prices in agriculture were somewhat more regulated than in non-agriculture, (only 58 percent of agricultural goods were in the free price category, in contrast to 69 percent for all retail trade), and the use of guidance mechanisms was also greater (20 percent of farm produce, compared to 10 percent of retail goods).

From 1991, more radical advances in price deregulation have been made. The total number of heavy industrial products and transport services subject to control was reduced from 737 at the end of 1991 to 89 in 1992. These included most machinery and electrical products, some steel goods and some petrochemicals. Many producer goods subject to central government price controls were deregulated, with new guidelines on material prices issued in July and August 1992. Of the 593 production materials on these lists, 571 were transferred to market pricing, and for another 22 goods, the control over prices was transferred from the center to local governments. In addition, for products still subject to controlled prices, these prices were adjusted upwards, towards their market levels.

Rapid progress has recently been achieved with those goods whose price controls had led to the need for heavy government subsidies; coal, transport, grain and edible oils.[1] For coal, where for several years only 5 percent of output was permitted to be sold at market prices, this ratio was raised to 20 percent in 1992 and to 57 percent in early 1993.[2] In the case of crude oil, selling price controls will be lifted on 22 million tons of output per year, at three major oilfields.[3] Price decontrols in 14 medium to small oilfields were also announced in May 1993. Transport tariffs have been raised for rail and water transport. Rail freight tariffs were raised in 1991, and then again in July 1992, from 2.85 to 3.85 fen per ton kilometer. A further 40 percent increase was announced on July 1 1993, to 5.35 fen, expected to generate Y8 billion worth of revenues. Among consumer goods, urban ration prices of grain, which had been constant since 1957, had an increase in seller prices in 1992 to match purchasing prices. By January 1993, urban ration prices for grain were free in 844 cities and counties and in March and April, the major urban centers Shanghai and Tianjin, as well as the province of Jiangsu, announced the decontrol of grain as well as edible oil prices for consumers, and the withdrawal of the coupons for their subsidized distribution.[4] Surplus provinces are now entering into market contracts with major purchasing areas.[5]

---

[1] World Bank (1992) 'China: The Achievements and Challenge of Price Reform' details the controls and subsidies for individual products.

[2] In 1992, China National Coal Corporation, the state coal monopoly, reduced its losses by some 500 million yuan as a consequence of the freeing of prices of 20 percent of output, as well as the layoffs of 100,000 workers. In 1993, market prices were permitted for 190 million tons of the total 370 million tons of state-allocated output, which was expected to further reduce operating losses by over 1 billion yuan. At the end of 1992, the CNCC, together with the Shanghai municipal government, put a coal 'futures market' into operation in the city. *Asian Wall Street Journal*, January 4 1993.

[3] Daqing, Liaohe and Shangli. The quantity of crude sold at market prices will also be increased by 22 million tons per year until 1995. Complete price decontrol will be introduced at the Jilin oilfield. From 1993, China National Petroleum and Natural Oil Corporation will purchase oil at the international price from these oilfields, and will then sell at fixed prices. *Summary of World Broadcasts*, BBC, 18 February 1993.

[4] However, in Jiangsu some compensatory cash subsidies were introduced; 6 yuan per worker and 4 yuan per student.

Prices of services are also being freed in some provinces such as Guangdong, where fees and charges have been lifted on 90 categories of services, and only 12 are still subject to controls.

Partly as a consequence of the accelerated lifting of price controls since 1992, the cost of living index of the 35 largest cities increased by 17 percent in the first quarter of 1993, over the same period last year.[6] To reduce the possibilities of escalating inflation, new price reforms will be suspended in the second half of 1992, as part of an overall economic plan to curb overheating.[7] This marks a halt in the latest phase of price deregulation.

Assessing Price Efficiency: Plan and Market Prices

How successful was the progressive decontrol of prices, in terms of the establishment of markets? If markets function efficiently, prices should accurately reflect relative scarcities, and the price of any given good should be the same regardless of the seller. For example, in the era of state controlled prices, parallel markets emerged for many scarce commodities where goods were sold at prices well above state regulated levels. With the introduction of dual-track pricing, which implied that a part of (above target) output could legally be sold on the free market, the gap between this price and controlled prices should have fallen, and the differential should be further reduced with progressive price decontrol. Thus one measure of the efficiency of markets is the extent of convergence between state regulated and market prices. As shown in Appendix Table A2.2, for consumer goods as a whole, free market prices were 80 percent above state prices in 1975. The gap declined to 48 percent by 1980, and further to 28 percent by 1985. By 1991, the differential was only 5 percent.

Disaggregating, to look at different categories of consumer goods (Figure 2.1), the general trend towards price convergence is clear for all products. However, as discussed above, residual controls until recently were much more important for some agricultural products, such as grain and vegetable oils. As a consequence, the graph clearly illustrates, official and market price differentials were much larger for these products. The effect of the reimposition of controls is also illustrated; the trend towards convergence was temporarily reversed between 1987 and 1989, notably for grain and meat products. However by 1991 the effects of this episode had been alleviated.

---

[5] At the national meeting for grain production and marketing in February 1993, Heilongjiang and Shandong, which are major grain producers, entered into an interregional grain sales contract with Yunnan, Shanghai and Beijing, marking the inception of a nationwide grain marketing system.

[6] Major macroeconomic factors are of course also involved, such as the credit expansion and high growth of investment.

[7] Sixteen point plan of the Central Committee of the Chinese Communist Party, announced in July 1993.

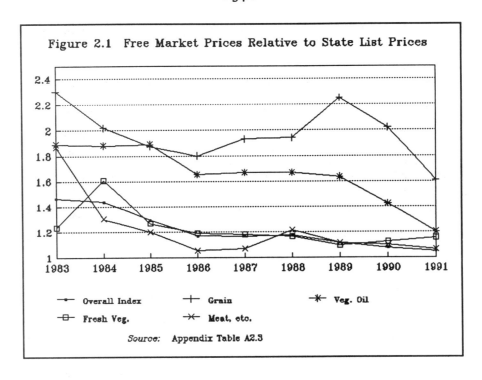

Figure 2.1 Free Market Prices Relative to State List Prices

Source: Appendix Table A2.3

Trends for producer goods also indicate convergence, but the result is weaker, and the temporary increase in the divergence of market and state controlled prices is more pronounced. In Table 2.1, price divergence increases for all products, around 1989, but declines, thereafter, for all products. Eventually, market prices in 1991, relative to 1986, are closer to planned prices for four out of six products; steel, cement, aluminum and timber. Market prices for copper are only marginally higher. The one significant exception is coal, although even in this case, prices do begin to converge after 1989. The reason for the slower convergence in coal prices is that controls on coal have remained more significant than for the other listed products, and the effect of this on market efficiency is well illustrated.

Table 2.1 Ratios of Market to State Prices for Main Materials

Market/State Price (percent)	1986	1987	1988	1989	1990	1991
Steel products	148	145	146	136	122	111
Cement	122	120	127	135	119	111
Coal	145	142	192	268	205	170
Copper	111	109	182	188	118	113
Aluminum	143	143	180	168	120	108
Lumber	145	153	169	169	161	140

Source: Appendix Table A2.4.

More evidence of price behavior for additional producer goods is given in Table 2.2. This table, like the preceding one, also shows that there has been price convergence over time in the producer goods described here, if we look at the end points 1985 and 1991. In this table too, prices have diverged in 1988, relative to 1985 for two of the products (steel rod and aluminum) for which data are available.[8]

Table 2.2 Plan and Market Prices for Selected Materials (1985-1991)
(Yuan per ton)

	1985				1988				1991			
	Plan ned price (a)	Non-plan price (b)	Price differe ntial (b-a)	(b/a)	Plan ned price (a)	Non-plan price (b)	Price differe ntial (b-a)	(b/a)	Plan ned price (a)	Non-plan price (b)	Price differe ntial (b-a)	(b/a)
Coal	26.4	77.4	51	293	61	148	86.8	243	83	141	58	170
Crude Oil	100	545	445	545					204	580	376	284
Steel Rod (20mm)	610	840	230	138	520	1513	993	291				
Cement(#425)	56	121	64.9	216	90	154	64	171				
Pig Iron	280	526	246	188					751	752	1	100
Aluminum	2760	5800	3040	210	4000	9426	5426	236	8436	9072	636	108
Zinc	1930	3131	1201	162					6789	7446	657	110

Sources: China Price Research; Tian Yuan and Qiao Gang, (1991); China Price, 1992 (February).

Assessing Price Efficiency: Regional Price Differentials

Another measure of the efficiency of the internal market, from the point of view of price behavior, is the extent to which there is regional price convergence. Once the system of allocation of specified quantities of goods to particular locations is terminated, and goods are free to move to those users who need them the most, there will be a tendency for regional market price differentials to converge as well, except for differences which reflect real costs of transportation. Looking at regional prices, the first observation is that variations have tended to be large. Some scattered evidence is available in Appendix Table A2.5, which details the plan and market prices for six major producer goods, at six different provincial locations, in 1987, 1989 and 1991, collected by the Ministry of Materials. In 1987, the 'all China' market price for steel was Y1516 per ton, but the regional prices at the six locations observed ranged from Y1080 in Shanxi to Y2000 in Zhejiang. In 1991, the 'all China' price was Y1984, with a minimum price of Y1857 (Hebei) and a maximum of Y2435 (Chongqing city).

A more comprehensive analysis of regional price differentials for producer and consumer goods has also been undertaken, covering all provinces in China (Appendix Tables A2.6 to A2.11).

---

[8] However, in this table, coal prices have converged steadily. The absolute values for prices per ton of coal and cement, which are available in both tables, differ, particularly for the official prices. Since the two sources of data are different, this may be due to different product standards. It may also be due to regional price differentials (see Appendix Table 2.5). The central finding, on eventual price convergence remains valid.

Looking first at seven broad categories of consumer goods from 1986 to 1991, it is observed that for all the products, regional variations in prices increased after 1986 (summarized in Table 2.3). For six of these products, price variations declined after 1989, but the levels of variation in 1991 were still higher than in 1986. For one of the seven products (color TVs), there has been no decline.

Table 2.3   Coefficient of Regional Variation of Retail Prices of Major Commodities
(1986-1991)

	1986			1989			1991		
	SD	Mean	COV	SD	Mean	COV	SD	Mean	COV
Flour (Y/kg)	0.05	0.50	0.10	0.16	0.55	0.28	0.16	0.74	0.22
Rice (Y/kg)	0.06	0.35	0.18	0.21	0.48	0.44	0.16	0.55	0.28
Vegetable Oil (Y/kg)	0.29	2.18	0.13	0.95	2.97	0.32	0.53	3.70	0.14
Apples (Y/kg)	0.29	1.92	0.15	0.69	3.34	0.21	0.75	4.21	0.18
White cotton cloth (Y/m)	0.14	1.18	0.12	0.49	2.25	0.22	0.41	2.73	0.15
Color TV (45 cm) (Y)	57.01	1383.55	0.04	233.05	2765.66	0.08	315.34	2250.69	0.14
Coal(resident use) (Y/100 kg)	0.89	3.37	0.26	1.38	4.00	0.34	1.94	5.87	0.33
Kerosene (Y/kg)	0.12	0.73	0.16	0.40	0.86	0.46	0.34	0.96	0.35

Note: SD: Standard deviation; COV: Coefficient of variation.

Source: Calculated from data in China Price Statistical Yearbook (various issues) (see Appendix Tables A2.6-A2.8).

For producer goods, the time period for which information is available is much shorter; December 1990 to June 1992. Looking at the prices of five major producer goods in all provincial capitals, from December 1990 to June 1992 (Appendix Tables A2.9-A2.11), we notice that the regional variations, for three out of five products, rose, but then decreased again. For two products, there was a continuous decrease. Although the pattern is not as clear as in the case of consumer goods, and the time periods are not comparable, the results generally suggest that regional price variations for many products, and clearly for consumer goods, rose after 1986, until around 1989. In more recent years, regional variations have begun to decline, but the decline is not consistent. In some cases variations appear to still be on the increase. And the recent declines in many cases are not sufficient, so far, to compensate for the earlier increases in regional price differentials.

Table 2.4   Coefficients of Variation of Materials Prices by Province (1990-1992)

Location	Steel Sheet (16-20mm)	Copper	Coal	Cement (#425)	Timber
COV December 1990	0.0765	0.08	0.3047	0.2145	0.2456
COV December 1991	0.0591	0.0382	0.2265	0.1835	0.2302
COV June 1992	0.0693	0.0211	0.3374	0.1312	0.2826

Source: Calculations in Appendix Tables A2.9 to A2.11.

One possibility is that, with the relaxation of controls, there was first a tendency for prices to diverge, as different markets each attempted to find out what the real demand and supply facing their products was. This, as well as the reimposition of controls in 1988-89, can help explain the initial divergences in market prices, by both sets of measures. However the failure of regional prices variations to even attain their 1986 levels, in the case of many consumer goods, cannot be thus explained.

To summarize the findings of the preceding paragraphs, there was clearly an increase in the efficiency of market price signalling, in terms of the movement from plan to market prices, at least until 1991. For convenience, we shall refer to this as 'vertical integration' of markets. The move was less pronounced in terms of producer goods than consumer goods. The data also indicate that this success is vulnerable to reversal when controls are reintroduced. The record in terms of 'regional market integration', as measured by regional price convergence, is not as encouraging. On balance it is clear that regional price variations were still significant in 1991 and have not noticeably diminished since 1986. The analysis so far reinforces the findings of the previous chapter on regionally segmented markets and suggests that this issue should now be the area of focus. However, one qualification to the above findings is that the effects of recently introduced price decontrols of 1992 and early 1993 have not been incorporated, for the most part, as data on these are not yet published. The analysis will have to be extended to take these into account when data are available.

B. Interregional Domestic Trade

One explanation for the findings above may be that the movement of goods between provinces is relatively little, so that prices in each province are relatively protected from prices elsewhere. There are also issues concerning segregation of markets across sectors of responsibility (such as governmental departments or ministries), which have been inheritied from the planning era. This could aggravate regional trade barriers set up by provincial authorities. In an effort to protect local industry, many provinces in China have set up barriers to internal trade. There are several anecdotal accounts of difficulties encountered in internal trade, due to a variety of factors, apart from transport associated bottlenecks. They include, first, restraint orders on exports or imports of certain goods. Physical restraints have sometimes been imposed, in the form of roadside barriers or checkpoints. Second, fees and fines have been levied on truckers transporting goods from one province to another. Procurement preferences given by local governments to producers in their jurisdictions are also mentioned, though there are fewer accounts of this, possibly because it is not unexpected.

Constraints on Domestic Trade: Some Anecdotes

Export Embargoes: The Commodity 'Wars'

During the latter 1980s, a number of agroprocessing factories in coastal provinces suffered from severe underutilization of capacity because of raw material shortages. Although China was a highly competitive supplier of both cotton and silk textiles, domestic capacity utilization in these industries declined year by year over the period 1985 to 1989. Raw materials from interior provinces were either diverted by regional governments towards local processors, or sold directly to overseas buyers. Embargoes or taxes were imposed on interregional exports. 'Wars' broke out between neighboring provinces, with barricades, roadblocks, and sometimes local militia, to enforce these.

Silk processors in Shanghai complained that Hunan refused to provide them with silk, preferring to export directly to Hong Kong, while Shanghai in turn was forced to import silk from Hong Kong for processing. State owned cotton processing enterprises only received 40 percent of their cotton requirements from the state in 1990 and many mills operated at only 50 percent capacity utilization. While state enterprise output increased only 28 percent over 1984 to 1989, output in rural enterprises increased five fold.

In the case of other commodities, local trade barriers led to market chaos, speculation and violence. At the same time as the fiber wars, a 'tea war' began, around 1985, continuing in some provinces until 1989. In May 1987, in Zhejiang province, peddlers and speculators forced up the price of tea, while crude processing factories hoarded and speculated, deliberately creating panic in the market. Collective and contracted fields of tea were plundered in Tishun county. In Shaoxing county, when tea was sold to neighboring Shangyu county at a more favorable price, the village head led twenty people in trucks and vans to attack the supply and marketing cooperative undertaking the sales.

Grain embargoes continued into the 1990s. Hunan province was approached by its neighbor, Guangdong, in 1990, to import rice. Guangdong felt that the price quoted by Hunan provincial officials appeared high. Guangdong officials then approached Hunan farmers directly, offering a price lower than this, but higher than the procurement price offered by Hunan province. Hunan put security guards on the borders to prevent the shipments and Guangdong retaliated with its own forces.

Export embargoes have not been restricted to agricultural commodities alone. Liaoning declared in 1992 that it would not permit exports of fertilizers, except under the central plan, as it could not meet its own requirements.

Tax Collection, Fees and Fines

In mid 1990, the Nanping railroad station, a transport hub for the ten counties of the Minbei region of Fujian province, became a tax collection point for 33 different taxes, for which the Nanping municipal tax bureau had enlisted the help of 30 agencies in the past. Tax collectors were commissioned in the baggage room, and the tax bureau set up a joint operation with the freight office to collect taxes when goods were collected for shipment. Revenue collection more than tripled. In Ningde county, a truck loaded with live eels for export was confronted on its way to Fuzhou airport with a demand for collection of a 3 percent special product tax. The owner responded that in the past, the foreign trade bureau had claimed responsibility for all taxes on exported eels and asked to discuss the matter with the foreign trade department. The truck was detained, the eels perished, and eventually the province suffered a loss of export earnings as well as a damaged reputation.

Apart from legitimate fees and taxes, there are illegal trade barriers in the form of 'inspection stations' which demand arbitrary traffic fees. In Baihuting, suburban Fuzhou, vehicles carrying scrap iron were stopped and fines were demanded, or else, the goods were confiscated for a token sum. A bamboo dealer in Sanming country in Zhejiang bought 1,524 yuan worth of bamboo shoots to truck to Shanghai. But by the time he had reached Tongxiang county in Zhejiang, a total of 546 yuan had been paid en route, for 13 taxes and fees. With several hundred kilometers to go, and no knowledge of how many more inspection stations there would be, the dealer decided to sell his cargo in Tongxiang and return.

Even in Guangdong province, reputed to be free trade oriented, a series of checkposts, barriers, local blockades, including those set up by the Guangdong Province Administration of Industry and Commerce (GPAIC) and the public security bureau, as well as numerous fees and fines, have been reported. In June 1992, orders were issued to close checkposts and the GPAIC reduced the checkposts from 51 to 5. Guangdong complains that its neighboring provinces of Jiangxi, Fujian and Guangxi have made no reciprocal attempts to reduce protection.

Import Restraints and Provincial Protection

Sichuan province says that it has lifted government restrictions and checkpoints on trade, since the beginning of the 1990s. However, in terms of government purchases, all other things being equal, local suppliers would be preferred. Meanwhile Beijing, in 1992, restricted imports of hogs, from Hebei. Elsewhere, according to a CASS field survey, a province in the southwest decided to protect 19 local products in 1989 and restricted the imports of these goods from other provinces. And an autonomous region in the west expressly prohibited the entry of 48 outside products.

Sources: Forster (1991), Agarwala (1992), Findlay et. al (1992), Watson and Findlay (1992), Lyons (1992), Huang (1992), *The Economist*, June 26, 1993.

It is possible to categorize these constraints and consider their likelihood of persistence or recurrence. The export embargoes on raw materials which occurred in the latter half of the 1980s, forcing the underutilization of some processing capacity, arose first of all because of the end of the unified purchasing system under mandatory plan, in 1985. Second, this was combined with a surge in demand. As free market prices rose above plan prices, there was a temptation to sellers to evade plan procurement and obtain the higher free market price. Local governments were forced to impose export embargoes to control outflows which occurred before mandatory quotas were fulfilled. The activities of hoarding and speculation were essentially a by-product of the market segmentation introduced with the new system. From 1989, there was a contraction in domestic demand, and a simultaneous reimposition, for some commodities, of the state procurement system. It may also be argued that by this time, a more orderly secondary market had developed, so that domestic 'exports' could now take place in a more orderly fashion, and the extent to which hoarding, speculation and disruptive market conduct could occur, might have diminished. The commodity 'wars' declined considerably for most products.[9] The more gradual reduction in government procurement quotas, as well as price controls, for these commodities since 1991 is likely to further reduce the likelihood of their recurrence.

Other factors which provoked the domestic export embargoes include an increase in the authority given to provincial and local officials to collect revenues, under the fiscal contracting system, and the export earnings retention system. Under the former, it was to the advantage of provincial authorities to extract monopsonistic rents for purchases and sales though public channels, and as the case of Hunan's grain exports illustrates, this factor is likely to persist to the extent that public procurement is channeled though provincial or county officials. The authority to collect revenues has also affected the flow of goods not subject to public procurement. The story of the tax collection at Nanping railway station illustrates the fact that transit points have sometimes proven convenient for the collection of a number of legitimate fees and taxes that would otherwise have large collection costs. However in addition, there are many instances of abuse of this authority, as well as cases of illegal checkposts and taxes, imposed on the highway. This form of ad hoc fee and fine imposition is likely to be more important, today, than the export embargoes of the commodity 'wars'

Another implication of the increased revenue collection authority given to provincial officials was the diversion of raw materials away from processing units in other provinces, towards processors in their own provinces, in an attempt to capture tax revenues from value-added. Import restraints issued by provinces are also a consequence of attempts by provincial authorities to protect local enterprises, at the same time increasing revenues from the profits and taxes of local enterprises. Local procurement preferences have the same effect, and are difficult to trace in the absence of formalized procurement guidelines. Finally, the factor that led to the diversion of goods away from the domestic market and towards the export market was the export retention system. Provinces were permitted to retain a part of export proceedings, and with the overvalued exchange rate, as well as the differentials in retention rates across provinces, each province attempted to increase its holdings of the undervalued resource, foreign exchange, by diverting sales away from the domestic market.

There are indications that such barriers may have loosened up in the 1990s. In November 1990 the State Council issued a circular banning restrictions on interprovincial trade. This is echoed in

---

9   It is reported, for example, that once grain rationing ended, grain began flowing from Hunan to Guangdong. *Baokan Wenzhai* (Periodicals Digest), 26 May 1992, p 1.

the new law against unfair competition of September 1993. Both major manufacturers and township and village enterprises in Shanghai and Guangzhou have established countrywide marketing networks for some of their products. This is particularly true of certain manufactured consumer goods such as wrist watches or radios, where firms from the south are now reported to be making inroads in the markets of northern provinces. Some larger products (for example, tractors), are less mobile, although a few heavy capital goods produced by a small number of state enterprises are also nationally distributed.

An Analysis of Domestic Trade Flows

The extent to which policy and real obstacles may have constrained internal trade may be gauged from an analysis of internal trade flows (Appendix Tables A2.12-A2.17).[10] In aggregate, for all provinces taken together, both domestic imports and domestic exports grew over time, in absolute terms. The annual average rate of growth of domestic interprovincial exports and imports, at 6.9 and 4.8 percent per year, were however slower than the rate of growth of total retail sales, and as a result, the share of domestic trade in retail sales (defined as {domestic imports+exports}/{domestic retail sales}) declined over time. The decline was pronounced between 1985 and 1990 (from 63 percent to 48 percent), with some marginal recovery since, to 50.3 percent in 1992. These results are in marked contrast to external trade. Over the last seven years, 1985 to 1992, international exports grew at 16.7 percent per year, while imports grew by 9.7 percent, on average, measured in dollar terms. Measured in domestic currency (for appropriate comparison with domestic trade), the rates are considerably higher, at 28 percent and 20 percent per year. These patterns imply that there has been a growing tendency for individual provinces to behave as independent countries, increasing their links with the external world, and in relative terms, reducing trade links with other provinces within the country.

There are some interesting differences between provinces in terms of domestic trade behavior. Looking first at export ratios alone, on average for all provinces, domestic interprovincial exports as a percentage of retail sales declined from 36.6 to 27.6 percent over 1985 to 1992. However, in some provinces, these ratios stayed virtually constant (Hebei) or increased over time (Liaoning, Jiangsu, Zhejiang, Fujian, Jiangxi, Guangdong, and Sichuan). With the exception of Sichuan, these are all relatively rapidly growing coastal provinces or their hinterlands. In terms of imports, Hebei, Jilin, Fujian, Jiangxi, Hubei, Guangdong and Guangxi were also able to raise domestic import ratios.[11] This suggests that more rapidly growing coastal areas may also be able to develop stronger trade links, in terms of domestic exports, with other interior areas. One significant implication is that 'trade diversion' does not appear to have occurred, as these areas simultaneously increased their domestic and external exports.

It is also notable that the three major cities of Beijing, Tianjin and Shanghai were the most 'open' areas at the beginning of this period, with higher ratios of exports and imports than most other provinces. However, in all three, both domestic export and import ratios have declined over time. This suggests that the municipalities directly under the central government may be growing somewhat more autarkic over time, and also relative to other provinces.

---

10   The source of the data in these tables is the State Statistical Bureau.

11   Import ratios also rose in some of the remote provinces; Sichuan, Yunnan and Shaanxi.

A more detailed time series analysis comparing domestic trade and external trade at the level of individual provinces was undertaken on a sample basis for five provinces.[12] The results are summarized in Figure 2.2. The data echo the finding that domestic trade ratios are highly variable across provinces. Shanghai had been the most open, in terms of links with other provinces and until 1990, the ratio of external trade exceeded domestic retail sales. However the ratios in Shanghai more recently have dropped to levels comparable to other provinces. These data also emphasize the finding that unlike domestic trade ratios, external trade ratios have been rising rapidly, and this is true of all the provinces illustrated here, except Shaanxi. This suggests once again that the relative attractiveness of the external and domestic markets favored the former, and that trade has tended to develop more easily with the external world than with other provinces.

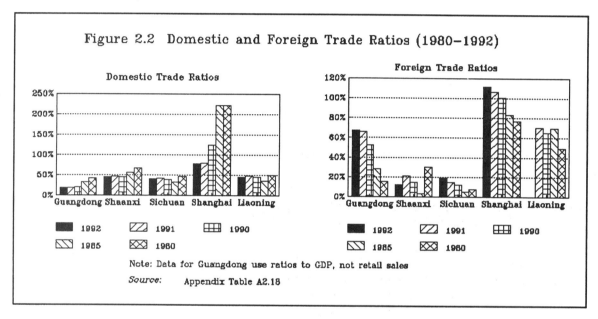

Figure 2.2   Domestic and Foreign Trade Ratios (1980-1992)

Note: Data for Guangdong use ratios to GDP, not retail sales

Source: Appendix Table A2.18

How does China compare, in terms of internal trade flows, with other countries? Detailed comparisons are available for the former Soviet Union (FSU) and its individual republics, as well as for the European Community. Although these are not single countries today, the FSU was a single country in 1990, which is the year referred to here, and the EC is a common market area. The results are summarized in Table 2.5.[13] The data show that, in terms of ratios to GDP, internal trade in selected

---

[12]   These data (Appendix Table A2.18) were collected by the CASS, unlike the above series, compiled by the SSB (Appendix Tables A2.12-A2.17). The absolute values of provincial data are higher in the CASS data, and the difference between the two series increases over time. However the CASS data are inclusive of urban and rural collective enterprises while SSB data refer to state units. This could account for the increase in the spread between the two series, as cooperatives have grown faster than state enterprises. In terms of direction, the results of the two series are the same for all provinces, except for Guangdong. However, in this case, the CASS data use ratios to GDP rather than retail sales.

[13]   Details are available in Appendix Table A2.19. It must be added that international comparisons are nortoriously difficult and that any interpretation of the data should take account of the possibility of a margin of error. The maximum difference in the ratios presented here, at 11 percent, could be vulnerable to such error.

provinces in China, at 22.1 percent, was lower than trade in the EC (28.3 percent), and also lower than trade among the nations of the FSU, excluding Russia.[14] This also suggests that there is considerable potential for expanding the internal market in China through increased internal trade.

Table 2.5 China and Other Regional Trading Areas: Interregional Trade

	Int. Imports	Int. Exports	Total GDP/a	Imports/ GDP %	Exports/ GDP %	Total Trade/GDP %
China (1989/1991): (Y million)/b						
Subtotal for 5 provinces/b	49085.8	36486.8	387878.0	12.7	9.4	22.1
E C (1989): (ECU million)						
EC Total	624.5	624.5	4406.9	14.2	14.2	28.3
F S U (1990): (Ruble million)						
Subtotal (Excluding Russia)	125752	95886	814602	15.4	11.8	27.2
Subtotal (all FSU countries)	182335	182335	2103179	8.7	8.7	17.3

/a The Chinese figures for the GDP column are GNP.
/b Guangdong, Jiangxi, Sichuan, Guizhou, Beijing. Various years between 1989 and 1991.
Source: Appendix Table A2.19.

The inferences drawn from these findings depend on the coverage of the data used. Data published in the Provincial statistical yearbooks cover only SOEs and rural cooperatives, which implies that private trade flows are not included. These are likely to have risen, over the recent reform years. At present no comprehensive data are available. Meanwhile, as data in Chapter 3 shows, the state continued to dominate the distribution system (see Appendix tables 3.4 and 3.5).

Taking this into account, how should China's relative decline in internal trade be assessed? First, some decline in the regional mobility of goods may be attributed to the decline in centralized allocation. At least a part of the centralized allocation was held to be inefficient, in terms of spatial planning, and some goods were transported unnecessarily long distances. To this extent, the decline in trade need not reflect a decline in efficiency. Second, the relative decline in internal trade between provinces, compared to the growth in total retail trade, may also be due to the rapid growth of township and village enterprises, and a consequent increase in production as well as consumption within provincial frontiers.[15] Third, some of the decline, in the years before 1989, may have been due to the adoption of the dual price system, and the embargoes on trade placed by some provincial authorities on the export of specific goods. However, these were not the only factors behind the decline in internal trade, and trade restraints were also a consequence of increased roadside tax collection by provincial and lower level authorities, as well as by unauthorized persons and the difficulties in arranging for financial flows (for payments) across regions. The increase in regional price divergence probably reflects some of these factors. If the decline in centralized allocation was the primary reason for the decline in internal trade, the trend decline in regional trade would have been arrested, as in the case of early plan-market

---

[14] The trade to GDP ratio for Russia was much lower than for other FSU countries, at 11.1 percent (Appendix Table A2.19). On account of its large weight in the sample, this brings down the national aggregate markedly, if included.

[15] A comparable analysis of intra-provincial trade, especially within some of the larger provinces, is desirable, but data are not available at present.

price divergence. The relatively low interprovincial trade in China, compared to the countries in Table 2.5, may therefore suggest some neglect of opportunities to benefit from specialization and local comparative advantages.

Some adverse effects of trade limitations are apparent. In the latter 1980s, the performance of large processing industries, for example in cotton and wool textiles, typically in the state sector, in coastal provinces, suffered, due to a deprivation of raw materials from interior provinces. This is likely to have been inefficient for the economy as a whole. It is also possible that rural collective enterprises in some industries, though profitable due to protection and captive markets, also suffered from the lack of scale economies. Today, revenue collection though ad hoc fees and fines, as well as protectionist import restraints, are probably more important than export embargoes. To the extent that the revenue collection is legitimate, it reflects the need for consolidation of numerous fees and charges in a more efficient way, and the devising of more efficient revenue collection methods. To the extent that the revenues collected are illegal, there is an urgent need to investigate remaining constraints and eliminate them.

Finally, there is a need to provide more transparent guidelines on interregional trade, at a national level. There have been no specific laws for this in China.[16] Some large federal systems, such as the USA, have constitutional clauses which specifically prohibit constraints against interstate commerce.[17] Some umbrella provision at the national level, which will of course have to be appropriate to the Chinese legal and governmental system, is required. Equally important, the implications of the fiscal contracting system for interstate commerce require deeper investigation. The ability to increase the extraction of revenues has probably fostered the development of some inefficient rural industry, and restraints against imports will have the same effect. Last of all, the drawing up of guidelines on the local preferences in provincial level procurement codes, will also be required, as the more transparent forms of trade constraints are removed.

C. Factor Mobility: Capital

Factors Affecting Interprovincial Investment

Parallel to the mobility of goods is the issue of factor mobility, also an essential element of an efficient internal market. Capital is usually considered the most mobile, among factors of production. One form in which capital mobility occurs is through enterprise investment. At a simplified level, enterprises may choose locations outside their current area of operation if there are favorable

---

[16]   Although the State Council has periodically tried to address this through other legislation, including, (1980), the Provisional Regulations relating to the Development and Protection of Socialist Competition, and again in 1982, with a Notice relating to the Prohibition of Blockades in the Sale of Industrial Products. In 1990, a circular was issued banning restrictions on interprovincial trade. Most recently, the new law against unfair competition (September 1993) also has an article restricting constraints on interregional trade.

[17]   Article 6 of the US Constitution, the 'Interstate Commerce clause'.

locational factors (input prices, infrastructure, communications, input availability), or policy-determined factors (taxes, subsidies or incentives and other cross-provincial investment regulations) which reduce costs. Special business links or tie ups, with other producers, buyers or suppliers, may also be an incentive. Another form in which capital may be regionally mobile is through the banking system, if there are inter-provincial bank deposits or loans. This requires that funds deposited at a given location may be loaned to investors in other locations, or alternatively that depositors may put their funds in banks outside their region of residence. There is also a variety of additional forms of markets for capital, for example, stock exchanges, which gradually evolve in market economies. This section first examines the various factors affecting regional investment flows and assesses the extent to which they have been conducive to capital mobility or otherwise, and then evaluates the available empirical evidence on capital mobility.

Profit Retention and Taxation

Arrangements between the central and local governments for the sharing of enterprise taxes and profits tended to discourage capital mobility, in the form of enterprise investment, in the early years of economic reform. More recent reforms in center-local fiscal arrangements over the past decade have removed some but not all of these effects. In the early 1980s, under the profit retention system, enterprises' transfers to other locations would have implied a loss in profits accruing to the local government.[18] At this time, the fiscal system was characterized by centralized revenue collection and centralized fiscal transfers. The revenue-sharing system distinguished between centrally fixed, locally fixed and shared revenues. Local revenues included the retained profits of enterprises owned by local governments, and consequently the system implied that local governments were reluctant to see their enterprises transfer resources outside their jurisdictions.[19]

In 1983/84 modifications to the revenue sharing system began, with the separation of taxes and profits at the enterprise level. However, the retention of profits, which was now permitted, accrued to local industrial bureaux, compared to central ministries, prior to this. The change was accompanied by new incentives to generate these now retainable profits, by the lowering of plan targets and permission to sell above plan output on the markets, together with further decentralization of plan formulation and implementation. A burst of investment resulted, but incentives to retain investments within local jurisdictions were high under this regime. To retain funds at their own level, and reduce tax remittances to the center, a number of items were removed from the enterprises' accounts and transferred to extrabudgetary funds, which grew rapidly after 1985.

Shortly after, the system of revenue contracts, first applied in agriculture, was modified and extended to state enterprises, under the contract responsibility system, which fixed profit remittances, retention rates and investment targets, usually for a three year period. By 1988, over 90 percent of all state enterprises were following this system. Parallel to the enterprise contracts, a system of fiscal contracting between central and local levels of government was also introduced, specifying which taxes were to be assigned to central and local governments respectively, and which were to be shared, and in what proportions. The income and adjustment taxes of locally-owned enterprises accrue to local

---

[18]   This has been described, for example, by Zhang (1992), in the context of the bicycle industry.

[19]   For further details of the evolution of central and local revenue-sharing arrangements, see World Bank (1990), Oksenberg and Tong (1990), Wong (1991) and Agarwala (1992) and Ma and Bell (1992).

governments, while certain other taxes, such as sales tax revenues from all enterprises, are shared between the center and local governments.

Regulations concerning the taxation of interprovincial investment under this system require that enterprises established wholly though investments from another region should pay turnover taxes (including product tax, business tax and value added tax) in the host area but continue to remit income taxes to the home jurisdiction. For a joint enterprise (set up with investments from outside as well as from the host area), turnover taxes are paid in the host area, while income tax can be paid in one of the following two methods. The first is to "first divide revenue then pay taxes," which means the two parties involved divide revenue according to their contract and then each pays taxes in its home area. The second method is to "first pay taxes then divide profits," which means the 'joint-venture' enterprise pays taxes in the host area, and the two parties then divide after tax profits according to the contract.

If the second method is adopted, regulations require that if the host area offers a turnover tax concession that is not available in the home area, the portion of taxes exempted in the host area should be submitted to the home area's tax or finance bureau. The method adopted in any given case is subject to negotiation between the two parties and the approval of the supervisory agencies and tax bureaus of both the host and the home area. In most cases, the home tax bureau objects to the second method, which reduces its revenue collection. No matter which method is chosen, according to these rules there is no **income** tax benefit for the investor from the host area. Although an outside investor can enjoy the host area's concessions on **turnover** taxes, this plays a less important role since in many cases turnover taxes account for a small portion of total taxes. The attractiveness of turnover tax concessions must be weighed against the uncertainties they involve. First, the offers of concessions are usually discretionary, and second, as soon as the fiscal contract of the host locality changes, its ability to offer tax concessions also changes, and many localities' commitments to favorable tax treatments are not credible. In sum, the present rules attempt to be neutral between location, at least to the extent that indirect tax rate differences permit. There do not appear to be any problems of double taxation due to ambiguities in the rules.

In practice these rules are not always adhered to and there is much regional variation in their application. Usually, the second method is applied, but investors do take advantage of turnover tax concessions offered by the host governments, without remitting the difference to their home provinces. Also, in practice, income tax frequently appears to be paid to the host government, contrary to the rules.[20] Some of these concessions are applied through the establishment of a variety of legal and illegal investment 'zones' and Special Economic Zones, where investment incentives in the form of both income and indirect tax concessions are offered.[21]

---

[20] Guangdong province responded in a survey that investors from other provinces had the choice of paying income taxes at either location (possibly in the hope of extracting some taxes which would normally be remitted to the region of origin) 'avoiding unnecessary financial and administrative restrictions in their place of origin'. Such arrangements have been negotiated in practice, and have also been undertaken by other provinces. Shaanxi province reports that its enterprises investing elsewhere and enjoying special concessions are indeed obliged to send the differential back but in practice this is difficult to enforce.

[21] World Bank (1993) Report No.11568-CHA, Wall (1992, 1993a&b), and Ma and Li (1992) provide extensive additional details of the zones.

Tax Concessions in 'Zones' Established by the Center

Under the open door policy launched in 1979, the central government opened some areas, particularly coastal provinces, to foreign investors, offering them various tax incentives. Some of these open areas provide similar tax incentives to domestic investment as well. The concessions had a profound impact on external capital inflows. Investments between the coastal and the inland regions were also affected to a modest extent. Five types of special regions were established; special economic zones (SEZs), 14 open coastal cities, Hainan, Pudong, and inland province zones along the Yangtze Delta.

Enterprises with foreign investment at the SEZs enjoy a 15 percent rate of income tax.[22] Still lower rates apply to investments of US$5 million and above, and projects with advanced technology. This is even more favorable than the standard concessional rates for foreign joint ventures, applicable in other regions.[23] Tax holidays have also been offered in the SEZs. Income tax is exempted for the first and second profit-making year and there is a 50 percent reduction for the third to the fifth years. Exemptions of import duties for production inputs and exemptions of income tax on profits for reinvestment are also offered. At many SEZs, the tax concessions for foreign investors have also been offered to domestic investors from other provinces, leading to capital outflows from many interior provinces to these zones.

Hainan, formerly one of the poorest regions in China, was granted the status of the fifth SEZ in 1988. According to the 1988 regulation outlining Hainan's special policies, the basic corporate income tax and tax holidays in Hainan are the same as in other SEZs and the Economic and Technological Development Zones (ETDZs) in fourteen coastal cities. The preferential tax policies for domestic investment applied in the other SEZs were also used in Hainan. In addition, Hainan provides more aggressive tax concessions in certain fields such as infrastructure and export processing.

The fourteen coastal cities' Economic and Technological Development Zones have also basically enjoyed the same preferential tax policy as the SEZs, since 1984[24]. An income tax rate of 15 percent is offered to foreign investors within the ETDZ, and to technology intensive enterprises with foreign capital of US$30 million or more in other parts of the cities. Tax holidays similar to those in the SEZs were also applicable. In other parts of the cities, a flat income tax rate of 24 percent prevails. The 10% profit remittance tax is exempt within the zone. However, there are no officially announced incentives for domestic enterprises in these cities.

---

[22]   The regulations are detailed in Economic Research Center (1981). The four original SEZs were Shenzhen, Zhuhai, Shantou and Xiamen.

[23]   Thirty three percent for equity joint-ventures and a progressive marginal rate scheme for contractual joint ventures and wholly foreign-owned ventures in 'non-open' areas. Equity joint ventures (*Hezi Jingying*) are limited liability corporations in which Chinese and foreign partners jointly invest in and operate a corporation, sharing the profits, losses and risks. In contractual joint ventures (*Hezuo Jingying*) the foreign partner typically provides technology, and may also provide a capital share which could take the form of a loan. Foreign investors are repaid on the basis of a predetermined schedule. The Chinese partner usually provides land, materials, the work force, basic buildings, services, etc. Wholly foreign-owned ventures (*Duzi Jingying*) enterprises are wholly owned and operated by foreign investors.

[24]   China Investment Guide (1989).

Pudong, a relatively underdeveloped area in east Shanghai, was 'opened' in early 1990. The regulation outlining the preferential policy for Pudong provides for basic income tax rates and tax holidays for foreign investment enterprises similar to those applied in SEZs. The 15 percent income tax rate and tax holidays also apply to domestic enterprises from other provinces. As a result, both foreign investment and investments from other parts of China have poured in.[25] In May 1992, the policy of special zones was extended into the interior, to a series of cities along the Yangtze.

Tax Concessions in 'Zones' Established by Localities

The attractive investment incentives in coastal zones put inland areas at a considerable disadvantage in terms of attracting external investment. In other parts of the country, foreign investors with equity contributions pay income tax at the rate of 30 percent plus a local surtax, or a total of 33 percent.[26] These rates are much higher than those in open areas. Investment from domestic state-owned enterprises or collective enterprises from other provinces is subject to the standard 55 percent nominal income tax rate and collectively-owned enterprises are subject to the standard progressive rate.

As an attempt to equalize tax treatment with the centrally-approved special zones clustered on the coast, all 30 provinces and thousands of counties and townships have launched their own 'zones.' This may be interpreted as the localities' natural reaction against the center's unequal tax policy. By early 1993, there were 1,800 zones (including special economic zones, economic development zones, economic and technology development zones, high- and new-technology zones, special zones for Taiwanese investors, border trade zones, etc.) at and above the county level.[27] These zones are approved by either State, provincial or county authorities. Most offer preferential tax policies similar to those which applied in the SEZs. Some zones offer even more aggressive tax reliefs, such as a five year tax exemption and further five year reduction by 50 percent.[28]

In some provinces, or in some counties within provinces, these concessions are offered to all incoming investment, whether foreign or domestic, while in numerous cases, domestic investors are accorded the concessions on a discretionary basis. The special zone for Taiwanese investors in Lanxi county, Zhejiang Province, for example, offers the same treatment to all domestic investment. Shaanxi

---

[25] While there are many real investments made by various central line ministries and other provinces, many domestic enterprises in west Shanghai moved their headquarters to Pudong and re-registered as new firms. Although all the production facilities still reside in west Shanghai, these enterprises now enjoy the preferential tax rate offered to new firms in Pudong.

[26] According to the foreign enterprise law of 1980. Income taxes levied on contractual joint ventures and wholly foreign-owned ventures were progressive, with the rates ranging from 20 percent to 40 percent according to total income. In July 1991 tax policy for foreign investment was unified across different types of enterprises with foreign investment.

[27] According to the Ministry of Finance. According to the People's Bank of China, 233 development zones at and above county level were proposed in Sichuan Province alone in the first half of 1992. By the end of 1992, Tai prefecture of Zhejiang Province had established 152 development zones, among which 134 zones were below the county level.

[28] The development zones in Jinin City in Inner Mongolia and Taiyuan City in Shangxi Province are examples.

province offers investors exemption from the business tax for a year, and from income tax for two to three years. Sichuan reported the same exemptions, adding that there was some flexibility in the application of the rates. Township and village enterprises and enterprises from minority regions are given longer exemptions. Sichuan can also exempt other funds payable by enterprises, notably the Two Funds; for Energy and Communication Development, and for Budget Adjustment. If investors from other provinces invest in industries where Sichuan appears to have a comparative advantage, or to infrastructure industries, bank loans are provided on a priority basis. Sichuan has now transferred the power to grant tax remissions or exemptions to governments at the city or prefecture level, and these cities or prefectures have introduced their own regulations on these issues. Liaoning, by contrast, maintains that it has no special incentives, except in its Economic and Technical Development Zones, where the 'two plus three' rule of corporate tax exemption applies.[29]

Most of these tax exemptions and reductions are not approved by the central taxation authority and are considered illegal by the center. In July 1993, the State General Bureau of Taxation issued a circular stating that the tax relief policies offered by these locally-approved zones should be stopped. The circular also required each province to 'clean' these unapproved zones. It added that all promises made by the localities regarding tax concession could only be fulfilled using the localities' own budgetary funds. The circular appears to have had some effect, since many provinces have reported a number of 'cleaned' zones to the center.

Other Tax Concessions by Localities

In addition to 'zones,' many areas offer tax concessions under other forms, legal and illegal. The current center-province revenue sharing system stipulates that provinces can only offer tax exemption and reduction on 'local-fixed' revenues, or revenues assigned to local governments.[30] Exemptions or reductions on centrally assigned or center-local shared taxes are subject to approval by the center, except for those to which special policies apply.[31] These regulations are frequently abused by localities for tax relief purpose. Most localities attempting to offer a tax concession can find regulations that are 'applicable.' In addition to using the centrally announced policies, many offer tax relief under the guise of implementing local industrial policy, or as 'subsidies to enterprises in difficulties.' Many taxes belonging to the center-fixed or center-local shared categories have been exempted without consulting the center.

---

[29]   The information refers to late 1992.

[30]   These include agricultural and animal husbandry tax, urban maintenance and construction tax, property tax, title trade tax, individual industrial and business tax, market tax, bonus tax, vehicle utilization tax, a special tax on forestry and agricultural products, slaughter tax, personal income tax and salt tax.

[31]   For example, enterprises in priority sectors (eg, electronics, exports) meeting certain requirements can enjoy income tax holidays. Enterprises that export more than 70 percent of their output value are eligible for income tax reduction. Newly established collectively-owned enterprises are permitted tax exemption for the first two years. Enterprises established by educational units, certain mass organizations, and social welfare units can also benefit from exempted or reduced income tax.

Regional Cooperation Zones

Another question to be examined in this context is the effect of the Regional Cooperation Areas in the promotion of internal trade and investment. The concept of establishing such regional zones began before the Cultural Revolution but the concrete introduction of six cooperative zones took shape with the Ten Year Development Plan of 1976 to 1985.[32] Guangdong, for example, is a member of the South China Region of Economic and Technological Coordination. The Shanghai zone, established at the end of 1982, originally embraced 9 other medium to large cities as well as 54 counties in Jiangsu and Zhejiang provinces. It was later expanded to include Anhui, Jiangxi and Fujian provinces as well.

Although much larger and less specialized entities than most of the special economic zones, these zones of cooperation are essentially an older variant of the many special zones discussed above, which did not carry any special incentives in the form of investment or tax concessions. The Planning Office of the zone was entrusted with the coordination and promotion of zonal cooperation. While there is some anecdotal evidence of resulting instances of cooperation, the general consensus is that such zones of coordination have had little effect in promoting investments, and in some cases, particularly in earlier years, had further complicated center-local administrative issues by the presence of another, 'area level' office between the center and the provinces.

Procedures and Practice

The procedures for setting up a new establishment for investors from other provinces could sometimes be discouraging. Taking a typical example, in Guangdong, individual enterprises from other provinces must first apply for a change of registration, at the Guangdong province bureau of the Administration of Industry and Commerce and then obtain approval from the local Office of Economic Cooperation, which undertakes a capital assessment and an examination of the certificate of real estate.[33] If investments are made as part of an enterprise group, the GPAIC is also required to examine 'related documents' such as the agreement of joint operation, corporation by-laws, notarial documents and financial statements. Property transfer procedures are additionally required in the case of mergers. Guangdong province assures equal treatment in terms of access to energy, water supply, transport and labor supply.[34] Difficulties with equal treatment have been reported at Shanghai, where enterprises from other provinces have complained that outsiders are charged higher rents for business space and they have difficulty in obtaining registration and operating permits for their business cars. At Liaoning, in addition

---

[32] Historically the Six Cooperative Areas have their origin in the Six Administrative Areas, established at the birth of the People's Republic. Apart from economic cooperation the concept was also intended to play a coordinating and cooperative role between lower levels of administration. There were also political considerations such as the prosperity of local ethnic minorities. Huang (1992) has details, and a case study of the Shanghai zone.

[33] On the whole the role of the provincial Administration of Industry and Commerce is more powerful than that of the Office of Economic Cooperation (OEC). The OECs were established in all provinces in the latter 1980s to facilitate external investment, but in practice their role has been limited and they have done little to facilitate interprovincial investment flows.

[34] An assurance that suggests that in some cases (possibly provinces other than Guangdong), equal treatment is not accorded.

to the permission of the Department of Economic and Technical Cooperation and the SAIC registration, a new enterprise must register its seal in the Public Security System, register in the tax department and open a bank account in the local branch of the Industrial and Commercial Bank.

Much of the interprovincial investment which has occurred has been intended to facilitate and 'internalize' buyer-supplier links, for example, the timely delivery of raw materials, or the marketing of finished products. Investments have also occurred in the tertiary industries, such as hotels and commerce, and in recent years, particularly in a few provinces, there have been large flows of investment into real estate, much of which has been speculative in nature. There have also been examples of investment flows which are essentially a form of compensation trade, intended to circumvent price or quantity controls.[35] However, on a more positive note, in a few rare cases, such investment has also occurred when enterprises have set up associated companies, producing goods with a common brand name and common quality control procedures.[36]

Summary: Tax Policy and Regional Capital Flows

The broad conclusions of the preceding sections are that first, in the past, regional capital mobility was discouraged, under the profit remittance system. Next, with the introduction of the separation of profits and taxes, as well as permission to retain profits and the concomitant increase in the local authorities' taxation powers, incentives to retain new incentives within local jurisdictions remained high. Third, the regulations governing cross-provincial investments are fairly clear, at least for regions which do not belong to special zones. These regulations are neutral across locations in terms of income tax; enterprises do not benefit from relocation but are not subject to double taxation as a result. Enterprises can take advantage of indirect tax concessions offered by host governments. However, fourth, the picture is distorted by the large number of special investment zones in China. Many of these have extended their offers of concessions to investors from other provinces, legally or illegally. Some of these incentives may be discretionary and subject to uncertainty. Nominally the granting of some of these concessions is controlled by the center alone. However, under current central-local fiscal relations, the only binding constraint that a locality actually faces is the fiscal contract with the level of government directly above. As long as the locality has fulfilled the revenue target specified in the contract, it tends to use exemption as much as possible to keep the resource in the locality. Moreover, there are no real, implementable, punitive measures against localities' illegal tax concessions. Finally, there may be practical and procedural difficulties in interprovincial investment flows which inhibit their growth.

The economic consequences of these findings for regional capital mobility are first, that under normal circumstances, regional capital mobility is likely to be limited. To the extent that it occurs, it is likely to be strongly influenced by the concessions offered by the large variety of special zones, being attracted to regions where such concessions are high. The implication is that even if interregional capital mobility does occur, it may not be efficiency enhancing for the economy as a whole, as it is based on competing regional tax differentials rather than on real differences in natural endowments or other costs.

---

[35] Guangdong International Trust and Investment Center (GITIC) jointly invested in an aluminum factory with Gongxian county of Henan province in 1986, in which GITIC provided a loan of Y 2 million, to be repaid with aluminum, at the market prices prevailing in 1986. Given the limited supply of aluminum at the time and its rising price, GITIC benefitted considerably.

[36] See the discussion on enterprise groups in Chapter 5.

The implications for policy adjustment are first, that disincentives to regional mobility due to local governments and local industry bureau interests in profit, revenue retention and extrabudgetary funds should be examined, with a view to their reduction. Such an investigation must necessarily form a part of a larger examination of the current system of fiscal contracting. Next, there is a strong case for more equal treatment of investors in all regions ('zones' and normal areas), and from all regions (domestic and foreign). Third, the current regulations on cross-provincial investments lack credibility because of a lack of enforcement procedures, as well as a lack of sanctions in cases of their violation. The development of regulations and enforcement procedures for this is a major undertaking which must be embarked upon if future flows of interregional investments, at the enterprise level, are to be facilitated.

An Analysis of Evidence

This section first examines the evidence on direct flows of interprovincial investment. Data are available for six provinces, Guangdong, Shaanxi, Sichuan, Beijing, Shanghai and Liaoning, over the period 1985 to 1992. These six provinces represent a cross-section in terms of location, coastal as well as interior, from the north as well as the south, and from developed as well as backward regions.[37] The total investment in these provinces accounted for around 30 percent of national investment, over the period, and the sample is therefore reasonably representative (Table 2.6)

The first observation is that interprovincial investment as a proportion of total investment today is very low in most provinces. In five of the six provinces examined, the ratio in the most recent year is less than 3 percent. The only exception is Shanghai, where interprovincial transfers account for almost a third of total investment. Second, in three of the six provinces, this ratio has declined over time (Guangdong, Shaanxi and Beijing). Sichuan has remained virtually constant and Liaoning has a small increase. Shanghai is the only province with a significant increase, which probably reflects inflows due to the Pudong investment zone. It also suggests that the declining internal trade ratio in Shanghai may be partially offset, in term of links with other provinces, by its increasing internal investment ratio. It is however clear that the case of Shanghai is exceptional.

It is also notable that domestic investment flows from other provinces are less significant than external investment. Foreign investment as a proportion of total investment in recent years has been as high as 10-13 percent in Shanghai, Liaoning and Beijing, and even higher in Guangdong (32 percent). In all these provinces, there has been an increase in this ratio over time. In the interior provinces, however (Sichuan and Shaanxi), external investment has been stagnant or declining. The high and rising external investment in Shanghai suggests that this is not 'crowding out' domestic interprovincial investment flows; rather, both have been able to significantly expand at the same time. It must also be recalled that the increasing foreign investment ratio of Shanghai has coexisted with a high and rising foreign trade ratio.

---

[37]   The data were collected as part of a background study for this report, undertaken by the CASS. Data are collected from provincial authorities and Departments of Cooperation.

Table 2.6 Interprovincial and Foreign Investment in Selected Provinces

	1992	1991	1990	1989	1988	1985
1. Guangdong (RMB Y billion)						
Total Investment	84.5	47.8	36.2	34.7	35.4	
% Investment from other provinces	1.7%	2.3%				
% Foreign Investment	31.7%	28.8%	26.6%	25.9%		
% Investment to other provinces	2.5%					
2 . Shaanxi (RMB Y million)						
Total Investment	15200	12493	10372	9518	9472	5799
% Investment from other provinces	2.4%	3.4%	3.7%	3.3%	3.7%	7.4%
% Foreign Investment/b	2.2%	1.9%	2.2%	4.8%	3.7%	
% Investment to other provinces		2.8%	2.9%	2.6%	3.2%	3.4
3. Sichuan (RMB Y million)						
Total Investment	36390	28252	20390	21219	14488	8047
% Inv. from other provinces	0.22%	0.25%	0.17%	0.07%	0.02%	0.01%
% Foreign Investment/b	5.4%		1.5%	4.5%	5.2%	
% Investment to other Provinces	4.45%	4.78%	5.64%	2.83%		
4. Beijing (RMB Y billion)						
Total Investment/c	19.38	19.19	17.92	13.95	16.3	
% Investment from other provinces	0.16%	0.14%		0.46%	0.44%	
% Foreign Investment			10.46%	12.87%		
5. Shanghai (RMB Y billion)						
Total Investment	32.5	25.8	22.7	21.5	24.5	11.7
% Inv. from other provinces/d	32.9%	30.6%		28.4%		
% Foreign Investment/e	13.4%	3.6%	6.8%	7.4%	1.5%	0.5%
6. Liaoning (RMB Y billion)						
Total Investment		31.8	26.29	24.32	26.13	
% Investment from other provinces		2.48%	0.72%	0.70%	1.30%	
% Foreign Investment			13.23%	6.01%		
% Investment to other provinces/f		0.75%	0.84%	0.41%	0.54%	

/a Shaanxi: There were only 18 foreign or foreign joint venture enterprises (1991)
/b Sichuan: The total for 1988 to 1992 was 6.6 billion RMB Y. Data do not include investments below 0.3 million RMB.
/c Beijing: Total investment for 1992 is an estimate
/d Shanghai: In 4550 enterprises, including the Pudong Zone
/e Shanghai: Joint Venture investment statistics
/f Liaoning: Figures for inward and outward investment in the context of 'horizontal integration'
Source: Provincial Yearbooks and CASS survey (see Appendix Table A2.20).

There are also some limited data from the same source (Appendix Table A2.20), though only for three provinces, on the outward investment of these provinces. It suggests that outward investments increase when investment flows inwards increase, and that the two may tend towards similar levels. Thus in Liaoning and Sichuan, inward investment has had a modest gain, or remained constant, over the period for which data are available, and outward investment has increased as well. In Shaanxi, there has been a general decline in inward investment as well as constant or falling outward investment in the most recent years. The inference is that provinces which are relatively more open tend to have both higher inflows as well as outflows. There are no cases of a successful 'beggar-my-neighbor' policy of high inward and low outward investments.

A second form in which the mobility of capital may be gauged empirically is through an analysis of differentials in returns to capital across different uses. If these differentials reduce over time, it suggests that capital mobility has increased. There is some evidence to suggest that capital is relatively more mobile than in the past, between different productive sectors. A study on sectoral profit differentials over 1980 to 1989 shows that these have declined over time.[38] A decline in sectoral profit suggests that administrative barriers across sectors (the vertical barriers) have weakened.

However, this has no automatic implications for capital mobility in regional or spatial terms. To analyze this, data on regional differentials in profit rates as well as enterprise tax rates were examined, using time-series data on state and private enterprises (Appendix Tables A2.21 to A2.25). The data separate the average profit rates and tax rates, by province, for each of the five years 1986-1990. Further, the average profit rates are computed separately for profitable and loss-making enterprises. Tax rates are also separated in terms of the total effective rate, and the effective rate for commodity taxes alone. Coefficients of regional variation have been estimated for each year's data. The results are summarized in Table 2.7.[39]

---

[38] Naughton (1992).

[39] Calculations are based on data from the CESSRI (China Economic Systems Reform Research Institute) data base, compiled by the SCRES on around 800 state and private enterprises, over six years, beginning in 1986. The data base is maintained at the STICERD, London School of Economics.

Table 2.7 Mean and Coefficient of Variation of Effective Tax Rates of 20 Provinces (1986-1990)

	Total Effective Tax Rates	Commodity Tax Rates	Profit Rate		
			Profit-maker	Loss-maker	Average
1986 Mean (percent)	84.51	16.92	65.85	-70.29	64.25
COV	0.085	0.559	0.148	0.791	0.193
1987 Mean (percent)	84.41	15.58	66.34	-71.67	65.00
COV	0.081	0.556	0.127	0.482	0.152
1988 Mean (percent)	85.14	15.05	68.27	-70.33	66.44
COV	0.099	0.546	0.144	0.238	0.176
1989 Mean (percent)	86.02	15.49	65.92	-84.79	58.29
COV	0.100	0.543	0.164	0.247	0.343
1990 Mean (percent)	89.78	16.10	71.33	-79.48/a	48.14/a
COV	0.102	0.579	0.185	0.459/a	0.657/a

/a   Adjusted value for 1990 (See Appendix Table A2.25)
Note: *Total effective tax rate* is defined as (commodity taxes + profit tax)/(commodity taxes + profit tax + retained profits);
          Commodity tax rate is defined as commodity taxes/sales revenue;
          Profit tax rate is defined as profit taxes/(sales revenue - material costs - depreciation).
Source: Calculated from data in Appendix Tables A2.21 to A2.25.

The results are an interesting contrast to the findings on sectoral profit rates. Looking at profit rates for all firms, on average, or at profitable and loss-making firms separately, coefficients of regional variation increased over time. In the case of taxes, the results are similar, for all enterprise taxes taken together, as well as for commodity taxes alone.   The overall finding is that there is no evidence to support a convergence of returns to capital across different provinces. Other things being equal, this suggests that capital mobility has not increased noticeably since 1985.

The Banking System: Interbank Borrowing and Lending

Another form of capital mobility is through the banking system and through financial markets. While there are a number of nascent forms of financial market in China, the interbank market is the main channel of cross regional capital flows today.[40] The interbank market, designed by the central bank as a short-term money market to meet the needs of banks which encounter a temporary shortage of funds for interbank payment, was first organized in a number of major cities in 1986. Initially, branches of the People's Bank of China (PBC) in these cities organized a regular meeting-- usually weekly--at which local bank branches could negotiate interbank loans for periods ranging from a week to several months. Currently, there are six visible markets, and interbank activities also take

---

[40]   Other capital markets include markets in short-term negotiable paper, bonds and securities. However their scope so far is limited (see below). In addition, some cities, such as Shanghai, have been able to directly attract bank deposits from persons outside the province, and these are now estimated to account for around 10% of Shanghai's total household savings accounts. However, cross-regional deposits are limited on a nationwide scale.

place directly and 'invisibly' between banks and other financial institutions.[41] Over the past few years, these invisible markets dominated interbank activities by accruing more than 90 percent of total transactions. Interbank borrowings include transactions taking place within or outside the same city or region, and within or outside a given specialized banking system. It is estimated that of the Y 96 billion of interbank transactions in Shanghai in 1992, about one third was across provinces.[42]

The country's interbank borrowing activity has shown an upward trend, but with significant pro-cyclical variations. Total borrowing activities amounted to Y 230 billion in 1987, which grew to Y 520 billion in 1988 when the economy was overheated. During the credit squeeze of the 'rectification program,' interbank borrowing shrank to Y 290 billion in 1989, and further to Y 260 billion in 1990.[43] From 1991, monetary policy began to loosen and interbank activities surged to a new record. In 1992, interbank borrowing was estimated to be about Y 800 billion.[44]

Although intended primarily for meeting short term liquidity requirements or placing short-term assets, these activities contribute to the breaking of administrative barriers between regions and sectors. The increasing interbank activities reflect that the current credit allocation mechanism is not efficient, and that the marginal productivity of funds differs across regions and sectors. According to some research, the faster-growing developed areas usually offer higher rates than the less developed areas.[45] High rates have been concentrated in the developed and fast growing eastern region, especially Shanghai, Jiangsu and Zhejiang. The study suggests that low rates prevailed in the western region and northern part of China, where capital productivity is relatively low.

The future growth of interbank market activities may be curbed by the policies of the government on instruments of monetary control. At present, credit controls are a key instrument of monetary policy, and the credit ceiling assigned to each local bank branch restricts interbank borrowing. The PBC stipulates that only those banks (branches) with unused credit allowance can borrow from the interbank markets. However, in many cases, banks that lack funds also lack a credit allowance. The control over the nominal interest rate in the interbank market, which is restricted by a ceiling set by PBC, is also an instrument of overall credit control, which depresses the supply of the funds in the interbank market. Recently, an increasing volume of lending has been taking place at parallel market rates, which are much higher than the nominal ceiling. In early 1993, the interest rate ceiling set by the PBC was about 8 percent, while the parallel market rates were close to 17 to 18 percent in some regions.

---

[41] Huadong (or East China, including Shanghai, Jiangsu, Zhejiang, Anhui, Shandong and Jiangxi), South Middle (including Sichuan, Yunnan, Guangdong, Henan, Hunan, Hubei), South West (including Xinjiang, Gansu, Qinghai, Ningxia and Shaanxi), Huabei (or North China, including Beijing, Tianjin, Hebei, and Shanxi), and North East (including Heilongjiang, Liaoning and Jilin).

[42] Shanghai branch of the People's bank of China.

[43] Figures are from Y. Huang (1992).

[44] Interview estimate provide by the Fund Control Department of the People's Bank of China.

[45] An examination of the weighted average interest rates in five major interbank markets during 1987-90 shows that in 1987, the reported weighted average rate in Huadong (East China) was 6.17 percent, the rate in South Middle was 5.99 percent, the rate in South West was 5.79 percent, and the rate in Huabei was 5.58 percent. The next three years followed the same pattern. See Shi and Yan (1991), p.61.

At the same time, there has been some abuse of the interbank market by banks, and as a consequence, the government has begun to look askance at its growth. The lending term is currently restricted to two months, as is appropriate for a short term liquidity management instrument, and borrowing from the interbank market for long term investment is prohibited.[46] Partly in response to the lack of adequate and flexible term lending institutions, at the time of the accelerated investment of 1992-1993, many banks tended to use the interbank borrowing for long term financing. In some cases this was undertaken by diverting funds to the banks' subsidiary non-bank financial institutions. In March 1993, the central PBC declared that this was prohibited.

These considerations point on the one hand to the need for the government to diversify its instruments of monetary policy away from credit and interest rate controls, which are still the primary means of monetary control. In the short term, within this framework, while it remains, there is a need to move away from regional and bank-specific credit ceilings, to enhance the efficiency of capital use. The PBC could consider the possibility of permitting the trading of credit allowances across regions and sectors. This will enhance the efficiency of the use of funds, although it will not substantially increase total outstanding credit while aggregate credit ceilings are in place. On the other hand, the supervision of the activities on the interbank market also needs to be strengthened, so that the misuse of funds from this source does not occur.

The Banking System: Payment Clearance and Settlement[47]

One of the factors affecting both interregional trade as well as interregional factor mobility is the degree of facility in interstate payments. If goods are bought or sold in other provinces, or if laborers are hired from outside their own province and wish to remit money to their home province, how easily can this be undertaken? This depends on the form of the interbank payment clearance and settlement system an how effectively it functions. There are many accounts of delays in payments, which indicates the merits of an examination of the payments mechanism.

A basic feature of China's interbank clearing system is that all non local interbank payment must first be cleared and settled between specialized banks on a local basis through the local clearing agency and then cleared within the specialized banks across localities or regions via the intrabank clearing mechanism.[48] Local clearings are made through approximately 2,200 local city and county level clearing houses throughout China. All local interbank and most local intrabank payments are exchanged and settled through the local clearing houses. All non local interbank payments are first exchanged and settled between specialized banks through the local clearing houses before being processed across geographic regions. After local clearings, non local items use intrabank clearing mechanism to effect payment. There are four different intrabank payment systems, and each has three stages, which are the physical exchange of payment instruments; the clearing of payment instruments and the settlement of the intrabank clearing. Instruments are physically exchanged by mail or telegraph, depending on the payment instrument used. This physical exchange is generally directly between the sending branch and the

---

[46]   The maximum term of interbank lending was six months before September 1989, when it was revised to two months.

[47]   This section draws from The World Bank (January 31, 1992) and The World Bank (March 1993).

[48]   Between branches of the same specialized bank.

receiving branch, irrespective of location. The clearing and settlement of the instrument is more complicated and takes place through different levels depending on the location of the sending and receiving branches of the specialized banks.

The Chinese settlement system is extremely complex by western standards since it includes separate settlements from local clearing, intra-county, intra-provincial and inter-provincial transfers. In addition, settlement is not undertaken daily for each settling participant, but only occurs when certain net balance thresholds are reached. These factors result in delays in the payment process. Payments made across regions also involve slow reconciliation since many specialized banks still use manual checking. Under normal situations, a payment made within a city may take one to three days, depending on whether it is across specialized banks. A payment made across banks and across regions may take from three days to many weeks, depending on whether the receiving bank is located in a city or in a remote county. As a consequence, branch banks have the incentive to keep accounts payable for longer than necessary, to guard against temporary difficulties in payment.

The problem of payment delays and hinders the efficient movement of capital across regions. Currently, the reconciliation system is being computerized within major banks, largely to overcome the long delays. In addition, an electronic interbank system, which uses satellite transmission techniques, has been adopted to increase the speed of payment clearing. This system has connected 21 branches and plan to cover some 200 branches nationwide. As the system spreads, disincentives to undertake interregional transactions will decrease. Meanwhile, the problem of post office clearance of IOUs also has to be addressed. It is estimated that by the end of 1992, money orders totalling 800 million yuan ($137.9 million) had still to be cashed in Sichuan province alone.[49]

In 1991, 320 million postal remittances were received, amounting to 101.78 billion yuan. The Ministry of Post and Telecommunications operates its remittances and accounts settlement with the Industrial and Commercial Bank of China, and with the Agricultural Bank of China. It claims that the process of remittance allocation and transfers between these rural branches is much slower because of weak computer links and the cash shortage which these banks suffer from. Many rural banks therefore find it hard to obtain sufficient cash for money orders. As a solution, the government is reconsidering the birth of a national postal savings bank to handle postal rremittances. It points out that postal deposits are already large. By the end of last year, more than 20,000 postal offices dealt with deposits. Postal savings totalled 47.6 billion yuan.

Although a specialized postal bank may have its merits, on other grounds, the establishment of such a bank is not likely to solve the problem of cross-regional payments, if settlements still operate through the existing commercial bank network. Setting up a parallel network is likely to be extremely expensive and there is no guarantee that this will function more efficiently. The answer seems rather to lie in strengthening and streamlining the current payments system operating through the banking system.

---

[49] *China Daily*. 19 February 1993. According to the Ministry of Posts and Telecommunications, the problem has grown more serious in the provinces of Sichuan, Hubei, Hunan, Jiangsu and Henan, which provide surplus rural labor. In Nanchong prefecture of Sichuan province, two thirds of the rural post offices were attacked by angry farmers before New Year's Day.

Capital Markets

Finally, interprovincial investments are also beginning to occur today through stock and bond issues. Some enterprises have begun to float these in numerous provinces. In the medium term, this may well develop into a promising vehicle for regional investment flows. Today however the scope of such markets is limited. By the end of June, 1993, over 120 enterprises were quoted on the Shanghai and Shenzhen stock exchanges, including enterprises from outside these municipalities. Another nine companies have ben approved for listing in Hong Kong this year, and one has already been listed in New York. Although there are a number of informal regional markets in shares, their operations tend to be local or regional in character. A major obstacle to the development to this market today is their imperfect supervision and regulation, which has led to well-publicized speculative activity well as fraud.[50] These problems will have to be corrected before this avenue of capital mobility can expand significantly.

D. Factor Mobility: Labor

China's policy towards the mobilization and deployment of labor in the prereform period was based on the twin principles of minimizing or eliminating unemployment, as well as providing lifetime job security and stability. These aims were largely achieved, through a set of complementary measures. Urban labor force entrants were allocated by government authorities to permanent positions in state enterprises, in predetermined quotas, and at the same time, rural urban migration was prohibited. This prohibition was effectively enforced by the household registration (*hukou*) system, and by urban grain rationing, which severely discouraged movement. However, the system engendered many unfavorable economic consequences. At the level of enterprises, their role in providing other services for their employees, such as housing or hospitals, combined with the lack of social security for unemployed persons, greatly increased the burden of their responsibility as well as financial liabilities and consequently increased the difficulties of dismissal of any staff.[51] The segmentation of the rural and urban labor force restricted the supply of rural labor to meet growing industrial requirements, and created a differential in wages, causing urban labor to be overpriced.[52] A further consequence, in combination with the underpricing and subsidization of capital, implicit in investment and interest rate subsidies prevalent at the time, was that enterprises had little incentive to use more labor-intensive techniques of production, and indeed sometimes accepted new recruits only if capital grants were also included. A

---

[50] Notably the stampede outside the Shenzhen stock exchange in late 1992 when new share issues were made. In terms of fraud, the Great Wall Company of Beijing has recently (early 1993) defrauded thousands of would be investors by promising them rates of return of 24 percent on a bond issue.

[51] Limitations on labor mobility also arose from the 'inheritance' of jobs in state enterprises by their families or offspring, according to the *dingti* system. The practice had been in existence for a long time and was formally permitted from 1978 (Christiansen, 1992). For a discussion of housing issues see World Bank Report No. 9222-CHA (1991) and for social security issues see World Bank Report No, 8074-CHA (1990).

[52] Putterman (1992), Jefferson and Rawski (1993) and World Bank (1992) Report No 10266-CHA discuss these issues in greater detail.

paradoxical consequence was that urban job availability became constrained.[53] Job security and wage rigidity in their turn implied that performance incentives and productivity were low, and underemployment was high, even among salaried workers.[54]

With the onset of reforms there has been a growing recognition of the adverse effects of the former policies, and attempts have been made to increase the flexibility of the labor market. Looking first at the supply side, the breakup of the commune system in the countryside in the late 1970s forced the massive disguised surplus rural labor force into evidence.[55] Millions of peasants became redundant in a few short years. Rapid new construction in urban areas provided a market for such persons. The temporary migration of rural labor to urban areas was permitted in 1983, with a State Council ruling that permitted rural households, without changing their residence, to embark upon 'cooperative joint ventures' in market towns. Permanent migration was permitted in 1984, for peasants who were self-reliant in terms of cash, food supply and accommodation. Although intended primarily for smaller townships, this ruling had the effect of legalizing the entry of large numbers of rural workers in all urban areas. From 1986, the sale of grain to urban migrants, at negotiated prices, was also legalized. Meanwhile, enterprises have also expanded their use of rural workers by setting up rural subsidiaries or 'associate' companies, and peasant entrepreneurs have also begun to employ rural labor.[56] Later, some provinces, such as Gansu and Sichuan, began to develop active unskilled labor export programs to labor deficit areas. In recent years, new moves have been made by the government to simplify transfers of skilled labor, in particular, between occupations. University graduates are now permitted to take jobs in township and village enterprises without losing their urban residence permits and their access to urban subsidies.[57] Talent exchange centers have been established for highly specialized personnel.

At the same time, larger cities have begun to acquire a number of illegal entrants from rural areas who contribute to a reserve pool of floating labor. This population differs from the migrant labor described above, as it is only eligible for 'temporary' residence, at best, in the locale to which it

---

[53] Other factors also contributed to the slow growth of jobs; the general bias against the creation of new service sector jobs in the early years of reform, the bias against agriculture implicit in grain price controls and the 'policy hierarchy', which gave preferential treatment to state-owned, collectively owned and private enterprises, in that order (Jefferson and Rawski, 1993).

[54] One survey shows that actual work time in industrial enterprises in Wuhan was 5.6 hours per day, instead of the statutory 7 to 8 hours (Jefferson and Xu, 1991).

[55] Based largely on Solinger (1992 and 1993).

[56] The Wuxi Boiler Factory, for example, started an enterprise in Xinguang village in Wangzhuang township in May 1985, exclusively to produce boiler parts. The initial investment was based on the transfer of machinery from Wuxi Boiler Factory, funded by an interest-free loan from the company. Initially the plant hired 205 workers from the village and in the mid 1980s, an additional 130 non-local persons were added from other neighboring counties (Christiansen, 1992).

[57] In Wuxi, enterprise leaders talked of 'buying' graduates (*daxuesheng*) from technical universities for a fixed sum of Y10,000 from other provinces or counties, to be employed as engineers or technical staff (Christansen, 1992). It should also be noted that in 1982 the State Commission of Science and Technology had promulgated a 'temporary regulation on the hiring of science specialists on second jobs'.

has moved.[58] It is estimated that in 1990 there were some 60 to 80 million persons in this category.[59] On average, according to public security statistics, at least a million or more persons 'floated' in each of the 23 largest cities with populations of over a million. In most medium sized cities the transients are provided by nearby areas. However in the largest cities of Shanghai and Guangdong floaters are drawn from much further afield. Estimates suggest that over two thirds of the transients stay on for half a year or more. These floaters provide a large and docile labor force, who however are extremely vulnerable to exploitation on account of their lack of formal status. Enterprises and even government departments have hired such laborers to reduce costs and increase flexibility.[60]

On the demand side, complementary instruments were introduced to increase the flexibility permitted to enterprises in the hiring of labor. As early as 1980, a State Council directive replaced the state monopoly on labor allocation with a system in which the official promotion of individual and private businessmen, as well as the possibility of individual job search, was accepted. The state also recognized the need for establishing special job promotion measures, in the form of 'labor service companies' (LSCs) for job vacancy registration, job training and placement.[61] The role of the LSCs gradually expanded to include the setting up and operation of new enterprises to create employment for surplus workers.[62]

At the level of the enterprise, greater latitude was granted in terms of hiring, and enterprises were permitted to hire temporary migrant workers in lieu of permanent labor. Not only were these cheaper, but they also provided greater flexibility in terms of increasing or reducing numbers to meet fluctuations in business activity. However the hiring of such labor still falls under the purview of the Ministry of Labor and local labor bureaux, who encourage the hiring of permanent staff to achieve aggregate employment and placement targets. More significant, a new flexibility has been introduced in the definition of jobs and job expectations, through the labor contact system.[63]

Under the labor contract system, new entrants to an enterprise are required to sign a contract, which typically specifies the duration of the agreement, the responsibilities and benefits of both parties (work requirements and performance standards on the one hand, and wages and benefits on the

---

[58] 'Temporary' residence is a legal category but it is estimated that probably only a third to a half of persons in this category are legally registered.

[59] Around two thirds of these are estimated to be peasants. The rest comprise tourists, or authorized business or individual travellers.

[60] However, due to the fact that such persons impose an additional burden for service on cities which are not equipped to deal with them, there are periodic moves to 'evict' the migrants and send them back to their villages. Beijing has recently announced that it wants to put tighter controls on unskilled transients who have 'flooded' the city. *China News Digest*, July 13 1993.

[61] The new 'three-channels-in-one' system (*san jie he*) for job placement.

[62] The *laowu fuwu gongsi*. These could be new urban collective or state-owned enterprises or their subsidiaries, set up by the labor bureau (Christiansen, 1992).

[63] The following two paragraphs on labor contracts and wages are based largely on World Bank (1992) Report No. 10266-CHA.

other) and terms for renewal or cancellation. The contracts greatly increased the flexibility provided to enterprises to reject unsuitable candidates, as well as to avoid the obligations of permanent recruitment, by not renewing contracts. The contract system covered only new recruits, and was first introduced on an experimental basis in 1983. It was formalized by a regulation of the State Council in 1986 and it is the intention of the government that it will eventually cover all workers.

New mechanisms for the linking of wages to performance were also introduced, initially through the bonus system, in 1978. Bonuses were allowed to cover 5 percent of the total wage bill initially and this was expanded to 12 percent shortly after. In 1985, a 'floating wage' system was introduced, permitting the linking of a portion of wages and bonuses to various performance indices. The concept was extended in 1988 to link wage funds to economic efficiency and meanwhile, the proportion of funds allocated to bonus and incentive funds was allowed to rise.[64] Within state enterprises, the share of basic wages in the total wage bill decreased as a consequence, from 85 percent in 1978 to less than 50 percent in 1990. The share of bonuses rose from 2.3 to 17 percent over the same period. In 1992, it was estimated that over 100,000 state-owned enterprises, with 41 million workers (over half the total state-owned enterprise workers) gave various forms of efficiency pegged gross wages.[65]

New managerial incentives to link rewards to performance were also introduced, in the form of both incentives and penalties.[66] First, considerably greater managerial autonomy was permitted under the enterprise contract responsibility system, which gave managers the authority to set production targets and gave them greater authority in decisions concerning pricing and sales. The selection of managers by competitive bidding was also introduced. The managerial role in risk-taking was also made more explicit. In a large number of enterprises, managers 'bidding' for a position offered to enter into a personal 'management contract', stating what their expected achievements would be, and offering a security deposit to back their promised undertakings. Managerial and professional 'demotion' for failure to perform was also introduced.

In 1985-87, a new experiment was launched to stem the severity of underemployment in state enterprises, known as the Optimal Labor Reorganization program. The program allows for a comprehensive reorganization of the work unit, with the retraining and redeployment of labor with the aim of increasing overall worker productivity, particularly of permanent workers. The identification and

---

[64] The link of wages to economic efficiency, known as '*gongxiao guagou* 'was an extension of the structural wage system, which was an alternative to the floating wage system, based on a delinking of the wage systems of public agencies and enterprises, but in other respects closer to the former (revised) structural system.

[65] 'Bulletin on the development of labor and employment in 1992', issued by the Vice Minister for Labor in early 1993. *Summary of World Broadcasts*, BBC, June 2, 1993. Analyses of the effects of such wage incentives on economic efficiency of state enterprises have shown that the links are significant (Chetty, et. al., 1993).

[66] Discussed in Groves, et. al., (1992, March) and (1992, September).

elimination of excess workers within an enterprise was aimed at, as well as the placing of remaining workers on contract.[67]

Achievements have also been made in the development of arrangements that mitigate the social dislocation associated with increased job turnover among urban workers.[68] The creation of systems for the compensation, training or retraining of workers, and the placement or dismissal of redundant workers, has begun. Contributory retirement programs for permanent, temporary and contract workers have been launched and some social welfare responsibilities formerly under the purview of the enterprise (such as medical care) are being transferred back to the state. Experiments with alternative means of commercializing the allocation of urban housing are growing widespread.

Partly as a consequence of these new cushions, from late 1991, the government began to permit bolder actions in the shedding of surplus labor by enterprises, to break the 'three irons'; the iron salary (inflexible wages), the iron chair (or permanent jobs for officials) and the iron rice bowl (or lifetime jobs for ordinary laborers). In July 1992, the government announced a new set of 'Regulations on Transforming the Management Mechanisms of State-Owned Enterprises'.[69] These rules provided enterprises with the right to 'make their own decisions about hiring', and the form of employment. The right to terminate contracts and dismiss and fire workers and staff was also included, and the right to demote managers and workers, and to reduce as well as increase pay, was made explicit. Enterprises in financial difficulties are expected to reduce wages and reduce or halt bonus payments, drawing on wage reserves to fulfil financial obligations. In the event of bankruptcy, firms may be disbanded.

The terms and conditions of layoffs and retrenchments were made more explicit through the 'Regulations on the Resettlement of Surplus Workers from State-Owned Enterprises'.[70] The regulations state explicitly that 'in case a layoff is necessitated by major changes to production and management, enterprises may terminate the labor contracts of staff and workers employed under these contracts before the term of their contract expires, and after such a move has been discussed and approved by the workers' congress'. However if the contracts do not provide for such early termination, compensation must be provided, with one-month standard wage for each year of service. There are also provisions for the option of lump sum compensation with resignation. Options for resettlement will depend largely on the enterprises' own programs, with society-assisted resettlement as a second choice. The livelihood of surplus staff and workers is to be ensured. Tertiary industry enterprises established by state enterprises to resettle surplus workers are exempt from income taxes for the first two years and pay 50 percent of taxes in the third year. The state enterprise is obliged to support labor service companies (LSCs) set up to provide employment for redundant workers, with funding, working space and materials and equipment. Provisions also exist for job training.

---

[67] Workers are encouraged to form labor groups to voluntarily contract for production. If an individual fails to be accepted, he may remain in the enterprise, on a reduced wage, or be asked to leave, if alternative employment opportunities are found for them. Many enterprises, especially before 1991, have relied on natural attrition to reduce the numbers of redundant workers.

[68] The paragraphs on new developments draw upon Jefferson and Rawski (1993).

[69] Also known as the 'New Operating Mechanisms' for State-Owned Enterprises.

[70] Xinhua News Agency, domestic service, 27 April 1993, announced the text of these regulations.

The consequences of the new regulations are already apparent. During the first half of 1992, the newly-created Economic and Trade Office of the State Council announced that 1.4 million urban workers had lost their jobs (in contast to 0.7 million in the entire year of 1989). Major instances of labor shedding were announced at large state enterprises. The China National Coal Corporation shed 100,000 workers in 1992, and it plans further reductions of 400,000 of its remaining labor force of 2.8 million over the period 1993 to 1995. Wuhan steel, one of the larger national steel plants, claims to have shed 80,000 of its 120,000 workers, with the aim of raising output per capita from 40 tons of steel towards higher international norms.[71] Most of the staff shed are not directly involved in production, but rather are from administrative or ancillary positions.[72] Meanwhile the Central government itself has announced its intention of laying off a fourth of its 34 million employees over the next three years. A reduction by a third in the staff of the State Council itself was proposed at the Eighth National People's Congress (March 1993), though the dissolution or merger of certain production departments under the Council.[73]

At present, the reforms are likely to find a natural limit as the ability of the enterprises as well as the state to provide new jobs is approached. According to a recent survey of 200 large and medium state enterprises in nine cities, around 17 million workers have been rendered redundant as a result of the reform process. The state will be able to provide jobs for no more than 7.32 million and the rest will be 'left to society'.

It has been pointed out that these new regulations do not completely abolish long-standing labor market restrictions, as state firms remain constrained to recruit ordinary workers (as opposed to managers or technicians) in their home localities. The right of ordinary workers to resign from their posts has not been established in the regulations. Moreover, the enterprises' autonomy in undertaking actions associated with labor-shedding may be challenged by local governments and branches of ministries. Nevertheless the new framework could represent a major transformation in China's labor market, in terms of the establishment of a market largely governed by economic forces. In terms of further progress, there is clearly some scope for further increases in flexibility, again especially in terms of regional transfers. Now that some of the constraints on providing for new urban entrants, such as the controls on sales of price-regulated grain and edible oils have been removed, with the large-scale lifting of grain price controls, and the ending of grain rationing in more than 400 counties and cities, the absorption of such transfers is easier than it was in the past.[74] Facilitation of the process of residence transfer could also include an examination of the legalization of 'illegal' migrants who, while providing a reservoir of cheap

---

[71] The UK produces around 12.1 million tons of steel with 40,000 workers, which amounts to around 300 tons per capita. The Japanese norm is higher, at 800 tons per capita.

[72] In this respect the path being followed by China today mirrors the path already followed by steel companies the world over, including the UK, USA, Italy and Germany. This is being undertaken despite the present profitability of Wuhan steel, and indicates that the Chinese internal market is becoming increasing aware of the standards of international production and markets.

[73] Such as the Ministries of Textile Industry, Chemical Industry, Metallurgical Industry and Light Industry. However in some cases it was proposed that the ministries spun off would be 'converted to company entities', which makes the real diversion of labor ambiguous.

[74] *China Daily*. September 28, 1992. But the permanent residence registration system remains a limiting factor, which has not so far been resolved.

labor, are easy to exploit and contribute to the wage segmentation of the urban labor market.[75] In the case of skilled workers, obstacles still remain in terms of the need to transfer each individual's dossiers from one official agency to another. Finally, new moves to increase the flexibility of enterprises in terms of layoffs and retrenchments are valuable, however, China has to tread a fine line between the the creation of a pool of unemployed persons without adequate security, and efficiency requirements of enterprises. Although protest strickes have occurred in recent years (in 1989, 1992 and 1993), on the whole, commendable parallel progress has been made on these fronts, and a maintenance of a balanced and synchronized approach in the future is to be hoped for.

E. Foreign Exchange Mobility[76]

Given the limited availability of foreign exchange, an important criterion of market performance is its efficiency of allocation among alternative uses, so that it can flow towards those uses where its marginal productivity is the highest. The extent to which foreign exchange can flow between alternative uses depends on the freedom of movement of foreign exchange among competing users and between competing regions. China traditionally combined an inconvertible currency with a rigid system of exchange control, under which any would-be importer had to depend on the State Planning Commission, which allocated all foreign exchange earnings via an annual import plan. Exporters turned over all of their foreign exchange receipts to a specialized bank, the Bank of China, in exchange for domestic currency. Exporters thus were left with no foreign exchange to finance their imports. With the onset of economic reforms, the government began to decentralize the administration of foreign exchange earnings in 1979 by allowing local authorities, departments, and enterprises to retain the rights to buy back a certain proportion of their foreign exchange earnings.[77] On January 1, 1994, China made major changes in its foreign exchange regime, with the unification of its exchange rates. A market-based managed float will be established. Other changes permitting greater flexibility in the foreign exchange management system have also been introduced, as discussed further below.

Retention quotas under the former system were transacted at the administered exchange rate, but by 1988, all enterprises with foreign investment as well as domestic enterprises with retention quotas were permitted to operate in the FEACs. Retention rates in 1984/85 were only 25 percent of export earnings. From 1988, specific priority sectors (light industries, arts and crafts, clothing, machinery, and electrical products) were permitted to retain higher proportions (between 70 and 100 percent) and higher retention rates were also allowed on foreign exchange earnings above planned targets,

---

[75] Migration into the tertiary sector and from rural areas is simpler than other forms of migration. Besides, the government now turns a blind eye to rural labor mobility, especially after the annual Spring Festival.

[76] This section draws largely upon World Bank (June 1993) Report No 11568-CHA.

[77] The full amount of the foreign exchange receipts was required to be surrendered to the state at the official rate by exporters. 'Retention quotas' for foreign exchange could be sold for renminbi at foreign exchange adjustment or "swap" centers (FEACs), which were established in late 1986, or used to purchase imports. Retention quotas could also be traded in the foreign exchange centers, or used for acquiring foreign exchange at the official rate to purchase approved imports.

during the period of mandatory export plans, until 1991. Some regions also enjoyed higher retention rates (provinces such as Guangdong and Fujian, several minority-dominated autonomous regions), and the SEZs, enjoyed retention rates of up to 100 percent. In general, retained foreign exchange was split evenly between the foreign trade corporation (FTC) handling the export transaction and the firm producing the good.

Expanded foreign exchange retention rights extended in 1991 were combined with easier access to foreign exchange markets. Quota controls on the utilization of retained foreign exchange, which had been imposed by the central government in 1985, were abolished, and the number of authorized local foreign exchange markets increased. Each province, autonomous region and centrally administered city was authorized to establish at least one foreign exchange swap center within its territory.[78] A national foreign currency swap center was also to be established in Beijing to facilitate currency transactions between central government agencies and to facilitate transactions between local swap markets in different administrative jurisdictions. In addition, the swap markets were formally opened not only to enterprises with foreign investment, but also to state-owned and collectively owned enterprises.

Major modifications to this system were introduced in 1991, and again at the end of 1993. In 1991, a uniform retention rate of 80 percent was set throughout the country, of which 10 percent accrues to the enterprise, 10 percent to the local government and the remaining 60 percent to the foreign trade corporation. However, special rates for certain sectors were retained and adjusted upwards. For machinery and electronics products, the retention rate is now 100 percent of which 10 percent accrues to the producing enterprises and 90 percent to the foreign trade corporation. Moreover, the central government ensured access to foreign exchange sufficient to meet its own requirements by reserving the right to purchase, albeit at the prevailing FEAC rate, an additional 30 percent of the foreign exchange initially retained; 20 additional percent points from the foreign trade corportations and 10 from export producers. Since it appears that the center fully exercised this option in 1991, an effective 50 percent of the overall foreign exchange earnings of the local authorities and enterprises was still appropriated by the central government, and producers of export goods were left with no retained foreign exchange. Even exporting firms which wanted to purchase imports outside the plan had to seek access to the FEACs.[79]

Under the former system, selling foreign exchange was considerably easier than buying foreign exchange. Sales of foreign exchange at the swap rate were virtually unrestricted after December 1991, when all domestic residents were allowed to start selling foreign exchange at the swap rate at designated branches of banks. These sales consisted of actual foreign exchange, sold mainly by enterprises with foreign investment, and of foreign exchange retention quotas by Chinese enterprises (since the actual foreign exchange was surrendered to the state).

By contrast, access to FEACs to purchase foreign exchange was subject to approval and was restricted mainly to enterprises which needed foreign exchange either to service their foreign currency debt or to import goods consistent with the industrial policy of the state. Purchases of actual

---

[78]   By end-December 1992, there were over 100 'swap centers' in operation.

[79]   The authorities have recently started experimenting with a cash retention system on a limited scale in several centers around the country. In such a system, the enterprise would only be required to surrender a portion of their foreign exchange earnings to the state administration of exchange control and would be allowed to keep a portion of its foreign exchange earnings in resident bank accounts.

foreign exchange were usually limited to enterprises with foreign investment, which could be used for purposes approved by the Ministry of Foreign Trade and Economic Cooperation (MOFTEC) including their own operating needs, debt repayment, and remittances. However, even domestic enterprises with permission to import were only permitted to purchase retention quotas in the FEACs; the purchased quotas had to be used within a six-month period to acquire foreign exchange from the state reserves, at the prevailing official rate, for approved uses. The priority list reflected plan objectives regarding key commodities, and it provideed for favorable treatment for exporting activity as well as for the acquisition of advanced technology. Requests for foreign exchange to finance imports of consumer durables, luxury goods or goods judged to be speculative in nature were not permitted.

Recent Changes

From January 1, 1994, the system of trading foreign exchange through the FEACs was shifted to the trade of foreign exchange through the banking system, wiht the development of a national interbank market in foreign exchange. The People's Bank of China (PBC) will publish renminbi buying and selling rates within floating margins set by the PBC. All domestic enterprises will be required to surrender their foreign exchange earnings to banks, and the retention system which prevailed until the end of 1993 will be abolished. However, 'cash' foreign exchange accounts can be held (in RMB equivalent) for foreign direct investment, proceeds of foreign borowings and individual foreign currency deposits. Retention quotas may continue to be used to purchase foreign exchange at the official rate through the 1st quarter of 1994.

The advantages of the new system are first, that all transactions will occurr at one rate. Second, if exporters or importers need foreign exchange, there is no need to be restricted by 'retention quotas'; foreign exchange can be purchased at banks. Third, with the interbank market, a national foreign exchange market will be established, to replace the former 18 foreign exchange swap centers. A national electronic exchange will be established with its headquarters at Shanghai, opening on April 1, 1994. Fourth, the system of the 'priority list' under the former system will be abolished.

Although it is too early to assess the new system, it certainly represents considerably more flexibility, as well as more more uniform prices for foreign exchange, across different forms of transactions. It represents a major improvement in the establishment of a unified market for foreign exchange. Its efficiency in practice, in terms of ease of access of different agents to foreign exchange, should be reviewed once the system is well established.

F. Conclusions

Drawing together the evidence of the preceding sections, a first general point which emerges is that while China has clearly made progress in improving the functioning of the market on the whole, and in substituting the former system of central guidance with a considerably increased reliance on market signals, there are still areas in which progress is required, particularly in the continuing segmentation of regional markets, but also in terms of market access, and uniform treatment to different economic agents. While detailed comments on the markets discussed above are discussed in each specific section, the key findings are reiterated below.

First of all, price behavior indicates that there has been a convergence in terms of plan and market prices, and there has also been some convergence in regional price differentials, after 1990. However, regional price differential still appear to be larger for many goods today than they were in 1986. The recent dramatic moves towards price liberalization of 1992 and 1993 however are not adequately captured in the information here and an assessment using these estimates should be undertaken when the data are available. It would be useful to establish an ongoing system for monitoring price differentials and trends in convergence, as undertaken here, to assess the real progress and impact of price decontrol. It should also be noted here that the rapid recent escalation of transport costs for cargo may have the effect of raising regional price differentials for some commodities, reflecting the increased and real cost of transport. To the extent that this is a factor, increased regional differentials are not harmful. Explicit treatment of the effects of transport costs will be necessary as their share in total cost rises towards significant levels.

The general conclusion on the mobility of both goods and factors is that such mobility appears to be low, and may in some cases have declined relative to the growth of output. Links with the overseas exterior appear to have been easier to develop than links with other provinces, both in terms of the mobility of goods and some factors, particularly capital investment. There has been some tendency for individual provinces to behave as separate countries, rather than as parts of a single large country. The continuous relative decline in internal trade is prima facie surprising and the reasons for this must be explored. First, some of this decline, in the early years of the reform, may have been the result of the introduction of the dual pricing system, in combination with output contracts and the increased revenue-collecting authority given to local officials, and this illustrates the difficulties of partial reform. Second, it may also be that with the rapid growth of township and village enterprises, intra-provincial consumption and production rose, relative to interprovincial trade. Third, the decline in the planned allocation and distribution of goods may itself have led to a decline in interprovincial trade flows. But it may also be argued that the continuation of this trend, as well as China's low relative levels of interprovincial trade, indicate that local protection, as well as the local government's incentives to keep local enterprises profitable, may be significant factors. Once more comprehensive data are available, the extent to which they support this conclusion should be reexamined, together with an assessment of the extent to which this phenomenon persists in the future. It also suggests the existence of other constraints to domestic trade, such as difficulties in interregional payments and in transportation. The rapid implementation and spread of the computerised interregional clearance mechanism is to be hoped for, and should be supplemented with an examination of procedural steps in intrabank and interbank payment systems.

The question which follows is, what form of regulation, or what changes in the structure of enforcement, could encourage increased mobility of goods and assist the breakdown of regional barriers. Experiments with unilateral freeing up of trade in some locations (Wuhan) met with no reciprocal response from other provinces and suggest that multilateral 'loosening up', guided by the center, may be more acceptable.[80] The adoption of regulations against constraints to domestic trade at the level of the center is called for. Attention will also have to be paid to the present incentives, at the level of provincial governments, to protect local industry, which emanate from the fiscal contract system and their assigned revenue bases.

---

[80] Cited in World Bank (1992) Report No 10479-CHA. However theoretically even a unilateral opening up of markets should lead to gains from trade. This illustrates the need to combine the politically acceptable with the economically rational.

The present revenue sharing arrangements probably also account for the limited flows of enterprise investment across provinces. It is also unfortunately likely that to the extent that capital flows do occur, they are motivated by the tax breaks offered, legally and illegally, in the multiple forms of special 'zones'. This process has itself aggravated internal differentials as in general inland provinces have benefitted less than coastal provinces. Although the government is now making a serious effort to remove illegal zones, a significant number of zones will remain and present indications are that regional differentials in fiscal incentives may therefore persist.[81] The examination of all such zones, with a view to reducing unequal treatment across provinces and across different categories of investors is required.

Constraints on regional flows of credit through the interbank market are in part related to the government's use of credit ceilings as the primary form of control on monetary expansion. The abuse of such controls by banks wishing to circumvent quotas, in the form of the misuse of interbank lending, has not assisted the development of this market. While a diversification in instruments of monetary policy in the medium term is required, this will need to be combined with closer monitoring of the interbank market, together with controls against its misuse.

In the field of labor mobility, there has been considerable progress over the last few years in terms of an increased capacity for both employers and employees to respond to performance based incentives and flexibilities in staffing requirements, through both systems of reward and penalty, Recent legislation on labor-shedding affords hitherto unprecedented opportunities to enterprises to adjust the sizes of their labor force. The issue here is how to find a balance, between the requirements of enterprises, and the requirements of society as a whole. China is making creditable progress so far in its recognition of these factors, and is gradually developing improved social 'safety nets'. One area in which the development of a flexible labor market is still lagging noticeably is in the spatial mobility of labor. Although some progress has been achieved here, the difficulties of regional transfers are still great and the rights of large numbers of illegal migrants are limited. Given the easing of rationing of urban grain and other essentials, this may be an opportune time to reexamine other constraints on regional mobility, such as the permanent residence registration requirement.

Finally, the market for foreign exchange has exhibited changes in behavior which in many respects parallel other markets, in terms of improving access and flexibility of use. In the case of this market, in 1993, there was an effort at eliminating regional differentials, in terms of retention rates, but in practice this did not work very well, and regional differentials in rates persisted, aggravated in periods such as mid-1993 when additional restraints on mobility were imposed by the central government. The recent changes introduced in the foreign exchange control and management system from January 1, 1994, in particular the exchange rate unification and the establishment of an interbank market, with the abolition of the retention system and the priority list, should considerably increase flexibility and reduce price distortions.

---

[81]   According to the Special Economic Zone Office, 1200 zones in 8 coastal provices have recently been scrutinized, and all but 200 of these have been declared illegal, and will be closed down and returned to agricultural land. UPI, August 12, 1993.

3

The Distribution System

While the previous chapters examined the structure of the internal market and policies concerning factor pricing and factor mobility, the present chapter evaluates the real side of market formation and product distribution. First, an assessment is undertaken at an aggregate level of the role of the state in distribution and the changes in its functions, in qualitative and quantitative terms. Next, the chapter examines the characteristics of the present distribution system to see whether it is successfully adapting to its expected role in a market economy. The emphasis here is on the distribution of producer goods, where the state has traditionally been more important and the process of transition is therefore more difficult. A review of the supporting infrastructure of the market, in terms of transportation and communication services, which critically affects the functioning of markets, supplements this examination.

A. The Changing Role of the State in Distribution

A fundamental part of the movement towards the establishment of a market economy has been the decline in the role of the state in material allocation. The total number of goods subject to centralized allocation through government procurement, and later contract, has declined from 837 to 19 between 1980 and 1992, or from 90 percent to 12 percent by value. Consumer goods allocated through the plan declined from 274 in 1978 to 14 in 1992. The allocation of producer goods, until 1993, was undertaken through the Material Supply bureaus of the former Ministry of Materials and Equipment (MME). Consumer goods were distributed through the Ministry of Commerce (MOC), through large state-owned trading enterprises in cities, and through the network of All China Supply and Marketing Cooperatives in rural areas. This segmentation of responsibilities for internal marketing ceased in 1993, with the merger of these two ministries, to form a single new Ministry of Internal Trade (MIT).[1] However, the separation of domestic and foreign trade continues, as virtually all foreign trade is conducted through foreign trade corporations (FTCs) under the Ministry of Foreign Trade and Economic Cooperation (MOFTEC).[2] FTCs do not have their own domestic distribution networks.[3]

---

[1] The extent to which this will lead to a real merger of distribution facilities will however only be known after the new ministry presents its organigram. Meanwhile the facilities continue to operate in a parallel fashion.

[2] FTCs handle over 90 percent of China's imports and at least 80 percent of exports. There are now an estimated 3,600 FTCs in operation, which are all owned by central or lower level governments. Enterprises with foreign investment, and a small number of individual enterprises (538, in mid-1992) also have the right to trade directly (World Bank 1993, Report No. 11568-CHA).

The largest group of goods still subject to planned distribution today are production materials, distributed by the erstwhile MME. Of the 19 commodities which remained under this ministry at the beginning of 1993, changes in the percentage of central distribution for ten principal products are given in Figure 3.1. As Figure 3.1 shows, even in the case of these products, the share of total production subject to supply by government contract declined markedly between 1985 and 1991.

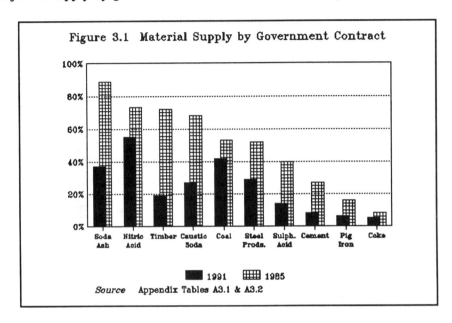

It must however be noted that while the general trend in the decline in the role of the government here is clear, the share of supply by government contract at the end of 1991 was still relatively high for some products; 25 percent or more for five of the ten products listed here. The variation between products was also high, and the decline in the role of the government has been more marked for some products relative to others. For example, the government's role in the allocation of timber and cement has fallen markedly, by 74 percent and 70 percent of their previous ratios. Relative declines are also significant for pig iron, steel and soda ash, (63 percent, 44 percent and 58 percent), although absolute levels, in the case of soda ash and steel are still fairly high (37 percent and 29 percent). In other products, such as nitric acid, the relative decline, by end 1991, was low, and the absolute level of supply by government contract was high. Coal has been a similar case. This suggests that specific bottlenecks may be operating in the case of products such as these, which retard their transfer to market allocation.[4] These factors require further investigation at a product-specific level.

---

[3]   For the most part, FTCs undertaking imports hand these over to importing firms, or to the internal distribution agencies of the erstwhile domestic ministries, MOC and MME. However, recently some specialized trading corporations have begun to sell their imports on commodity exchanges, thereby engaging directly in domestic trade. The China Metals Import and Export Corporation is an example (Chapter 4).

[4]   Nitric acid is used mainly by the machinery industries as a heavy chemical and cleansing agent. Coal has both industrial and domestic uses and the efficiency of coal use is discussed in World Bank (1991) Report No. 8915-CHA.

In the case of agricultural consumer goods, it must first be noted that the rate of marketization of agricultural products has increased. Thus, the proportion of retail sales by agricultural residents, to persons outside agriculture (as opposed to consumption within the agricultural sector), has increased for all major agricultural products (Figure 3.2). This again reflects an increase in the role of markets in the allocation of goods. While the absolute proportions sold outside agriculture are more significant for fruits and vegetables, the proportional increase in grain and vegetable oils has also been high; fom 7.5 to 9.6 percent, and 8.6 to 15.9 percent, respectively.

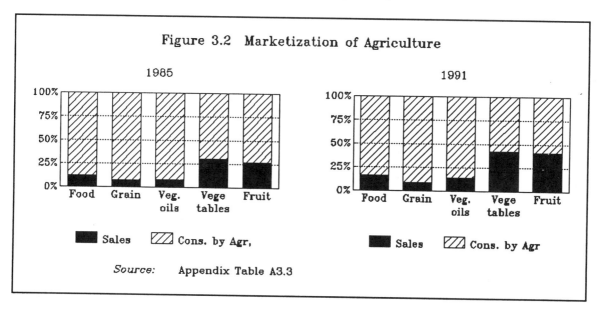

Figure 3.2 Marketization of Agriculture

Source: Appendix Table A3.3

The increased role of the market in terms of the allocation of goods, and in terms of the marketization of produce, is clear. As discussed in the previous chapter, the role of the state in price regulation has similarly diminished considerably. It might therefore be expected that the role of the state in distribution has declined in the same fashion. However, as Table 3.1 indicates, this does not appear to have been the case. While the table shows that there has been a clear decline over time in the proportion of state-owned units in retail sales, most of this decline occurred in the period 1978 to 1985, when the share of the state in the ownership of retailing fell from over 53 percent to around 40 percent, in terms of the value of retail sales. Between 1985 and 1991, there is little perceptible change in this proportion. This finding is unexpected, and parallels the findings of Chapters 1 and 2, of the simultaneous observation of remarkable change in some aspects of the movements towards a market economy, and virtually no change in other directions.

Table 3.1 Composition of Total Retail Sales Value by Ownership (1960-1991)
(Y 100 Million and Percent)

Year	Retail Sales By Ownership					Sales of Agricultural to Non- Agr. Residents (%)
	Total Value of Sales (Y 100m)	State-Owned Units %	Collective Units %	Jointly Owned Units %	Individual Units %	
1965	67.03	53.0	43.2	0.0	1.9	1.9
1978	158.97	53.5	42.4	0.1	2.0	2.0
1985	430.5	40.4	37.2	0.3	15.4	6.8
1991	941.56	40.2	30.0	0.5	19.6	9.7

Source: Appendix Tables A3.4 and A3.5.

One reason for this finding may be that although new distribution and retailing units have been established by the non-state sectors, their share in the total value of distribution remains small, because of their relatively small size. This is partly correct, but is not a sufficient explanation. As indicated in Appendix Tables A3.6 and A3.7, individual and collective units have dominated for years, in terms of numbers of units, on account of their small size. Thus in both 1985 and 1991, the share of the state sector in terms of numbers of units, was just over 5 percent. However, it remains true that the absolute increase over this period in individual and collective units has been negligible. While the 6.2 million individually owned units, accounting for 75.6 percent of domestic trade units in 1985, grew to 7.8 million, and 79.8 percent of the total number of units by 1991, the absolute number and proportional share of collective units declined (from 1.6 to 1.4 million units, and 19.1 to 14.7 percent of the numbers of units). Looking at different provinces within China, the relative shares of state and non-state units are, on the whole, similar.

Table 3.2 Number and Share of Domestic Trade Units by Ownership and Region
(1985-1991)

	1985				1991			
	Total	State Owned Units	Collective Units	Individually Owned Units	Total	State Owned Units	Collective Units	Individually Owned Units
Numbers of units	8250472	429424	1578953	6238600	9797708	534145	1443617	7817454
Percentage	100.0	5.2	19.1	75.6	100.0	5.5	14.7	79.8

Source: Appendix Tables A3.6 and A3.7.

Not only was there no change in the state's share in the value of retail trade, and a relatively constant state share in the total number of distribution units, there was also a steady absolute increase in the number of outlets under the Materials Circulation system, between 1985 and 1991 (Appendix Table A3.8). In terms of numbers, the outlets of the material supply system grew from 32.5 thousand in 1985 to 51.2 thousand in 1991; an annual average rate of growth of 7.9 percent. There was also a large increase in the numbers of persons employed (over 300,000, or an increase of 5.5 percent per year. In regional terms, increases appear smaller in relatively developed areas and larger in more backward areas. Thus, the growth of personnel in Beijing, Shanghai and Guangdong, in terms of personnel in the materials circulation system, much lower than the national average (at 1.1, 0.4 and 1.7 percent per year on average). The growth of state-owned units in storage and transport (3.4 percent per year) has also been faster than collectives or supply and marketing cooperatives for storage and transport (2.6 and 0.2 percent per year, respectively) (Appendix Table A3.9).

The data above show that while the role of the state in allocation has declined, it continues to play a large role in distribution, growing in absolute terms and perhaps increasing its share relative to the non-state sector. This finding is particularly surprising, in view of the overall sharp decline in the share of state owned enterprises in output value (Chapter 1). It must be concluded that while the share of the state in productive enterprises has declined sharply, the state has not withdrawn from its dominant role in distribution.

How can the declining role of the state in allocation and price controls be reconciled with the maintenance of the state in distribution? One explanation is that, despite the steady presence and dominance of the state in distribution, there may have been a change in the orientation of state-owned units, towards more market-based functions and behavior. In the past, state owned stores were largely intended to focus on the sales of state-allocated goods. However, as the state withdrew from planned allocation, the facilities for distribution remained, and state-owned stores continued to serve as distribution centers, for enterprises wishing to sell their output on the free market. State enterprises within the Materials Supply system have made strong efforts to become more competitive and more market-oriented. This is reflected in Appendix Table 3.9, which shows that personnel employed at state-owned 'administrative units' grew relatively slowly, between 1985 and 1991, from 1.35 to 1.5 million, or 1.9 percent per year. At the same time, personnel at state-owned 'business units' grew at 4.8 percent per year, and their numbers rose from 5 to 6.6 million. New forms of retail outlets appeared over this period, for example, outlets owned by the state but run by collectives, and outlets leased and run by individuals. By 1991, 522,000 persons were employed by such enterprises. The number of persons employed in jointly owned enterprises grew faster than the other categories (5.3 percent per year in all, and 26 percent per year for Sino-foreign joint ventures), though absolute numbers are still small (50,000 persons in all joint-venture distribution enterprises).

It should be mentioned here that whether or not the new enterprises belong to the state sector, the general trend towards an increase in the number of retail trade units is desirable. Most planned economies suffer from relatively limited retail trade services, and as such the rapid growth in these stores in the early 1980s, and the continued, though slow, growth in more recent years has helped to place China above the league of other formerly planned economies. As Table 3.3 shows, retail trade services per capita in China have been well above the former Soviet Union. In terms of numbers of persons employed in retail trade China is still well below West Europe, although in terms of numbers of stores the figures are comparable.

Table 3.3 Retail Trade Services in China and Other Countries
(per 10,000 of Population)

	Number of stores			Number employed		
	1978	1985	1991	1978	1985	1991
Soviet Union		20			177	
United States		61			491	
United Kingdom		61			412	
Germany		66			383	
France		86			335	
Japan		135			527	
Italy		175			350	
China	11	74	80	46	170	190
state ownership	1	2	3	10	27	34
collective ownership	9	13	10	35	63	58
individual ownership	1	58	67	1	79	98

Sources: China Statistical Yearbook (1992) and Woo (1993).

The conclusion of continued strong state presence, albeit with a rapidly changing face, is corroborated by the following sections of this chapter and the next, which describe the new measures and experiments adopted by government marketing agencies to improve their systems of distribution. This overview also emphasizes the importance of assessing the efficiency of the state-agencies' efforts in this direction.

B. The Efficiency of the Present Distribution System

Evolution of the Materials Distribution System

Prior to the launching of economic reform, the distribution of production materials was undertaken in conjunction with allocative plans of the State Council, which assigned the output of these goods to specific users. The function of distribution was conducted by individual ministries or departments which oversaw the production of these goods in conjunction with the State General Office of Materials, for major production goods.[5] With the launching of economic reform, the decentralization of the distribution function began and in 1979, 'production goods service companies', the precursors of distribution enterprises, were established. Also at this time, some producer goods were removed from the central plan allocation system, and the production service companies began to assist their sales through supporting the organization of large 'fairs', where buyers and sellers would meet and examine

---

[5]   Distribution during the pre reform period also had its phases, which are not detailed here. However, to synopsize, there was a Ministry of Materials in the period prior to the Cultural Revolution, which was dissolved in 1967. In 1975, the State General Office of Materials was set up, and administrative departments for materials were partially restored. By the end of 1978, many provincial and ministerial bureaux of materials had also been restored. (See MME Background Note 5 for details).

the goods available for sale outside the plan. It was believed at the time that markets for these goods would emerge, more or less automatically, after their removal from central allocation. The state became aware of the need for maintaining at least a supervisory role in the distribution of these goods, and in August 1981, the first directive on market regulation was issued by the state council; Regulation No. 120 of 1981, the 'Temporary Provision on Regulating Markets for Industrial Production Goods'. The provision defines the industrial production goods which could be freely traded, as well as the qualifications and business scope of firms dealing with their distribution. This is still the only major legal regulation of markets for goods.

Shortly after, the State Bureau of Material Supply, which had until this time had no more than a guidance function in the allocation of goods, was given increased importance. In 1982 the State Council decided that the materials office could be made into a department of the State Council, and placed this department below the State Economic Commission. The importance of the function of distribution was given increasing recognition, and the State Council provided Y6 billion in the form of bank loans to material supply and marketing units, to augment their working capital. Half this sum went to the General Office of Materials, of the State Bureau of Material Supply and half went to the supply and marketing organs of the material departments. At the same time, materials enterprises were given some control over price fixing, for certain goods, and the possibility of profit retention was also introduced.

The process of materials market reform accelerated over 1984 to 1986 as a consequence of the introduction of production contracts and dual-track pricing. A given commodity could now be sold partially under the plan, and partially outside the plan, with a proportion subject to fixed prices, and the balance under free prices. However, there was only a single distribution network in existence for the sales of all these categories of goods. As a result, the material supply bureaus began to establish facilities for producers to sell their non-plan output at the same location on a commercial basis, through the establishment of permanent 'on-site' trade fairs for a variety of goods. This led to the emergence of a new form of market, the 'comprehensive distribution center', set up initially to facilitate the sales of above-plan output of producer goods on a commercial basis.

Specialized material bureaus for individual products were also set up, as the State Council gradually began to transfer the function of distribution from the production ministries or departments responsible for these goods, to the Material Supply bureau. The organization of specialized markets for specific products, in addition to the comprehensive trading centers also began. The establishment of markets for steel products was approved in 1985 and in March 1987 steel markets were set up in 68 cities, including Beijing and 20 provinces. An automobile trade center was approved in the same year.[6]

Another significant experiment launched at this time was the introduction of sales on a margin or commission basis by the Material Supply bureaus, for producers outside the plan. The 'Shijiazuang market' experiment, as it came to be known, as a consequence of its city of origin, initially came into being due to the fact that producers selling goods outside the plan had greater flexibility in terms of meeting customer requirements in terms of quality and price. The Material Supply bureaus on the other hand had the physical infrastructure for distribution, in the form of warehousing, and contacts

---

[6]   By the end of 1992, the Ministry of Materials and Equipment (MME) reported the existence of 3,000 retail markets, as well as some 500 "comprehensive trading centers", whose combined turnover totalled 45 billion RMB Yuan in 1991. By now, it has also created over 300 wholesale markets specializing in the sale of steel products, whose turnover exceeded 21 million tons of products in 1992.

with buyers. It was agreed that the Material Supply bureau would undertake to sell the non-plan goods, on the condition that it could sell these at the same price as the goods which it was obliged to sell under the plan. The difference would then be returned to the producer. Later, the system grew more flexible, and the Material Supply bureau kept a part of the difference in price (10 percent) as its own fee. Although this represented a form of price maintenance, the experiment was significant as it also represented the provision of distributor services on a commercial basis by the Material Supply bureaus, and thus represents the beginning of the commercialization of the functions of these government agencies.

There was a considerable degree of regional diversity in the experiments launched at this time. For example, in the province of Guangdong, the material offices were converted to General Companies of Materials and accorded considerable commercial freedom. In 18 provinces, distribution was under the charge of the Material Bureau offices, advised by local economic and technical coordination offices. In other provinces however distribution plans were made by the provincial planning council, and the only role of the materials offices was to supply the goods according to these plans.

Over this entire period, 1979 to 1987, the State General Office of Materials and local material departments helped to develop product markets, but the various departments of production of these goods still retained their roles. In April 1988, at the first session of the 7th National People's Congress, the State General Office of Materials was dissolved and the Ministry of Materials (MME), a more autonomous and powerful organization, was set up in its place. Twelve ministries signed contracts with the new MME on the transfer of their supply and marketing organs to the new ministry. The staff, working systems and channels, however, were to remain unchanged. A liaison department between these production departments and the MME was established at the MME. In 1991, the MME issued provisional rules on the Approval of Qualification for National Firms Trading Important Industrial Means of Production and their Trading Scopes; thus defining the activities of major marketing organizations. More radical changes in the distribution system began from this time, with the establishment of a series of commodities exchanges and 'futures markets'. The development of these is discussed in detail in the following chapter (Chapter 4).

The importance of this history of institutional change is threefold. First, it illustrates that the process of deregulation, in terms of planned allocation or price decontrol, did not, in China, automatically lead to the creation of markets for these goods. Even when goods could have been sold by other means, producers continued to find efficiencies in using existing distribution systems. Second, the state-owned distribution system, however, adapted to changing circumstances, with progressive new experiments. Third, this process has taken considerable time, and is still far from resembling the distribution network of a moderately developed market economy.

Specialized Distribution Companies: Recent Developments in Fuel Distribution

Coal Distribution in Shanghai

The Shanghai Fuel General Corporation is one of the largest fuel distribution companies in China. Its 1992 distribution volume was 14.5 million tons of coal and 1.1 million tons of heavy oils, resulting in sales of Y2.2 billion.

Today it faces increased competition. Users can now buy coal direct from mining companies or middlemen. In 1991, the Corporation accounted for 94 percent of coal sales in its trading area, but in 1992, this had dropped to 90 percent as some middlemen began to solicit business actively. Most of the 30 or 40 middlemen represent trading companies from other provinces. Lacking facilities to warehouse coal, they must ship directly to their customers. At present, this constrains their expansion.

In response, the Shanghai Corporation is improving and adding value to its services, through coal blending for power use before sale, to reduce pollution and evenly raise combustibility value. The Corporation's physical distribution system is also improving. Coal delivery used to be the responsibility of a separate trucking company over which the Coal Corporation had no control. With the takeover of the trucking company in 1992 the Corporation has instituted regular delivery schedules, important for the several customers who lack space to hold large inventory.

There is scope for improvement, however, in the handling of incoming coal. Much of Shanghai's coal arrives by ship. Incoming coal is unloaded onto a dock, then loaded again, into smaller boats, for transportation to the coalyard. At the coalyard it is once again unloaded and stored until it is loaded onto trucks for delivery to customers/users.

This system is inefficient as it involves more rounds of materials handling than strictly necessary. It would be preferable to load coal directly into smaller boats at the docks. Today this is out of the Corporation's control, as the port is under separate management and dock space limits a collier's time at dock to 10 hours, which is evidently not enough for direct loading into smaller boats. Moreover, arrival times for shipments in are not always predictable, and this, together with multiple storage sites and slow handling, results in actual inventories of around 1.8 million tons; much larger than the desired inventory level, of 1 million tons.

If the Coal Corporation could control or contract with the warehouse company, large gains could be realized through better control of the timing and mode of inward and outward shipments and mode of storage. Introducing cross-docking (loading coal directly from incoming ships into trucks that transport it to customers) would also help eliminate much dock to coalyard shipping. Where this is difficult, warehousing facilities at or near the port should be added, so that coal can either be unloaded directly into a warehouse or transported to a holding area by conveyor or other mechanical means.

Household Propane Gas Distribution in Shenzhen

The Shenzhen Gas Company bottles and distributes cooking gas to households and restaurants. It maintains a filling facility, a fleet of over 80 delivery trucks, and 6 stores. Each store maintains its own fleet of tricycles for local delivery to households. The company owns a total of about 140 tricycles. Its sales are around Y100 million per year, with a profit of about Y2 million on gas sales.

The filling facility receives imported LPG (liquefied petroleum gas) and stores it in large tanks. The storage tanks are connected by hose to a canister-filling carousel, which is located on a raised, covered concrete platform. The platform serves all the functions performed by the company. It is the storage facility for both returned and filled canisters, and the loading dock for delivery trucks.

The operation works virtually on a 'just-in-time' system because there is little storage space available. Five workers load 12 empty canisters on the carousel, where they are automatically filled, in 40 seconds each. The canister's valves are closed manually by the workers, who then place them in the loading area where other workers load them onto waiting delivery trucks. When a truck is fully loaded with about 200 canisters, it leaves almost immediately for one of the stores. A store has room for a maximum of about 1000 canisters (including empties), and the trucks go back and forth all day. There are about 300,000 canisters in circulation in Shenzhen. Most customers request the stores to transport gas to their homes by tricycle delivery, which costs around Y2 per canister.

The system is labor intensive. For example, a truck is loaded at the filling plant, then unloaded at the store. A tricycle is then loaded at the store and then unloaded at the customer's apartment. The company is planning to reduce wage costs, through (1) the installation of a new filling line at a second location that will fill containers much faster and will require only one worker to manage. (2) It has also received a license to pipe gas directly to the users in certain neighborhoods. The company would like to expand its use of pipeline distribution.

Further improvements to be considered for the future are (1) the institution of scheduled regular deliveries direct to users' apartments, instead of the present ad hoc and unscheduled deliveries. Since most dwellings in Shenzhen are multi-family, and clustered, it might then be possible to deliver to one location in truckload quantities, distributing to each apartment directly from the delivery truck. (2) As gas usage increases, it might be feasible to pipe gas within buildings and feed gas to individual apartments from one large canister centrally located somewhere in the building. It is considerably less expensive to pipe only the inside of a building than to pipe to each building from a central location. And it is less expensive to deliver one large gas canister to a building than a number of apartment sized ones.

Sources: Background Papers.

The System Today

The structure of the distribution system in China today reflects its gradual evolution as it followed the process of economic reform. With the growth of the non-state sector, as well as the shift in administrative systems of SOEs, a change in marketing system has been a natural corollary.[7] Clearly there has been considerable progress in the development of a producer goods market.[8] The state's dominance of distribution functions, particularly of producer goods, has continued, despite the decline of the state in planned allocation. Nevertheless the system today represents a hybrid which includes core elements of distribution geared towards central planning, but with several modifications and adjustments, in response to the phased decline of planned allocation, and also in response to competitive forces emerging in the economy. As with many other elements of economic reform, the new elements have been introduced gradually, on an experimental basis, and with wide regional variations.[9] Examples of the adaptive ability, as well as of continuing inefficiencies and difficulties carried over from the former system, are illustrated in the descriptions provided of the distribution of coal and household fuels in Shanghai and Shenzhen.3.1 At the apex, the major city of each region has a parent organization, which is a Materials Supply and Equipment bureau, which is delegated by the local government to organize the distribution of producer goods. The Bureau reports to the MME interns of business policy. This parent organization supervises approximately a dozen distribution organizations. Most of these specialize in a particular commodity, such as coal or steel, or a range of goods, such as electrical equipment, which represent the goods currently or formerly allocated under the plan, and which were formerly transferred to the MME from specialized ministerial departments.[10] Although these goods may no longer be subject to distribution under the plan at all, or the proportions subject to planned distribution may be negligible, the material bureaus still dominate their distribution, as existing distribution facilities and networks are still the only ones still available on a large scale, to carry out the distribution function. This distribution function is in some cases undertaken on a purchase and sale, or on a commission basis. The range of goods so far does not appear to be driven by specific customer needs; there appears to have been little change in the merchandise assortments carried by individual distribution organizations over the course of reform.

---

[7] The reorientation of SOEs is referred to as *Zhuan Gui Bian Xing*; or 'shifting rails and transforming functions', in China.

[8] In the distribution field, the Chinese government launched experiments with ownership reform several years ago, with the "'Three Various's' (various economic ownership, operational models and distribution channels) and One 'Less'(reduction of distribution links and levels)".

[9] See in particular Solinger (1989), who describes the new form of hybridized relations of exchange.

[10] Examples of these material distribution companies, for individual product lines, are given in Appendix Tables A3.10 to A3.12, for machinery and electrical equipment, metals and fuel. Each table lists the 20 largest product specific corporations in the country.

Material Supply Bureaus in China Today

The Wuxi Municipal Goods and Materials Bureau

The materials bureau at Wuxi, one of the fastest growing areas in China, consists of 12 companies, each specializing in a single commodity or a range of goods, covering the principal goods subject to state planning. Very few of its products are now distributed by plan; less than 2 percent in 1992, compared with 85 percent in 1986. Individual distribution companies can shop for merchandise in any province. Moreover, this bureau can import directly through its own import/export agency. The Bureau sells at largely market determined prices. The Bureau has competitors; it estimates there are some 4600 companies trading in one good or another in the Wuxi area. Today the emphasis of the bureau is on providing places for trading activities to take place.

The Bureau's distribution firms maintain a staff of some 5000 salespeople who are responsible for procurement as well as sales. Salespeople today receive a basic salary plus incentive compensation based on their volume of sales.

The distribution companies instituted customer delivery in 1991, and their latest initiative is a "comprehensive delivery center." If customers require products handled by different distribution companies the comprehensive center provides a single central ordering point, and assembles and delivers the order. The customers, however, will receive separate bills from each distribution company.

The Bureau also processes certain materials. For example, it owns sawmills and will cut timber to customers/users' orders. It wants to extend its processing activities to other materials as well.

The Bureau maintains a building that houses a showroom, and offices that it rents to sales representatives of manufacturing firms that want to do business in Wuxi. These firms may be located in any province and may sell direct to customers in the Wuxi area. They do not have to go through the distribution company. Also included in the building is a materials trading center.

The Suzhou Materials Bureau

This Bureau encompasses the usual 12 companies. One of the 12 is a real estate company, established in 1991. The real estate company is building offices and hotel blocks. It also has enterprises attached to it, including a knitting company.

The Bureau would like to expand both horizontally (into more enterprises) and vertically, (into

manufacturing). The reasons offered are that price decontrol has made trading too risky and profits are low and uncertain. Too many competitors are entering the field. Both large manufacturers and construction firms are increasingly bypassing the Bureau's distribution firms and buying materials they use in large or predictable quantities directly from suppliers.

The Shenzhen Materials General Company

The Shenzhen Materials General Company is the oldest State-owned company in Shenzhen, also the largest and most widely diversified. It is the largest of the national materials trading companies. It has thirteen subordinate companies and owns interests in fifty-six joint ventures. Of the latter, 20 are with foreign firms and 36 are with inland Chinese firms.

In addition to the usual distribution companies, the Materials General Company also owns a taxi fleet, an auto repair business, assembly plants, and real estate. The Company engages in compensation trade. It also engages in bonded storage of imported raw materials and components. It has opened foreign branches in Hong Kong and Thailand to do trading.

The Company controls its enterprises very tightly by means of a "financial settlement center" which functions as a bank. All of the Company's enterprises deposit their receipts in this center daily. The center then pays all of the enterprises' bills.

This system, of course, gives the Company almost complete control of its enterprises' cash. It also minimizes the Company's needs for working capital since all the enterprises' balances are available to offset any enterprise's needs for disbursement. On the negative side, though, the individual enterprises are not free to take advantage of any opportunities that require funds without the Company's express permission.

The Materials General Company is an independent legal entity with its own general manager and its own board of directors. All the stock in the company is now held by the Shenzhen Municipal Investment Management Corporation. Plans are in place to reorganize as a joint stock company and to sell some of the stock to the public. The proposed stock offering will raise, management believes, several hundred million RMB Yuan, which the Company plans to use to finance some ambitious expansion plans. It wants to expand its trading activities, storage and warehousing capacity, build a multi-function materials and equipment mall and producer goods wholesale market, an exhibition center, start a bus line for passenger transportation, expand its goods transportation business and open more overseas offices. It also wants to develop more high technology manufacturing.

Sources: Background Papers.

In addition, many materials bureaus also have a 'comprehensive trading center' as one of their companies. By and large, delivery systems are still traditional and distributors deliver to their customers.[11] The distribution companies have salespeople who call on customers. In some companies, the salespeople perform a procurement function also, acting as buyers for the goods the distribution company offers. These persons' functions strongly resemble those of the old factory purchasing agents (*caigouyuan*), who served enterprises whenever the plan proved inadequate.

In other respects, the system today has new features, which have developed in response to the reforms in the allocation and distribution system. The first major tool that has been used is the introduction of competition into the distribution system by broadening the geographic reach within which distribution enterprises can buy and sell. Second, purchases are now permitted from or sales to any entity. Distribution companies today can buy from producers in any province, and can sell to state, private or collectively owned customers/users anywhere in China. Distribution companies can also sell to independent (privately or collectively owned) distribution organizations. Third, new privately or collectively owned distribution organizations are allowed to enter, and to compete with the State-owned distributors, in most product categories. Fourth, at the level of the production enterprise, 'zero-level channels' are permitted, in which producers sell direct to users, bypassing the distributor.[12]

Fifth, a system of incentive compensation for managers and workers in the State distribution enterprises has been instituted. Managers and salesmen in distribution companies receive incentive pay based on performance. A typical performance pay formula takes into account sales, gross margins, capital employed and profits. The companies are now expected to show a profit. Sixth, innovations have been introduced in delivery systems. Some material bureaus have a separate delivery organization that takes orders that encompass goods sold by more than one of the distribution companies, and combines and assembles the goods into one order. Seventh, distribution centers are now undertaking some value-adding functions such as the further processing of materials.[13]

In addition to their distribution companies, the municipal materials bureaus have entered other ventures, some related to distribution, some not. Typically, as the example of Suzhou illustrates, the materials bureau owns a hotel catering to businessmen, and has built or is building a large, high rise structure to house its offices, a commodities trading operation and offices and display space for producers who want to sell direct to customers in the area. In Shenzhen, the municipal materials bureau has diversified into automobile repairs, and operates a taxicab fleet. It maintains a showroom which displays a wide range of imported items such as plywood and bathroom faucets for use in goods manufactured in Shenzhen for export. This bureau also participates in some forty-six joint ventures, many with foreign partners. In addition, the Shenzhen bureau acts as banker for all its enterprises. All funds collected go to the municipal "bank" which then makes all disbursements on behalf of the enterprises, including payroll. The diversity in the functions of apex material supply bureaus is illustrated in the examples provided, of Wuxi, Suzhou and Shenzhen.

---

[11] Appendix Table A3.13.

[12] See the annex to this chapter, Annex III.1.

[13] A new nationwide Outline Plan for Commodities Markets is under preparation, under the newly-formed Ministry of Internal Trade (MINT), which emerged from the merger of the former MOC and MME. The plan should be ready by March 1994.

The Efficiency of the Present Materials Distribution System

Strengthening the distribution system in the future requires changes that may be grouped into two broad categories. First, those which are derived from the unique evolutionary origins of the Chinese system, and which are therefore highly specific to China. The second set of recommendations are derived from features of the Chinese system which are observed in other countries at a similar stage of evolution towards a market economy, and are therefore based essentially on China's stage of development. Experience in other countries with more advanced industrialized economies indicates that distribution systems must continually improve and change as industrialization proceeds. Actions should however be taken to ensure that changes are made in the right direction. One method of gauging the efficiency of a given system is by comparing it to 'best practice' elsewhere. The annex to this chapter (Annex III.1) details the key structural elements of a producer goods' distribution system in any market economy, detailing the range of options and describing 'best practice' techniques that could be applied to China today.

Looking at features specific to China, a first issue is the diversity of functions being undertaken by the materials distribution bureaus today. Some bureaus are branching out into a variety of activities beyond distribution.[14] This can be detrimental to the building and maintenance of a strong, efficient distribution system. Some of these activities, such as investments in real estate, are speculative. In many cases the material bureaus have made use of their relative ease of access, through links with local administrations, to prime real estate, to undertake these activities.

Materials bureaus have also taken on a variety of highly diverse industrial and commercial activities. The ability to diversify into such a broad range of areas probably stems, originally, from the very diverse products whose distribution they were entrusted with. However these activities go well beyond the processing or trading of production materials. In order to ensure that local materials bureaus focus their activities on distribution, consideration should be given to regulations on the breadth and scope of the businesses these bureaus own or control. Expansion into real estate should be seriously questioned and diversification into manufacturing, or service businesses other than distribution, merits examination. One disadvantage of this diversity is the potential for creation of a large, cumbersome bureaucracy. Another is the possibility of cross-subsidization that masks inefficient enterprises or leads to investments that are not market justified. It is also not clear that the ownership of new industrial assets should be in the hands of the local Materials Bureau. However, the restriction of other activities may not be necessary if different activities can be separated, so that the performance of each is more transparent. A separate group or groups should own and control manufacturing enterprises.[15]

---

[14] Some industrial enterprises undertake their own distribution of producer goods and other industries have entered the distribution network. The diversification of distribution enterprises is partly a response to this.

[15] At Shenzhen, for example, the vastly different characters of the various businesses presently under the control of the Corporation require very different management skills. Consideration should therefore be given to breaking the conglomerate up into smaller, separately controlled units. A possible structure might be to break the Materials General Corporation into five units containing respectively: (1) distribution and trading, including import/export; (2) infrastructure, including terminals and port facilities; (3) service businesses, such as auto repair, trucking and taxicabs; (4) domestically owned manufacturing and related businesses; and (5) joint ventures with foreign partners.

An issue to be examined in this context is whether the diversification of materials bureaus occurring today may not be in part a response to the restrictions placed on the deepening of their trading activities. In a market economy, such bureaus may evolve towards general trading companies, which integrate external and domestic distribution functions.[16] Restrictions against directly undertaking foreign trade have already been mentioned. Even the right of approving the volumes of quotas for imports and exports, for products under the control of the MME, such as steel, has been transferred to the State Planning Commission. This restricts the functions of the MME in adjusting demand and supply.[17] In August 1992, following the promulgation of the New Operating Mechanism for state enterprises, the MME formulated a set of implementing rules, regarding materials enterprises, where continuing restrictions on the autonomy of these enterprises were pointed out. Apart from requesting import licenses for large and medium-sized material bureaus, the MME also requested permission to make swaps or changes in the varieties or specifications of materials still to be distributed under the mandatory plan, if the products did not meet with customer approval. Greater independence in price setting, for the products they are obliged to sell, and greater flexibility with labor management was requested. The MME also proposed that materials enterprise be allowed to set up of joint ventures, trans-departmental, and trans-regional undertakings, including cooperative arrangements and mergers, if required, with other enterprises. Greater flexibility to undertake imports and make decisions on quantities purchased and sold would assist whichever agency is responsible for the distribution of these products, whether the MME or any other private or public agency. These requests are therefore efficiency-enhancing and will help the present distribution companies to deepen rather than widen their activities.[18] The essential point concerning scope of activities is that fewer controls at the operational level on such agencies' decisions will permit them greater flexibility to achieve the efficient execution of their tasks.

Actions to increase future competition through new entrants in the distribution system are required as well. The present situation makes it more difficult than necessary for competitors to enter distribution businesses presently controlled by bureaus. Producers from anywhere in China should be encouraged to set up sales offices and, where profitable, distribution facilities in the municipalities, and should be allowed to sell directly to customers in those municipalities. Local distributors should be encouraged to expand into municipalities other than their own. Entry into distribution by private individuals and collectives should also be encouraged. The small organizations that may result can serve some business sectors and customers more efficiently than the large ministerial distribution organizations.

Another feature of the present distribution system which is specific to China and merits review is the core eleven to twelve company structure below the materials supply bureau which is still frequent today. This is the result of the transfer of former material supply organs of other ministries under the State Council to the MME. However, the maintenance of these intact in the future may be detrimental to efficiency.[19] Regions as diverse as the heavy industrial city of Shenyang and the light-

---

[16]   For example, the *sogo sosha* of Japan (see World Bank 1993 Report No 11568-CHA for details).

[17]   MME Background Paper No. 5 (1992).

[18]   However, the MME also requested permission to launch new industrial undertakings, a proposition to be treated with greater caution.

[19]   Before this the MME already had more than 40 directly subordinate general companies, with their own subsidiaries, or levels of subsidiaries.

industry city of Suzhou have identical groups of companies below the material supply bureau. The future structures should be given greater flexibility, to adapt better to the requirements of local industries and activities. Greater flexibility may be aided by the emergence of a modern enterprise system permitting greater executive independence. Elsehere in the world, a producers' goods distributor typically serves an application or an industry (or a cluster of industries with similar needs) because this is the most efficient arrangement. Municipal distribution companies in China should start moving in this direction where clusters of industries or applications are emerging.

The delivery companies some municipalities have instituted recognize that some customers' needs transcend the goods assortments carried by individual distribution companies. These delivery companies may provide a basis for reorganizing the present companies. It is worth noting, in this regard, that it is not necessarily inefficient if two or more distribution companies' goods assortments overlaps. The goal is to maximize efficiency in merchandise handling and delivery, and small targeted companies may be more efficient than large institutions with very broad product lines.

Similarly, the 'comprehensive distribution centers' which originally developed in response to the liberalization of a portion of production from planned allocation for various producer goods, may also be grouped into industries which provide similar goods, or related goods, in the future. Some of these new groupings will emerge naturally, provided distribution centers are permitted the flexibility of responding to industries' needs.

Other specific difficulties faced by the distribution system today in China include the organization and costs of the order-placing conferences; a tradition which continues today and is estimated to cost Y100-300 million each year. The scale of the conferences has grown, despite the decline in planned allocation. This is partly because of the additional stalls for 'non-planned transactions', that have sprung up alongside the planned exchange of goods. Many production enterprises are urging distribution departments to hold another trade fair for such non-plan production. Some fairs are held more than once a year and each time the locations differ.

Dealing with the trade fairs is problematic. Clearly they serve a purpose, in terms of the dissemination of information. The issue here is the extent to which such a system could be replaced by other more convenient and less costly methods of contact and exchange, such as catalogs, newsletters, and of course telephone and computer communications. One hindrance to the development of these indirect methods of contact is that buyers and suppliers are no longer able to see the goods transacted. This calls for a high degree of standardization in product specification, to remove buyers and sellers concerns.

Material distribution enterprises have expressed a desire to undertake more value-adding activities, such as the processing of some of the materials they receive, as well as research on the qualities and properties of their materials. In market economies it is recognized that value-adding though sorting, packaging, grouping, blending, etc., is a part of the normal range of functions that may be provided by a distribution channel, the functions of which extend well beyond the simple task of distribution (see Annex III.1). These suggestions, if shown to be profitable, are to be encouraged. Primary research on materials is however not a normal function of distribution systems, although the institution of standards and quality control systems is. A careful extension towards these additional functions is also desirable.

Materials enterprises have also pointed out the relatively poor condition of warehousing facilities and the high capital costs for their replacement or extension. Around 90 percent of the 110 million square meters of goods yards in the country have floors of earth, gravel or stone, and were constructed mostly in the 1950s or 1960s. MME bureaus claim that these are older than the warehouses of the ministries of commerce or foreign trade. The poor moisture proofing of these warehouses leads to large losses due to corrosion and rot. Major actions must be taken to assess the capital investment requirements of the distribution system, and a program for progressive upgrading over time must be launched.

Finally, a major issue to be examined in the context of China's distribution system is its profitability. According to the MME, profits on sales of materials enterprises have declined over time, from 2 percent in 1988 to 0.7 percent in 1990. Materials distribution enterprises attribute these to losses on sales of goods still subject to planned allocation as well as price regulation. High costs of carrying inventory, due to difficulties of transportation, also reduce profitability.

An examination of the extent to which the recent changes in the distribution system may have led to long term gains in efficiency was undertaken, by estimating the ratios of inventory to total sales (Appendix Table A3.14). First, looking at a long time series of inventory to sales ratios in commercial units, it appears that there was indeed a decline in this ratio in the early years of the reform, between 1982/83, when the ratio was between 63 and 65 percent, and 1985-86, when the ratio dropped by 12 percent, to just over 51 percent. The extent to which there was a drop after this is appears to have been much lower.[20] This suggests that efficiency gains were the most pronounced in the earlier years. A more detailed examination of these effects was also undertaken, for 1986-1991, for three producer goods sectors, steel, cement and coal (Appendix Table A3.15 to A3.17). The data are based on small samples of production as well as distribution enterprises, looking at ratios of inventory to turnover as well as working capital to turnover. No clear trend emerges from these. In the case of coal and steel, there are some indications of reductions in inventory and working capital requirements around 1989, with a rise again by 1991. However, this could well be the effect of cyclical movements. No such trend was observed for steel. Overall, there is no clear indication of a change in inventory management in the materials distribution system after the mid-1980s.

An examination of the profitability, cash-flow management and inventory management of the distribution system is clearly called for. With the merger of the MME and MOC in mid-1993, a parallel examination of distribution systems for consumer goods should also be considered. This will be a major undertaking and should be taken up through a team of marketing as well as financial consultants. The exercise should attempt to separate the impact of policy-induced costs (such as costs associated with price controls or essential distribution) from other operational or capital costs. Given that the last major round of price decontrols and adjustments has just been concluded, this would be an appropriate time for such an exercise.

Regarding more general recommendations, at this stage in China's development, the key activities where the distribution system should be strengthening its performance are (1) product search and procurement, (2) inventory holding and storage, (3) financing, (4) delivery, (5) personnel incentives

---

[20] Interpretation of the data after 1986 is difficult as the definition of the series changes to include non-state retailing units. The data show a continued decline, but this may be due to lower holdings of inventory among non-state firms. The decline may also have been due to the cyclical boom of the late 1980s which would have had the effect of lowering inventory. Besides, by 1991, the ratio had risen again, and stood only 5 percentage points below the value of 1986 (Appendix Table A3.14).

and (6) making better use of backchannels and recycling. Promotion is a secondary consideration under most circumstances. Further details of some of the necessary functions, and how they are generally conducted in a market economy, are given in Annex III.1.

Product Search

Product search and procurement are important because not all prospective sellers appear to be in touch with all potential customers. Similarly there are many prospective buyers who may not have the experience or ability to search efficiently for sources of supply. The functions of the former *caigouyuan*s must now be now professionalized. In a rapidly industrializing economy, the variety of goods produced increases steadily, and manufacturing firms need a continually broadening assortment of inputs and capital equipment.

Personnel Incentives

While the introduction of incentives for sales persons is a move in the right direction, the specific factors used in determining incentive pay today may be encouraging behavior that is counterproductive for the system. The typical incentive formula today takes into account sales, expenses, capital employed and profits. Factoring profits into the equation encourages managers to look toward raising prices as the easiest way of earning incentive compensation. They should instead be focusing on holding down expenses while serving as many customers as possible. An incentive system that rewards managers for minimizing gross margins while maximizing sales may encourage behavior more specifically focused on efficiency.

Shipment and Delivery Techniques

Distribution companies should encourage producers to ship direct ('drop ship') to customers/users where such shipment is more efficient than shipping to the warehouse and then reshipping. In such cases, the distribution company can act as the customer's agent and take a commission on the sale. Comparing the size and frequency of customers' orders with the quantities a producer can efficiently ship (e.g. a truckload or a boxcar load) can also identify opportunities to obtain such savings.

Warehousing and Computerization

As wages increase, the distribution companies may have to replace warehouse labor with capital and office personnel and paper with computers. The distribution companies should recognize these needs, and prepare plans for the timely introduction of mechanized materials handling and computers. The distribution companies should recognize that they may have to relocate some of their physical facilities as the configuration of customers' locations and local and long haul transportation systems may change. They should be identifying such future needs and planning to take action in response.

Reverse Distribution

In addition, the cities and provinces should begin at once to develop backchannels (also known as a reverse distribution system) for recycling used materials, especially of plastics and metals. In other countries, scrap steel, rather than iron ore, has become the major feedstock for steel mills. Virtually all lead used in manufacturing automobile batteries comes from reprocessing the lead from dead batteries. As China's automobile stock increases, so will its stock of scrap batteries and automobile bodies. At present there seems to be no organized means for retrieving scrap and delivering it for reprocessing and reuse.[21] Specialist organizations have emerged in such countries that pick up the used material and deliver it for reprocessing. These organizations have emerged because there are markets for the scrap and facilities to transport it. China should encourage its smelters and mills to develop the ability to use recycled material. Given free entry into the trucking business, a reverse distribution system will emerge. Wherever possible, reprocessing should be done locally so as to minimize the use of an already burdened transportation system.

C. Parallel Changes in Agriculture

It should be mentioned that while changes were taking place in the distribution of producer materials, new directions in the marketing of agricultural produce were also being explored. Markets for specific agricultural commodities have been studied more intensively elsewhere, however, an overview of the pattern of change in wholesale distribution is presented here, which illustrates the parallels in the development of the various segments of the distribution system.[22] In addition, and again in parallel to certain producer goods, new forms of commodity exchanges have been established for producer goods. These are discussed in the following chapter (Chapter 4).

Agricultural Wholesale Markets

The reduction in the role of the state in the procurement and distribution of agricultural products accelerated after the back-to-back good harvests of 1989 and 1990, which imposed a heavy burden on the state's resources devoted to the procurement and stockpiling of foodstuffs.[23] Spending on price supports for grain and edible oils rose from Y3.6 billion in 1978 to over Y40 billion by 1990, representing 14.5 percent of government revenues.[24] As a result, the government began to gradually withdraw from the purchasing of grain, and more rapidly, from the rationing and controlled distribution of grain to urban consumers. In 1991, the State Council released a 'Communique on Further Revitalizing the Distribution of Agricultural Goods, which authorized the establishment of agricultural markets and

---

[21] In the industrialized countries, every place that sells automobile batteries is a recycling point. Battery distributors pick up used batteries when they deliver new ones and consolidate them for pickup by a lead smelter. Unserviceable automobiles are taken to scrap yards. In these yards, useable parts are removed, and the car bodies crushed and cut up for shipment to a steel mill.

[22] See World Bank (1991) 'China: Options for Reform in the Grain Sector, and later, World Bank (1993) Report No 11671-CHA on grain distribution. More attention is being paid today to the marketing of agroindustrial products as well, as discussed in Landell Mills Commodities Studies (1993), in the case of rubber and sugar.

[23] In 1991, despite extensive flood damage, food production was reduced only 11 million tons from the previous year, and stood at 435.3 million tons. This was still historically the second highest level of output achieved, and illustrates the new security in food supplies.

[24] This section draws extensively upon Kobayashi (1992).

provided incentives for the diversification of distribution routes, including the participation of individuals and village collective organizations in the distribution sector.

Smaller 'periodic agricultural markets', or general markets, that were traditionally the center of local agricultural produce are also growing rapidly in numbers and sophistication. In 1991, there were close to 75,000 such markets, which accounted for a fourth of all retail sales of the agricultural products traded in the market, countrywide. Thirty percent of the taxes from these regional markets go to local governments, and the funds are used to build permanent markets and improve the hygiene and sanitary controls of existing ones.[25] Expenditure on the construction of these general markets in 1991, at Y2.8 billion, was almost double that of 1990. Clusters of these smaller markets have developed around larger centers; for example in Henan province, where the Zhengzhou grain 'futures' market is located, almost 150 general markets grew up in the second half of 1991 alone and Y140 million was spent on the construction of new transaction facilities (1.63 million square meters).

Many of these small general markets are growing into larger and more established wholesale agricultural markets, serving growing areas. For example the private market established at the Dazhong temple in Beijing's Haidian district in 1986, (now renamed the Dazhong Agricultural and Secondary Foods Wholesale Market) today supplies a quarter of the vegetables consumed in Beijing city, procured through out China, and brought to the market by a force of over a thousand seasonal or permanent drivers. However their growth has been constrained by the difficulties faced by 'own-account' farmer drivers due to restrictions and difficulties with long-distance transportation. Due to the perishable nature of agricultural goods, such difficulties have been relatively more important in their case.

D. Transportation, Telecommunications and Services

The efficiency of a distribution system is necessarily dependent on the efficacy of the available infrastructure for the movement of goods, in the form of transport, primarily, and also on communications and services. At present, the level of transportation and services available in China (as measured by the combined share of employment in trade as well as transport), at around 15 percent of total employment, is roughly comparable with other large developing countries, such as Brazil and India, or even the former Soviet Union, but considerably below the level of advanced countries such as Germany (over 20 percent) or the US (over 25 percent) (Table 3.4).

The growth of transportation routes over the last decade has fallen considerably behind the overall rate of economic growth (Appendix Table A3.18). For railways, new routes grew by only 0.43 percent per year over 1983 to 1992, and the rate of growth of waterways was lower still (0.09 percent). The rate of growth of highways has been somewhat higher (1.63 percent per year), but is still low in absolute terms. In per capita terms, the rates of growth of railways and waterways has been negative, and of highways only marginally positive (Appendix Table A3.19). Although there has been a gradual but steady increase in average shipping distance of freight over the last three decades, which has compensated for this to some extent, even these rates of growth are low (Appendix Table A3.20).

---

[25] According to the 'Regulations on the Collection and Management of market Taxes from General Markets' of January 1983.

The average shipping distance by highway, for example, which is the most dynamic part of the market, has grown at only 3.1 percent per year, from 19 to 46 kilometers, between 1961 and 1991.

Table 3.4 China and Other Countries: Employment in Trade and Transport
(000)

	Total employment	Employment in trade		Employment in transport	
		Number	Share(%)	Number	Share(%)
China (1989)/a	101087	9806	9.70	6400	6.33
India (1988)/b	25712	421	1.64	3063	11.91
Brazil (1987)/c	57410	6656	11.59	2161	3.76
Germany (1989)/d	27742	4092	14.75	1545	5.57
USSR (1989)/e	127057	9877	7.77	10233	8.05
U.S. (1989)/f	117342	24230	20.65	6588	5.61

a/ State-owned and collectively-owned enterprises.
b/ employment in 'proprietary establishments' only.
c/ Civilian labor force employed.
d/ Civilian labor force employed.
e/ Employment in state-owned units only.
f/ Civilian labor force employed. Hotels are not included in "trade."
Source: Statistical Yearbook 88/89, United Nations, 37th issue.

These issues have been the subject of detailed independent investigations.[26] This section restricts itself to discussing the linkages between these issues, and the problems of distribution, discussed in the preceding section. An inability to get goods to where they are needed in a timely and predictable manner leads to difficult consequences for the manufacturing sector, particularly (i) production downtime due to lack of input materials; (ii) the holding of excess inventory as a buffer against late shipments; and (iii) spoilage of perishable goods while in storage awaiting shipment or during shipment.

The discussion on transportation focuses on railroad and highway transportation, which are the most important in China, and also the most extensively used for the transportation of materials. However the development of inland waterways is becoming increasingly important and the use of air

---

[26] World Bank (September 1992) 'China: Reform and Role of the Plan in the 1990s' describes the constraints of transportation on overall economic growth. A chapter in (World Bank 1990) 'China: Macroeconomic Stability and Industrial Growth under Decentralized Socialism' discusses transportation issues specifically in the context of regional trade. Two regional transportation studies have also been undertaken; a three volume study on the Yangtze Economic Zone (World Bank December 1990) and another on Southern China (Harral, 1992). Railway investments and strategy are discussed in World Bank (1992) Report No. 10375-CHA, and World Bank (1992) Report No. 10592-CHA. A study of the trucking industry is under preparation. A recent study (World Bank 1992 Report no 9413-CHA) has also been undertaken on the telecommunication sector in China. It points out that China's telecommunications system grew at over 16 percent per year in the late 1980s, and is now the 10th largest in the world. Although service quality may be poor, and sophisticated business services are lacking, over 70 percent of the population has access to some telecommunication services, well above most developing countries. The role of communications development and vertical and horizontal contact across regions is also discussed in Liu (1991).

transportation for exports has increased. It is clear from existing studies that China does not at present have sufficient capacity in its transportation system to sustain a high rate of economic growth. China therefore faces the need to make considerable investments in transportation over the next several years, both in railroads and in roads and highways.

The Railroad System

Transportation needs for goods may be classified in three categories: (i) long haul, 1000 km. or longer. For long hauls, railroad or water are usually the most economical shipping methods; (ii) medium haul, less than 1000 km. As the hauling distance becomes shorter, highway transportation, using trucks becomes more efficient; and (iii) local transportation. Road transportation is usually the most efficient for local hauling. China's lack of capacity is most severe in its railroad system, and the major impact of this capacity shortage is therefore on long distance hauling.

It has recently been estimated that demand for about 200 million tons of freight remained unsatisfied in 1989.[27] This amounted to almost 10 percent of freight capacity. Bottleneck links on the railroad network occurring when traffic reached 95 percent of capacity rose from 7 percent of the network in 1985 to 37 percent in 1989. The problem was identified to be underinvestment in facilities, and was not ascribed to poor management or organization. China has been investing in its transport at an average rate of 1.3 percent of GNP over the last few decades, while other developing nations' investments were at a rate of from 2.0 to 3.8 percent of GNP. To bring supply into balance with demand by the year 2000, China must raise its rate of investment in railways to at least 2 percent of GNP. With an appropriate adjustment of tariffs to reflect costs, the railway system could enjoy a profit rate of 30 percent or more. In the long run, the railroad system will have to become more responsive to its customers needs as the economy becomes increasingly market driven. The railroad system will have to compete with other modes of transportation, especially for medium and shorter haul business.

One difficulty which has been observed in the utilization of railway capacity is the distribution of quotas for the use of available freight space. For example, grain traded at certain wholesale centers may be eligible for a rail transportation 'quota', while at other locations, the quota may be unavailable. As a result of its potential mobility, the price of grain purchased at the first location rises, relative to the second, and this may occur even if this region enjoys a surplus. At the other region, which cannot offer freight quotas, demand and prices fall. In this example, the rail quota is implicitly included in the price paid for grain, and the overall price represents a proxy element for the transportation quota in addition to the price for the grain itself. It is advisable to separate the two markets, making the freight space available to all and raising tariffs to reflect availability. Proxy markets distort price and production signals and could lead to inefficient long term resource allocation.

Truck Transportation

First of all, looking at the road network, it is clear that intercity road capacity is severely strained by recent economic development, and traffic congestion within cities and on major intercity routes, is intense. There are plans in place for development of an extensive intercity highway network, the National Trunk Highway System (NTHS). While still in its infancy, many important links are under construction. Municipalities are also working to improve their street networks.

---

[27] World Bank 1992 (Report 10592-CHA) .

Next, looking at the vehicles used in highway transportation, a first observation is that in contrast with the railroad system, trucking capacity is relatively less efficiently used. The reasons for this are a combination of the fragmentation of ownership of the trucking fleet, as well as legal constraints that inhibit many truckers from maximizing the efficient use of the equipment. A series of reforms introduced since 1983 have made entry into the trucking business easier and pricing of these services more flexible. Licensing of for-hire vehicles is now open to state, collective as well as privately owned enterprises. State trucking enterprises have more autonomy vis-a-vis their bureaus and rate-setting has been progressively deregulated. Guidelines on a spread of tariff groups have been formulated across products and a 10 to 20 percent variation within the band is permitted.[28] More recently, in 1992, the fuel allocation system was abolished, and the sector has now been opened to partial foreign investment.[29] As a result, the share of state enterprises in the sector has declined by 17.6 percent over 1986 to 1990.

However, barriers and constraints on entry remain. For example, business licenses are required for the provision of 'for hire' services and the criteria include not only vehicle and facilities safety and security, but also a minimum number of vehicles (10) to start an enterprise. Driver and vehicle licensing and registration, which prior to 1984 was the responsibility of the local Transportation Bureau, is now undertaken partially by the Public Security (police) Service. There appears to be some duplication in the function of the two offices.[30]

'Own-account' trucks (those owned by say, a manufacturing or distribution firm) must obtain a special license to use their trucks on a for-hire basis. These licenses are short-term and may contain severe constraints on their use. This means that a manufacturer's truck that makes intercity or interprovince deliveries from its factory to, say, a distributor must return empty. To complicate the problem, a manufacturer who wants to hire a trucking company or individual trucker to make such deliveries will find this difficult because of interprovince and perhaps even intercity licensing problems. Possibly as a consequence, there appear as yet to be few private sector trucking companies. There are still municipal and provincial bureaus that maintain trucking fleets and there are some individual truck operators, but there are no trucking fleets which are common in most other countries.

Given the constraint on highways and streets, and the high cost of trucks and trailers, good utilization of whatever capacity is available is critical, and regulations which restrict such use should be revised. A first recommendation to improve capacity utilization is that firms with own-account trucks should be allowed to operate for hire as well. If allowed to do so, these firms are likely to look for business that will fill their empty and partially filled trucks. In the process, some may even become quasi freight forwarders. Second, individual ownership of trucks should be encouraged, because this will in itself promote good truck care and efficient truck utilization. One of the factors which inhibits greater use

---

[28] The authority for tariff-setting within these guidelines has been vested in the local Departments of Communications, and in practice, there are known to be considerable regional variations in tariffs.

[29] Up to 50 percent. However in most productive sectors, a hundred percent foreign ownership is allowed. New joint venture trucking enterprises have begun in coastal provinces such as Guangdong.

[30] Public Security bureaus look into drivers' licenses, vehicle registration and safety inspection, while the Transport bureaus look at the same vehicles from the point of view of 'economic inspection'.

of private trucks may be the tolls, fees and fines on highways, described in the previous chapter. The extent to which private truckers are more vulnerable to such exactions should be investigated.[31]

Another, more concrete way to further encourage the efficient use of individually owned trucks, would be to provide support services in the form of consolidation and forwarding terminals. Today, freight forwarding or consolidating terminals that could serve as collection points for goods shipped in less-than-truckload quantities are lacking. It difficult and inefficient to send and receive goods in small quantities. Individual truck owners may be efficient haulers, but may find it difficult to find steady sources of goods to haul. Terminals could provide marketing assistance for these individual truckers. Once aware of its benefits, individual truckers might later group together to build and maintain such terminals.

The growth of trucking companies that will specialize in intercity and interprovincial hauling should also be encouraged, by giving them the ability to participate in intermodal arrangements and operate terminals. Provincial licensing requirements should be made uniform and the mutual and reciprocal recognition of individual provinces' (or municipalities') licenses should begin. In the medium term, however, if large trucking companies become a force in the market and gain a virtual monopoly position, it may be necessary to accompany this growth with a regulation of shipping rates. In addition, municipalities particularly, should keep shipping needs (both shipping in and shipping out) firmly in mind when planning or approving manufacturing plant and distribution center sites. One of the best ways to ship efficiently is to minimize road time by careful facilities placement.

Finally, and apart from recommendations specific to the railroad or road freight industries today, for the medium term, China should consider the introduction of intermodal systems. These are increasingly being used for long hauls in industrialized countries. These systems require that freight be shipped in containers. Containers are then moved from truck to railroad (or barge) and back as efficiencies dictate.[32] Eventually, China must look at its producers' goods distribution system as part of a larger system that includes both producer/ sellers and customers/users.[33] The long-term goal should be a system that results in the delivery of finished goods to their final buyers at the lowest possible cost. In China, the long-distance transportation system is a major constraint towards this today.

---

[31] A detailed account of how the 'three malpractices' (the extortion of unsanctioned fees, the collection of arbitrary 'fines' and the apportionment of 'expenses') have operated in the case of the long-distance transportation of agricultural goods is available in Kobayashi (1992). During an 800-km journey, a private truck loaded with garlic cloves was stopped 15 to 16 times, and was forced to pay a fine every 45 to 50 km on average. No receipts were issued.

[32] For example, in the U.S., containers of goods destined for New York (on the East coast) might be unloaded from a ship in Los Angeles (on the West coast) onto trucks, carried by truck to a railroad freight depot, carried by rail to somewhere near New York and again loaded on to trucks for final delivery.

[33] In the early 1980, certain transportation activities, required for trade in agriculture, were restricted. In February 1986, the State Council issued a communique allowing the use of powered transportation (trucks and boats), and also freeing long-distance transporters from certain restrictions on volume, administrative district and distance (Kobayashi 1992). However, in some quarters, 'long-distance transportation' continued to be viewed as speculative and 'capitalist' in ideology.

E. Summary and Implications

The first key finding of this chapter is that the state's withdrawal from the task of distribution occurred primarily prior to 1985, over the first phase of reform. Since then, there has been virtually no ownership change in the undertaking of distribution. In the latter period, the state's withdrawal from allocation has been far more noteworthy than its withdrawal from distribution. However, a second finding is that the nature of the ownership function has changed over the more recent period. There has been a rapid increase in distribution services available over the last five years, and now, the distribution services available in China far exceed those available in other large transforming economies, such as the former Soviet Union, although the level of these services is still well below the norms of Western Europe. It is also noteworthy that many innovations have been introduced by the state sector in distribution. The overall position therefore is, a distribution system with continued strong state dominance, although with a rapidly changing face.

Third, the distribution system today is a hybrid, and some of its structures such as the comprehensive distribution centers, reflect the partial transition of China towards a market economy. some features of the present system bear strong characteristics of the former period (such as the 12 enterprise structure of most material bureaus). There are other features, at the same time, which are very innovative, such as the multiple agencies and branching out of operations at bureaus such as Shenzhen, and the value-adding processes adopted at many specialized distribution centers. It is desirable that, on the one hand, greater flexibility is introduced into the frequently encountered 11 or 12-enterprise structures, and on the other hand, that the growth of the new style bureaus is orderly. Thus, speculative activities should be checked, value-adding functions should be encouraged, and constraints within the distribution system, in the form of obligatory sales at controlled prices, should be reduced, to make genuine distribution-related functions more attractive.

Fourth, there is much which is still to be done to improve distribution functions, through better handling, delivery and warehousing procedures. A detailed set of recommendations on specific measures which can be introduced, which are considered 'best practice' elsewhere, is given in the annex to this chapter. Fifth, there is a need to review the physical warehousing facilities available. Preliminary investigation suggests that new investment is desirable, to upgrade and relocate existing facilities. Sixth, there is also a need to undertake a detailed examination of the present financial situation of the materials distribution system. Again, preliminary observations suggest that profits are declining and it is essential to find out why this is so. As with the physical appraisal of warehousing, such a financial appraisal is a major undertaking which should be launched with specialized expertise.

Finally, the role of transportation in distribution is critical, and it is clear that there are difficulties here. On railways, the problem has been prolonged underinvestment, in turn due to insufficient funds, resulting from low tariffs. This situation has recently improved and it is hoped that fresh investment will follow. In trucking and highway transportation, there are more issues relating to regulation; multiple regulatory authorities, the lack of synchronization of tariff schedules across regions, and problems of entry. An integrated approach to all these issues is required to achieve the successful physical development of markets.

Annex III.1 A Note on Producer Goods Distribution Systems

Efficient Distribution Systems

A distribution system is a link between producer and user, who, in most cases, are separated geographically. The primary function of a distribution system is to get the right goods from the right producer to the right customer/user as efficiently as possible. In many cases, the mix of goods needed by a user do not match the output of any one producer. Given this situation, an important function of distribution systems is to provide time, place, and assortment convenience based on the physical movement and storage of goods. Distribution systems also help to match supply and demand, both by moving goods where they are most needed and by providing demand and supply information to producers. Time and place convenience implies that goods are more easily and quickly available to users than if the user had to pick them up at their places of manufacture. Assortment convenience implies that the distributor can combine in one place and ship to a user the output of more than one producer.

An efficient distribution system is essential to an efficient economy because without a good distribution system manufacturers cannot plan their production efficiently, the country's transportation system is not well utilized, and buyers end up paying too much for goods for which delivery is unpredictable. Efficiency in the distribution of producers' goods is, in fact, a virtual necessity for a country that wants to avoid inflation at home or to compete in world markets. Such inefficiencies affect the price of all finished goods because they add unnecessary costs to inputs. Inefficiency in consumer goods distribution may result in a penalty paid only by domestic consumers that may hold down demand, but may also contribute significantly to inflation. Inefficiency in producers' goods distribution affects also the price of finished goods that firms may want to export.

There is no particular structure that is most efficient in all circumstances. The structure that will be most efficient depends on several factors including (but by no means limited to) the relative size of sellers and buyers, their geographical location with respect to each other, and the services the buyer requires from the seller. As described below, channel members typically perform additional functions in addition to physical distribution. Channels of distribution are very dynamic; given the opportunity to do so structures and functions keep changing to accommodate to the ever changing needs of buyers and sellers.

Alternative Channel Structures

Channel structure has two dimensions, length, and ownership. Channel length is described in terms of levels. In a zero-level channel, goods go directly from their manufacturer to the customer-user. In a one-level channel, goods go from producer to a middleman, commonly referred to as a wholesaler or distributor, and then to the customer-user. A two-level channel has both a distributor and a sub-distributor between manufacturer and customer-user, and so on. While a producer might have only one manufacturing site in a given country, a one-level channel will typically have several distributors, each located to best serve a particular geographic area. A two-level channel will have a larger number of more localized distributors.

Channel structures are categorized as direct or indirect depending on who owns the channel institutions. In a direct channel, the manufacturer owns all the distribution institutions.

Typically, direct channels are either zero- or one-level. In a one-level direct channel, the distributor is simply a branch owned and operated by the manufacturer. In an indirect channel, the manufacturer does not own the institutions at one or more of the distribution levels. Indirect channels can be, and often are, multi-level.

Channel Functions

The functions of a distribution system, extend well beyond just the physical distribution of goods. Distribution systems are also systems for information transmission, for the performance of promotional and related marketing activities, and for financing and funds flow. In some cases, they can even become 'shoppers' for their users. Some of the major functions that distribution systems provide are:

- Product Search and Procurement: A channel member can act as its customers' purchasing agent, identifying the best sources for the products its customers need and then procuring those products for its customers.

- Consultative Advising: A channel member can be an authority on a particular manufacturing process or product category, recommending product specifications and manufacturing processes to its customers.

- Customer Prospecting: Finding potential customers for the manufacturer's products.

- Customer Selection: Choosing the particular customers the seller wants to serve.

- Promotion: Devising and promulgating information designed to induce potential customers to buy a particular manufacturer's products or to buy from a particular distributor. Promotion encompasses both advertising and personal selling.

- Inventory Holding and Storage: Keeping a supply of the manufacturer's goods at a place where they will be readily available to customers.

- Ordering: Placing orders with the manufacturer to ensure that stock will be available for customers.

- Delivery: Transporting or arranging for the transportation of goods to the customer-user. In a zero-level channel, goods are transported only once. In a one-level channel, of course, goods are typically transported twice, once from producer to distributor (long haul), and once locally from distributor to customer/user.

- Allocating: For goods in short supply, deciding how to apportion them among customer-users.

- Negotiating: Coming to agreement with customers on matters such as costs and terms.

- Financing: Extending and receiving credit; collecting and transmitting payment for goods.

- Installing: For capital goods, putting the item in place at the customer/users site and readying it for use by the customer.

- Servicing: Providing after-sales service and/or spare parts for equipment sold to customer-users.

- Information transmission: Collecting and disseminating information about market and economic conditions from customer-users to manufacturers and from manufacturers to customer-users.

- Recycling: Picking up scrap and used material and sending it to the appropriate place to be re-used in one form or another.

The Evolution of Distribution Channels for Producer Goods

As economic development proceeds in countries in which market forces operate, distribution systems are in a continuous state of change. Indeed, channels continue to change even in a mature economy in which market forces operate. The stimuli for change come primarily from the changing needs of customer/users that competing sellers vie to serve and from a changing supply/demand situation. There are four kinds of change that are of interest for analyzing the efficiency of a distribution system: (1) changes in the **modal length** of channels, (2) in the **size of channel institutions**, (3) in the **controller** of the channel, and (4) in the **number and type of alternative sources of supply** available to a prospective buyer.

Studies of industrialization suggest some generalizations about the changes that are likely to occur in distribution systems in market economies. (There are, however, many exceptions to the generalizations and they should be not be taken as completely representative). At very early stages of a country's industrialization, channels are short, even zero-level, and the selling institutions are few and large. The major distribution institution is likely to be an importer, either an independent importer acting as agent for a foreign producer or a sales subsidiary of a foreign producer. Customers/users are likely to be small, but despite their small size the importers may sell direct to their customers. At this early stage, demand for many goods is likely to exceed supply.

As industrialization proceeds, domestic producers appear, supplanting some imports, but imports are still important, especially for more sophisticated products. Larger and larger customer/users appear as the domestic manufacturing sector grows. Smaller firms may proliferate also, at both the buying and selling end of the channel. Supply begins to catch up with demand, and for some easily produced products, supply may exceed demand.

Later, some longer channels using indirect distribution appear because of (1) a larger and more diverse base of consumers, who require an increasingly diverse list of products and (2) the appearance of small, specialized sellers who cannot afford the expense of direct zero-level distribution. This lengthening occurs in part because the needs of particular customer/users encompass a wider breadth of products than any one producer can supply.

As some customers/users grow larger, the zero-level channel becomes more important for goods those large customers/users purchase in substantial quantities. Multi-level channels become more important in serving the needs of smaller customer/users and in serving the smaller quantity purchases of larger customer/users. As independent distributors appear, they are likely to be small, rather than large, and to specialize in a narrow, rather than a broad range of products.

In virtually every economy channel alternatives proliferate as industrialization proceeds. Zero-level and one- or two-level channels exist side-by-side, dealing in the same goods, with each specializing in a particular kind or size of customer. Sellers may themselves employ more that one method of distribution, using for example both a zero-level direct channel and a one-level indirect channel, depending on the relative efficiency of different channels in different circumstances.

Channels that are one-level or longer are typically indirect, with middlemen that are owned independently of the producers they represent. There is a set of conditions that particularly favors the appearance of one-level (or higher) channels employing independent distributors. These conditions are:

- Large numbers of potential customers.

- Standard and stockable items.

- Typically small quantities of sales.

- Requirements of fast delivery and/or service by customers.

As potential supply begins to exceed demand, control of the channel passes from producer or distributor to customers/users. Producers compete for good distributors and both distributors and producers must compete for good customer/users. At this stage of industrialization, they are competing for customers/users who have enough experience to shop intelligently, and can evaluate the offerings of different sellers.

In response to changed market conditions, the functions that channel members perform change in importance. At early stages of industrialization, product search, procurement and allocation are likely to be key functions, while customer prospecting and promotion are not. As industrialization proceeds, consulting advice may take on added importance as potential customer/users confront opportunities to develop new products requiring inputs with which they may not be familiar. Information transmission, both up and down the channel, increases in importance. Customer/buyers want more information about the alternatives available to them. Sellers want to know more and more about the customers to whom they sell and want information that allows them to better forecast demand so they can produce more efficiently.

Producers' and distributors' competitive strategies become more diverse. For some, price becomes their key competitive weapon. These competitors strive simply to offer the lowest delivered prices to their customer/users. Other channel members base their competitive strategies on offering quick delivery, liberal credit terms, after-sales service or consulting advice. Regardless of the specific competitive strategy they may pursue, virtually all use promotion very heavily, especially personal selling. Wherever possible, producers try to differentiate their product offerings as well. Some try to differentiate only by offering lower prices; others try to add more features to their products, raise their quality, or build a brand image. Producers, too, use promotion very extensively.

The result of all these efforts is a marketplace characterized by an increasing proliferation of product alternatives and a wide diversity of distribution channels, all coexisting and competing strongly for customers. They coexist because of the diversity in their customers' desires and are successful when they can meet the needs and desires of a particular customer group more effectively than competitors pursuing similar strategies.

Independent distributors, especially in industrialized countries often specialize, either in an application or product category or in a particular industry. For example, a distributor might specialize in hydraulics, offering a complete line of equipment and supplies to a potential customer who has a need for hydraulics. Alternatively, a distributor might specialize in supplying hospitals. Such a distributor would endeavor to supply everything a hospital would need.

In an advanced market economy, where supply frequently exceeds demand, distribution institutions can come reasonably close to the economist's definition of perfect competition. This is especially the case when a modicum of regulation allows free entry and restricts the use of predatory market power. For independent distributors, entry and exit barriers are low, provided they can gain access to goods that are in demand. Neither large amounts of capital nor great expertise are required to become a successful distributor. In a market economy, distributors and distribution systems come and go as the needs and desires of customers/users dictate. In such economies, especially in industrialized countries, many forms of distribution will coexist.

Some Comments on Distributor Efficiency

While some customers may not be purely interested in obtaining the lowest possible price from a distributor, in a market economy every distributor must operate efficiently in order to survive. The gains from efficient operation, if not passed on to customers in the form of lower prices, can support promotion, service, delivery or other elements of the distributor's competitive strategy. There are several major elements of distributor operations that affect costs and, therefore, efficiency. They are:

- Inward Shipping: The cost of shipping goods from the producer to the distributor's warehouse. Using partly loaded trucks or railroad cars, or slow-moving equipment can add to costs.

- Inventory Holding: Holding inventory ties up capital which could otherwise be invested. Inventory holding also increases costs because it increases the amount of space the distributor needs to operate. Unreliable inward transportation means that distributors must carry higher levels of inventory.

- Goods handling: The more times goods are handled or moved, within the distribution center, and the greater the distance over which they are moved, the higher the cost.

- Order processing and billing: Pushing and processing paper costs money, and inevitably leads to mistakes in billing.

- Payload planning and delivery scheduling: Poorly scheduled vehicles, or only partially filled vehicles, can add substantially to costs even if delivery is local.

- Worker productivity: Regardless of the particular systems or techniques a distributor may employ, the efficiency with which workers perform their assigned tasks affects distribution costs.

- Labor costs: The cost of warehouse labor has been a major cost item in distribution. The trend in virtually every country is toward steadily increasing wages for labor, thus raising costs.

- Physical location: Land costs for warehouses and offices obviously affect distribution, and hence the location of many large warehouses outside urban centers. Location can also affect costs depending on how efficiently a location fits into local and long haul transportation system.

'Best Practice' Tools and Techniques to Minimize Costs

Inward Shipping

Inward shipping is the cost item that is least controllable by the distributor, and therefore the most difficult to minimize. Where possible, distributors can take a variety of actions to minimize these costs. One action is to locate directly on the line of the long haul carrier most accessible to the supplier. This means locating, as appropriate, at a dock, on a railroad spur, or contiguous to a major highway. A related action is to choose suppliers, where possible, that are located in such a way that they will minimize shipping costs. In some cases, this is not a matter of choosing the closest supplier, but is a matter of choosing a supplier with direct access to a connecting railroad, highway, or water system. Placing orders of a size that fits the shipping capacity of the transportation mode to be used also lowers costs. A full load invariably costs less per unit to ship than a partial load. Placing orders well ahead of need or buying on a contractual basis can also lower costs because these actions allow suppliers to plan their production more efficiently.

Inventory Holding

Minimizing inventory requires predictability in receiving incoming orders and in the size and timing of orders from customers/users. This requires not only reliable shipping but information from customer/users as to the size and timing of their needs. Predictability allows for smaller buffer stocks and can also result in less handling of goods. Inventory minimizing systems are most beneficial when producer, distributor, and customers/user are all linked together with a common information system. These linkages are becoming more and more common in the industrialized world.

In a typical system, customers/users enter product use information into the system as they use the product in their manufacturing process. This allows the distributor to anticipate customer/users' needs, permitting the distributor to plan both inventory and customer/user delivery schedules. The distributor then collates this information from all customer/users of the product and reports it to the supplier of the product. The supplier can then plan both production and shipping more efficiently.

Any sophisticated system to minimize inventory requires computerization. This is not just a matter of having a micro-computer at each site. The customer/user's, distributor's and producer's computers must all be tied together. This means the systems each use must be compatible and electronically linked. Typically, local linkages use telephone lines, while, in sophisticated systems, more distant linkages are by satellite.

The well-known Japanese 'just-in-time' system is designed to minimize inventory stored at the customer/user's site. In this system, a distributor or producer delivers goods to the customer/user according to a preplanned schedule of when the goods will enter the customer/user's production process. In this system, the customer/user might receive several small deliveries each day. A by-product of the system is that it also allows the distributor or producer to minimize their inventory as well.

However, continuous change and adaptation is necessary. Japanese firms instituted just-in-time systems in part because of the high cost of space in Japan. These high space costs, of course, make inventory expensive to hold. The system worked well because supplier firms located very close to their customer/users and because both roads and trucks were in ample supply. But in the past few years, the efficiencies produced by the system have been questioned. As adoption of just-in-time broadened, the streets and roads have become clogged with delivery vehicles.

Goods Handling

Goods handling has become a capital intensive activity, even in industrializing countries. As wages go up, the only way to increase labor productivity is to replace hand trucks with fork lifts and conveyor belts, and introduce palette handling systems. Other tools and techniques have also been adopted to minimize handling. Warehouses arrange their inventories so that goods frequently appearing on the same order are stored close together to minimize order pick-up time and effort. Heavy and bulky items are stored near the loading and unloading dock for the same reasons.

Warehouse efficiency is also improved by the arrangement of the computerized printing of customer orders in the sequence in which goods are stocked in the warehouse. This technique also minimizes pick-up time and effort, as an order can be picked and assembled with one orderly 'pass' through the warehouse. Cross-docking is another recent innovation. It is a variant on the just-in-time system. In a cross-docking system, the supplier's vehicle arrives as vehicles that will deliver goods to customer/users are preparing to leave. Incoming goods go straight from the incoming supplier's vehicle to the outgoing delivery vehicle without ever entering the warehouse.

Order Processing and Billing

Distributors are replacing manual procedures using people and paper with computerized processes as quickly as they can. In a typical system, in more and more common use in the industrialized countries, customers/buyers transmit their orders to distributors or producers via a computer link.

4

New Forms of Markets

As the previous chapter described, the progressive withdrawal of the state from the functions of procurement and allocation of large numbers of goods accompanied the decontrol of their prices. However the withdrawal of the state from distribution activities was more gradual, due first to the need to develop entire chains of buyer-seller links as well as new distribution techniques, in addition to the need for the physical infrastructure for distribution. Second, the state's role in distribution itself grew more innovative over time. The majority of the newly-established centers cater purely for retail trading, and constitute an adaptation of traditional retail markets. The next largest group of such markets is represented by wholesale markets. New retailing techniques and new forms of wholesale markets for producer goods were discussed in the previous chapter.

Third, in addition to the changes in wholesaling and retailing, more innovative forms of new markets have recently and rapidly been introduced for both agricultural and industrial commodities. These markets comprise highly automated Exchanges in which both forward and prompt trading occurs in a comparatively narrow range of products.[1] In an effort to hasten the switch towards a market economy, there has been a deliberate effort to establish formal exchanges in which commodity trading is undertaken. Government agencies at every level, as well as national production and import-export corporations have come together to create commodity Exchanges. This chapter evaluates their functioning, drawing in detail on examples of the new metals Exchanges.[2] The interlinkages between these markets and other areas of the economy are pointed out and the future direction in which these markets may evolve is discussed.

---

[1]   By early 1993, three independent Exchanges, trading metals, coal and agricultural inputs were already in operation in Shanghai (the leader in this field), and two further independent Exchanges, trading petroleum and agricultural products such as grains and vegetable oils, began trading during the year. Each of these Shanghai Exchanges has its own geographically separate and distinct facilities, even though there can be no doubt that the benefits from sharing telecommunications, computing, banking, training, regulatory supervision, settlement procedures, brokerage and trading facilities would be very substantial, and could be achieved (as is done in New York and London, for example) without forcing the individual Exchanges to lose their identities.

[2]   These are the best established and most important exchanges today for industrial products. Examinations of the markets for agricultural products have been undertaken earlier (see Chapter 3 Section C) and exchanges for agricultural goods are examined below (in Chapter 4 Section B).

A. China's Distinctive Pattern of Development of Commodity Exchanges

The rapid mushrooming of commodity marketing centers in China has no parallel anywhere else in the world, except the former Soviet Union. In all other countries, commodity markets have been allowed to evolve at their own pace, and it is virtually unknown for a fully-fledged Exchange, complete with Exchange members, computer systems and detailed rules for the payment and delivery of products, to exist without having spent some considerable time passing through much less sophisticated patterns of trade. For example, all of the world's main metal markets - in London, New York and Tokyo - have their origins in very old informal markets, in which metal trading occurred between dealers whose offices were all near one another, so that trading could be undertaken in person. The markets then evolved towards a more formal framework, with traders meeting in one convenient centrallocation, and with the standardization of contracts. For a long while, trading was purely on a spot basis, but eventually forward markets emerged - at first, purely informally, and later under formal rules - in which traders agreed to buy or sell metals for physical delivery at some mutually acceptable date in the future.

The next stage of the development of Exchanges in world trading centers was the standardization of forward contracts and the buying and selling of these contracts between traders in the period before the contracts matured. Only when forward trading was very well understood, and the buying and selling of forward contracts in the period between the date of the opening of a forward contract and its expiry was common, did proper futures contracts come into existence. The distinction between forward and futures markets lies in the degree of standardization of contracts.[3] Whereas forward markets may permit buyers or sellers to stipulate one particular brand of a product or one particular point of delivery, futures market contracts are designed in one completely standard form, in which typically a number of brands and a number of delivery points are permitted completely freely and interchangeably. Unlike with forward contracts, therefore, the buyer of a futures contract who takes delivery of copper at the expiry of the contract merely knows that the seller will be allowed to deliver any one of the permitted range of brands, and that the delivery will take place in any one of a number of permitted delivery points.

In China, several stages in the evolution of commodity markets are being compressed into one single step. After only a few months of a fledgling free market, several commodity sectors are suddenly being offered access to formal Commodity Exchanges, some of which are more complex and sophisticated in certain respects than their counterparts in the industrialized world. Before producers, traders and users of commodities have become accustomed to spot physical trading between themselves, they are being invited to trade on a forward or futures basis on a Commodity Exchange.

The proliferation of commodity marketing centers reflects some lack of understanding about the nature and functions of Commodity Exchanges and futures markets. There is a misconception that building a special trading room and installing computers programmed to record trades constitutes a futures market. Therefore, many "futures markets" are now claimed to exist; but almost all of these are little more than an adaptation of existing formal or informal markets, in which products free from

---

[3] Forward and futures contracts are typically used for different purposes. A forward purchaser usually intends to take delivery of the product at a certain date, while a 'hedge' purchaser of a futures contract does not intend to take delivery at that date, but rather to cover his current position in the commodity against its future price variations.

government price controls and marketing quotas are traded on a spot basis, for immediate payment and delivery. Speculation has rapidly become the primary source of turnover, and therefore commission income. However, there is also a small, but nonetheless significant, proportion of trading which is based upon conventional techniques of "hedging" against price uncertainties.[4] The following sections describe and evaluate the functioning of specific new Exchanges, and then draw together common findings in terms of their effectiveness.

B. Agricultural Markets

Following the accelerated reduction in the role of the state in the procurement and distribution of foodstuffs, from 1991, large wholesale markets in agricultural products were set up at a number of locations, dealing mainly in foodstuffs, such as grain (Zhengzhou in October 1990; Hubei, March 1991; Heilongjiang, October 1989), edible oils (Heilongjiang, October 1989), rice (Anhui, January 1991), corn (Jilin, March 1991), poultry (Jiangsu Wuxi, June 1991) and sugar (Guangdong Yujian in June 1991, Southern sugar at Guangzhou and Northern sugar at Tianjin, in January 1992).

Most of these were relatively large wholesale markets, under the control of the national or provincial governments, and at some of these centers, formal Exchanges have been established. Established on a no-profit basis, they operate on a membership or agency system. Most agricultural exchanges require the payment of deposits based on the contracted values of transactions and most have a system of 'insurance' against price fluctuations, which in practice is a form of government intervention that limits the normal price variation that characterizes a commodity exchange.[5] The experience of the first of the country's major agricultural commodity exchanges, the Zhengzhou Grain Wholesale Market in Henan Province, which started trading in October 1990, has been one of only a slow move away from spot trading. The market was established by the Ministry of Commerce in conjunction with the Henan Provincial Government. In March 1993, the Zhengzhou grain market was "officially turned into a futures market". Announcements about its price movements are made in the Chinese and foreign press.[6] Nine separate Government agencies, including the Ministries of Railways, Agriculture and Finance, and the People's Bank of China, were involved in the approval of the establishment of the Zhengzhou Market.

---

[4] Annex 4.1 explains how gains and losses from forward and futures trading are distributed between hedgers and speculators. It shows how trading on Commodity Exchanges is a "zero-sum game"; the profits made by those who are successful in their trading are exactly balanced by the losses suffered by those who are unsuccessful. On average, a participant in trading on the Exchanges should not expect to make money consistently from such trading.

[5] At the Zhengzhou grain market, if there are price fluctuations below 6 percent of the contracted price, the buyer bears 40 percent and the seller 60 percent of the loss. However for fluctuations between 6 and 10 percent, the state bears the loss. For variations over this level, an application may be made by one of the parties to cancel the contract and the security deposit is used to compensate the other party. These provisions are intended to be preliminary and in the future all government intervention is to cease.

[6] Information provided by the Ministry of Internal Trade in January 1994.

Special dispensations had to be obtained from the State Administration for Industry and Commerce to allow brokers trading on the regular Zhengzhou grain market to have their trading licenses amended to permit them to trade on the Exchange.[7]

The Zhengzhou grain exchange uses a sequential auction system of trade, in which an auctioneer oversees the trading of individual lots of grain one after another, with the prices displayed on a screen.[8] The auctioneer announces prices verbally, and adjusts prices upwards, when competitive bidding is occurring, or downwards, when there is a lack of offers, until a single price is reached at which the lot of grain being auctioned is sold. The lots traded are far from uniform in terms of quality, location and delivery time. In practice, the majority of transactions are for spot sales; only 10 percent of all trades are estimated to be for forward delivery. In view of the highly specific nature of each lot traded in Zhengzhou, and the frequent problems associated with securing freight capacity to transport grain, it is difficult to find secondary buyers wanting to purchase existing contracts from other buyers, with the result that there is minimal speculative interest in trading on the Zhengzhou Market.

Government intervention in the grain market is a serious barrier to the more active use of China's first formal Grain Market. The government-enforced price ceilings and quota prices for grain reduce, and often remove entirely, the incentive to use the Zhengzhou Market, since the nature of price risk is distorted by the government's actions. Moreover, the government's efforts to defend fixed price ceilings remove the attractions of storage and potential "cash and carry" business in the grain market.[9]

It is therefore not surprising that the volumes traded on the Zhengzhou Grain Market are low. On many trading days, there are few, or none, transactions which are completed. To summarize, therefore, the failure of the grain sector to support an active commodity exchange can be attributed to (i) the lack of standardization of the lots being traded, (ii) the transport cost barriers to the existence of a truly national grain market and (iii) the extent of government intervention. Nevertheless, the institutions (notably the Shanghai Municipal Government and the Ministry of Commerce) behind the proposed Shanghai Cereals and Oils Exchange have not been discouraged, and the Exchange opened for the trading of wheat, rice and maize in July 1993. By January 1994, according to the new Ministry of Internal Trade, it had a healthy level of trade.

In other agricultural sectors, these problems should pose less of an obstacle to a thriving market and active two-way trading. For example, the liberalization of the sugar and rubber markets over the past two years has been very comprehensive, and in recent months the domestic prices for both of these products have moved closely in parallel with world market movements. Neither sugar nor rubber are very perishable, and they can therefore be stored safely for relatively long periods. Recently, no serious transportation difficulties have been reported for these products. Further, there are large numbers of both sellers and buyers of these two commodities. Sugar and rubber prices are free to fluctuate, and

---

[7]   This was because 'speculation' is not permitted as a trading activity. Similar special dispensations were required for the Shanghai Metals Exchange (see below).

[8]   This system is much simpler, and less costly, than those adopted on the two Metal Exchanges (see below).

[9]   The recent reduction in government procurement, price control and intervention in grain trade may go some of the way towards reducing this obstacle (see Chapter 2).

have often done so substantially over the past year. It therefore appears that the pre-conditions exist for the establishment of a thriving commodity exchange, trading spot and forward contracts in each of these commodities.

The first large scale commodity exchange opened its doors for trading in these products in 1993. The South China Commodity Exchange in Guangzhou was to start trading natural rubber spot and forward contracts in May 1993 on a trading floor that is largely modelled upon the design of the Shanghai Metal Exchange, established by the Guangdong Bureau of Land Reclamation and State Farms, in conjunction with the Guangdong Provincial Government and the Ministries of Agriculture and Chemical Industry. At present, however, this is another example of an Exchange being imposed upon the sector from outside rather than evolving naturally from an existing actively traded market. Currently there is only a very limited volume of even forward trading in the rubber sector. Companies involved in the physical production or trading of natural rubber did not clamor for the establishment of the South China Exchange, which did not represent an obviously useful tool use for their day-to-day commercial business.

Unlike rubber, the sugar sector did not opt for the creation of large and costly Exchanges. Instead, the sugar industry has seen the creation of two specialist wholesale markets, under the aegis of the Ministry of Commerce, in association with the Sugar, Wine and Tobacco Corporation (an enterprise under the control of the Ministry, and the former monopoly distributor of sugar within China). One market is in Tianjin, for beet sugar, and the other is in Guangzhou, for cane sugar. It is reported that a third market will be opened soon in Zhanjiang, the largest sugar producing region of the country, lying in South West Guangdong. However, at present, there is no trading in either Tianjin or Guangzhou. The main explanation offered by users and traders is that they tend to trade directly with their customers or suppliers, and do not see the need for an intermediary in the process. It is relatively simple to contact traditional buyers or sellers and terms for the delivery of sugar to the desired location can then be negotiated, without involving third parties.

Within the direct buyer-seller trading system for sugar, there is very little forward trading, even though there has been substantial price volatility of sugar since 1991. Possible difficulties with contract enforcement are mentioned as one reason, if one or other party felt that prices had moved excessively in the period since the forward contract was signed. Another and possibly more important barrier to forward contracts appears to be the feeling that such contracts represent an unacceptable degree of speculation.

Notwithstanding the reluctance on the part of people in the sugar sector to get involved in forward trading, there is growing pressure in Guangdong to establish a sophisticated forward and futures market for sugar, possibly in association with the South China Exchange. It is quite conceivable, therefore, that Guangzhou will soon be host to two commodity markets, trading agricultural forward and futures contracts, yet without a clear indication of interest in these contracts on the part of the companies involved in production, consumption and trade.

C. The Metals Exchanges of Shanghai and Shenzhen

Looking at producer goods, two commodity Exchanges have been set up for the trade of non-ferrous metals, and in the summer of 1993, a petrochemicals Exchange was also established. This section focuses on the experience of the metals exchanges, due to their relative stability and length of existence. The development of metals markets and exchanges in China has followed a different course from that seen in the agricultural sector. In the metal market, spot and forward trading is facilitated by four main factors, which distinguish the trade in metals from that in agricultural produce. First, metals tend to be relatively high unit value products, so that internal transport costs constitute only a modest barrier to inter-regional trade. Second, metals are not perishable; therefore, delays in transporting metals from one part of China to another do not create undue difficulties. Third, the Chinese government's intervention in the determination of domestic prices is much weaker in the metal sector than it is in several major agricultural sectors, such as the grains market, and therefore, the metal sector behaves much more like a free market than the domestic agricultural sectors. Finally, the most successful contracts for the trading of metals are those in copper and aluminum, and in both of these markets, China is a net importer (where the volume of metal in unprocessed raw material is taken into account) (Appendix Table A4.1). Consequently, the domestic prices of copper and aluminum follow the world market very closely; this is in marked contrast to some of the leading agricultural sectors, in which China may be self-sufficient, and where there is often in any case a very limited link between world market prices and those prevailing domestically.

The metal markets are undoubtedly moving rapidly through several stages of evolution which took decades, or even centuries, in Europe and North America. Both the Shanghai and Shenzhen Exchanges have moved from spot to forward markets, and are now not far from becoming fully-fledged futures markets, in which standardized contracts form the basis of trading.

The Shenzhen Metals Exchange: Structure and Methods of Operation

Ownership: The Shenzhen Metals Exchange (SME) is a private company, which charges members for the provision of services, and hopes to be profitable. This is unlike the Shanghai Metals Exchange (SHME), which is government-owned, but which is not intended to be a profit-making company. At present, the SME provides all of the services required for the operation of the Exchange; however, the Guarantee Fund and Clearing House will be taken over and operated by the SME's members later in 1993.

Supervision: The Shenzhen Municipal Government published and approved the regulations under which the SME operates. These have three main elements, the charter of the SME, the regulation of the management of the exchange, and regulations governing trading. The Municipal government has established the supervision committee which oversees trading and has the ultimate power to enforce penalties in the event of breaches of exchange rules.

Management and Admission to Membership: The admission of new members is recommended by the Management Committee of the SME, but all applications have to be approved by the Municipal government. The Management Committee includes representatives of the shareholders, but over half the Committee is made up of members of the SME.

Financial Conditions of Membership: Upon joining, members of the exchange have to deposit 200,000 RMB in cash with the SME Guarantee Fund. In addition, they pay an annual fee, which was set at 20,000 RMB in the first year, but which has been increased to 30,000 RMB in 1993. The members also pay a fee of 0.1 percent of the value of each contract to the SME; however, the SME then pays 20 percent of its fee income into the Guarantee Fund, which serves to augment the Fund as turnover increases.

Margin Payments: There is an initial margin payment equal to 5 percent of the value of a contract, and daily variation margins are called if prices move against a trader. Thus, if someone has sold a forward contract at 20,000 RMB/ton and the price rises by 200 RMB the next day, a variation margin of 200 RMB/ton is called by the SME Settlement Department in order to ensure that there remains the cushion of 5 percent against the risk of a default by the trader. These margins are all held in bank accounts in the name of the member; therefore, members receive the interest earned on their margin payments during their commodity trading on the SME.

Trading Sessions: Trading sessions are held between 9 a.m. and 11 a.m. daily from Monday to Friday. The two hours are divided into five trading sessions of 20 minutes each, with a break of five minutes between the sessions.

Sessions 1 and 4 are devoted to the trading of copper; Sessions 2 and 5 are devoted to aluminum trading and Session 3 is reserved for all of the other metals - lead, zinc, tin, nickel, manganese and antimony. There is no "kerb" trading outside the official trading sessions.

Types of Contracts: Trading occurs in both spot and forward contracts for each metal, and also occurs in futures for aluminum alone. A number of different brands of metal are approved for each spot and forward contract, as well as a number of different delivery points. The aluminum futures contract specifies just three delivery points: two in Guangzhou and one in Shanghai, and also specifies that the metal must be of an acceptable quality, and therefore delivery is restricted to registered brands which meet the SME quality criteria. The lot size on the SME is 10 tons.

Nature of Trading: Trading is undertaken in a trading floor in which members have access to telephones. Members submit their bids and offers to the representatives of the SME who are seated by computer terminals. These bids and offers specify the price, quantity, month of delivery, brand and location of the delivery, and identify the member who is making the bid or offer. All of this information is then entered into the computer and is displayed anonymously (so as to conceal the identity of the member) on a large computer screen which dominates the trading room. The screen lists details of all of the bids and offers that have been made by traders in the metal that is being traded during that session. When one of the members decides to accept the bids or offers that are listed on the computer screen, it submits a note of acceptance to the representatives of the SME seated by their computer terminals, and the Clerk announces that a deal has been struck and reads the details of the deal into a microphone. The computer terminals list bids and offers in chronological order, and ensures that if there are several bids or offers at the same price, those bids or offers which were made first are the ones which are filled before any others. If there are several acceptances submitted for the same offer at the same time, the tonnage on offer is divided equally between the different members accepting the offer.

Settlement Prices: At the end of each day's trading, settlement prices are determined and published by the Settlement Committee of the Exchange, which is composed of a representative of the SME and five trading members.

Price Limits: There is a daily limit on price movements of 3 percent. Thus prices in one day's trading are not allowed to move more than 3 percent, either upwards or downwards, from the previous day's settlement prices.

Physical Delivery: The physical delivery at the expiry of a contract occurs between the 21st and 25th of the month of expiry, and payment settlement is between the 26th and the 30th of the month.

Sources: Background Papers.

The Shenzhen Metal Exchange

The first fully-fledged metals exchange to be created in China was the Shenzhen Metal Exchange (SME).[10] The Exchange was formed in June 1991, and the formal opening of the exchange for the trading of contracts was in January 1992. In total, 81 companies were trading on the Exchange by March 1993.[11] The SME was modelled primarily upon the London Metal Exchange (LME) Ring-dealing system, using "open outcry" methods of trading, but its trading methods have evolved towards a system that now is a close approximation to the screen-based trading methods of the Shanghai Metals Exchange (SHME). The key features of the structure and methods of operation both exchanges are provided below.

The structure of trading on the SME has evolved considerably since the exchange first opened. Having started with a high percentage of spot trades and with a large proportion of forward contracts leading to eventual physical delivery of metals, the proportion of spot trades is now typically below 10 percent of turnover, and the proportion of forward trades which result in physical delivery is also below 10 percent. During 1992 as a whole, spot trades accounted for 18 percent of total turnover; forward trades for 75 percent; and futures trading for 7.2 percent. The total volume of turnover during the course of 1992 was 483,000 tons, with a value of 6.3 billion RMB (implying a fee income from commissions alone of 6.3 million RMB).

An indication of the expanding pace of trading volume is given in Appendix Table A4.2, describing trading during January 1993 (which was shortened by the Spring Festival holidays) and February 1993. In January, trading exceeded 53,000 tons, with a value of 795 million RMB, and in February, the volume was over 73,000 tons (implying a daily trading average of almost 3,700 tons) and the value was 1,023 million RMB (equivalent to 51 million RMB per trading day). By mid-March, the

---

[10] The local Bureau of the MME and the Municipal government in the Special Economic Zone first created a Trade Center, in which 52 producers, users and traders were able to trade and exhibit their products, but by 1989, they had decided, in conjunction with the China Non-Ferrous Metal General Corporation (CNFMGC), to move towards the establishment of a formal metals exchange. To this end, the Shenzhen branch of the CNFMGC formed a Hong Kong branch in 1989, from which to gain trading experience. After two years of this experience, the Corporation acted as the instigator in the creation of the Shenzhen Metal Exchange Company. The CNFMGC was the majority shareholder in the new company (with 60 percent of the equity), and the two minority shareholders were the Shenzhen Non-Ferrous Metal Corporation (with 25 percent of the equity) and the Shenzhen Materials General Company (an enterprise of the MME, with a share of 15 percent in the SME). The total investment in the facilities of the SME totals 12 million RMB Yuan. At present, the SME owns and operates the Exchange's Guarantee Fund and Clearing House, but it is planned that these will both be owned and operated by SME members later in 1993.

[11] The SME has been selective in accepting applicants for seats on the Exchange, and has so far tried to select mainly producer and user companies. In March 1993, there were only seven members from brokerage companies, but their numbers are expected to be increased in the next round of admissions of new members.

daily volume reached almost 8,000 tons.[12] For 1993 as a whole, it is forecast that total trading volume will be of the order of 20 billion RMB.

Over time, the volume has become increasingly concentrated in just one or two active contracts. In both metals exchanges, the active metals are copper and aluminum, with copper dominant in Shanghai and aluminum in Shenzhen. A second form of trading concentration, which can be interpreted as a healthy stage in the move towards fully fledged futures trading, is the growing proportion of trade in what are effectively standardized contracts. A growing proportion of forward trades specify LME brand metal (rather than particular individual brands, which are of a lower quality), and specify either Shanghai or Guangzhou as delivery points). As much as 80 percent or more of all forward trading would be eligible to qualify for delivery against an aluminum futures contract.

Today, hedge-buying and selling account for only a relatively small proportion (10 to 15 percent) of trade. The primary interest of the participants was speculative, with a major proportion of this speculation linked to expectations about the unofficial swap exchange rate for the RMB Yuan against the US dollar. Since aluminum and copper are both products in which China is a regular net importer (Appendix Table A4.1), China's domestic prices follow world prices closely, with a relatively stable relationship between the world price (expressed in RMB yuan at the unofficial exchange rate) and the domestic market price, quoted on the SME. Thus, the purchase or sale of a forward or futures contract on the SME can be used as a means of speculating on movements in either the world prices of these two metals or in the unofficial exchange rate.

The link between local and world prices for metals is highlighted by the practice of the SME of listing the latest world market quotations from the LME and Comex in the trading room and on boards outside the room, together with details of exchange rates, and of listing the conversion of the SME's settlement prices into dollars for comparison with the quotations on overseas markets. One possibility that is actively being considered is the denomination of all of the SME's contracts in US dollars, rather than RMB Yuan. Such a change would require the approval of the State Administration for Foreign Exchange Control.

The overriding interest in speculation has led to an almost total neglect of one major aspect of commodity trading in other countries, namely the arbitrage between physical and forward markets and the use of forward and futures contracts as a means of reducing the cost of holding and managing inventories. It can be shown that the differentials between the prices for different forward contracts on the SME reflect apparent failures of arbitrage to bring these differentials into line with the costs of storage.

There are several possible reasons for the failure of arbitrage to take effect in the differentials in the structure of forward prices. One is ignorance about the scope for such arbitrage; another is poor access to storage facilities; but the most important are undoubtedly the high costs of margin deposits for such arbitrage operations, and the perception that the scope for speculative profits

---

[12] The turnover figures for both the SME and the SHME count one transaction, involving the combination of a buying and selling order for, say, 100 tonnes as 200 tonnes of turnover. However the convention adopted by Exchanges elsewhere is to count each transaction only once. Turnover on Chinese Exchanges should therefore be halved for purposes of comparison with the quantities mentioned on Exchanges in North America and Europe.

from these operations is limited in relation to the potential gains from speculation in forward and futures markets.

The Shanghai Metal Exchange

The Shanghai Metal Exchange (SHME) was formed as a joint enterprise of the Shanghai Municipal Government and the former Ministry of Materials and Equipment in Beijing.[13] The investment costs of the new exchange were raised by the Shanghai Materials and Equipment bureau, through bank borrowings. The management of the SHME was entrusted to the Shanghai MME, which was also responsible for drafting the regulations under which the exchange would operate. The MME secured the approval of the Shanghai Municipal State Administration for Industry and Commerce for the amendments to government policy which were essential before the commodity exchange could operate. Trading began in May 1992. The Exchange Company has five departments (Dealing, Delivery, Settlement, Information and Administration) and employs some 60 people. The Settlement department acts as the Clearing House for the SHME and oversees the daily settlements of margins. Another two departments (Development and Engineering) have been added and the number of employees has consequently increased.

---

[13] In 1979, when the government first started to encourage the operation of a market economy within a socialist framework, Shanghai was the first city to establish a spot commodity market, which operated within the broad guidelines set down by the State Plan. The commodities that were traded on this first exchange were predominantly geared towards the needs of heavy industry, and included wholesale products such as cars, steel and electrical machinery. The success of the first moves towards the creation of commodity markets encouraged the establishment of other such markets, and in 1984, the Shanghai Municipal Materials and Equipment Bureau (Shanghai MME) established the Shanghai Materials and Goods Trade Center in the Wu Mao Building in the city to promote spot trading in metals and related industrial products. The acceleration of the adoption of a socialist market economy encouraged the Shanghai MME to examine the potential viability of a commodity exchange in which forward and futures contracts could be traded. In April 1991, the Shanghai MME invited representatives of overseas metals markets to visit the Trade Center and lecture on the functions and operations of futures markets, who presented the Shanghai MME with a proposal to open a full metal exchange in the Trade Center.

The Shanghai Metals Exchange: Structure and Methods of Operation

Regulations: The Shanghai Metals Exchange (SHME) is a non-profit-making institution. Any surplus it makes is ploughed back into its facilities. Regulations for the SHME were drafted by the Shanghai MME, with special permission and waivers to overcome obstacles presented by existing regulations concerning domestic trade. The first concerned forward trading. Speculation is illegal in China, and since all forward trading involves the possibility of gains or losses to market participants, such trading could be considered speculative and hence illegal. By special amendment the Shanghai SAIC permitted the SHME to undertake forward trading.

The second restriction concerned trading licenses. Any diversification by a company into a new field of activity requires the approval of the SAIC and granting of a new trading license. By special permission, the SAIC will allow SHME members to trade on the Exchange without amending their current trading licenses. Third, and also on the issue of trading licences, the Shanghai SAIC approved new regulations which allowed SHME members to operate as brokers, representing outside companies, without needing to obtain special licenses as agents.

Finally, an amendment was agreed with the Price Bureau, to allow metal prices to fluctuate on the market.

Supervision: At the top of the administration and supervision of the Exchange is the Management Committee, composed of representatives of the Municipal government and the former MME. Shanghai Municipal Council is represented by the Vice-Mayor, who is the 'Director Member'. Other government agencies who nominate representatives include the Municipal Planning Committee and Economic and Trade Commission, the Administration for Industry and Commerce, the Finance Bureau and the Price Bureau. The Management Committee coordinates relations between ministries and local governments, drafts and revises trading rules and is entitled to cancel transactions, fine members or even cancel membership of any offending company. Next, a smaller Supervision Committee, also composed entirely of government representatives (from the SAIC, Price Bureau and MME) which monitors trading on a more detailed basis, and is intended to resolve contract disputes.

The SHME has a Board of Directors; the highest executive body, two thirds of which consists of representatives of member companies and a third of which is nominated by the government from certain government agencies. The Board implements decisions of the member congress, presents proposals for revision of rules or by-laws and approves applications for admission.

Management and Admission to Membership: Admission requires SHME Management Committee approval.

Financial Conditions of Membership: Upon joining, members of the exchange have to deposit a performance bond, such as a bank Letter of Credit, of 200,000 RMB with the SHME Guarantee Fund. (This differs from the practice in Shenzhen, where cash deposits are required). In addition, they pay an annual fee of 50,000 RMB. The members also pay a fee of 0.1 percent of the value of each contract to the SHME.

Margin Payments: Identical to the Shenzhen Exchange. The SHME calls for an initial margin payment equal to 5 percent of the value of a contract, and daily variation margins are called if prices move against a trader. Bank L/Cs are accepted for partial margin payments. This ensures that members receive all the interest earned on their margin payments during their trading.

Trading Sessions: Sessions are now daily (originally they took place only on Mondays, Wednesdays and Fridays). The first session is devoted to copper (50 minutes), the second trades aluminum (50 minutes). There is a 20 minute session for zinc and the other four metals - lead, tin, nickel and pig iron, are traded in separate 15 minute sessions in the afternoon.

Types of Contracts: Trading occurs in both spot and forward contracts for each metal. There is no trading of standardized metal futures contracts. A number of different brands of metal are approved for each spot and forward contract, (12 separate brands of copper) as well as a number of different delivery points. The lot size is 25 tonnes.

Nature of Trading: Each member has a two seat cubicle on a trading floor, with telephone and computer facilities. In place of the Shenzhen system, where individual members pass their bids and offers by hand to the Exchange staff for entry into the computer system, each SHME member enters its own bids and offers directly onto the screen. The information is displayed anonymously (to conceal the identity of the member) on the screens which each member can summon up.

If there are several bids at the same price, the central computer satisfies orders on a first-come-first-served basis.

Throughout the trading session, the central computer prepares up-to-date details of remaining unfilled bids and offers that have been made by traders in the metal traded during that session, but keeps the identity of each buyer or seller anonymous. While they are trading, individual traders can list the full details of all bids and offers made during the session, as well as details (keeping the identity of the participants confidential) of completed deals.

Settlement Prices: At the end of each day's trading, settlement prices are determined and published by the Settlement Department of the Exchange, in conjunction with representatives of the trading members.

Price Limits: There is a daily limit on price movements of 10 percent. (This compares with daily limits of only 3 percent on the Shenzhen Metal Exchange).

Physical Delivery: The physical delivery at the expiry of a contract occurs between the 16th and 25th of that month.

Sources: Background Papers.

The Exchange had 62 member companies by January 1994. The largest single group of members is traders on the domestic market, who provide 31 members. The next largest group consists of 19 members which have interests in the production and processing of metals; these 19 include several major companies which are end-users of copper, such as in the manufacture of wire and cables. The membership of the exchange is completed by companies which are active in the import and export of metals and by financial institutions, such as brokerage companies. The SHME has been highly selective about admitting companies to the Exchange, and has a large number of unsatisfied applications. As with the Shenzhen Exchange, the SHME was modelled primarily upon the London Metal Exchange (LME) Ring-dealing system, but instead of the "open outcry" methods of trading used in London and on Comex, the SHME's trading is entirely screen-based.

Like the Shenzhen exchange, the SHME has made very rapid progress in its first few months of operations. In the period of just over seven months from its opening until the end of 1992, it traded 2.93 million tonnes of metals with a total value of 48.8 billion RMB.[14] This implied that the SHME received 48.8 million RMB in 0.1 percent transactions fees alone, a figure which dwarfs the 2.4 million RMB received as annual membership fees.[15] Over the next two months, from the start of 1993 until March, turnover totalled 2.05 million tonnes, worth 39.8 billion RMB, even though this included the Spring Festival holidays, implying an average daily volume of the order of 100,000 tonnes, with a value of close to 2.0 billion RMB (Appendix Table A4.3). During its first seven months of existence, the proportion of contracts that resulted in physical delivery was 26 percent. However, the proportion has fallen steadily; it was 86 percent in the first month of trading, and was down to 17 percent by December.

The two forms of concentration that were discernible from the patterns of trading in Shenzhen have been repeated in Shanghai. As in Shenzhen, volume has become increasingly focused upon just two metals, copper and aluminum, with copper increasing its turnover, and hence its share of overall volume, at a faster rate than aluminum. In 1992, the two metals accounted for over 90 percent of total volume, of which aluminum contributed almost 35 percent; in the first two months of 1993, copper's share had increased to 60 percent, while aluminum's contribution to the total had slipped to 32 percent.

The other form of concentration of activity represents a major step in the evolution towards futures market trading. As volume has expanded on the Shanghai Exchange, so also has the share of total business that takes place in grades of metal and locations of delivery which are more or less standardized in the way that one would expect on a futures market. By March 1993, nearly all trading specified Shanghai (where three warehouses have been registered with the SHME) as a delivery point, and it was estimated that in excess of 80 percent of trading volume was in LME-registered brands of metal.

Participation in trading on the SHME appears less heavily dependent upon speculation than in Shenzhen. Leading traders here include importers of concentrates who use the SHME as a means of hedging their price risk in the period between purchasing the concentrates and selling the refined metal

---

[14] It should be remembered that this means that there were 1.465 million tonnes of metals that were actually sold on the Exchange. (The other 1.465 million tonnes represented the other (purchasing) side of the same transactions.)

[15] At both exchanges, both buyer and seller pay the 0.1 percent commission fee. Fees at overseas futures markets are much lower.

produced from the same concentrates to Chinese customers. Others obtain their initial futures market price hedges on their overseas purchases of metal through the LME. Later, once their LME hedges were in place, they gradually reduced their LME futures positions and moved their hedging protection to the SHME.[16] Among domestic producers of metals, there was a significant use of the SHME for physical hedging up to three months forward, with the possibility of making physical deliveries at the expiry of a contract if that appeared to be advantageous. Nevertheless, there can be no doubt that the dominant force behind trading on the SHME is the same as that in Shenzhen, namely speculation about the unofficial exchange rate for the RMB Yuan, or hedging against future foreign exchange rate variations.[17] With the new exchange rate system, it will be interesting to see whether this decreases. To the extent to which access to foreign exchange is free, it may well lead to a decline in trade.

D. An Assessment of Trading on China's Two Metal Exchanges

The System of Trading on the Exchanges

The developers of commodity exchanges in China clearly have a specific model in mind when they establish such exchanges. They profess a desire to incorporate the main features of the leading exchanges, such as the Chicago Board of Trade and Comex in the US or the London Metal Exchange in England, but have chosen to adopt a computer-based trading system, rather than the open outcry methods employed on almost all of the world's main commodity exchanges. This approach is both more costly and technically more complex than those found on the world's leading commodity markets. The choice has been defended on the ground that the open outcry methods of trading in other countries have a long historical tradition and have evolved over many decades or centuries. They may be difficult to create from scratch in an economy that has not been governed by a market economy for a period of 40 years. Moreover, even the exchanges that rely upon open outcry methods are becoming increasingly computer-based, while many of the newer forward and futures markets, such as those in foreign exchange and interest rates, are using screen trading, rather than open outcry. Therefore, it was felt that China should opt directly for the most modern methods of trading, rather than evolving slowly towards them.

Those exchanges which have adopted computer-based trading have often done so because the volume of trading has become too great, and the number of market participants too large (as with the markets in financial instruments) to be handled by open outcry methods. Volumes of trading on the Chinese exchanges are nowhere near the limits possible with open outcry. It may have been preferable for China too to adopt an evolutionary approach with 'open outcry' to begin with, moving towards screen-based trading as volumes pick up and live contracts are assured for specific commodities. Choice of technique should be determined in part by the technology available and the costs of the alternatives.

---

[16]   The differential between the LME and Shanghai is said to be fairly stable in the region of US$250 per ton (where the Shanghai quotations are translated into dollars at the swap market rate); consequently, there is not too much risk in the switching of hedged positions from the LME to the SHME.

[17]   The key point is that the metals exchange serves as a proxy for a market in foreign exchange.

Where wages are high, as in Europe and North America, there is a stronger economic incentive to hold down costs by substituting computers for employees than in China.

Establishers of exchanges in China argue that the less well regulated framework of open outcry markets would lend itself to possible corruption and falsification of deals. By contrast, computer-based trading methods in which the identity of traders was kept confidential, were felt to be less prone to cheating. However, those exchanges which practise open outcry methods of trading have all established rules which permit other members of the exchanges or the regulatory authorities overseeing the exchanges to question the validity of the prices at which individual transactions occur. Where the exchanges keep sequential time records of the details of each trade, it is simple for outside authorities to evaluate the pattern of trades over time and detect if there are transactions whose prices are significantly out of line with other trades. It may also be questioned whether the use of computers avoids problems of cheating. Besides, the most important forms of cheating are typically those which occur off the trading floor.[18] In early 1994, cases of 'computer fraud' were reported in the Shanghai stock exchange, which demonstrates the vulnerability of screen-based trading to fraud.

Since the investment on these two exchanges at least has been made, it may be too late to reopen the debate about the form of trading in these, but the same principles should apply to other exchanges being established. However, there are other factors that should be taken into consideration in determining how to develop the current trading systems in future in these exchanges. The first is the suitability of present computer systems for an expansion of trading volume. From observing the two Metal Exchanges in operation, it is doubtful whether the current systems can be said to be suitable to handle much greater volumes of turnover.[19] When the computer systems are working as intended, the speed of response of the systems is inadequate. It takes traders several seconds to input a fairly complicated sequence of details (including brands of metal, delivery location, price, month of contract and quantities) onto the screen in the Shanghai Metal Exchange, and the task is not helped by the use of long sequences of number codes, extending up to eight or so digits, to represent different brands or locations. During trading, when traders want to view the details of bids and offers and of the strike prices at which deals have been agreed during the session, the computer system is again somewhat slow. Instead of the instant response that is needed, it often takes several seconds to go through the listing of bid and offer prices.[20] This suggests, at least, a need for reprogramming the software used.

A second issue that seems to have been inadequately appreciated during the design of the Metal Exchanges and of the other commodity exchanges established in China relates to the physical

---

[18] For example, when a broker receives several different trading orders during a session, it may require sophisticated methods of scrutiny to ensure that all of the customers of the broker receive equally good service, and that the broker does not reserve the best prices during the session for the most favored customers and relegate the worst prices obtained during the session to the least favored customers. (One means of avoiding the danger of cheating would be to adopt the Japanese system whereby one price is determined each session, at which the tonnages of all bids and offers are exactly matched. It is interesting to note that this is being adopted for the Guangzhou Rubber Exchange.)

[19] In one of the two visits that were made to trading sessions on the exchanges the start of trading had to be delayed by half an hour because of computer failure.

[20] Some of these problems may be reduced if and when the markets move over to futures trading with standardized contracts, since less information is required for each transaction.

facilities and infrastructure that are needed for alternative forms of exchange. Trading floors are essential when trading occurs through means, such as open outcry, in which all participants need to be able to see one another and to respond to the waves and shouts of other traders. Trading floors become much less necessary, and may not be needed at all, if trading is entirely computer-based. The lack of contact between traders at the Shanghai Metal Exchange suggests that they have no need whatever to be located nearby. In effect, there is no need for the trading floor, and all traders could be situated more cheaply in their offices, linked to one another and the central computer of the Exchange via a computer telephone network.

The situation in China's Metal Exchanges represents a hybrid, combining the physical infrastructure (and associated cost of a trading room) of an open outcry market with the computer infrastructure (and the associated cost of the networked computer system) of a screen-based market. One of these expenditures is redundant: either the trading floor should be used more fully for open outcry trading, and the computer system adapted to link individual traders with their offices, or the trading floor can be eliminated or used for other purposes and the computer system altered so that the terminals are located in traders' own offices, rather than on the trading floor.

The time is already approaching when both existing Metal Exchanges have to consider expanding their present computer systems. The Shanghai Metal Exchange is reviewing an investment of $1 million in new facilities for trading, in which added computer capacity will undoubtedly loom large. Before making these investments, the inconsistency between a trading floor suitable for open outcry methods, on the one hand, and a computer-based trading system which does not require such a floor, on the other, should be resolved. This provides an opportunity for a serious review of the present screen-based system as well as software presently used. Although sunk costs may dictate that it is too late to change the present system, these factors should be evaluated in any new exchanges to be set up in the future. To reduce the risk of cheating, if this is felt to be a major concern, serious consideration should be given to modelling the trading system upon the Japanese auction method (see below) which is to be applied to the Guangzhou Rubber Exchange.

It is sometimes argued that the benefit of computer trading is that trade is not monopolized by traders in the geographic proximity of an exchange, and greater regional integration of trade is encouraged. It should be pointed out that in an 'open outcry' system, distant participants can be represented by traders or brokers. Eventually, however, if the voume of trade proves sufficient to justify the costs of screen-based trading, this option should be considered, but its selection at the outset is an expensive choice.

The Japanese Auction System

Many Japanese commodity exchanges, such as the Tokyo Grain Exchange, have adopted an auction system which provides an effective means of establishing a commodity price without any danger of cheating. The Guangzhou Rubber Exchange, which was officially opened on March 28th, 1993, is being established initially so as to trade along the lines of the Shanghai Metal Exchange, but, as turnover increases, it will then switch to the Japanese auction system.

In the Japanese system, the trading floor consists of floor traders who are linked to their offices by telephones. At the start of each session, the Exchange representative starts the proceedings by announcing a price for the contract that is being traded at that time (say, June 1993 wheat). Each of the floor traders then informs her/his office of this price, and this office lets the trader know how many lots it would like to buy or sell at that price.

To arrive at this quantity, the office holds its own mini-auction, which is almost a replica of the situation on the exchange, in that the office is in touch with all of its clients, and gets each of them to inform it of their buying or selling intentions at that price, and the office then combines all of its clients' bids and offers to arrive at a single net tonnage. On the trading floor, the floor traders pass on these net buying and selling quantities to the auctioneer, whose colleagues immediately compute the net balance. If there is an excess of buying orders over selling orders, the auctioneer announces a slightly higher price; if selling orders are larger, the auctioneer lowers the price.

The process continues until there is an exact balance between buying and selling, and the price that emerges is the single price at which all of the buying and selling orders are implemented for that trading session, without any possibility at all of cheating, since the single price is known to everybody. In practice, the process of arriving at a balance is less prolonged than might have been expected, since some of the bids and offers are flexible, in the sense of someone offering to buy whatever is on offer at a certain price, thereby clearing the market.

Source: Background Papers.

The Costs of Trading on the Exchanges

Chinese Exchanges charge extremely high fees by world standards (even if they may seem relatively small in relation to the value of the metals being traded). On the two Metal Exchanges, the fees paid to the Exchange were originally set at 0.1 percent of the value of the commodities being traded, and other new Exchanges are known to be considering charging fees of as much as 0.15 percent of the value of the commodities changing hands on their trading floors.[21] In developed countries, the size of the fees charged by Commodity Exchanges is determined partly by competition with other Exchanges and partly by pressure from members (who own the Exchanges) to hold down the cost of transactions. Since, with very few exceptions, Exchanges in Europe and North America are non-profit-making bodies, their fees are designed merely to cover their actual operating costs.

The world's two leading Metal Exchanges, in London and New York, operate on a non-profit-making basis. Consequently, as their turnovers have risen, fees have been reduced per lot traded on the Exchanges. Currently, the fees charged by the London Metal Exchange amount to approximately 0.5 percent of those charged by the two Chinese Metal Exchanges. In other words, instead of 0.1 percent of turnover, the LME charges a mere 0.0005 percent as its fee; and this very low figure includes the Clearing House fees payable on each transaction!

The remarkable disparity between the fees charged in China and those charged overseas will not be able to persist if and when Chinese companies have much freer access to foreign Commodity Exchanges. If Chinese Exchanges are to succeed in maintaining their turnovers, they will have to lower

---

[21] The Ministry of Internal Trade has state in January 1994 that the Shanghai metals exchange will revise its charge to 0.7 percent.

their fees towards the levels charged by their major international competitors. When this happens, there will be much greater pressure than there is at present for the Chinese Exchanges to reduce their costs towards international norms. It is to be expected that this may bring to a head the issue of the appropriateness or otherwise of the current computer-intensive trading methods employed in China.

The Nature of Trading Activity on the Exchanges

Speculation

The importance of speculation as a source of trading volume on these exchanges has already been pointed out. Since the trading is in metals contracts, it is inevitable that the speculation appears at first sight to be centered upon metal prices; however, the contrast between the complete lack of trading interest in those metals in which China is self-sufficient and the active two-way forward trading in those in which China is a regular net importer is powerful evidence of the extreme importance of exchange rate speculation as the primary cause of speculative interest. Only for those metals in which China is a consistent net importer are domestic prices linked closely to world market quotations. When world prices of copper or aluminum increase, Chinese prices follow suit. The same is not true of lead, zinc or tin, for example, since China's self-sufficiency has led to a much weaker correlation between local prices and world market values.

Speculators who trade copper or aluminum forward contracts in Shanghai and Shenzhen are speculating on two prices: the world market quotations for these metals, expressed in US dollars, and the unofficial exchange rate between the RMB Yuan and the dollar. Moreover, provided that the variations in the world market quotations are uncorrelated with changes in the exchange rate (as is likely), it can be shown that the volatility of the Chinese domestic price of these two metals will be greater than the volatility of either the world metal price or the exchange rate.[22] Since price volatility is one of the main pre-conditions for active speculation, the enhancement of price volatility by the introduction of exchange rate uncertainty adds to the attractions of speculating in copper and aluminum contracts. When the price volatility of these two non-ferrous metals is low, then the forward contracts acquire another allure: as a proxy for a speculation in the value of the RMB Yuan. In the absence of a more direct method of taking forward positions in the currency, these metals contracts become a major arena for foreign exchange speculative interest at times of heightened uncertainty about the international value of the Chinese currency.[23] With the growth in the number of participants on their own account or as

---

[22] In the absence of correlation, the volatility will vary with the sum of the variance of each price series; ie, with the sum of the squares of price movements in metals and in foreign exchange.

[23] However, China is now making moves towards the establishment of foreign exchange futures markets. In late 1992, the government cracked down on several unauthorized foreign exchange companies, but in mid 1993, the Guangdong SAIC authorized the setting up of the Guangdong Wantong Futures Brokerage, and further such brokerages are to be approved (*Flemings Research*, May 1993). On June 9, 1993, the Central Bank approved provisional regulations on foreign exchange futures trading. According to these rules, the eligible traders are financial agencies, or traders and brokers cosponsored by financial institutions, and approved by the State Administration of Foreign Exchange (*Economic Daily*, June 27).

brokers, the scope for further development of this speculative interest in trading on the two Exchanges is considerable.[24]

A general implication is that in a partially deregulated market, 'proxy markets' will form, in which trade in goods where prices and quantities are allowed to vary freely sometimes become 'bundled' with other goods, where there are constraints on such flexibility. (The example of grain prices reflecting freight availability for grain (Chapter 3) was another example of this phenomenon. These consequences demonstrate some of the costs of partial deregulation.

Hedging

The use of the Exchanges for conventional hedging purposes and for price protection is still relatively limited. It would appear that hedging accounts for a higher proportion of futures turnover in Shanghai than in Shenzhen, but it is still doubtful whether hedging, defined broadly to include those transactions for which it is difficult to distinguish hedging motives from more speculative trading, accounts for as much as 25 percent of the total volume of turnover in Shanghai.

The main origins of the current hedging business on the Exchanges are twofold. One important category of users of forward contracts consists of import/export trading corporations and processors, such as smelters and refineries. Both of these groups face operating margins which are very sensitive to fluctuations in commodity prices between the date when they purchase their raw materials and the date when they sell their products to their customers.

The other major category of users of the Exchanges for hedging is producers who employ the Exchange as a means of "locking in" prices for forward delivery, in order to reduce the uncertainty about their future revenues. By the very nature of these transactions, it is difficult to know the degree to which forward trading represents a form of speculation or whether it is part of a deliberate strategy of controlling price uncertainties.

Physical Deliveries

In their early days, the majority of trading on both Exchanges was for prompt delivery, and a majority of total turnover led to the physical delivery of metals to buyers. Since then, the proportion of spot trading has fallen towards 10 percent of turnover, as has the proportion of trading volume which results in final delivery to buyers. The reduction in both proportions is a natural part of the evolution of trading towards one that is close to conventional futures trading, in which only a small percentage of turnover ever results in physical delivery. Nevertheless, the possibility of physical delivery is still very important in generating interest in trading on the Exchanges, since it enables users to become accustomed to viewing trading on the Exchanges as a valuable extension of their trading and marketing

---

[24] At present, the method of trading on both Exchanges is cumbersome and is not designed to stimulate the active participation of potential customers located outside the Exchange buildings. There are, as yet, no computer screens displaying either SHME or SME prices to participants away from the Exchange premises. Indeed, apart from telephone contact with the "red jackets" (the floor traders) in the Exchange trading rooms, there is no link between the outside world and trading on the Exchanges. Customers of the brokerage companies have to rely upon faxes transmitted to them by their brokers each day for their information on the market.

of physical metals to customers. For example, producers who need to supply metal at short notice to customers in Shanghai can buy it from the Exchange, rather than having to arrange urgent shipments from their refineries.

Inventory Management

One of the most important omissions by member companies in the present range of trading interest in the two Exchanges is an active use of forward contracts as a medium for managing inventory financing.[25] Until the time profile of forward prices reflects the costs of holding inventories, the markets cannot be considered to be functioning at their full efficiency. The causes of the failure of forward prices to reflect storage costs are both informational and institutional. They are informational in that users of the Exchanges do not yet appear to be aware of the scope for using the forward and futures markets as a tool for inventory management. This deficiency will presumably be overcome as trading becomes more sophisticated. The failure is also institutional in the sense that the methods of margin payments on the Exchanges mean that, in relation to straightforward speculation or hedging in a single forward contract, a comparatively large sum of money has to be tied up in margins when trading the "spreads" between forward prices (the differentials between forward prices for different contract months).[26]

This is in marked contrast with the situation on Exchanges in other countries. On these Exchanges, the Clearing Houses calculate the degree of price volatility and associated risk of fluctuations in the magnitude of spreads. For example, in recent months, copper spreads have displayed greater price volatility than those for aluminum; therefore, the London Metal Exchange charges relatively higher initial

---

[25] An analysis of the structure of forward prices on the Shenzhen Metal Exchange during the week of 8th to 12th March, 1993 was undertaken, which demonstrated that the structure of price differentials between the prices quoted for different contract months does not yet reflect the costs of financing and storing inventories. The same is true of the structure of prices on the Shanghai Exchange.

[26] When buying or selling a single forward contract at a price of, say, 20,000 RMB per ton, for the June 1993 contract, the initial margin deposit on both Exchanges is 5 percent of this value, i.e., 1,000 RMB per ton. If, however, a trader makes a "spread" between the June 1993 contract and the September 1993 contract by buying the June contract at 20,000 RMB at the same time as he sells the September contract at 20,750 RMB, he has to make two initial margin deposits, one of 5 percent of 20,000 RMB and the other of 5 percent of 20,750 RMB, making an initial deposit of 2,037.5 RMB even though the spread which is being traded is one of only 750 RMB (20,750 minus 20,000). From the perspective of a trader with limited access to working capital for the payment of margins on the Exchanges, a single forward transaction ties up a mere 5 percent of the value of the contract that is being traded. However, the initial margin required to buy or sell a spread on China's two Metal Exchanges ties up over 270 percent of the value of the spread itself. The leverage that can be secured from 100,000 RMB of margin finance is therefore very much greater with straightforward trading in a single forward position than in a "spread" between two contracts.

margins on copper spreads than for aluminum.[27] This limits the usefulness of the Chinese exchanges to their participants.

The Role of "Market Makers" or "Locals"

An important component of a successful Commodity Exchange in other countries is the existence of a group of traders, known as "market makers" or "locals", who trade actively on their own account, often buying and selling many times during the trading session. These traders are vital in providing the market with liquidity in the very short run. If someone appears on the Exchange floor with a large buy or sell order, it is these market makers who will adjust their prices slightly and take the other side of the transaction, in the expectation that they will be able to make a small profit from disposing of their position in steps over the remainder of the trading session. In effect, they act as small wholesalers, who earn their living from the small profits that they hope to earn by providing very brief "storage" for commodity futures contracts.

This group does not yet exist on any of China's Commodity Exchanges. One reason is that the contracts that are currently being traded are forward (rather than futures) contracts, so that potential market makers run the unacceptable risk that they may find that they have bought contracts for delivery of a certain brand in Beijing with the intention of a rapid resale, only to discover that prospective buyers either want delivery in Shanghai or specify a different brand of metal. This particular problem will be overcome once the trading shifts to a standardized futures contract.

The other barrier to the emergence of a group of locals lies in the nature of the screen trading methods that have been selected for use on all local Exchanges. Despite the substantial tonnages that are recorded in turnover on each Metal Exchange every trading day, the actual number of distinct transactions is surprisingly small. Appendix Table A4.2 reveals that the Shenzhen Exchange actually handled an average of fewer than 20 transactions per trading day in January and February 1993. In Shanghai the flow of transactions is significantly higher, but there are several *longueurs* when trading may be very slack.

The present cumbersome screen-based trading is largely responsible. Even if someone wanted to trade actively within the course of a single session, the methods of trading employed in China will impose a constraint upon the number of transactions that can be completed within the session. This runs the risk of violating one of the cardinal rules of many market makers, which is that they will never end a day involuntarily as a net buyer or seller of contracts. Their intention is to profit from trading that occurs entirely within the session. The other problem with screen-based trading is that it lacks the sense of contact with other traders of the traditional trading pit. In such a pit, they can adjust their buying and selling prices instantly, as they see how the other traders are behaving. With a computer, they have to

---

[27] In March 1993, the initial margins for each 25 ton lot of copper futures amounted to $2,500 (equivalent to approximately 4 percent of the value of the contract), and those for 25 ton lots of aluminum futures totalled $1,250 (roughly 3 percent of the contract value). However, for three months' futures spreads, the initial margin stood at a mere $1,000 for copper (which contrasts with the margin of $5,000, i.e., twice $2,500, which would have been charged if the rules of China's two Metal Exchanges had been applied); and for aluminum, the initial margin on three months' futures spreads was only $150 (as against the $2,250, i.e., twice $1,250, which would have been applied in China).

wait until they can list the bids and offers of other traders, and lack the sense of immediate reactions to sudden changes in circumstances within the session.

E. Policies and Regulations for Commodities and Futures Markets

The Difficulty of Reconciling Free Markets and Continued Government Intervention

The rapid adoption of the socialist market economy has led to a situation in which some aspects of official policy, such as continuing forms of government intervention in commodity pricing, distribution or storage, are incompatible with most recently adopted policies, such as the development of thriving commodity exchanges. The development of 'proxy markets' in foreign exchange through the metals exchanges, or in scarce transport facilities through the grain exchanges, has already been described. Any systematic form of government intervention in the pricing of commodities or in their distribution and storage runs the same risks; either of undermining the price uncertainty on which any futures market depends, thereby making it impossible to keep newly established commodity exchanges in existence, or, alternatively, in the cases in which forward markets succeed in surviving, of generating potentially unsustainable upward pressure upon the financial costs of government intervention.

Another example of this is provided by storage subsidies. Futures (or forward) markets are by their very nature concerned with inter-temporal price differences, and the physical counterpart of these markets is storage. On a commodity exchange, the premium of today's futures quotation for one particular calendar month (say, March 1994) over today's quotation for a less distant month (say, October 1993) represents the market value placed upon storage between those two periods. In a truly free market, this storage value reflects (i) the physical costs of warehousing, (ii) the financial costs of stock finance and (iii) expectations of relative scarcity of the commodity in question in the two months.[28]

However, there are cases in which the structure of forward prices can be distorted by government actions. In China at present, in several markets for major agricultural products, government agencies provide cheap storage finance to enterprises under their control. At present, the Ministry of Internal Trade (formerly Commerce) provides finance for the storage of certain commodities at preferential interest rates. It does so, for example, for enterprises in the oilseed crushing and cotton ginning sectors, and has done so in the recent past for sugar. The Ministry of Chemicals has intervened in a similar manner in the natural rubber sector. It is to be presumed that the government's objective in

---

[28] The first two items are straightforward since they represent the actual financial costs incurred when commodities are stored. The significance of price expectations can best be understood by considering the situation which may arise if supplies of an agricultural product are seasonally very tight in the immediate future (in October), but are then expected to ease when the new crop becomes available (in October, for example). Under these circumstances, it is quite normal for the more distant (March 1994) price to stand at a discount to the nearby (October 1993) price, because this set of price differentials gives a clear signal to any holders of surplus stocks that they should sell them to the market as soon as possible, and help to ease the immediate scarcity of supplies, instead of holding on to them. The premium that is paid for nearby supplies in this example represents an illustration of the forward market providing valuable price signals to the holders of surplus stocks.

providing these storage subsidies is to ensure that the economy at large benefits through lower price premia for forward delivery than would otherwise be the case.

Provided (as may be expected) that SOEs pass on the benefits of their storage subsidies in the forward prices that they quote to their customers, private firms without access to these credit subsidies will find it attractive to "arbitrage" the market by leaving the main responsibility for commodity storage to the government sector, and shifting as much of their inventory as possible to these subsidized SOEs. Under such circumstances, the futures market will lose a considerable proportion of its two-way flow of trade, and will be turned into one in which participants from the sector without access to subsidized credit will tend to be consistent buyers of futures contracts (in order to save on their storage costs), with subsidized SOEs acting as the major sellers of futures.

In this situation, a 'proxy' has been established through the futures market, which ensures that every enterprise, state-owned or otherwise, has access to the benefits of subsidized credit for storage. However, the government may find that it has to face a larger cost of storage subsidies than it had anticipated. If it is unwilling to continue to underwrite subsidized storage and see stock-holding increasingly left to SOEs, it may impose a strict limit to the money spent on storage subsidies. In this event, the weight of futures or forward buying will provide a mechanism through which the effective premium for storage will be pushed up to the unsubsidized free market level. Under these circumstances, the government storage subsidies will have achieved nothing but a transfer of income (in the form of the subsidized credit) to the SOEs, without any benefit in terms of reduced premia for forward prices for the economy at large.

Thus, if forward/futures markets are allowed to operate in sectors in which government agencies are involved in the subsidized financing of storage, the arbitrage in the financing of storage will mean that the situation should tend towards one of two outcomes: either the companies without access to subsidized credit will shift as many as possible of their storage activities onto the government by selling physical metal and buying their stock requirements forward (thereby taking advantage of the subsidized credit embodied in the "carry"); or the government will give insufficient subsidized credit to the Ministry to allow it to defend the low, subsidized "carry", and the "carry" in the forward market will reflect the cost of capital to the private sector, rather than the government's subsidized interest rate. In the latter case, the subsidized credit acts as a direct transfer (in effect, a gift) to the Ministry which receives it.

Financial Safeguards for Participants on the Exchanges

Financial safeguards which form an integral part of any Exchange's operations are typically reflected in up to three different categories of payments. The first is the deposit by each member of an Exchange of a significant sum of money, or some form of bank guarantee, such as a Letter of Credit, to create a Guarantee Fund to provide reassurance for other members of the ability of the member to meet any reasonable commitments.

The second is the payment of margins, both as initial and variation margins, which are adjusted daily to maintain a sizeable financial deterrent against a member defaulting on a commitment, and to provide a cushion (equal to the initial margin), which can be applied to prevent any other member from being put at a disadvantage if a particular member does not meet its margin calls, and has its position closed out by the Exchange.

Both Metal Exchanges have somewhat similar regulations regarding the size of their initial margin payments and variation margins, and both require a payment of 200,000 RMB to the Exchange's Guarantee Fund. The main distinction of note is that Shenzhen requires a cash payment, while Shanghai accepts Letters of Credit.

The most important discretionary item in these two categories of payment is the size of the initial margin. At normal times, a 5 percent deposit should be more than ample to cover one day's price movement; but there are occasions when market prices can become very volatile, and the Exchanges reserve the right to make adjustments to the size of this deposit. Under ideal circumstances, changes in the size of the margins, and special margin requirements for "spreads" between two different forward contracts (which were highlighted in our earlier discussion of the obstacle that current margin requirements pose to the use of the Exchanges for financing and hedging inventories), are issues that should be resolved in regular contacts between the Exchange's Management Committee and the proposed Commodities and Futures Management Commission (CFMC).

A third form of payment is made into what is commonly known as a Fidelity Fund. This differs from the Guarantee Fund and from margin payments in one crucial respect. The other two payments apply solely to payments between members of the Exchange. Thus, the margin calls and the Guarantee Fund are intended to reassure members that other members' debts to them will be paid in full when a forward trading position is settled. Yet, many members of Exchanges act as brokers for non-members. An active broker may be at one and the same time both a large buyer of contracts for some clients, and a large seller for other clients. In terms of the broker's commitments, such as margin calls, the quantities that are relevant are <u>not</u> the total <u>gross</u> numbers of contracts bought and sold by members, but are the <u>net</u> numbers, after the buying orders are set against the selling orders.

The significance of this distinction between gross and net positions is that it means that individual clients of brokers do not necessarily receive any protection against a default by the broker. The interests of other members of the Exchange will be protected, but the Exchange's procedures do not provide an unequivocal guarantee against possible default by an individual member in its dealings with brokerage clients (other than the requirement that member companies demonstrate that they have considerable financial backing before they are allowed to join). To avoid this risk, many Exchanges have established a Fidelity Fund, which accumulates reserves to insure the clients of individual brokers against precisely this eventuality.

A major omission from all of China's current Committee Exchanges is a Fidelity Fund, to protect outside users of the Exchange from possible default by their brokers. The creation of such Funds should, therefore, be given priority by the Department of the CFMC that is responsible for the Regulation of Futures Brokerage Companies.

A Framework of Regulation for Commodity Markets in China and Other Countries

A first observation on all the new commodities and futures exchanges which have recently opened in China is that the speed with which these agencies have been opened has been far ahead of the national government's ability to lay down clear rules for the operations of such exchanges. Consequently (and as illustrated by the preceding examples) there is a disturbing absence of uniformity in the regulation and supervision of exchanges. Without a nationwide legal and regulatory framework, different exchanges are operating under quite different forms of regulatory control, depending upon which precise group of provincial and municipal governments or bureaus has been active in establishing the individual exchanges.

This does not imply that there are no regulatory policies. On the contrary, most Exchanges appear to have two or three levels of regulatory supervision, but the selection of institutions for the membership of the various regulatory bodies is different in every case. Typically, the top level of regulatory supervision - usually known as the Management Committee - comprises representatives of the provincial and national government agencies actively involved in the establishment of the Exchange in question, as well as representatives from those government agencies, such as the State Administration for Industry and Commerce, which have a broad responsibility for the control of trading activity.

Although there have been no scandals involving the operation of any of the major Chinese Commodity Exchanges (though some of the small local trading centers have fallen victim to problems of contract defaults), the dangers of the current approach are self-evident. In the absence of a single specialized agency which can monitor all commodity forward and futures trading, the expertise needed to supervise complex trading systems is not developed properly. Further, with the present membership of the Management Committees of each Exchange, there must be a risk that Ministries and provincial governments which have invested in the development of an Exchange will face a conflict of interest when applying controls over commodity trading.

There is a fine line to be drawn between permitting an excessively lax approach to issues, such as the supervision of the market power of individual participants (in order to monitor whether that are acquiring an unhealthily large share of the contracts - the so-called "open interest" - in a particular forward month, with the consequent risk that they may try to "squeeze" the market in an artificial manner), on the one hand, and an excessively restrictive approach, which may obstruct a free flow of trading on the Exchanges. It is not wise to allow different standards to be applied to different Exchanges. If just one Exchange were to founder on a failure of supervision in its early years, the damage which would be done to the entire system of Commodity Exchanges would be tremendous, and could undermine the official support for the continued operation of such markets.

Regulation of Commodities and Futures Markets: The UK and USA

All countries with large and successful Commodity Exchanges have nominated one government agency to oversee and regulate all such Exchanges. In the USA, the Commodities Futures Trading Commission (CFTC) is the agency. In the UK, it used to be the Bank of England, which is the Central Bank. However, the changes to UK financial legislation in 1986, when the Financial Services Act took effect in advance of the "Big Bang" liberalization of British financial markets, led to the removal of the Bank of England's regulatory control over the British commodity markets. Initially, the Department of Trade and Industry assumed the major role in regulating these markets, with the Treasury in a minor role, but in 1992, the main responsibility for the supervision of commodity exchanges was transferred to the Treasury, under the ultimate control of the Financial Permanent Secretary.

The contrast between the system in the US, where a single Federal agency, the CFTC, oversees the commodity markets, and the UK system is far-ranging, and highlights the scope for quite different philosophies of regulation. In essence, the US method of supervision is straightforward and unambiguous; the CFTC maintains a close eye on virtually all aspects of trading, ranging from daily analysis of open interest (which is divided into categories such as "Trade Long Hedging" and "Speculative Short Trading") to occasional detailed reviews of the computer records of second-by-second trading during a market session, in order to determine whether floor traders and brokers are executing customers' orders fairly. Thus, the CFTC covers the entire gamut of commodity market trading from the actual behavior of traders on the trading floor to the actions of financial intermediaries, such as brokers.

Until the 1986 Act, the UK method of regulation was much less formalized. The Bank of England had monitored the actions of the commodity exchanges and of commodity traders, largely as a legacy of the foreign exchange control powers held by the Bank. Ultimately, the Bank had extreme draconian powers to implement its decisions on aspects of commodity trading, but these powers were not intended to be invoked, other than as a means of ensuring that the committees in charge of Britain's commodity markets took full notice of the "quiet words" that the Bank of England's officers might have with them when certain aspects of commodity trading caused concern among the regulators.

The situation was transformed after 1986. The Financial Services Act was designed to emphasize the self-regulation of every segment of the financial services sector. Different financial service companies were allocated to specific "authorizing bodies", the so-called Self-Regulating Organizations (SROs), which are owned and operated by the companies under the regulatory control of the these same bodies. For example, the Securities and Futures Authority (SFA) is responsible for ensuring that customers and investors are protected in their trading on the Stock Exchange and in a wide variety of derivatives. All brokers who do business on the British commodity exchanges have to be registered with the SFA, which has very strong powers to discipline members. Other SROs cover sectors such as life insurance (under LAUTRO) or financial service companies dealing directly with the general public (under FIMBRA).

All of the SROs report to the Securities and Investment Board (SIB), which in turn is directly answerable to the UK Treasury. Because commodity exchanges are in a rather special legal position, since they exist to provide services and facilities for their members, and do not act as brokers or traders in their own right, they do not fit neatly into one of the SROs, and therefore, they report directly to the SIB, which monitors their activities. However, at its heart, the system retains the key feature of the former method of regulation undertaken by the Bank of England, in that it is intended that the ultimate sanction of intervention by the SIB will not be required. Instead, the emphasis remains strongly upon self-regulation by the exchanges.

Regardless of the precise institution nominated to oversee commodity markets, the agencies such as the CFTC in the US or the SIB in the UK have to develop the skills needed to ensure that three different aspects of commodity trading are undertaken in a proper way. They ensure that the regulations under which the Exchanges operate are appropriate, including aspects such as the size of initial margins and of Guarantee Funds; they have the power to monitor the daily variations in the positions of each member of the Exchanges (the number of contracts bought and sold by each individual member of the Exchanges in each forward month, so as to prevent undue influence being exercised by a single member); and they also have the power to oversee the details of trading that occurs second-by-second on the Exchanges, in order to prevent members cheating their customers (for example, by making several sales of a particular forward contract at different prices for different clients on the same trading day, and then allocating to preferred clients the sales that were made at the highest price, and to least favored clients the sales that were made at the lowest prices).

These skills are potentially very complex, especially the monitoring of computer records of second-by-second trading. Therefore, it makes good economic, as well as regulatory sense for one single body to be given this power.

Sources: Background Papers.

Confronted with a lack of uniform methods of regulation in the securities market, the government has created a National Securities Administration Committee to monitor and regulate stock trading. A similar body, the China Securities Supervision and Administration Committee, has recently been set up to administer and supervise futures trading. 'Interim Regulations on the Registration and Management of Futures Brokerage Companies' were announced by the State Administrative Bureau for Industry and Commerce (SAIC) in April 1993.[29] It was also announced, in June 1993, that regulations governing trading on the exchanges would soon be issued.[30] The newly-established Ministry of Internal Trade expressed its expectation, in mid-1994, that a new 'Outline Plan for Commodities Markets' would be released later in the year.

The creation of the China Securities Supervision and Administration Committee was overdue. It would have been much better to have had it in place before the proliferation of Exchanges got under way. It should now, as a matter of urgency, ensure that all of the existing Exchanges adapt their regulations to implement good regulatory practice and apply brakes to the creation of new Exchanges, in order to limit the numbers in existence and prevent unviable ones from being established. In the case of the two Metals Exchanges, it appears that these represent a good basis for operating in the absence of a single national administration; but the situation would be improved by the establishment of such a Committee.

F. Future Prospects for China's Commodity Exchanges

The Pressures for the Rationalization of the Number of Chinese Commodity Exchanges

There is no evidence from any other country in the world that China will, in the long run, require anywhere near as many exchanges as have been established since 1990. It is certain that, as the Chinese domestic economy continues with the liberalization of markets, most of these exchanges will become redundant in terms of meeting either regional or national needs. There are two main pressures that will hasten the process of reducing the number of exchanges.

First, the improvement in communications within China, both in the standard of the telecommunications links between different regions of the country and of the physical distribution of commodities within China, will reduce the differences in prices between different regions, and will make it easier for traders in one center to have immediate telephone contact with their counterparts elsewhere. As a result, a single exchange will be able to serve institutions in many parts of China without forcing the participants to suffer any appreciable loss in their ability to protect themselves against adverse price movements.

---

[29]   Xinhua news agency domestic service, 28th April 1993. The regulations contain 17 articles providing specific stipulations on the establishment, behavior and registration of futures brokerage companies. The SAIC is entrusted with their interpretation.

[30]   *China News Digest*, June 10, 1993.

The second force tending to reduce the need for a large number of exchanges in China is that, with price and foreign trade liberalization, Chinese domestic commodity prices will move increasingly closely in parallel with world prices. In the absence of barriers (such as import licenses) to the importation of products, and in the absence of distortions in the exchange rate for RMB Yuan, the Chinese local price for imported products should equal the f.o.b. price of imports plus freight costs plus Chinese import tariffs. Provided the levels of tariffs and freight rates are stable, prospective users of futures markets in China will be able to hedge their price risk on imported commodities in overseas markets just as easily as they can in domestic markets. However, exchanges catering for worldwide customers have the special attraction that they are usually more active and offer more competitive prices than markets catering only for Chinese customers. Eventually, many domestic exchanges will lose trading volume to those markets that serve a global audience.

The combined impact of these two forces leading to a reduction in the attractions of local commodity exchanges to domestic participants is demonstrated by the results of empirical analysis which illustrates the correlation between the number of viable futures markets that trade major commodities and the value of world trade in these commodities.[31] Even a commodity as important as copper appears to have only sufficient world trade volume to be able to support two viable and thriving futures markets serving international customers. This implies that if one of the new Chinese exchanges is to succeed in establishing itself as an economically viable institution in the global free market trading of copper, it will have to supplant one of the two existing major exchanges in London or New York. This will not be easy.

The Likely Development of Trading on the Exchanges

The most important feature of the development of both Metal Exchanges over the next year or so will be the further expansion of turnover and an associated improvement in the liquidity of trading, making it easier for buyers and sellers to have an immediate response to their buy/sell orders. An essential element in the increases in turnover will be the development of means for the prompt dissemination of price trends within a trading session to interested potential customers located away from the Exchange premises.

Once such information is available immediately, so that outsiders can follow the trading that occurs during the course of the session, it is to be expected that, as the hectic activity on the country's two Stock Exchanges illustrates, there will be much larger demand from institutions such as financial institutions and money management funds (most of which are operated from Hong Kong or Taiwan), which already use the Metal Exchanges to some extent. Even now, weekly brokerage commissions of over one million RMB per month have been reported by one of the largest brokerage companies on the Shanghai Metal Exchange; but once the full potential for outside trading interest is tapped, the value of these commissions is likely to rise many times over.

There is no doubt whatever that, hand-in-hand with the expansion in trading volumes, it will be only a short while before both Exchanges evolve towards conventional futures markets. At present, there is only one futures contract that is traded (without very much success); the aluminum futures contract on the Shenzhen Metals Exchange. Instead, both Exchanges are acting as forward markets, but it is very significant that they are forward markets in which already the vast majority of turnover consists of the trading of forward contracts between traders. In view of the degree of

---

[31] Landell Mills (1993), Annex 3: An Evaluation of the 'Critical Mass' in Futures Contracts.

standardization that has already occurred in the contracts that are actually being traded, it will be comparatively simple to make the transition to futures contracts specifying certain acceptable brands for delivery and just one or two permitted delivery locations. Such a transition would not constitute a great imposition upon users of the two markets, since they have already accepted the same restrictions for most of the trading that they undertake at present.

The question that arises at this point is why the sole futures contract that is currently available on the two Exchanges - namely, the aluminum futures contract in Shenzhen - has fared so poorly. The answer lies in the limited liquidity of the market. At present, forward contracts are attracting sufficient trading volume for users to be happy to continue to concentrate their trading volumes in these forward contracts, in the knowledge that it is relatively straightforward to resell, or buy back, these contracts when the time comes to do so. By contrast, the Shenzhen aluminum futures contract continues to languish with a very low trading volume, which does nothing to attract prospective users of the contract, who may fear that they may find it difficult to extricate themselves from a futures position when they want to do so. In effect, given the choice between a successful forward contract and an illiquid futures contract, they have opted for success and liquidity. There is not sufficient and distinct volume of forward and futures trading to generate a large volume of turnover in both kinds of contract.

Nevertheless, the expectation must be that the two Exchanges will soon move to a futures-dominated trading structure, and that, at that time, forward trading will rapidly decline in importance. This is because futures trading is technically much simpler than forward trading. Instead of having a large number of different details (of brands and of delivery points) confronting users of the computer screens, and creating artificial barriers to a smooth flow of trading when volume is heavy, it will be much easier to have all bids and offers expressed in terms of standard contract terms.

The timing of the switch-over from an emphasis upon forward trading to an emphasis upon futures trading is likely to be determined principally by these practical considerations. Once the Exchange authorities decide that their existing computer systems are at the limits of their capacities, and once members decide that they are no longer willing to work with a sluggish computer network, which has to display long lists of bids and offers, differing only in small degrees from one another in terms of brands and locations of delivery, then there will be strong support for the launching of futures contracts, which will offer much simpler methods of trading. Other changes that will materialize more slowly are likely to include the gradual emergence of a group of market makers, who will provide a strong boost to liquidity within the course of individual trading sessions. As our earlier remarks imply, however, the emergence of this group is likely to be faster if open outcry methods of trading are adopted.

Another change that must be anticipated within a matter of a few years, at most, is the creation of foreign exchange futures markets, which will, at a stroke, eliminate the basis for a great deal of current trading volume on both Metal Exchanges. In order to survive the traumas that this could cause, the Exchanges will have little choice but to facilitate the use of their contracts for the regular needs of the physical buyers and sellers of metals. Already the Exchanges provide a valuable service for standard hedging purposes. The avenue in which new initiatives are most urgently needed is in the use of the Exchange as a means of financing inventories. The current set of registered warehouses for each Exchange provides a valuable basis for the encouragement of this more sophisticated use of Metal Exchanges, but the Exchanges themselves can hasten this trend by reducing the margin requirements for "spreads" between two futures positions, so as to reduce the current excessive imbalance in the trade-offs between risk and margin requirements when contrasting a single futures purchase or sale with a spread. The earlier example revealed that, as against a margin-to-price ratio of only 5 percent for a straightforward purchase or sale of a forward contract, the ratio of the margin to the value of the spread can easily reach several hundred per cent.

A further change that can be expected is that both exchanges will eventually decide to drop their unsuccessful contracts. Shenzhen currently trades eight metals, while Shanghai trades seven; yet, in practice, only two metals dominate their trading: copper and aluminum. Once a contract has attracted a bad reputation for low turnover, it is almost impossible to revive it.

The final change which could be hastened by the proposed new CFMC is a rationalization in the physical facilities provided by the various Exchanges which have been created in China. Each of these Exchanges makes substantial investments in their own offices, trading floors, computer systems, and back-up administrative and financial infrastructure. These are all respects in which there is great scope for reducing costs by bringing different Exchanges under one roof. This does not imply the demise of the individual Exchanges: in New York, Chicago and London, it is common to find quite different markets and independent Exchanges trading alongside one another, without in any way losing their independence. It is to be hoped, for example, that the five different Exchanges shortly to be in operation in Shanghai, covering Metals, Coal, Petroleum, Agricultural Inputs, and Grains and Vegetable Oils, can be persuaded to share their facilities, to mutual benefit.

G. Implications for Government Action

It is clear that China today has moved remarkably rapidly towards the adoption of some of the most sophisticated forms of market of an advanced market economy. Due to the limited evolutionary experience with these marketing systems, there are many areas of the operation and economic consequences of such markets which today are not fully understood. The differential speed of change, in different areas of the economy, with only partial reform in price or quantity control mechanisms in other areas of the economy, also has implications for the nature of trade in these markets.

Details of potential problem areas, and measures that may be taken to address them, are presented in the preceding sections. Some of the key points which emerge, for the attention of policy makers, may however be summarized here. First, caution should be exercised in the setting up of additional such exchanges. It must be recognized that today a substantial part of trade on some of these markets is speculative in origin, and in part is a proxy for trade in less freely tradable goods, notably foreign exchange, and also that many of these exchanges are likely to die out, as China grows better integrated with world markets.

Second, and related to the preceding point, if exchanges function effectively, controls on price or quantity (subsidies or quotas) assoicated with the traded products, for example, freight or storage, are undesirable. First, differential application to different individuals (as in freight quotas, or as in storage subsidies for SOEs) will be arbitraged through the exchanges, and second, some of the real advantages of forward trading, (such as trading forward in lieu of paying warehousing costs) are obscured.

Third, given the existence of a number of exchanges today, efforts should be made to adapt their trading systems to increase efficiency, reduce information requirements and reduce expenses, as the number of traders grows. Apart from a reexamination of the present screen-based trading system, this also calls for an evaluation of the possibilities of combining the facilities of different exchanges in a single location, to reduce overheads.

Fourth, the overall framework of regulation on the exchanges has to be developed, and the present differences in systems in different locations, or for different products, should be ironed out. The role of the supervisory agency (or agencies) will have to be defined, and adapted to other areas of economic policy. Finally, a large part of this common framework of regulations must also include safeguarding the interests of users, through the introduction of a Fidelity Fund. The need for reductions in the cost of trading (for example through adjustments in margin deposit rates, an increase in the flexibility with which these rates are determined, and reductions in commission fees) should also be investigated.

Annex IV.1 Commodity Market Trading - A Zero Sum Game

Trade on commodity futures markets occurs for two main reasons: either to speculate, or to avoid speculation (by hedge-selling or hedge-buying). Although these reasons are the exact opposites of one another, both groups of participants find great value in the operations of futures markets. However, the ways in which these three groups use futures markets are quite different from one another. Hedge-sellers of futures are consistent sellers of more distant futures contracts and are then, subsequently, purchasers of these same contracts when they approach their expiry dates. Hedge-buyers are undertaken exactly the opposite form of transaction. They are consistent buyers of distant futures contracts and, later on, sell back these contracts when they approach their expiry dates. Speculators can be either buyers or sellers of any particular futures contract, according to whether they believe that prices are more likely to rise or fall.

In theory, it is possible that the activities of hedge-sellers and hedge-buyers could exactly balance one another, so that hedge-sellers were wanting to sell a particular futures contract at precisely the same time that a hedge-buyer wanted to buy that contract. In practice, it is highly unlikely that the two operations will be so perfectly synchronised. Speculators play a vital role in providing the volume of trading, sometimes on one side, and at other times on the other, which ensures that every hedge-seller or hedge-buyer can find someone to take the other side of their transactions, whenever they want to hedge-sell or hedge-buy futures.

Since for every buyer there is a seller, it follows that, on balance, all trading in futures markets is a true *zero-sum game*. All of the profits that are made by certain participants are exactly counter-balanced by the losses made by the other participants. This is explained briefly below. First, looking at contracts purchased over a certain period of time, t_1, suppose altogether n lots of copper futures contracts are bought at prices of $p_1 t_1$, ..., $p_n t_1$. These same n lots are subsequently sold, at prices of $q_1 t_2$, ..., $q_n t_2$. Then the profits (or losses) on these purchases and subsequent sales are given by

$$\Pi p = \sum_{i=1}^{n} p_i t_1 - \sum_{i=1}^{n} q_i t_2, \qquad p = 1, 2, \ldots, n; \quad q = 1, 2, \ldots, n ,$$

$$\ldots (1)$$

Next, we look at contracts sold. When the original futures contracts were bought, there were people on the other side of the market who had sold these same contracts at these same prices, $q_1 t_1$, ..., $q_n t_1$. These same people will eventually buy back their contracts. The company which sold the first contract at the price of $p_1 t_1$ will not necessarily be the company which buys it back at a price of $q_1 t_2$, but it will buy it back at a price of $q_j t_2$, where j lies in the range 1,...,n. To each of the original sellers of futures at specific prices p_i there will be its own value, q_j, of the price at which it buys back these futures. Therefore, the profits (or losses) on these contact sales and subsequent purchases are

$$\Pi q = \sum_{i=1}^{n} q_i t_1 - \sum_{i=1}^{n} p_i t_2, \qquad p = 1, 2, \ldots, n; \quad q = 1, 2, \ldots, n ,$$

$$\ldots (2)$$

Adding together the two sides of the market, one can calculate the overall combined profits or losses that are made from futures trading. These equal:

$$\Pi p + \Pi q = \sum_{i=1}^{n} p_i t_1 - \sum_{i=1}^{n} q_i t_2 + \sum_{i=1}^{n} q_i t_1 - \sum_{i=1}^{n} p_i t_2 , \qquad \ldots (3)$$

But since the contracts purchased in period 1 matched the contracts sold in period 1, $\sum_{i=1}^{n} p_i t_1 = \sum_{i=1}^{n} q_i t_1$. And similarly, since contracts sold in period 2 match contracts purchased in period 2, $\sum_{i=1}^{n} q_i t_2 = \sum_{i=1}^{n} p_i t_2$. Thus the profits on one side are exactly offset by the losses on the other side, and $\Pi p + \Pi q = 0$. This demonstrates that futures trading is a zero-sum game. Over any period, all of those people who make profits from futures trading are only able to do so because all other market participants are suffering losses on futures trading, where these losses are exactly equal to the profits made by the first group.

5

Market Regulation

A. Regulation in a Market Economy

As the previous chapters have demonstrated, China's move from a command economy towards an economy regulated by a system of markets requires not only the dismantling of procedures of control, but their replacement by new instruments which ensure and safeguard the functioning of the market. This necessitates a new framework of regulation, and the previous chapters have already discussed the need for new regulation, or the modification of present regulations, in the areas of pricing, internal trade, distribution, and the creation of new forms of markets. The central theme linking these separate areas of regulation together is the creation of a competitive market environment, to enable enterprises of production or distribution to make the correct allocative decisions, based on accurate market signals. The creation of a competitive market has many aspects, and these include the existence of a large number of buyers and sellers, free entry and exit of producers or distributors, trade in goods and factors without physical or tariff barriers, and independent price setting decisions by all producers. From a theoretical standpoint, 'perfect' competition also has requirements such as constant returns to scale in production or full information, which are rarely obtained even in functioning market economies. The aim should however be to at least steer the economy towards a situation of greater rather than lesser competition.

Translated to regulation, this requires the creation of a range of instruments, required to ensure competitive behavior, which may affect the number of economic agents, or the behavior of these agents, in terms of 'fair' competitive practices, freedom of entry to the market for new firms, and ease of exit or dissolution, in addition to issues pointed out in earlier chapters, such as the mobility of goods and factors, and flexibility of prices. There is a range of regulatory instruments which safeguard the market in these areas, which include laws on the number of agents and freedom of entry, such as licensing and regulatory procedures, laws on competitive behavior, such as regulations on monopolies, or on restrictive or unfair trade practices, or laws to maintain or safeguard competition, and laws on exit, such as bankruptcy law. Other regulations also safeguard or uphold the operation of enterprises in a market economy; the system of contract law and contract enforcement, safeguards to producers (such as patent or copyright) and safeguards to consumers (such as trademark or advertizing rules, or consumer protection laws).

In China today, some pieces of this canvas of regulations exist already in some form, and recent modifications to adapt these to the framework of a market economy have been introduced in many cases. In other areas, there was virtually no regulation until recently, and the process of creating this *ab initio* is now under consideration. An initiative to accelerate the pace of economic legislation was launched in early 1993, by agreeing on a blueprint for the development of a legal framework for the market economy, to be implemented over the next five years. The plan is being formulated by the Standing Committee of the National People's Congress, along with the Bureau of Legislative Affairs and the State Commission for the Restructuring of the Economic System. The legislative plan of the State Council for 1993 alone includes 89 elements, of which 12 are laws and 72 are administrative statutes.[1] These include (1) standardizing and maintaining market economic order (through laws on competition, contract, consumer protection, insurance, domestic trade and market regulation for commodities, securities and futures markets); (2) laws for macroeconomic control and regulation (such as laws on the budget, taxation, and central banking); (3) social security law (labor law, unemployment insurance); (4) laws to aid the process of opening up the economy to the outside world (laws on foreign trade, on foreign banks and other financial institutions, arrangements for foreign enterprises oil exploration); and (5) laws for improving administrative organizations (such as regulations on civil servants).[2]

There are some features of the Chinese economy which are unique, even if compared to other transitional economies, or even other market economies, and it is essential to take this into account when preparing the legislation to be introduced in these areas. The following sections selectively discuss some major areas concerning the creation of a competitive market in China, where there are issues of special interest to China, and from an economic viewpoint. The current state of legislation in other areas affecting competition has recently been reviewed elsewhere, and as far as possible, duplication of issues has been avoided here.[3]

B. Competition and a Competitive Environment

Appropriately designed competition laws can play an important role, complementary to liberal trade policies, in *maintaining* well-functioning, competitive markets. In addition, such laws also can be instrumental in *creating* more competitive markets, through their impact on the existing and future structure of markets, and on the behavior of market participants. The drafting and widespread dissemination of detailed and transparent guidelines can help to accelerate the otherwise protracted development of specific rules through precedent and would provide both consumers and producers increased certainty regarding the rules themselves, and the mechanisms by which they will be enforced.

In formulating rules for competition, the economic environment in which these rules are to be applied is of critical importance. In many centrally planned economies undertaking a move towards free market systems, there are pervasive problems of monopoly, due to the typically large size of firms set up under the planning period. The breakup of these large enterprises, or the introduction of safeguards against the exercise of monopoly power stemming from high concentration ratios and the presence of 'dominant firms' then become important issues in the formulation of new economic regulations.

---

[1]   The program is described in a press release of the State Council's Legislative Affairs Bureau, of 18 May 1993. The text of the release is available in *Summary of World Broadcasts*, May 22, 1993.

[2]   BBC, *Survey of World Broadcasts*, 22 May 1993.

[3]   An overview of the legal framework confronting enterprises in China today, which spans a broad spectrum of issues, is available in Lichtenstein (1993).

In China, as the first chapter points out, the industrial structure today is far from concentrated, in a sectoral or spatial sense. The following sections provide further evidence on market structure in China today, looking at sectoral concentration, and also discuss its likely future evolution. In view of this evidence, it appears that while there is indeed a need for market regulation to safeguard competition, the emphasis may have to lie on market conduct, rather than market structure related issues.

Market Structure: Firm Size and Industrial Concentration

In contrast to countries of the former Soviet Union, where specialization took place at the countrywide level and often resulted in single monopoly enterprises producing specific goods, specialization in China historically has taken place at the provincial or even local level. The emphasis on local self-sufficiency in the Maoist era led to a duplication of industrial pattern by province, a pattern that was reinforced by the decentralization of investment decisions to the provincial level in the early 1980s. Looking first at anecdotal examples, a large part of the Chinese automotive sector is characterized by fragmentation and small scale, with 2531 enterprises producing motor vehicles or related parts and components, with an average employment of only 620 employees. Shanghai Volkswagen, arguably the most important producer of passenger cars in China, produced about 17,000 Volkswagen Santana cars in 1990, and there are over 110 producers with less than 10,000 units. In contrast, the new Saturn division of General Motors of the US is designed to produce at least 200,000 cars a year.[4] A very diversified number of enterprises also characterizes the machine tool sector, with every province in China (except for Tibet) manufacturing machine tools. While the top 5 machine tool enterprises in Japan account for 42 percent of national production share and 69 percent in the USA, the corresponding figure for China is 20 percent.[5]

Data on industrial size distribution (Appendix Tables A5.1a to A5.3c) provides a more comprehensive source of information on industrial concentration. Aggregates for all sectors of industry are given in the summary Table 5.1 below. Details for individual subsectors are available in the appendix tables. First, classifying firm size in terms of number of persons employed, the number of firms, the numbers of persons employed and the value of output is measured, in each size category. Next, an alternative measure of firm size is used; classification by value of output, at current 1991 prices. The same three measures of concentration are undertaken.

---

[4] World Bank (1991) (Automotive Sector Report). However, there are also some large automobile enterprises and enterprise groups in China, such as Second Auto Works.

[5] Strong efforts at restructuring the sector in terms of mergers, alliances, joint production and marketing arrangements have been recommended for China to compete effectively in international markets. World Bank (1992) Report No 10688 (Machine Tool Sector).

Table 5.1 Size Distribution of Industry by Alternative Indices (1991)

I. Firms Classified by Numbers of Employees:	Total	Above 3000	1000-3000	100-1000	Below 100
1a. Number of Firms (%)	100.0	0.5	2.2	30.4	66.8
1b. Numbers of Persons Employed (%)	100.0	23.9	18.5	45.1	12.5
1c. Output Value (%)	100.0	28.4	21.8	40.4	9.4
II. Firms Classified by Value of Industrial Output:	Total	Above Y30m	Y10m-Y30m	Y1m-Y10m	Below Y1m
2a. Number of Firms (%)	100.0	2.7	5.8	31.9	59.5
2b. Number of Persons Employed (%)	100.0	36.0	18.5	32.4	13.1
2c. Output Value (%)	100.0	58.5	18.3	19.6	3.6

Note: Data in the table are of independent accounting enterprises at and above the township level.
Source: Appendix Tables A5.1a to A5.2c.

As the table shows, using any measures of size, the number of firms in the large size categories is very small, 0.5 percent in terms of number of employees and 2.7 percent in terms of output value.[6] Although the large firms are important in terms of the proportion of persons they employ (around a quarter, on the first measure, or 36 percent, in terms of the second), firms in the medium categories dominate in all measures. Looking at the firms with over a hundred but below 3,000 employees, they account for three quarters of total employment and over 60 percent of total output value. If classified by output value, firms with a turnover of over Y1m but below Y30m account for around half total employment and around two fifths of total output value. Looking at disaggregated figures, there are indeed sectoral size differences, with a relatively larger concentration of large firms in industries such as ferrous metals, chemical fibers and tobacco processing and lower ratios in food, clothing and construction materials.

More evidence on industrial concentration is provided in Table 5.2, in which regional concentration indices are estimated, in terms of the share of the leading province, and the leading four provinces, in the value of output, by sector. The data are ranked in descending order of concentration.

As the data show, for all industries except railway coaches and power generating equipment, the share of the leading province is typically below a third of total output. In most cases, even the top four provinces account for less than two thirds of total output. Taking the evidence from all sources together, it suggests that concentration, in the sense of size or geography does not appear to have been a serious issue in China so far.[7] However, industrial structures evolve, and the question of the extent to which this may alter over time, in view of the process of economic reform, should also be examined. Apart from the natural growth of existing firms, there are two processes which could accelerate industrial concentration; the growth of firms by merger and acquisition, and the growth of associations between firms, in the form of enterprise groups. Both these processes have gained momentum

---

[6] Since the sample of firms includes only those with the relatively new independent accounting system, it is likely that a large number of very small firms are omitted already.

[7] These results are however preliminary and more detailed analyses are required, as well as more 'yardsticks' from other countries to evaluate the implications of the findings.

in China over the last few years. The following sections evaluate, on the basis of qualitative evidence, the possible implications of these tendencies for industrial concentration.

Table 5.2 Industrial Concentration Ratios for Selected Industries
(1986, 1987)

Product	Share of Commodity Output Value		Leading Producer
	Top Province	Top 4 Provinces	
Railway coaches	57	100	Hebei
Railway freight wagons	38	82	Heilongjiang
Motor Vehicles	24	62	Liaoning
Transformers	22	49	Hebei
Electric wire	22	53	Tianjin
Washing machine	16	55	Shanghai
Sulfuric acid	9	34	Liaoning
Ammonia	9	33	Hebei
Insecticide	25	57	Tianjin
Silicon	12	29	Hebei
Cotton cloth	15	41	Jiangsu
Bicycles	16	50	Tianjin
Sewing machines	33	66	Shanghai
Power generating equipment	45	70	Anhui
Machine tools	17	50	Zhejiang
Large/medium tractors	28	84	Shanghai

Sources: Data for the first eleven products ('Railway coaches' to 'Cotton cloth') are taken from 'China's Large and Medium - Scale Industrial Enterprises', Summary Volume, 1989. Data for the last five products ('Bicycles' to 'Large/medium tractors') are from the China Statistical Yearbook. Calculations are presented in Rawski (1993).

Potential Changes in Market Structure: Mergers

Enterprise mergers were initially exclusively government-initiated. In February 1989, guidelines on mergers were issued which applied to the mergers of enterprises through purchase, including the principles of mergers, the identification of merged enterprises, the forms and procedures for undertaking mergers, the ownership of assets and their valuation, and issues concerning taxation and employment.[8] Among the stated principles of this document are provisions that mergers must promote economic benefits, prevent monopoly and promote competition. The document was addressed directly to provincial authorities in charge of economic reform, and in response, local governments began to take increasing interest in mergers and by the end of 1989, 17 separate regional authorities (provinces, autonomous regions, municipalities and cities with independent planning powers) had specific provisions

---

[8] February 19, 1989, by the State Commission for the Restructuring of the Economic System, the State Planning Commission, the Ministry of Finance and the State Assets Administration.

for the merger of enterprises, each with their own preferential policies.[9] The increasing number of mergers led to the organization of specific enterprise property rights markets to promote enterprise mergers. Twenty five such markets were established by the end of 1989.[10] Gradually, the process of voluntary merger, or mergers initiated by the concerned enterprises, was also accepted.

In 1992, the policy of voluntary mergers was formalized in the 'Regulations on Transforming the Management Mechanisms of State-Owned Industrial Enterprises', where the right of enterprises to merge operations with other units was explicitly recognized.[11] The approval of a merger may be witheld if the authorizing government department considers the merger to violate state laws and prevent competition. Merging enterprises must comply with registration regulations, to indicate their change in status.[12] Some limited experimentation in these procedures is taking place. In Shanghai, for example, line bureau approval has been required only from the supervisory authorities of the larger party since the beginning of 1993.

In practice, enterprise mergers to date appear to have been used mainly as a government-driven vehicle to rehabilitate loss-making enterprises. There are comparatively fewer cases of voluntary, market-driven mergers to achieve economic efficiencies or increase market power. It is also less common for enterprises of different regions and different sectors to annex or be annexed, because the relations between different supervisory departments become more complicated and the coordinating work more difficult. In 1989, the number of enterprises that merged with enterprises of other provinces dropped relative to earlier years (in part in response to efforts by localities to promote intra-regional mergers). The number of mergers or takeovers of enterprises of different areas within the same province was also low, at 84, and a decline relative to 131 in 1988. These represented barely 3.5 percent of all merged

---

[9]   For example, the city of Chengdu released a document in 1988 allowing debt-ridden enterprises that merge with another enterprise to keep enjoying all former subsidies. The newly formed company is exempted from income tax for a certain period of time and enjoys a reduction and exemption of other taxes and overdue fines according to its financial condition. Banks are prevented from classifying the annexed enterprise as part of the annexing enterprise so that the latter can continue to raise loans. Cited in 'New Progress Made in Enterprise Mergers During Economic Rectification', in Gao Shangquan and Ye Sen (eds)(1990) pp. 54-61.

[10] These local property rights markets provide a common location for sharing information (where potential annexing and annexed enterprises can be informed about possible partners) and for coordinating merger-related activities (where representatives of government departments and organizations can discuss feasibility studies, asset evaluation, liabilities liquidation, personnel placement and other registration procedures). The development of these markets was reported to have been promoted by the State Administration of Industry and Commerce (SAIC).

[11] The 'New Operating Mechanisms' for state enterprises, of July 23, 1992. The regulations define the sphere of enterprise autonomy, though the rights are not absolute.

[12] Discussed in greater detail in section C below. Approval by the original supervisory authorities of both parties and 'other relevant documents and certificates' are required before any merger can take place (including government departments in charge of land, real estate, tax, labor, banking, and the State Property Management Agency).

enterprises within China in 1989. Mergers or takeovers across different industries are also low. In 1989, only 697 enterprises merged with partners in other industries, or roughly 27 percent of the total.[13]

Although the aggregate number of mergers has declined, the number of voluntary mergers, cross-industry (vertical and conglomerate) mergers and cross-regional mergers appears to have increased somewhat since 1989. However a number of obstacles still appear to constrain efficiency-enhancing mergers. There are separate fees for the transfer of land, the transfer of buildings, notarial fees, and auditing fees. These are burdensome payments. There is also insufficient local audit capability to value the assets of firms to be merged, especially the value of intangible assets. Perhaps most important, government officials still have discretion to determine which enterprises should merge, and this discretion is often exercised for non-commercial objectives. Even if approval for voluntary merger is finally granted, it may take the annexing and annexed enterprises several months to get the approval of the first administrative department in some areas, a requirement which is still only the first of many. Administrative, financial and fiscal hurdles must then be several times multiplied in magnitude for cross-industry, cross-regional transactions. Only once some of the more significant of these constraints are removed does there seem to be a case for competition law which emphasizes a review of mergers, to consider the impact of future mergers on efficiency and market power.[14]

Potential Changes in Market Structure: Enterprise Groups[15]

Origins and Growth

Another question which can be raised about potential changes in the competitive structure in Chinese industry concerns the emergence, over the past decade, of a large number of 'enterprise groups'. Do these new structures signify an increase in concentration? An answer to this first requires an understanding of nature of the new enterprise groups. The stimulus for the formation of enterprise groups in China arose from different sources.[16] First, the reduction of mandatory planning lent impetus to large state enterprises to set up 'horizontal linkages' with other firms. Since the planning system had previously assured inputs required to meet planned output, new linkages were developed, with the decline of planning, as a means of creating alternative channels, or consolidating existing links, with supplying and purchasing enterprises. Such linkages were also established for efficiency-enhancing purposes, such

---

[13]   Gao Shangquan and Ye Sen (eds) (1990) pp. 54-61.

[14]   The new competition law of September 1993 does not concern itself with mergers, but the new Company Law, or Enterprise Law, of 1994, has articles which clearly provide for the process by which a merger may be approved (Articles 182-184).

[15]   This section draws on Tidrick and Chen (1987) and Wu (1990).

[16]   The sources are not necessarily mutually exclusive. Some of the early informal horizontal associations were 'encouraged' to a greater or lesser degree by government authorities.

as the better utilization of capacity, sharing of technical knowhow or trademarks, and more rarely, in the form of capital investments.[17]

Second, some enterprise groups have been initiated by ministries and local administrative authorities. Such groups include a number of administrative line bureaus, at the provincial and local levels, that have essentially changed their name from 'line bureau' to 'enterprise group' and in the process have taken control over companies that they previously supervised.[18] Third, in some cases, individual powerful enterprises, with the consent and sometimes support of local authorities, have 'taken over' other enterprises, in many cases without their full understanding or consent. A final category includes those groups that have been voluntarily organized, through nongovernmental channels. This category is the smallest nationwide, reported to include around a hundred groups by the end of 1992.

In the first phase of their establishment, which began in 1980, enterprise groups were 'horizontally associated' in relatively loose structures. From 1986, these horizontal associations were upgraded into more formal enterprise groups, and some large enterprise groups were accorded special status in the state economic plan (likened sometimes to the treatment of 'off budget' items) which allowed them direct dialogue with the central government. Today there are 55 large enterprise groups which belong to this category. Of these 55 large groups, 16 have their core activities in machine building/electronics, 7 in energy, 6 in defense, 4 each in steel, building materials, chemicals and pharmaceuticals, 3 in banking, and 2 each in forestry, transport and foreign trade. Prominent among these are the Nanjing Zhongshan Electronic Works, Great Wall Computers, and Second Auto Works. Exceptionally, the 55 large groups are permitted to establish their own financial companies. Other preferential policies granted to these groups include import/export rights, business promotion-related foreign travel rights, and rights of independent planning (unrestricted by line ministry or locality plans). With the new enterprise regulations at the end of 1988, which permitted the establishment of shareholding companies and mutual share participation, a third phase in enterprise group formation began, in which ownership participation in group enterprises could be conceived of.

---

[17] In the Chinese context, 'horizontal links' or *hengxiang lianxe* refers to links between producers which could be either upstream or downstream suppliers or buyers, or with other enterprises, in trademark or technology associations. The critical distinction is that the links cut across normal administrative barriers of jurisdiction and may be formed across regions, across supervisory bureaus and across ownership categories. 'Vertical linkages' in contrast, in the Chinese context, are between supervisory line bureaus and supervised enterprises.

[18] This transformation of administrative line bureaus into enterprise groups, motivated by self-preservation given the expectation that many line bureaus will be abolished in the course of reforms, has strong parallels with a similar transformation of 'branch ministries' into 'concerns and associations' in countries of the former Soviet Union (FSU). Members of these organizations in Russia typically 'own shares' of the concern, and portray themselves as industry associations of the type common in industrialized countries. Yet most of these national or regional concerns are almost exact replicas of the former branch ministries, and are headed by high officials of the FSU. The economic environment in which these concerns operate is critical in determining whether the concerns play a limited 'facilitating' role or whether they are perpetuating centralized planning.

Enterprise Groups in China

An Example of a Major Enterprise Group: The Aeolus Group is an example of one of the larger enterprise groups in China. Second Auto Works is the central enterprise. Of the 305 enterprises with which Second Auto Works has established relationships, five are deemed to be tightly linked to the center, although Second Auto Works does not hold any of their equity. This is because their annual output plan and contract is included in the plan for Second Auto Works, and their production, investment and financial decisions are also made by Second Auto Works. These 'tightly linked' enterprises however are separately responsible for the payment of taxes and other obligations to local governments. The remaining 300 enterprises are independent legal entities that have signed sales contracts with Second Auto Works. Of these, 36 are 'half-tightly linked', (Second Auto Works holds between 5 and 20 percent of their shares and in return receives an assurance that its input needs will be met before the enterprises sell to any other customers). Supervisory control over these enterprises is exercised by their home province line bureaus.

Benefits of Enterprise Groups - Supplier Links and Subcontracting: Groups help ensure input supplies. The Anshan Iron and Steel company formed a group with a coal mine and provided investment and management to ensure their future supply of coal. Links with suppliers of components have sometimes been established to circumvent inflexible labor or wage legislation, which makes direct hiring a liability, or to similarly circumvent constraints on labor mobility. When the Wuxi Boiler plant could not get cheap additional labor from neighboring provinces, it subcontracted plate manufacturing operations to 'associated' component suppliers. The Chongqing Clock and Watch company ships components to member companies in other provinces for assembly, which helps bridge the ties between regional markets.

Efficiency Improvements: The Wanbao Refrigerator Group expanded its annual production capacity to over 1 million by lining up over 85 firms and became the world's eighth largest refrigerator producer. One third of output is now exported, although it had not participated in the foreign market before. Many enterprise groups are reported in the textile industry (wool producers, textile mills, garment manufacturers and export marketing groups) which have helped improve the efficiency and profitability of these firms.

Links to Improve Capacity Utilization and Increase the Flexibility of Resource Allocation are exemplified by the Jaling Motor Association, originally an ordinance factory under the supervision of the Armed Forces. With cuts in the defense budget and a consequent under-utilization of capacity, Jaling formed an association with five other enterprises (two state and three collectives) and became a successful producer of light motor cycles. Another example is provided by the Shenyang Air Pressure Works company, which responded to a shortage of workshop space by moving a part of its production to 11 other member firms, which increased gross industrial output value by 25 percent.

Sharing of Trademarks and Improving Technology has occurred in enterprises which enjoy prized brand names, and are able to get royalty fees from other producers by allowing them to use these brand names. An example is the Shenyang Double Happiness Pressure Pot Plant (manufacturing pressure cookers), which has links with 19 enterprises in other provinces who use its brand name in return for a 3 percent royalty on sales. Double Happiness maintains some quality controls on the output. Mergers and technology pooling among bicycle producers (Phoenix and Flying Pigeon) have also been reported. Groups have also been used to better integrate the links between research institutes and industrial enterprises. For example, the Panda Electronic group's 134 entities include 10 universities and 4 research institutes. The combination of research and experimental production has shortened the development time for new products.

Cross-Sectoral and Regional Links: A variety of enterprise groups now have activities spread across numerous industrial subsectors and across a number of different provinces. The Jinjiang group in Shanghai, for instance, begun with 11 hotels and has diversified into an export-oriented entity which combines tourism with foreign trade, industry, commerce, science and technology, real estate and information services. The five tightly linked firms of the Aeolus Group are located in five different provinces; the 36 half-tightly linked firms are in 10 provinces and the remaining loosely-linked firms are scattered in 29 provinces.

Involuntary Groups: One example of enterprise group formation used as a mechanism for an involuntary takeover of a number of enterprises is provided by the Beijing Building Materials General Company. The company prepared a form, which was presented to a number of managers of construction materials enterprises, to sign on as group members. Over eighty enterprises signed on, but later some wanted to leave the group and found that independent legal status, voluntary participation or withdrawal were not provided for. In some cases, the central enterprise then demands some share of the profits and depreciation funds of group members. Managers are resentful of their loss of independence. In some cases it is claimed that product quality has deteriorated as a consequence. For example, a Beijing-based group of 18 companies requires all members to use its trademark. As a result of product quality variations, demand has declined and prices have fallen. Due to the group's insistence on a 4 percent annual increase in exports, goods are virtually dumped on the international market.

Sources: Tidrick and Chen (1987), Wu (1990), background papers.

Since the early 1990s, the number of enterprise groups has increased dramatically, with over a thousand 'national level' groups recorded by the end of 1991 and over 6,000 enterprise groups at all levels by the end of 1992. The most rapid development occurred in the coastal provinces, with over 47 percent of the national level groups in the regions of Guangdong, Shanghai, Jiangsu and Shandong. Over 65 percent of these groups have their core activities in electronics, light industry and textiles.

Structure and Forms of Enterprise Groups

In terms of formal definition, enterprise groups were recognized by the government in 1980, when the State Council issued a regulation explaining, probably for the first time, the basic principles and organizational issues relating to enterprise associations.[19] According to the regulation, economic associations must be based on voluntary and mutual benefits. Enterprises' associated entities could be established regardless of differences in locations, sectors, ownerships and administrative levels. In 1986, a second second fundamental regulation, on 'horizontal economic association', was issued, which, while confirming the basic principles of the 1980 regulation, promoted economic association as a reform strategy, to promote the rationalization of structure, separate administration from ownership and management, and promote the markets for capital and technology.[20] This regulation provides that large or medium enterprises producing superior products are encouraged to be the backbone of economic associations.[21] The voluntary principle is emphasized and administrations are prohibited from interfering with the formation of economic associations. The change of administrative agencies to economic associations is also prohibited.

The third, and so far latest, core piece of legisation on enterprise groups consists of the implementing principles for the regulation of 1986, issued in 1987.[22] Further definitions of enterprise groups are offered, with the group described as a multi-tier organization, with a core tier, and less closely associated tiers. According to these, enterprise groups are allowed to choose the management system suitable to their needs, but requests that the system should combine centralized and decentralized management, for different categories of issues.

Partly as a result of these regulations, many typologies of enterprise groups are in simultaneous use today. The classification adopted by the SAIC, defines 'regular enterprise groups' which are composed of a center (or 'mother') enterprise and three or more subsidiary enterprises (or 'daughters') that are 'tightly linked' to the center. Firms 'tightly linked' to the center include wholly owned subsidiaries, majority owned subsidiaries, state enterprises whose rights and responsibilities concerning resource use (including production, input purchase and sales decisions) have been transferred to central enterprises after consultation with the supervisory departments even though there is no formal

---

[19] Interim Regulations on Promoting Economic Associations, issued by the State Council on July 1, 1980.

[20] Regulations on Certain Issues Concerning Further Promoting Horizontal Economic Associations, issued by the State Council on March 23, 1986.

[21] This regulation introduced the distinctions between the 'closely associated', 'semi closely-associated' and 'loosely-associated' enterprise groups (see below) and also distinguished between equity and contractual or other forms of association.

[22] Views on formation and development of Enterprise Groups, of December 1987, issued jointly by the SCRES and the State Economic Commission.

ownership of shares, enterprises under a long term contract with the center, and enterprises or assets whose management have been transferred to the center through the State Property Management Bureau.[23] There are also 'half-tightly linked' subsidiaries (where the center is not a majority shareholder), or 'loosely linked' subsidiaries (with stable, long-term contractual relationships with the center but no management links). It is reported that over 80 percent of enterprise groups in China are of the loosely linked type. Enterprise groups which were launched at the initiative of a central enterprise, in terms of the links described above, are referred to as 'mother first' groups. By contrast, those which are established at the initiative of an organ of the government, such as a supervisory bureau which transforms itself into an 'enterprise group', are referred to as 'daughter first' groups.[24]

Other typologies of enterprise groups exist. Statistics published by the State Statistical Bureau (1989), on the 6,780 enterprise groups existing at the end of 1988, classify 7.9 percent of these (536 groups) as 'dominant firms with a leader', 4.2 percent, or 285 groups, as the 'specialization type', 24.4 percent (1,674 groups) of the 'vertical integration' type, 14.9 percent (1,008 groups) of the 'horizontal integration' type, and finally, 40.6 percent (2,754 groups) as the conglomerate type.[25]

An Evaluation: Implications of Enterprise Groups for Competition and Efficiency

Since over 80 percent of the enterprise groups in China are of the 'loosely linked' variety, their significance in terms of concentration of capital assets is limited. Cartel-like activities within the members of a group are however possible, and these are market conduct issues (see below). The development of large, multi-enterprise corporations of the 'tightly linked' variety is impeded today by a range of factors. First, the restrictive 'three no' principles of the government continue to apply to most enterprise groups. According to these guidelines, there can be no changes in (1) affiliations with government agencies; (2) ownership structure, and (3) the fiscal channels for taxes and profits. Groups may produce consolidated, or at least aggregated, financial accounts, and combined planning of output, and technology sharing, are possible. Some groups have unified planning and management systems (over issues such as personnel, finance, production, supplies and marketing). Nevertheless, each enterprise in a group typically continues to report to its own local industrial bureau and tax authority, and each firm continues to be an independent legal entity, individually responsible to the state for mandatory production plans and for tax and profit remittances. Consolidated treatment for taxes and profits is not possible. The group as a whole has no direct link to any government agency, but individual members may retain links to several government organs.

The resulting structures typically suffer from a lack of clear governance mechanisms, continued state intervention, and the difficulties of multiple authorities to answer to. Moreover, the formation of enterprise groups, as in the case of mergers, may be prevented by the failure of line bureaus in different subsectors or provinces, to give the necessary approvals. These approvals today are not based on considerations of potential market power, but rather, rest upon considerations such as potential

---

[23] This final type was part of an experiment which began in 1992.

[24] There has been much resentment over the formation of such 'fake' enterprise groups, expressed in the press. The government has recently announced its intention of tightly controlling the authorization of further such 'daughter first' groups.

[25] The remaining 8 percent are defined as 'other' groups. Cited in Wu (1990).

conflicts with local authority revenue or tax sharing agreements. Provincial or municipal authorities may also sometimes introduce non-neutral requirements, for example, that the enterprise group conforms with the region's industrial policy, or that it meets specific export thresholds.

Even if the formation of the enterprise group is approved, lack of financial consolidation implies that the resulting group is of limited significance, especially if combined with a lack of independent planning rights. This prevents resource reallocation across enterprises in a group, tax offsets or profit offsets. In some cases even the setting of prices of products is regulated by different line bureaus in separate provinces. Without its own financial company (and obtaining approval to set one up is alleged to be difficult), the transfer of funds between group enterprises is complex. For example, if a group member producing industrial parts wishes to reallocate funds to an agriculture-related enterprise within the group, it must first transfer funds to the local Industrial and Commercial Bank, which in turn transfers funds to the other firm's local Agriculture Bank; a process costly in resources and time.[26] Even though enterprises decide to constitute an enterprise group, consolidated financial treatment is prohibited without the formation of an 'enterprise group financial company'. Setting up such a financial company requires the approval of the People's Bank of China (PBC), which is reputed to be hard to obtain. However, the 55 large groups are an exception to this framework, and many of them do have their own finance companies. Moreover, these groups are permitted to liaise directly with the central government, instead of a number of independent regional authorities.[27]

---

[26] It must be recognized that financial consolidation also provides enterprises greater scope to cross-subsidize or transfer-price internal transactions.

[27] Eleven separate regulation documents for these 55 enterprise groups, authorizing them to experiment with increased autonomy, are in the process of being drafted or already completed. These regulations include rights of independent planning, for materials management, for labor and wage management, for accounting, for the establishment of financial companies, for registration, for asset transfers, for import/export rights, and for travel abroad/foreign visits.

Competition Law in a Market Economy

A modern competition law is a legal code that is intended to create and maintain a competitive and predictable business environment, by addressing market failures due to the exercise of 'market power'. A competitive and predictable business environment, in turn, is desirable not as an end in itself but as a vehicle to promote economic efficiency and consumer welfare, so that consumers can enjoy the benefits of lower prices, increased product choice and improved product quality. While some competition laws, such as the U.K. Restrictive Trade Practices Act have traditionally pursued other public interest goals as well including regional employment and export performance, there has been a growing consensus in international enforcement practice over the past years to focus on economic efficiency as the sole objective of competition law. Such a unique focus is desirable because it reduces the likelihood that the competition enforcement authorities will be deflected from their central purpose, since the pursuit of any other objective is more visible whenever there is deviation from a simple rule. Explicit focus on clear and transparent objectives also reduces business uncertainty regarding enforcement practices.

Competition law is typically a law of nationwide application. In principle, competition law should apply to all sectors of the economy and all regions of the country. Although there are specific sectors that are exempted under most countries' competition laws, there has been a trend reduction in these. Utilities, transport, telecommunications and energy markets as well as banking and insurance are increasingly subjected to the same rules of competition as other sectors.

South Korea provides an example of a country that adopted a competition law despite initial resistance. In the 1960s, government intervention in the economy was widespread and there was strong opposition in the business community to the adoption of a competition law. However, once the economy became more open, it became clear that government allocations and controls could not allow a complex economy to adjust efficiently to the oil price rises of the late 1970s. In addition, economic groups had accumulated large profits as a result of government protection, at the expense of consumers and smaller firms. Both these developments were instrumental in leading to widespread support for a competition law. In response to public pressure, the Korean Fair Trade Act was enacted in 1980.

For economies characterized by a legacy of mandatory planning and an initial low level of competition law related skills and enforcement resources, gradual institution-building is desirable, with an initial focus on a limited number of tasks. Key priorities include a general competition advocacy role, promoting the role of competition throughout administrative bodies nationwide, an emphasis on reducing entry barriers (including lowering of policy-induced interregional mobility barriers), clear rules against cartel agreements, with stricter enforcement and penalties against horizontal agreements and more lenient treatment of vertical agreements, and provisions regarding abuse of dominant position and mergers that are used only sparingly at first and limited to instances of gross misconduct.

The main agency responsible for administering the competition law also should play a role in the formulation of government economic regulations. Although the agency should be reactive toward anticompetitive business practices, it should be proactive in seeking to remove government determined policies which limit competition. Korea's Fair Trade Commission, for example, lists 'reform of anticompetitive government regulations' as the first item in its list of major activities over the past ten years. The Commission reviews draft regulations to prevent the introduction of restrictive elements and every ministry which intends to issue regulations must consult the Commission.

There is widespread agreement in all countries with competition laws that explicit horizontal, cartel-like agreements to fix prices, allocate customers or rig bids should be banned. Just as independence among competing suppliers in the same market is at the core of competition, prohibitions against cartel behavior are central to appropriate competition law. The general approach for such practices where the harm to competition is obvious is to make them *per se* illegal, that is, proving guilt requires only the demonstration that the alleged conduct has occurred. To act as a strong deterrent and convey a clear message that such practices are unacceptable regardless of context, countries such as the U.S. and Korea have criminal sanctions against this. However other practices, such as abuse of dominant position, or the implementation of mergers, are generally reviewed according to civil rather than criminal provisions. Rather than being outright illegal, they require a balancing of probabilities or the 'rule of reason' approach, where the harmful effects on competition are balanced against possible beneficial effects on economic efficiency.

Rules on cartel agreements, abuse of dominant position and mergers should be used sparingly at first and limited to instances of gross misconduct. To limit the abuse of administrative power, it may be desirable to restrict the scope of activity of the competition authorities in the control of 'dominant enterprises' by having a 'safe harbor' clause, so that enterprises with less than a specified percentage of market share would explicitly lie outside the purview of those rules. In the control of mergers, it may be desirable to start with a high prenotification thresholds, so that only mergers beyond a large size would be reviewed. Such thresholds could then be lowered over time, if necessary, as administrative capacity increases.

Source: Background Papers for this study.

The discussion suggests that the concentration of economic power by the formation of large, multi-plant or even multi-enterprise corporations is not a major issue, at present. Indeed, the benefits of the formation of multi-plant enterprises are often difficult to reap, because of the difficulties confronting enterprises which wish to expand through the setting up of new subsidiaries, or the formation of affiliated companies. In some areas, greater flexibility to permit such group formation is desirable, for example, the possibility of answering to a single profit or tax authority, and permitting consolidated financial and tax treatment, at least for majority owned subsidiaries. For the 55 large corporations, however, which are more 'tightly linked' today, it may be advisable to set up some process of monitoring their further growth in size, and their market behavior. This will have to be reviewed in the context of an examination of the overall need for legal safeguards for competition. At the same time, it must be recognized that the formation of 'fake' enterprise groups, from former line bureaus, is not likely to be economically beneficial. The formation of groups through coercive processes ('hostile takeovers') needs to be more carefully defined, in terms of the conditions and the processes under which this can be permitted to occur, and the formation of groups through fraudulent means has to be guarded against.

Market Conduct Issues

There appears to be a substantial incidence of agreements between enterprises in the same market (within or outside enterprise groups) regarding price and output decisions, as part of practices inherited from the era of planning, when such decisions were required to be made collectively. Such agreements take place, for example, within subsectoral producer groups. While these practices appear to leave scope for competition (through spreads between maximum and minimum prices agreed during annual 'price meetings', as well as a lack of effective enforcement mechanisms to monitor pricing), continued close communication between enterprises in the same industrial subsector could lead to more cartel-like output restriction over the longer term. In early 1993, five top commercial outlets for electrical appliances in Beijing formed an association to add ten percent to the price of washing machines at their outlets. These five enterprises account for around a third of the capital's washing machine market. In May 1993, eight large commercial firms in Nanjing, capital of Jiangsu province, established an association to jointly reduce the price of airconditioners. They were undercutting a small firm which had previously beaten their prices and had taken their business.[28]

Legal Provisions on Competition

The preceding sections suggest that while there are issues concerning competition in China, they are related not so much to market structure as to market conduct and behavior. The cases of price collusion and predatory pricing behavior above illustrate the requirement for legal protection against such behavior. Until recently there was no comprehensive competition law in China. A somewhat obscure 1980 regulation on the promotion and protection of competition was never invoked or implemented in practice.[29] Through the 1983 State Enterprise regulations, the state safeguarded lawful

---

[28] *China Daily.* June 23 1993. The five washing machine sales outlets of Beijing are the Xidan and Beijing Department Stores, the Dong'an and Chang'an Markets and the Longfu Emporium.

[29] According to the 'Provisional Regulations on the Promotion and Protection of Socialist Competition' (approved by the State Council, October 17, 1980), 'Except for products which are under the special management of the departments concerned and units appointed by the State, no one is allowed to exercise a monopoly on the remaining products or act as the sole operator of a business'. According to one source (*China Daily*, June 23, 1993) these rules were put into effect in 1987, but have had little effect.

competition and prohibited inappropriate methods of competition (such as fraud, price collusion, bribery and illegal competition). The 1988 State Enterprise legislation did not continue these provisions. More recently, there were provisions under the 'Standards for Limited Share Companies' of 1992, which empowered authorized government departments to withhold share company merger approval if the merger 'violates state laws and regulations and policies prohibiting monopoly and unfair competition'.[30] However, this provision lacked force.

In 1993, three significant pieces of legislation affecting competition policy in China were passed. The first (February 1993) was the Product Liability Law. Second, a Consumer Protection Law was adopted in November 1993. Third, an Anti Unfair Competition Law was enacted by the Standing Committee of the National People's Congress in September 1993 and was declared effective on January 1, 1994. On December 31, 1993, the Congress also passed a new Enterprise Law which has implications for competition.

Legal provisions regarding holding companies or enterprise groups are less developed than provisions for mergers. Comprehensive legal definitions of rights and liabilities for concerned parties for both holding companies and enterprise groups are still lacking. According to the 1988 enterprise registration regulations, enterprise groups and subsidiary/branch companies of national corporations require official examination and approval. In practice, however, it appears that formal registration of enterprise groups only began following the issuance of the specific 1992 registration rules for enterprise groups; only since that time does SAIC have authority to intervene through administrative means if enterprise groups are not registered, requesting that they do not do business as a group.[31]

From the point of view of maintaining market competition, the new law on unfair practices is timely. Its purpose is fourfold: to ensure healthy development of the socialist economy, to encourage and protect fair competition, to stop unfair competition and to protect the lawful rights of business operators and consumers. The focus of improper competition in the new law is on deceptive trademark and advertizing, practices injurious to reputation and violation of trade secrets (although the provisions here are not reconciled with existing legislation on these issues). There is a specific provision against interregionally restrictive trade practices. While collusive pricing practives are outlawed in the context of submitting tenders, there is no allusion to the legality of cartel issues or oligopolistic price coordination in general - a key element of competition legislation in other countries. It is noteworthy that the new legislation includes in its scope both domestic and foreign enterprises and its general provisions apply to private and public companies alike. The new law certainly represents an important step forward, although its links to existing legislation need clarification, and its coverage needs to be strengthened.

Provisions on enterprise groups or holdings, when drafted, will have to find a careful balance between promoting the potential efficiencies to be gained through such groups, which so far have been difficult to achieve in China, and the implications of such groups for future market power. Market power through such groups today is not, for the most part, a size-related issue. Provisions on forming enterprise groups will also have to look at the mechanisms of group formation to provide adequate

---

[30] Article 90 of the 'Views on Standards for Limited Share Companies'. SCRES (May 15, 1992).

[31] In May 1992, regulations on the 'Temporary Method for Formation of Enterprise Groups' were jointly issued by SCETO, SRC, SPC and SAIC. The new Enterprise Law of January 1994 does not make any reference to enterprise groups.

safeguards into coercive or fraudulent behavior. Finally, the economic merits of encouraging the formation of enterprise groups from ministries or industrial bureaus should be scrutinized before they are permitted.

C. The Entry of New Firms

Maintaining ease of entry of new suppliers, domestic or foreign, provides a highly effective source of competition in a market economy. Entry has many dimensions, and some aspects of this, concerning the regional mobility of goods and factors, have been discussed in previous chapters. The following section examines a specific, and immediate aspect of entry, the registration of new firms. Since 1980, this process has been dominated by a single government agency, the State Administration of Industry and Commerce. Requirements for entry and the administration of the entry process are reviewed below.

The Role and Functions of the SAIC

The State Administration for Industry and Commerce (SAIC), set up in 1980, is a ministerial-level government department directly under the State Council, and at the apex of Bureaus of Industry and Commerce throughout the country. The SAIC and its bureaus are entrusted with the responsibility for the supervision and regulation of the economy and with administrative power to enforce laws affecting economic markets.[32] Established with the onset of reform, the original function of SAIC was largely limited to the supervision of the distribution of goods by private proprietorships and the administration of local consumer goods markets, for daily necessities such as agricultural produce, clothing and small industrial products. In this context, the SAIC administered local trading facilities throughout the country where individual sellers could come to sell their produce. The SAIC was allegedly responsible both for providing market-related facilities and services, as well as for protecting the interests of consumers. Over time, with the rapid growth of private and collective enterprises, and the increased market orientation of the economy, the role and functions of the SAIC have increased rapidly, to cover a large spectrum of market regulated activities. Indeed, with the reforms to build a 'socialist market economy', the Bureaus of Industry and Commerce have gained authority and business scope, even as the economic ministries lose authority to control the planned economy.[33]

The principal functions of the SAIC today consist of (1) enterprise licensing and registration; (2) market organization and administration, including rural and urban markets, consumer

---

[32] During the Cultural Revolution, a department was established under the Ministry of Commerce with the enforcement of prohibitions against private sellers as its main task. Preparatory work for the establishment of a specialized agency to regulate markets began following the third plenary session of the XIth Central Committee of the Communist Party, in 1978.

[33] Manion (1993) analyzes the structure and operations of the SAIC in depth, from the point of view of process and insulation from corruption. From an economic standpoint the growth in power and stature of this agency provides an excellent example of the shift in external authority from one group of agencies (the planners) to another (the regulators) in a process of economic transformation.

goods markets and the market for the means of production and production components (as well as stimulating the establishment of new markets such as futures markets); and (3) market supervision (for investigating and providing redress for violations of economic laws and regulations). This includes the monitoring of unfair trading practices, cases of fraud, false advertizing, violation of patents and trademarks, as well as out-of-court dispute resolution. The central priority within the SAIC today is to protect the legitimate interests of consumers in order to create an environment of fair competition. In addition to separate departments responsible for enterprise registration, market administration and supervision, there are also functional departments at the central SAIC and at all local Bureaus of Industry and Commerce, responsible for advertisements, trademarks, economic contracts, the private economy, and the development and review of laws and regulations. The total staff employed by all SAIC branches must number in at least in the tens of thousands, since the Shenyang city SAIC bureau alone employs roughly 4,000 people while the Shenzhen city SAIC bureau employs over 1,000 people.

Enterprise registration in China is intended to ensure compliance with existing legal requirements governing new enterprise entry (registration for starting operations), entry of existing enterprises into new markets (alteration in scope of operations), enterprise expansion (alteration in registered capital) and other changes in enterprise status.[34] All enterprises must register with the appropriate central or local SAIC to acquire legal status prior to undertaking any economic activity. Enterprises applying for 'legal entity' registration must have at least eight full-time employees and registered capital above minimum thresholds; those not qualifying as legal entities must apply for 'business' registration, in which case the investors, in an individual capacity, shoulder civil responsibilities for the enterprise. Upon fulfillment of all registration requirements, enterprises receive a business license; they can then open bank accounts and carry out operations within the approved business scope. Business licenses are only valid for one year, after which a mandatory annual inspection is required for renewal.[35]

According to the present requirements for enterprise registration, which date from 1988, all enterprises, state-owned, collective or private, applying to begin operations as legal entities, require a series of documents. These include (1) a certificate for eligibility as a 'legal person', (2) a certificate of creditworthiness, (3) documents 'from the department in charge or responsible for examination and approval', and 'other relevant documents and papers', which consist in the main of (4) an application to the SAIC, (5) the organization charter, and (6) certificates for the use of residence and locations of operation.[36] The distinction in registration regulations for state versus collective or local enterprise lies in the nature of documents required within these categories, and by whom they are approved. For example, the certificate of creditworthiness is issued by the State Property Administration Bureau for state

---

[34] Registration rules for industrial and commercial enterprises are contained in the 'Regulations of the People's Republic of China On the Management of Registration of Enterprise Legal Persons', promulgated by the State Council on June 3, 1988 (effective July 1, 1988). Administrative guidelines are contained in the 'Detailed Rules for the Implementation of the Regulations of the People's Republic of China concerning Registration Administration of Legal Entities', Announcement No. 1 of the SAIC, November 3, 1988 (effective December 1, 1988).

[35] An annual examination report and financial statements must be submitted. As part of the annual inspection, checks are conducted by the relevant SAIC on the major items that constitute the enterprise legal person registration.

[36] Regulation On the Management of Registration (1988), Article 15.

enterprises but by an accounting or auditing firm for private enterprises. Documents required 'from the department in charge' usually include approvals from the supervisory administrative line bureau under which the economic activity was expected to take place, the Planning Commission (so that the project is included in the local plan), the Economic Commission (that deals with construction and factory buildings, among others), and the Environmental Protection Bureau. For enterprises from outside the locality, investment flows are monitored by the local Cooperation Office as well, and their approval is required.

In addition to the principal regulations on enterprise registration, there are allegedly over 130 other rules affecting enterprise licensing, which specify the various documents required to accompany the application, in the form of permits (*xuke zheng*) from various government departments. In some instances up to 100 or even 200 permits may be required. Apart from the standard documents, an enormous number of enterprise-specific special requirements may be invoked in individual cases.

According to the 1988 registration regulations, enterprises are only permitted to engage in economic activities in accordance with their initially approved business scope, operational methods and amount of registered capital. If the enterprise wants to enter a new market by producing or selling something else, expand or contract its operations (increase or decrease its registered capital by more than 20 percent) or change the location of operations, it must apply for an alteration in registration. For all such alterations, requirements include a letter of application to SAIC, approval by the original controlling authorities, as well as the usual 'other relevant documents and certificates'. The key point of significance here is the measure of flexibility accorded to officials in granting a license. Bureau officials have effective control over the time it takes to process an application, through the degree of flexibility or strictness applied to the evaluation of acceptability of an application.[37] As a consequence, there is considerable scope for corruption. In 1990, a campaign to combat corruption in the SAIC was launched. However, penalties for abuse have not always been serious.[38]

In terms of process, the apex SAIC does not dictate or prescribe operating procedures of lower level Bureaus of Industry and Commerce, and variations have arisen in different parts of China. In a typical process, however, licensing is sequential and requires the successful completion of four tasks: (1) the receipt of application materials (*shouli*); (2) investigation and verification of materials (*shencha*); (3) approval of a license (*hezhun*) and (4) issue of a license (*fazhao*). Once the formidable process of application is complete, the task of investigation and verification begins, by administrative departments under the Bureaus of Industry and Commerce, separate from the licensing departments.

Entry-related fees must be paid to the relevant SAIC, and these include charges for initial registration, for all alteration of registrations, and for the annual examination. Penalties for opening a

---

[37] Manion (1993). For example, a strict application of rules may allow an enterprise to produce one specified type of computer software; a more flexible application may not require specification of the type of software, and a truly flexible application may allow an applicant to specify production of computer accessories as its main economic activity. Licensing authorities may also approve activities which are clearly inappropriate in scope, such as 'scientific and technological exchange', in one instance.

[38] Officials in one district in Beijing were reported to have refused 93 invitations to dinner, 29 bribes amounting to over Y1,000 in cash and Y5,000 in gifts in a period of a few months, following the campaign (Manion, 1993).

business without approval and registration include immediate halting of operations, confiscation of illegal proceeds, and an additional fine of up to Y20,000. Fines are also levied for failure to register alterations or to comply with the annual license renewal process, together with confiscation of illegal proceeds and an order to rectify the violation as appropriate.

Though new central instructions on registration have not been issued since 1988, an attempt to simplify the enterprise registration procedure was launched in 1992.[39] In May 1992 the SAIC convened a national meeting on the management of private and household enterprises, following which an internal circular was issued, calling for fewer steps in investigation and approval procedures and a revision of the requirements for permits from other departments. Many regulations issued by government departments as well as by provincial Bureaus of Industry and Commerce were invalidated as a consequence.[40] For commercial enterprises, for example, the minimal thresholds for initial registered capital have been lowered, the minimal premises/facilities size requirement for wholesale trading has been lifted, and the legal person eligibility requirement for state enterprises no longer requires nomination by the relevant line bureau. Line bureau approval requirements in the registration process have been eliminated completely in Shenzhen in 1985, and for selected subsectors in Guangdong in 1992. In Shanghai, supervisory agencies' approval requirements for changes in business scope also have been eliminated in 1992, though the relevant SAIC must still be notified of all changes.

Other Agencies Concerned with Entry

It is difficult to gauge whether the problems of entry and licensing are to be attributed solely to the operations of the SAIC, or whether the other departments concerned also play a major role. In practice, it appears that the influence of line ministries and other administrative bodies on resource allocation remains extensive in many subsectors. In the automotive sector, for example, the China National Automotive Industry Corporation (CNAIC), the focal point of Chinese government authority, is active in sectoral planning and has a strong say in national regulatory decisions affecting the sector. In early 1989, CNAIC was strengthened and has gained renewed authority over investment decisions.[41] For key enterprises in the machine tool sector, there is also a strong influence of the line ministry regarding allocation of resources, product development and production orientation.[42] As recently as 1990, in electronics, the responsible line ministry was planning to use industrial licensing for large projects to prevent what it views as 'excessive entry' in critical areas.[43] And in the fertilizer sector, the marketing system was remonopolized in 1991, with the China Agricultural Means of Production Company (CNAMPC) given the sole right for wholesale fertilizer distribution, while the China National Chemicals Import and Export Corporation (SINOCHEM) remains the only corporation with the right to import fertilizers. SINOCHEM tends to favor the better-off coastal provinces which have easier access to import

---

[39]   Following Deng Xiao Ping's Spring Speech earlier that year which signalled a new political environment for public and private enterprise.

[40]   Circular of 20 June, 1992. The simplification applied to enterprises in all ownership categories.

[41]   World Bank (1991) (Automotive Sector Study).

[42]   World Bank (1992) Report No 10688-CHA. pp 12-13.

[43]   World Bank (1990) Report No. 7962-CHA. p. 22.

licenses and foreign exchange.[44] As the economy relies more on market-based mechanisms, less restrictive entry and expansion rules would encourage more competition and banks should increasingly perform most of the screening functions currently undertaken by administrative authorities.

Enterprise registration requirements, including the mandatory annual inspection, impose a burden on the scarce entrepreneurial resources of new entrants. They divert scarce resources from producers when they should be focusing their time and attention to the requirements of successful entry. There clearly appears to be scope for a great deal of procedural simplification. In many respects the multiple and discretionary requirements of the licensing process resemble the myriad taxes, tolls and fees levied on goods in transit from one jurisdiction to another. Both illustrate the need for greater transparency, simplification, and reduction of the scope for discretion in application. Although these deterrents have not prevented new firms from entering the market, they may well have restricted their scope or form, and have likely extracted a tax in the process. Easing these procedures would certainly assist the growth of market competition.

D. Other Regulations Affecting Market Structure

In addition, a number of regulations exist that affect both the structure of economic markets and the conduct of enterprises within those markets, ranging from rules on smuggling, deception, advertising, trademarks, contract and dispute settlement. An 'anti unfair competition' law, prepared by the SAIC, which includes some competition law elements (such as provisions on cartel-like agreements in tender submission) and consumer protection elements (such as fraudulent sales practices and false advertising) was enacted in 1993. In addition, new laws are under preparation, and amendments to existing regulations have recently been enacted, in a number of areas affecting market conduct and competition. Recent developments in this area are reviewed below.

Consumer Protection Related Rules: Advertising and Fraudulent Practices

There are over 70 separate rules and regulations governing illegal economic activities, including prohibitions on fake products and pornography, on smuggling and traffic in smuggled goods, on speculation, and on deception and swindling. There are also separate laws on advertising, trademarks, and contract dispute settlement and arbitration. The 1987 advertising regulations replace the former 1982 rules, and offer some degree of progress towards a market economy by allowing individuals (sole proprietors) to engage in the advertising industry, allowing advertisers to set their own fee scales, and extending the scope of judicial review to SAIC decisions.[45] The 1987 regulations also address consumer protection and competition law concerns. For example, advertisements are prohibited from deceiving consumers, and consumers are empowered to lodge complaints with their local SAIC. Advertisers are also prohibited from denigrating other similar products. 'Monopolization or unfair competition' are also

---

[44]   World Bank (February 1993). Mimeo.

[45]   Administration of Advertising Regulations, promulgated by the State Council and announced on November 10, 1987, followed by Administration of Advertising Regulations Implementing Rules, promulgated by SAIC on, and effective from, January 9, 1988.

prohibited, though the law provides no details regarding the enforcement of this provision. Regional laws on the same topic also exist such as the 'Fujian Consumers' Lawful Interests Protection Regulations', which allow consumer redress for misleading advertising.

The local SAIC enforcement authorities are closely involved with the combatting of illegal economic activities. Interviews suggest that the most frequent complaints and interventions occur in the production and distribution of fake products and fake trademarks, followed by smuggling, deceptive advertizing and fraud, in addition to registration-related infractions.

In 1992, the nationwide 'antifake' campaign against counterfeit production and marketing resulted in the uncovering of over 116,000 cases, accounting for 62 percent of the country's total economic crime. Defective goods handled by SAIC were valued at 366 million yuan, with fines amounting to roughly one third of that total value (114 million yuan). Over the year, 1,300 'fake-product centers' have been discovered and eliminated, and more than 2,200 law-breakers were arrested. As an example of illegal private activities and their links with state-run oversight, two apprehended individuals had been producing tons of useless fertilizer over a period of four years, labelled with fake trademarks of SOE factories. Without a production permit, business license, necessary technology and equipment, the individuals had carried on their illegal production under the protection of the local town government, which received sizeable side-payments for its complicity. In October 1993, a new law on Consumer Protection was adopted by the Standing Committee of the National People's Congress, which for the first time represents a unified umbrella of legislation on consumer protection issues. This represents a major step forward in the area of competition policy.

Consumer Protection Law

Consumer protection laws form a part of the legislation which defines a framework for retail trade. Retail transactions in market economies are underpinned by laws that define the rights and responsibilities for buyers and sellers. Additional laws prohibit fraudulent sales practices, false or misleading advertising, and other harmful practices that cannot be efficiently addressed through market-based remedies.

Consumer protection policies are motivated by a concern that enterprises operating in a market economy may exploit informational disadvantages faced by their customers and thereby expose them to loss or harm. Such policies seek to address two main sources of market failure in terms of consumer information. First, markets do not always provide sufficient incentives for producers to reveal the true characteristics of their products and services (referred to as 'asymmetric information' problems), and second, markets do not have adequate incentives for individual consumers to assert their rights after transactions (referred to as 'public goods and coordination' problems).

The general approach of consumer protection policies in most market economies is first to adopt market-supportive measures that promote the supply of accurate information by market participants, and only to adopt regulatory remedies for those specific problems where market-based remedies are not sufficient. Competitive markets and their accompanying legal infrastructure, if functioning properly, help solve many information-related problems so that detailed specific legislation is generally inappropriate. Experience from other countries has shown that arbitrary restrictions on the number of entrants, such as guarantees ensuring secure markets to one 'responsible' enterprise while presuming that all potential rivals are 'irresponsible', are one of the most ineffective and counterproductive ways to protect consumers.

The first priority in this area for a transitional economy is to have a transparent set of rules governing the rights and responsibilities of buyers and sellers in market-based transactions. With such a nationwide legal infrastructure in place, more competitive markets should help solve many information-related problems. For example, high warranty claims in an environment where unmet claims can be challenged can become a relatively low-cost market signal of quality, since producers of defective products will be driven out of the market through competitive forces. The consumer protection agency should play a market-supportive role to encourage markets to supply accurate information on their own, for example by establishing recognizable metrics to measure product characteristics for certain classes of goods (such as the lumens scale for light bulb brightness and R-values for insulation). Sellers who score well on these metrics will adopt them on their own and promote themselves without administrative enforcement. More interventionist rules are desirable in the protection of health and safety, including the regulation of foods, drugs and consumer products.

An important issue to consider, in the context of enforcement of consumer protection-related laws, is whether or not to combine the consumer protection authorities with the competition authorities. Though the competition laws of various countries include specific consumer protection-related provisions, other countries have chosen to separate the enforcement of both sets of legal provisions. Consumer protection often involves a very large number of small transactions, and it would be undesirable for the competition authorities to be overwhelmed and fail to address other issues. On the other hand, for a country that is adopting new measures in both areas, there may be sizeable synergies from having both offices at least located nearby, since economic staff adept at analyzing competition-related issues may also have useful insights into consumer protection issues.

Source: Background Papers for this study.

Protection to Producers: Trademarks, Patent and Copyright[46]

The 1982 trademark law is another example of a law that addresses consumer protection concerns, as well as the rights of producers.[47] Consequently, the law recognizes and protects trademarks as an exclusive right, while imposing certain liabilities on trademark owners. It requires that

---

[46] This section draws on a series of articles in *Development Business*, on March 31 and April 16, 1993.

[47] The Trademark Law of the People's Republic of China was adopted by the National People's Congress Standing Committee on August 23, 1982, and entered into force on March 1, 1983. The Implementing Regulations under the Trademark Law of the People's Republic of China, promulgated by SAIC on January 13, 1988 replace the earlier implementing regulations of March 1983.

(a) any changes on a registered mark must be approved by the Trademark Office; (b) a trademark owner must be responsible for the quality of the goods; (c) a trademark applicant must be a lawfully registered legal entity or self-employed business person; (d) the trademark cannot be used for goods which exceed the approved scope of the business, and (e) compulsory trademark registration is required for pharmaceuticals and tobacco products.

Registered trademarks are valid for ten years, after which they must be renewed. The law empowers the SAIC to be the authority responsible for the registration and administrative control of trademarks throughout the country, to supervise the quality of goods and stop any practices that deceive consumers. Foreign enterprises dealing with matters concerning a trademark in China must entrust an organization designated by the SAIC to act on their behalf. According to the law, if a registered trademark is used for goods whose superior quality has been replaced by inferior quality so that consumers are deceived, the SAIC can order rectification, together with a notice of criticism, a fine, or cancellation of the trademark. If anyone infringes the exclusive right to use a registered trademark, SAIC is empowered, at the request of any person, to order cessation and compensatory damages to be paid to the infringed party; alternatively, the infringed party can institute proceedings directly with the people's court.[48]

In February 1993, nine amendments to the law were promulgated, and entered into force on 1 July. The major improvement introduced was the extension of exclusive trademark rights to services; previously only products could be covered. The significance of this is that service industries, such as advertising, insurance, banking or transportation, can now register their trademarks. The law also opens up the possibility of 'multi-class' filings, for different categories of goods. The new law is also more specific about requiring prosecution of infringers, in cases where the violation falls under criminal law. Meanwhile criminal law penalties for counterfeiting have been raised, from three to seven years. Some experts are however concerned that the new law does not go as far as expected in certain areas, for example, the rights of any company to obtain any trademark provided it files first, in China, among other requesting foreign or domestic companies. This is clearly of concern to foreign companies. Protection against certain types of infringement have been alleged to be weakened.

A second area of recent reform concerns patent law. China's first patent law was put on the books in April 1985. While the law was generally considered 'satisfactory' by critics, and comparable to similar legislation in third World countries, gaps were considered to exist in coverage, for key industries. One industry where the US had repeatedly pointed out difficulties was the pharmaceutical industry, and in January 1993, the patent law was revised to include new provisions in this area. In the amended version, additionally, the duration of protection for invention patents is now 20 years (relative to 15 in the past) and 10 years for utility designs (relative to eight in the past). Patent protection can be extended directly to drugs made by protected processes, and not only to the processes themselves. Production methods used for making animal or plant varieties can also be protected now. Licensing requirements for patented products have been tightened and penalties for fraudulent representation of patented products have been raised.

Copyright law was promulgated on September 7, 1990 and became effective on June 1, 1991. The law extends protection to works of Chinese citizens legal persons, as well as non-legal persons

---

[48] Accession to GATT will have implications for stricter enforcement of trademark regulation, especially abuses by Chinese enterprises regarding use of foreign trademarks.

in China, as well as foreign persons, under international treaties or bilateral agreements. Unlike provisions in the Trademark Law and the Patent Law, the Copyright Law does not impose criminal penalties for serious infringements. China has also promulgated computer software protection regulations, in 1991, which provide protection for 25 years. Copyright owners of software may also pursue civil remedies.

China has also taken a tougher stand on intellectual property laws, as copyright infringement allegations escalated. Since the beginning of 1992, a series of measures have been adopted in rapid succession. In January 1992 China entered into an agreement with the United States to upgrade intellectual property protection, and shortly after (October 1992), China acceded to international copyright conventions.[49]

E. Conclusions

China today is making enormous efforts towards the establishment of a framework of regulations appropriate for a market economy. In the last year, at least three landmark pieces of legislation in this area have been adopted - a law against unfair trading practices, a law on consumer protection and a Product Liability Law. These laws suggest that the thrust of the new framework at present is broadly speaking the protection of consumers against fraudulent marketing practices. Preoccupations against size, cartel formation or mergers are not predominant. This may well reflect the current economic issues facing the development of the market economy in China today. The remaining proposed agenda of new legislation and regulations is large and complex, and the comments offered here refer to the areas selectively discussed in the preceding sections. However, an examination of the economic implications of all other areas of proposed legislation is clearly desirable, as well as a review of the implementation experience of recently issued or adjusted regulations. This is a major undertaking which should be launched in the short to medium term.

With regard to the issues raised in the preceding sections, concerning the need for regulation to enforce competition, there is clearly a need to carefully assess the need to adapt any proposed legislation to the structure of China's economy. The problem in China today is not firm size, *per se*, or asset concentration, but rather, market conduct. In terms of structure, China has the opposite problem, of difficulties of growth in enterprise size, in terms of difficulties in growth through mergers or enterprise groups, even when this may be economically desirable. At present there appears to be scope for efficiency gains from encouraging such formations, in some circumstances. New regulations must be careful to permit their orderly growth and distinguish between cases when such formations may be economically desirable from cases where they would not be.

There are difficulties in granting a blanket permit to the development of some enterprise groups, such as the 'fake' groups set up through the transformation of administrative bureaus, or groups formed through coercion or 'hostile takeovers' or other fraudulent means. There is also an unusual degree of difference in the treatment granted to the 55 large enterprise groups, relative to other groups. The basis for differences in treatment, and the means of distinguishing between different forms of groups, require

---

[49] The Berne convention in July and the Universal Copyright Convention in October, of 1992.

clarification. Meanwhile, the present focus on market conduct, as opposed to size, as indicated by the 'anti-unfair competition' law currently under review appears appropriate. However, the draft law has not been reviewed and detailed comments on this must await such a review.

Next, regarding the process of entry, it is clear that the present process is (1) complex, and (2) has a large discretionary element. Both issues need to be addressed. The two recent drives, against corruption in implementation, and in favor of a procedural simplification are both to be welcomed. The problems in this area bear a strong resemblance in their nature to the myriad fees, fines, taxes and tolls levied on interprovincial trade, and as such may be symptomatic of a generic issue in the present forms of market regulation. In this instance too, it is desirable to have greater homogeneity in application and procedure across the various regional Bureaus of Industry and Commerce, and to make the requirements and processes more transparent.

Regarding the SAIC itself, its rapid growth is likely to continue, as the need for market regulation increases, if there are no interventions. It would be desirable, as this organization continues to expand, to consider alternative means of separating its very diverse spectrum of activities. For example, the functions of competition enforcement, enterprise licensing, consumer protection and the regulation of commodities and futures markets usually lie with different authorities, in a moderately advanced market economy. Although the limited age and experience of the organization, in the context of China's rapid evolution towards a market economic system, account for and explain its present structure, there is a case for beginning now to examine alternatives for its future structure.

With regard to other legislation, it can only be said that rapid changes have been introduced, many of which appear to be in the right direction. China has clearly begun to develop a more sophisticated system of producer protection, in the form of patents, trademark, and copyright laws, from predatory market behavior. It is hoped that consumer protection against fraudulent and fake products will also be reinforced. Ultimately, however, it must be recognized, that the passage of laws alone is not enough. In some cases laws are passed without adequate prior review, and there may also be cases where regulations reflect to some degree the self interest of the departments which prepare the draft legislation. And finally, the process of administration of the laws cannot be separated from the legal framework itself, and will require a detailed simultaneous examination.

6

Markets and Government: Future Perspectives

A. General Themes - A Synthesis

It is clear from the discussion of the preceding chapters that China has made remarkable strides, over the last decade, towards the establishment of a market economy. Particularly notable, in this regard, is its progress in replacing the allocative mechanisms of the former planning regime with allocation through the market, based on signals through the price system. The reduction in the proportion of goods allocated though the plan, as well as the increase in the proportion of goods subject to market prices, has been remarkable. As the analysis here shows, there has been a significant consequent reduction in the disparities in prices in different markets. Recent price reforms in early 1993 have consolidated and extended the progress achieved since the introduction of the dual track system in the mid 1980s. China has also taken bold steps towards exploring the establishment of new forms of markets usually found in mature market economies, as a part of its program of structural change.

However, as the report shows, the progress achieved so far has been uneven. In some areas of its transition towards a market economy, China is still well below its potential. The foremost among these concerns the spatial or regional fragmentation of its markets. China has not taken advantage of the benefits of specialization of other large countries and its economic structure still tends to be relatively 'cellular', with a striking similarity of industrial pattern by region, and relatively little change in this structure over time. As a consequence, many benefits, such as scale economies in plant size, and the spreading of overheads in management, technology and learning, communications and infrastructure associated with the development of industrial 'clusters', have yet to be exploited. Moreover, despite the rapid decline in the number and level of price controls, there are still persistent regional price differentials among both producer and consumer goods.

Data presently available on trends in the development of interregional trade, as well as cross-provincial investment, suggest that individual provinces are tending to behave like independent countries, with an increase in external trade and a relative decline in trade flows with each other. While data coverage issues require caution in interpreting the final results, Another explanation for the decline in trade, the sustained downward trend, continuing until the present, is still difficult to explain. A part of this decline may be ascribed to the reduction in the forced movement of goods under the plan system, over 1985 to 1988, in the period of the interprovincial 'trade wars'. The partial deregulation of the output and selling price of some goods led to incentives to evade public procurement, in favor of free market prices. These attempts at evasion, in turn, were countered by provincial authorities by the erection of export embargoes. The absence of any overarching regulations on interprovincial trade leaves the country vulnerable to such whims at the provincial level. However, with further relaxations in price and quantity controls, as well as the decline in the short-lived demand boom of that period, such export embargoes became much less significant. Other possible reasons for the continuing decline include the problems of numerous fees and fines, extracted on the road, legal as well as illegal, and also, the difficulties of transportation, especially by rail.

The role of the fiscal system, and the incentives and authority given to provincial and local governments to raise revenues in contributing to the relative increase in provincial autarky, from the point of view of investment, is clearly significant. The separation of profits and taxes was accompanied by the introduction of profit retention, as well as an increase in local authorities' taxation powers. It is therefore to the advantage of local governments to retain enterprises within their jurisdictions. Besides, incentives for interprovincial investment are confused by the large number of special zones, with their various authorized or unauthorized tax rebates or deductions.

If regional trade and specialization are to be promoted, there should be credible mechanisms in place for the redistribution of benefits among the various regions. Today, with the marked relative decline in the proportion of total revenue accruing to the central government, the scope for such redistributive mechanisms is more constrained. The reforms in the fiscal system introduced in January 1994 should help to alleviate the situation.

China's transition experience shows that the withdrawal of the state from allocation, and even pricing decisions, need not lead automatically towards the withdrawal of the state from distribution. It may argued that the state in China was reluctant to abandon its former role in this area, but it appears more likely that it was more difficult for the state to withdraw, whether or not it wished to. Markets, it appears on the basis of the evidence presented here, do not emerge automatically. The innovative changes in the distribution system, which is still state-dominated, in response to other changes in market mechanisms, do not suggest a conservative attitude. Moreover, they illustrate that the state sector has been able to respond to competitive stimuli, and that changes in operation are being effected despite relatively gradual changes in ownership. The combined requirements of capital-intensive infrastructure and the need to build information networks across large regions and many entities may well make it more difficult for the non-state sector to enter the business of distribution, relative to production. There is however scope for greater encouragement from the state in diversifying the ownership base and range of services of distribution.

Continuing state intervention in distribution has also taken the form of intervention in the prices (or quantities) of distribution services, for example, freight and storage. As the examples of the preceding chapters clearly illustrate, it is not possible to isolate these controls, and the effects of controls in these spheres will spill over into the prices of goods which are allowed to vary. Two cases which provided examples were the effects of controls on freight availability, which are reflected in grain prices, and the effects of differential storage subsidies, for state and non-state enterprises, which are arbitraged through forward prices on metals contracts. If markets function, such transmissions of price controls through the creation of 'proxy' markets are normal, and reinforce the case for proceeding with the lifting of residual controls on prices and quantities.

The most striking example provided here of the effects of controls in one market, on the rest of the economy, is the story of foreign exchange speculation through trade on the metals exchanges. If there are markets which deal in forward and futures contracts, and engage in the exchange of internationally tradable commodities, these markets will inevitably also reflect movements in the foreign exchange rate, if foreign exchange is a non-tradable. In the absence of free tradability of foreign exchange, a large part of the *raison-d'etre* of such exchanges will be speculative. The considerable and rapidly growing volume of trade on the exchanges already, and the large part of this which is speculative, suggests that the foreign exchange market is more constrained today than is, at first, apparent. The consequences for the rest of the economy, in terms of distortions in price signals elsewhere (ie, in the metals exchanges) are also obvious. With the removal of the dual exchange rate system, and the introduction of an interbank market in foreign exchange, this situation should improve, provided there is free access to foreign exchange for all traders.

The uneven pace of China's movement towards a market economy is nowhere felt as strongly as in the realm of regulation. It is clear that in many areas, China has plunged ahead, in terms both with the elimination of controls, as well as with experiments with major innovations in market forms, without providing the necessary framework of consistent regulation for the new system. This does not necessarily imply an absence of regulation, on the contrary the difficulty sometimes is the presence of a large variety of mutually inconsistent regulations. This is clearly illustrated in the case of the new commodities and futures markets, where today a bewildering array of regulations exist, in the different exchanges, depending on by whom they were established. There are wide mutual differences in terms of financial conditions of membership, restrictions on price variation, the treatment of profits and the role of supervisory agencies. There are also some considerable differences between these exchanges today, and standard regulation in more mature economies, for example, in commission fees charged. Recent moves towards the establishment of common oversight bodies are to be welcomed. It is to be hoped that these will be established before the proliferation of commodities exchanges proceeds much further. The more detailed tasks of harmonizing the legislation of individual exchanges must soon follow.

The need for adapting existing regulations or devising new regulations is also apparent in several other areas, particularly those laws which affect the degree of competition in the economy. Until 1993, there was no single competition law in China. In September 1993, the 'Anti-Unfair Competition' law was adopted, which has a heavy emphasis on unfair trading practices such as false trademarks or false advertizing, as well as the violation of trade secrets. Although the new law does not emphasize the control of monopolistic practices, referring back to China's fragmented and cellular industrial structure, the need for this so far has not clearly emerged. Any new law must be adapted to the structural conditions of the economy, which in this instance implies not an emphasis on size, per se, but rather, the exercise of market power in terms of behavior. The new legislation has some provisions for this, which may in the future require fortification.

A new law on contracts, as well as a new version of the company law, were presented to the State Council at the same time as the 'anti-unfair competition' law. The company law was finally adopted on January 1, 1994. Another new law relating to market conduct, the Consumer Protection law, was adopted in November 1993. There are other pieces of legislation affecting various areas of competition. For example, entry for new enterprises or units is largely, though not entirely, governed by laws relating to the activities of the State Administration of Industry and Commerce. This agency is already overburdened and it is not clear that in the future it will be able to discharge these multiple responsibilities efficiently. Laws on exit until recently were governed by the Bankruptcy law of December 1986. Since then, considerable flexibility has been introduced in the context of enterprise downscaling by amendments in labor laws, which eased the conditions for partial or complete exit. The new company law includes detailed provisions for the implementation of bankruptcy procedures. Laws on patents and on copyright protection have been introduced, and the law on trademarks was modified in 1993, partly as a result of China's efforts to accede to the GATT.

Based upon these general themes, which have emerged from the preceding analysis, the following sections explore a set of actions which could follow, to fortify and strengthen the present functioning of the market economy. A first set of actions discussed here refer to policy variables affecting the functioning of the markets, and here it must be understood that since policy recommendations may require trade-offs, only broad directions for change are prescribed. In the following section, however, which deals with the less ambiguous area of the functioning of 'real' markets, (such as improvements in the distribution system, or modifications to the trading mechanisms in the new commodity markets), more detailed recommendations are possible.

B. Policy, Regulation and Administration

Price and Quantity Controls

A first area to examine, in terms of policy, is China's control over decisions on prices and quantities, or resource allocation. Over the reform period these have been the key areas of focus of policy makers, and a principal tool towards the movement towards a market economy. These instruments have been extensively used and have had a demonstrated effect already, in terms of price convergence and market unification. A question which therefore arises today is, has their use been exhausted?

The present report suggests that this is not the case; there is still scope for adjustment in prices and in quantitative controls. **It is recommended that residual controls on prices continue to be lifted.** So far, the emphasis has been on the prices, or allocation, of goods. **In the next stage, the emphasis must move towards residual price and quantity restraints on services and on factors of production.** One finding here, which underscores the need for such further action, is the fact that there are 'leaks' from residual controls, which affect and distort the pricing of goods whose prices are not controlled. In the service area, these prices included freight quotas and subsidies, and storage subsidies. In factor markets, foreign exchange is a prominent example. The argument many also be extended to the pricing of labor (where much progress has been achieved in the past few years) and the pricing of capital, although this has not been demonstrated in the present report. Establishing functioning markets in these areas has been a slower process, so far, than in the case of goods.

Internal Trade

A second broad policy area to be examined is the issue of regional trade and the integration of regional markets. Looking first at trade in goods, China relative to most other large countries today suffers from the disadvantage of a lack of a general framework of legislation on interregional trade, which would prohibit certain kinds of trade barriers, including export embargoes or import restraints. **First, the drawing up of an overall framework of regulation on domestic trade is necessary,** whether as a constitutional clause (as in the US, and India, for example), or in the form of other national level legislation. **Second, the myriad fees and fines, legal and otherwise, levied on interprovincial (or even intercounty) trade today must be clarified.** Ideally, if provincial approval is possible, **a nationwide standardized list of genuine charges should be prepared.** Third, if a common list cannot be agreed upon, **the transparency of the procedure followed in each local jurisdiction can be improved through the collection and periodic publication of schedules of tariffs, taxes and other charges, at a provincial or national level.** Then if a specific item was not on the 'masterlist', it would be know to be suspect. Fourth, **the collection agencies for each of these fees should also be** standardized, or once again, the details of persons or agencies responsible for collection should be made evident and readily available.

Internal trade is also affected by regulations on transportation. Although detailed recommendations on transport are available in other reports, some key issues affecting distributional efficiency are pointed out or reiterated here. Producer goods have been particularly dependent on the railroad system, which has suffered over a prolonged period from severe underinvestment. One reason for this was the lack of adequate revenues from railways, due to the low passenger and freight tariffs. Recent successive raises in tariffs are expected to improve the profitability of the system. In parallel, the assignment of freight quotas to specific producers or users must also be examined. This practice has led to distortions in the prices of commodities requiring rail freight. **The removal of subsidies to railway freight users should be combined with the removal of the practice of assigning freight quotas to specific individuals or agencies.**

Another policy issue of concern in this context is the regulation and administration of the trucking business. Although the entry and pricing of trucking services has become more flexible since 1983, **the overlap in some of the functions the multiple agencies whose permits are required for licensing and registration (the local Transportation Bureaux as well as the Public Security Office) should be removed. There are also severe constraints on the time period, and permitted uses, of 'own account' trucks, which should be relaxed to permit greater flexibility.** The deregulation of trucking tariffs has taken the form of 'decentralized regulation', with the transfer of the authority for setting tariffs to the local Departments of Communications. As a result, there are now considerable regional variations in tariffs. The need for such decentralized regulation is questionable and some of these tariffs could probably be deregulated altogether, which would remove some tariff disparities. **To the extent that truck tariffs could be deregulated, this should be undertaken; if tariff regulation is still considered imperative in some areas, large regional variations in these tariffs should be reduced, through a harmonization of regional rates.**

Another factor affecting the movement of goods, which is likely to become more evident as the more obvious barriers are dealt with, is the question of government procurement. At present there are no transparent regulations for this at lower levels of governments. It is considered normal today to give preferences to local suppliers. This is unusual in other federal countries and also in larger economic trading areas, such as the European Community. **Government purchases should focus on obtaining the best value and should not grant more than limited and transparent local preferences, at best. This requires that the procedure for bidding for local government financed contracts should be made transparent, and as far as possible unified across regional governments at the same level. It should also be assured that there is no discrimination between suppliers of different regions.** Once the question is raised more frequently, these issues will follow.

Factor Mobility

Even more major issues arise in the context of capital mobility and interprovincial investments. It is clear today that the present fiscal system has inbuilt disincentives for permitting the mobility of enterprises to other jurisdictions, if this implies a loss of both income and corporate taxes. It is necessary to reexamine the assignment of taxes, from this perspective. Although income taxes would not be lost if guidelines are followed on the transfer of such taxes to the originating province, it is clear that there are both legal and illegal circumventions of this regulation in various jurisdictions, as a result of the establishment of special 'zones'. **While many illicit zones have recently been removed, the 200-**

odd which have been permitted to remain are still a non-negligible number. The undesirable consequences for the economy as a whole, despite short term local advantages, have to be recognized and acted upon.

Many other issues arise on the subject of capital mobility, which could not be treated in depth in the present work, as they are too large to be explored in adequate detail. However, to enumerate, these include issues on interstate flows of deposits or loans through the banking system, as well as new, alternative markets for capital. Today, these have been developed little, and these questions are likely to loom larger in later years. It is not too early for China to begin devising appropriate regulation, which would also help develop these new markets into major alternative channels for interregional capital flows.

Additionally, government contributions to capital investments, which today are much lower than in the past, have to be considered in this context. One positive role played by these in the past was as a vehicle for some form of regional redistribution. Although the withdrawal of the state from direct support for industrial investment is normal in a market economy, the redistributive role of these contributions should not be forgotten. The need for setting up alternative new structures such as the European Community's Structural Funds, to undertake these functions, should be explored.[1]

Concerning the labor market, it is true that the flexibility in the deployment of labor has increased considerably over the last few years, and so has de facto wage flexibility. There has been less progress however in increasing the regional mobility of labor, which is still strictly regulated. One important reason for restricting labor mobility in the past was urban grain rationing. However, since many of these rations have been lifted in early 1993, this is an appropriate moment to reconsider the need for maintaining the present restraints on labor mobility under the permanent residence registration system. While the shortage of urban residences and the very limited market in housing is still a constraint, an increase in regional mobility, over the present levels, could certainly be effected.

Under the 'swap center' system, constraints on the mobility of foreign exchange clearly existed, as demonstrated by the volume of speculative activity on the metals exchanges.[2] At present, the system is in transition, and in principle, with the interbank foreign exchange market and the unification of the exchange rate, direct access to foreign exchange could be greatly improved. This will have to be carefully monitored especially in its initial stages to ensure that the market fulfils this expectation, so that the new commodities markets can fulfil their primary function.

---

[1] This is explored in the recent report on China's budgetary policy and intergovernmental fiscal relations; (World Bank 11094-CHA; July 1993). This report also points out the erosion of the redistributive capacity of the central government (para. 3.98) and recommends the setting up of a closed-end, interprovincial equalization fund (para. 3.114), filled with a certain percentage of taxes shared between central and local governments, administered by a body with both local and central representatives.

[2] World Bank (1993), Report No. 11568-CHA, discusses the foreign exchange market in detail; the present recommendations are focused on the links between this and other markets, and the repercussions of the method of regulating mobility in foreign exchange on the rest of the economy.

Market Regulation

China's rapid moves towards experiments with sophisticated instruments of a market economy are bold steps, and care must be taken to ensure that these experiments do not founder because of a lack of adequate definition of a framework of regulation. **The predominant concern in this area so far has been the lack of an overall framework of supervision for the new exchanges.** At present, the task of registering exchanges has been entrusted to the State Administration of Industry and Commerce, and the responsibility for their supervision has very recently been assigned to a new body, the China Securities Supervision and Administration Committee. Regulations for the latter are under preparation, and this report presents different options for the approach towards the supervision of such agencies, in terms of their scope and method of functioning. **The early adoption of a standard framework of regulations is necessary today.** Once the overall umbrella is in place, **the task of reconciling the differences in operating rules of different exchanges must also be undertaken.** Finally, a critical element of the legislation on these exchanges, which so far has been neglected, is **to put in place appropriate financial safeguards for participants on the exchanges, through the establishment of a Fidelity Fund.**

It is not clear that the SAIC is the body best suited to handle the process of registering or approving new exchanges. Although this appears to be a natural extension of its present duties, of registering other new enterprises, **the approval of commodities exchanges requires far more specialized knowledge of trading systems and would be better handled by a separate department of the new China Securities Committee.** While the SAIC is now expected to re-register the exchanges after their scrutiny by the Securities Committee, the role of the SAIC in this process should be limited and not discretionary. Another issue here concerns the regulations, recently adopted by the SAIC, for traders and brokers on the exchanges, which may restrict the number of participants on the new exchanges. **It is more desirable to have a smaller number of exchanges, but with a relatively large number of participants on each, than vice versa.**

The recent history of the operation of the commodity exchanges also emphasizes a point raised earlier, in the context of 'proxy markets' and price controls; the difficulty of reconciling continued government intervention in some areas of these markets, with the concept of commodity exchanges. As illustrated here, continued government intervention in activities related to the exchange of commodities, such as setting price ceilings or floors (as in the case of the Zhengzhou grain center), or warehousing (through the provision of differential subsidies, in the metals trade) runs the risk of either undermining the price uncertainty on which such exchanges depend, or raising the pressure to continually increase government subsidies, as these are transferred through arbitrage to all participants on the market. **Once again the message is that market economies are made up of a single price 'system', and that residual ad hoc controls today would generate 'interference' in other price signals. The early removal of such constraints is required to permit the new markets to function effectively.**

A key issue which China must confront in its experiments with new market forms, and specifically in the area of establishing commodities markets, is the fact that the present large numbers of such exchanges will probably diminish over time due to a number of factors; the improvement in internal communications, closer integration with the world economy and consequently closer links with exchanges outside the country. The reduction in speculative activity as the 'zero-sum' nature of such trade is better understood, and the establishment of independent markets, most importantly in foreign exchange, will hasten this process. **The likelihood of considerable waste in the establishment of several new** exchanges, **especially in view of the presently preferred capital-intensive methods of trading, must be recognized and more exchanges should only be established if expected to be sustainable in the medium term.**

China is already aware of its need to develop regulation appropriate to the functioning of competitive markets, and has made considerable progress in this direction in 1993, through the laws against unfair competition, the law on consumer protection, and the product liability law. Laws to safeguard market competition through the protection of patents and trademarks have already been approved. It must be recognized, in this context, that the problem of monopoly in China is not pervasive, unlike many other transforming socialist countries, and consequently, **the emphasis should be on the promotion of competition, and the control of unfair trading practices, rather than safeguards against, or dismantling of, large enterprises or groups of enterprises.** The new competition law adopts this focus. The law has relatively little detail on more traditional areas of competition policy such as price maintenance or cartels. These aspects may have to be reinforced in the future.

China is today experimenting with the fostering of links between enterprises and the formation of enterprise groups and some of the experiments are likely to increase operational efficiency, and facilitate interregional investments, given the backdrop of the cellular structure of the economy. Care must be exercised to not snuff out these experiments with unduly restrictive regulations on mergers or enterprise groups.

It must also be remembered that competition law is far from being the only, or even the principal, vehicle of regulation for establishing a competitive economic environment. Laws on entry, or exit are at least equally important. The administration of the process of entry and exit, moreover, may sometimes be as important as the law. In this regard, the present study suggests that **the procedures for establishing new enterprises are still relatively onerous.** Many different agencies' permits are required, and the discretionary role given to some of these, especially, today, the SAIC, is large. The role of the SAIC has expanded enormously over the last few years, as the market economy has developed, and it is undertaking the work entrusted to several different agencies in market economies (including the licensing of establishments, the safeguarding of competition and the approval of new commodity exchanges). **It is recommended that the functions of the SAIC and other agencies should be redefined to make them more transparent and reduce the discretionary element. It is also recommended that some of the SAIC's functions** (such as, monitoring unfair practices, monitoring cases of fraud in labelling and trademarks, and taking care of enterprise entry requirements), **be delegated to more specialized agencies in the future.**

The agenda for legal reform appropriate to a market economy which is now being launched, as part of the Five-year plan for economic legislation is ambitious in scope. A number of different agencies will tackle different aspects of reform, and the process could be slow, especially in view of the need for drafting assistance required by some of the agencies concerned. **Care must be taken to temper the universal enthusiasm and determination for setting up the legal framework for a market economy, with the recognition that a proliferation of new laws, sometimes conflicting in scope, or in terms of agencies concerned, could be counterproductive.** Care must also be taken to counter any tendencies to permit the interests of the agencies drafting the laws to dominate the new draft legislation. The World Bank has indicated willingness to assist the Chinese government in this process of legal reform through an Economic Law Reform Project, which is currently under preparation.

C. Physical Constraints and the Management of Distribution

Distribution Practices and Distribution Facilities

Prescriptions for solutions to the physical difficulties of establishing markets, as well as the minutiae of the management of marketing systems are less controversial, but equally necessary, to ensure that the 'real' side of markets develops in tandem with the new policy environment. Looking first at the process of materials distribution, the slowness of the state to detach itself from this sphere of activities requires that the state bears a significant responsibility for the continued streamlining and improvement of the marketing and distribution process. **It is first necessary to carefully examine the wide range of activities with which the MME is involved, in some of its bureaus, including industry, real estate and construction.** It may be advisable to limit the scope of some activities, a part of which are speculative in nature, such as the real estate dealings. However, it is also essential to perceive the rationale for its involvement in these activities. One possible explanation may be that **some of the distributional activities in which a normal distribution agency in a market economy may be involved (for example, warehousing or transportation) are not attractive to the MME bureaus, because of price regulation or other curbs. Such constraints should be removed, so that the expansion of the materials distribution bureaus into activities related to their main business will be more likely.**

Action to increase future competition through new entrants is also required. **Local bureaus should be permitted to, and encouraged to, expand into other localities, and entry into distribution by individuals and collectives should also be facilitated, for example by permitting them to lease warehouse space from government bureaus.**

One direction of diversification undertaken by some materials bureaux is the adding of value to their products, through processing, blending or packaging. **Such value-adding activities, which provide additional quality or convenience for buyers should be encouraged.** Quality control and testing facilities are also desirable. However some materials bureaus talk about the undertaking of research on the materials they distribute. Such industry facilities may be better integrated with production enterprises than with distribution enterprises.

Another issue on the organization of the materials bureaus concerns their typical twelve-enterprise structure, below the central materials bureau of each location. This structure is the result of the takeover of the marketing and distribution functions of some production bureaus, with agreements to maintain their structures intact. As a result, **the present material bureau 12-enterprise structures lack the flexibility to adapt to local needs. It would be desirable to permit the materials bureaus full flexibility to rationalize (expand, merge, separate or even close down) these individual materials enterprises.**

Similarly, the comprehensive distribution centers (which had emerged as a consequence of partially deregulating the output of some goods, and the need to create marketing opportunities and outlets for the portions of output sold outside the plan) may also require, or naturally undergo, structural rationalization. **In the future, goods which are similar, or related, in terms of customer requirements, should be sold at a single center, or store.**

More detailed **attention must be paid to the physical facilities of the distribution system.** Many of the warehouses owned by the materials bureaus are old, in some cases with inadequate protection against the elements, leading to spoilage and damage in storage. However this demands a detailed review of existing facilities and appraisal of the costs of any proposed additions. The location of the new facilities at the sites of existing storage centers may not be optimal. **Many warehouses today are located in urban areas, and their relocation to points outside major cities, but well connected by road or rail, should be considered.** In the future, the mechanization of materials handling and the computerization of order placement and inventory management will require introduction.

There is scope for **better management of distribution functions of existing warehouse facilities.** For example, **the reduction of partly-loaded truck shipments, the reduction of the number of times goods are handled or moved and improved inventory management** through more reliable shipping from producers as well as more information from users. Better physical management of warehouse space by arranging goods on a computerized customer order in the order in which they will be picked up from warehouse shelves will reduce pick-up time and effort. The introduction of 'cross docking' practices to permit vehicles bringing in supplies to be transferred directly to delivery vehicles to purchasers, will also reduce materials handling and increase distributional efficiency. The development of backchannels for the recycling of used materials should also be introduced.

There is also a need to **examine the financial condition of the materials bureaus.** The extent to which the decline in profitability of the materials bureaus may indeed be attributed to losses made on goods which remain under planned allocation will have to be ascertained. Given the recent considerable reduction in these goods, the profit rates of the materials bureaus should improve as a consequence. The materials bureaus have also ascribed poor profitability to transportation difficulties. The extent to which profitability could improve as a result of the adoption of more efficient distribution practices must also be considered. **A detailed examination of the profitability, cash-flow and inventory management of the materials distribution system should be launched as an exercise which combines marketing as well as financial expertise. Since the last major round of price decontrols has just been concluded, this is an appropriate time to begin such an undertaking.**

Road Transportation

Transportation by road is important for many raw materials, and agricultural goods. Apart from the policy issues affecting entry, and tariff structure, which have been raised above, there are issues here too concerning the efficiency of management of trucking operations. For example, one practice that would aid the growth of private 'own account' truckers is the **development of freight forwarding and consolidation centers, to serve as collection points for goods shipped in less-than-truckload quantities.** In the medium term, the growth of intercity and interprovincial trucking would be facilitated by the **development of intermodal transportation systems, which enable goods to be moved from rail to truck, or to barge or back, as efficiencies dictate.** Such systems require the development of containerized shipping, which China is now beginning to explore.

Commodities and Futures Markets

Scope for improvements in the operational and cost efficiency of the many new exchanges in China can be pointed out, and can be effected independently of the policy issues concerning these exchanges given above. A first issue here concerns the nature of trading practices. The Metals Exchange at Shanghai is a fully computerized screen based system, where, as has been pointed out, the existence of a trading floor is redundant. The Shenzhen exchange is a combination of an 'open outcry' system, with a large central screen recording bids and buys. In both cases, **a simple open outcry ring dealing system** would not only have sufficed, but may have been preferable, and considerably cheaper. The computerized information entry requirements slow the trading process and will become a hindrance as the pace of trading accelerates. The growth of trade by 'market makers', trading on their own account and providing essential liquidity to the system, is also impeded by the present systems. Although it may arguably be late to change the present system in these exchanges, these are important considerations for the many new exchanges in the process of being approved. Objections to 'open outcry' based on its vulnerability to fraud, are exaggerated. However if this is a major consideration, the 'Japanese Auction System' could be introduced, in which there is a single price for all buying and selling orders for a given trading session.

Even at the existing exchanges, there will soon be a need for a major extension of computer facilities. This may be an opportune moment to reconsider the adoption of a cheaper and more effective trading system. Meanwhile, **trading costs could be reduced with the utilization of the facilities at a given trading center by more than one exchange.** Since most exchanges at present do not trade every day of the week, or all hours of the day, this should certainly be feasible.

To encourage the continued growth of the use of these exchanges, **it will be advisable to reduce the costs of trading extracted at the exchanges, in the form of fees.** Fees in China today (at least at the metals exchanges) are unusually high, at 0.1 percent per transaction, compared for example to the average 0.0005 percent at the London Metal Exchange. **Some of the exchanges are set up as profit-making entities, in contrast to exchanges in market economies, which are typically operated through a break-even membership basis.** There are similar questions concerning the **margin deposit requirements, which are also extremely high, and discourage the use of commodities exchanges as a medium for managing inventory financing.**

D. The Future Role of the Government

In a market economy, the role of the government in the realm of economic activity is that of indirect intervention, to create an enabling environment for economic agents. The economy is then regulated through market signals, which determine prices and resource allocation. The economic functions of the government are therefore very different from the dirigiste role required in a centrally planned economy, where decisions on resource allocation and price levels are determined to a greater or lesser degree by the government.

China today is confronted by the task of transforming the economic role of its government from that required in a system of central planning, to a role more appropriate for a market economy. While China has made huge, and successful, efforts to disengage the State from the role bestowed upon it under the period of planning, it has been less clear about the role of the government in a decentralized market economy. A first issue here is that in some areas of economic activity, controls have been relaxed, but there are no regulations to replace these controls. Second, in some instances, the difficulty is not the absence of new regulations, but rather, a proliferation of regulations, put forward by a variety of agents. Not surprisingly, there are sometimes contradictions between these independent regulations. Third, in some cases, the new regulations reflect the interests of the agencies who have drafted them to a greater degree than they safeguard the interests of the affected individuals. China's emerging new commodities markets, to take an example, illustrate all these difficulties. First, there is an absence of umbrella legislation for all commodities and futures markets. To the extent that regulations exist at the individual exchanges, there are wide differences between them, in terms of supervisory responsibility. Moreover, in many areas the regulations are not in the best interests of users (the profit-seeking basis on which they are established, the high commissions per transaction, and the lack of financial safeguards for users). These are the broad areas to which the government will have to pay increased attention, in its future role as regulator, rather than controller, of economic activity.

One style of deregulation which has frequently been adopted in the context of China's economic reform program is the decentralization of regulatory authority, to lower levels of governments. This is true not only of some areas of prices (procurement prices for agricultural products, tariffs for transport), but also in terms of licensing requirements for transport operators, and a multitude of fees and charges levied on persons trading or transporting goods in any given province. This form of 'decontrol' can be misleading. Decentralized regulation can have the effect of creating large differences in economic regulations between local jurisdictional levels and consequent problems of differences in economic behavior. The preceding analysis has shown that the spatial integration of China's markets represents a major issue in its move towards a market economy and the difficulties already present here could sometimes be exacerbated by this form of decentralization of the authority to regulate. It is clearly necessary to demarcate and distinguish between economic functions where such decentralization is desirable, from others where this is less clearly so.

In the medium term, China may wish to seriously consider the possibility of an enumeration of all internal barriers on trade and factor movements, in the same fashion as was undertaken in the European Community, in its White Paper of 1985, and prepare an agenda for dismantling these. China's version of such a document would look very different from that of the EC, where many barriers took the form of technical specifications, or capital mobility constraints due to the independent financial systems of member countries. These are not issues in China today. However, China will have its own list, which will include fees and fines on the movement of goods, tax regimes and factor mobility, and unique problems in the sphere of labor mobility. There will also be many issues, (both including and in addition to those in the five year legal reform program) concerning the drawing up of umbrella legislation on market management, as well as the harmonization of existing legislation, in different parts of China.

Finally, the government at all levels would have to pay more attention to the enforcement of its new regulatory framework. If direct intervention is to be limited, indirect intervention can only be credible if it can be successfully enforced. In this regard there are many instances today of ad hocism in the application of regulations, with wide discretionary margins at all levels of authority. If this situation persists, it will undermine the plausibility of 'market regulation', and lead instead to a situation where decontrol is replaced by anarchy, rather than monitored indirect regulation. The many tax 'zones' and exemptions provide one example; the equally numerous fines, fees and levies on interstate transport and freight, by authorized and unauthorized personnel, provide another. The issue of enforcement must be confronted as part of China's transformation towards indirect regulation and the establishment of a market economy.

REFERENCES

Agarwala, Ramgopal (1992) China: Reforming Intergovernmental Fiscal Relations. World Bank Discussion Papers No. 178. China and Mongolia Department.

Albouy, Yves (1991) 'Coal Pricing in China'. World Bank Discussion Papers, China and Mongolia Department Series, No. 138. Washington D.C.

Altrogge, Phyllis, and Pitman, Russel (1992) 'Some Principles for an Effective Competition Policy in Developing and Transforming Economies'. US Government, Federal Trade Commission and Department of Justice. Mimeo.

Balassa, Bela (1961) The Theory of Economic Integration. R.D Irwin. Homewood, Illinois.

Baldwin, Richard (1989) 'The Growth Effects of 1992'. Economic Policy. pp. 277-99. October.

Banister, Judith (1989) 'The Migration of Surplus Laborers in China'. Mimeo, US Bureau of the Census.

Berglöf, Erik and Perotti. Enrico (1992) 'The Governance Structure of the Japanese Financial Keiretsu'. ECARE (European Center for Advanced Research in Economics), Free University of Brussels and the London School of Economics. Mimeo. November.

Boner, Roger and Krueger, Reinald (1991) 'The Basics of Antitrust Policy: A Review of Ten Nations and the EEC'. Industry Series paper No. 43. World Bank. February.

Buiges, P. and Sheehy, J. (1993) 'Recent Developments and Trends of European Integration'. Commission of the European Communities. Mimeo, March.

Byrd, William A. (1987) 'The Impact of the Two Tier Plan/Market System in Chinese Industry. *Journal of Comparative Economics*. Vol. 11, No. 3 pp. 309-18. September.

Ceccini, Paolo (1988) The European Challenge 1992. The Benefits of a Single Market. The Commission of the European Communities and Gower, UK.

Chetty, V.K., Ratha, D., and Singh, I.J. (1993) 'Wage Incentives, Labor Productivity and Economic Reforms'. Mimeo, Policy Research Department, World Bank.

China Investment Guide (1989) (4th edition). 'Regulation Concerning Preferential Tax Policy in the SEZs and 14 Coastal Cities'. CITIC Publishing House.

Chinese Academy of Social Sciences (CASS) (1992) 'The Current State of Inter-Provincial Trade in China and its Development Strategy'. Mimeo, November.

Chinese Academy of Social Sciences (CASS) (1992) 'Background Data on the Chinese Consumer Commodity Circulation Channel'. Mimeo, November.

Chinese Academy of Social Sciences (CASS) (1992) 'The Evolution and Change of the Purchasing and Marketing System for Consumer Goods in China'. Mimeo, November.

Chinese Academy of Social Sciences (CASS) (1992) 'A Study on the Consumer Goods Circulation System in China'. Mimeo, November.

Chinese Academy of Social Sciences (CASS) (1992) 'Background Data for Research of China's Price Management System of Consumer Goods'. Mimeo, November.

Christiansen, Flemming (1992) '"Market Transition" in China: The Case of the Jiangsu Labor Market, 1978-1990'. *Modern China*. vol. 18, No. 1, pp. 72-93. January.

de Melo, Jaime, Panagariya, Arvind and Rodrik, Dani (1992) 'The New Regionalism: A Country Perspective. World Bank and CEPR conference on New Dimensions in Regional Integration. Washington DC. April.

Development Research Center, Government of China (1992) 'The Principles of Economic Zoning of China'. Mimeo, November

Development Research Center, Government of China (1992) 'Marketization in China: Progress in the past Decade'. Mimeo, November

Dongsheng, Chen (1990) 'The Regional Economy', in P. Nolan and D. Fureng (eds.) *The Chinese Economy and its Future*. Polity Press, Cambridge, UK. pp. 259-267

Donnithorne, Audrey (1972) 'China's Cellular Economy: Some Trends since the Cultural Revolution.' *China Quarterly*. No. 52, pp. 605-19. October-December.

Economic Research Center, State Council of the People's Republic of China (1981) 'Regulations on Special Economic Zones in Guangdong Province' in the Almanac of China's Economy, 1981.

Emerson, M. et. al. (1988) The Economics of 1992. Oxford University Press, Oxfrod.

European Commission (1985) 'Completing the Internal Market'. White Paper from the commission to the Council. Luxembourg.

European Commission (1992a) 'Completing the Internal Market. Current Status 1 January 1992'. Paper from the Commission to the Council. 5 volumes. Luxembourg.

European Commission (1992b) Seventh Report of the Commission to the Council and the European Parliament concerning the Implementation of the White Paper on the Completion of the Internal Market. Luxembourg.

Findlay, C., Martin, A., Watson, A. (1992)
'Policy Reform, Economic Growth and China's Agriculture' University of Adelaide and the World Bank. Mimeo.

Forster, Keith (1991)
'China's Tea War'. Chinese Economy Research Unit, The University of Adelaide. Mimeo.

Gao Shangquan and Ye Sen (eds.) (1990, 1991) China Economic Systems Reform Yearbooks. China Reform Publishing House. Beijing.

Groves, Theodore, Hong, Yongmiao, McMillan, John and Naughton, Barry (1992) 'Autonomy and Incentives in Chinese State Enterprises'. University of California at San Diego. Mimeo, March.

Groves, Theodore, Hong, Yongmiao, McMillan, John and Naughton, Barry (1992) 'China's Evolving Managerial Labor Market'. University of California San Diego. Discussion Paper 92-36. September.

Halpern, Nina P. (1993) 'Changing State Functions: The 1988 Reorganization of the State Economic Bureaucracy'. Department of Political Science, Stanford University. Mimeo.

Harral, Clell G. (ed.) (1992) Transport Development in Southern China. World Bank Discussion Paper No. 151, China and Mongolia Department Series.

HMSO Stationery Office (1975)'A Review of Monopolies and Mergers Policy'. London.

Huang, Yinfei (1992) 'Basic Situation of China's Financial Markets'. *Financial Research* (Jinrong Yanjiu), February.

Huang, Weixin (1992) Economic Integration as a Development Device. The Case of the EC and China. Nijmegen Studies in Development and Cultural Change. Vol 9. Verlag Breitenbach, Saarbrücken and Fort Lauderdale.

Hufbauer, Gary C. (ed.) (1990) Europe 1992: An American Perspective. Brookings Institute. Washington DC.

Hufbauer, Gary C., and Schott, Jeffrey J. (1992) North American Free Trade: Issues and Recommendations. Institute for International Economics, Washington DC.

Jacobs, Jane (1968) 'The Economy of Cities'. Vintage Books, New York.

Jefferson, Gary, Rawski, Thomas G., and Zheng, Yuxin (1992) 'Growth, Efficiency and Convergence in China's State and Collective Industry'. *Economic Development and Cultural Change*. No. 40, pp. 239-66. January.

Jefferson, Gary and Rawski, Thomas G. (1992) 'Unemployment, Underemployment and Employment Policies in China's Cities'. *Modern China*. vol. 18, No. 1, pp. 42-71. January.

Jefferson, Gary and Wenyi Xu (1991) 'The Impact of Reform on Socialist Enterprises in Transition: Structure, Conduct and Performance in Chinese Industry'. *Journal of Comparative Economics*. vol. 15, No. 1, pp. 45-64.

Jefferson, Gary and Rawski, Thomas G. (1993) 'Labor Markets as a Constraint on Reform in China's Urban Economy' Mimeo, Universities of Brandeis and Pittsburgh.

Keidel, Albert (1993) The Third Japan US Symposium on China: Foreign Economic Relations. The Johns Hopkins University. Mimeo, July.

Khan, A.R., Griffin, Keith, Riskin, Carl, and Zhao Renwei (1992) 'Household Income and its Distribution in China'. *China Quarterly*. (U.K.) No 132, December. pp 1029-61.

Kobayashi, Hironao (1992) 'Rural Economy and Distribution Problems in China'. *China Newsletter*. No. 98, pp. 13-20. May-June. Jetro, Tokyo.

Krugman, Paul (1991a) 'Increasing Returns and Economic Geography'. *Journal of Political Economy*. Vol. 99, No. 3, pp. 483-99. June.

Krugman, Paul (1991b) Geograpy and Trade. The MIT Press, Cambridge, Massachusetts USA and London England.

Krugman, Paul (1991c) 'History and Industrial Location: The Case of the Manufacturing Belt'. *American Economic Review*, papers and proceedings. pp. 80-3. May.

Landell Mills Commodities (1993) The System of Commodity Exchanges in China. Mimeo, Oxford, U.K.

Langenfeld, James and Blitzer, Marsha W. (1991) 'Is Competition Policy the Last Thing Central and Eastern Europe Need?'. The American Journal of International Law and Policy. Vo. 6, No. 3, pp. 347-398. Spring.

Langhammer, Rolf J. and Hiemenz, Ulrich (1991) 'Regional Integration Among Developing Countries'. UNDP-World Bank Trade Expansion Program Occasional Paper 7. Washington D.C.

Lardy, Nicholas (1978) Economic Growth and Distribution in China. Cambridge University Press, New York.

Lardy, Nicholas (1983) Agriculture in China's Modern Economic Development. Cambridge University Press, New York.

Lichtenstein, Natalie G. (1993) 'Enterprise Reform in China: The Evolving Legal Framework'. Annex 4 in 'China: Enterprise Reform Strategy'. World Bank, Washington D.C. Draft. August.

Liu, Alan P. (1991) 'Communications and Development in Post-Mao Mainland China'. *Issues and Studies*. Vol. 27, No. 12, pp. 73-99. December.

Liu, Yuelin (1993) Public Policy and Competition Amongst Foreign Investment Projects: a case study of the Daya Bay Economic Development Zone in South China. *Public Administration and Development. Vol. 13, pp 65-800.*

Lou Jiwei (1992) 'On Division of Economic Power between Central and Local Levels', in *Chinese Economic Studies*, (eds.) Christine Wong and Dai Yuanchen. Vol. 25, Fall 1991-Summer 1992.

Lyons, Thomas P. (1987) Economic Integration and Planning in Maoist China. Columbia University Press, New York.

Lyons, Thomas P. (1990) 'Planning and Interprovincial Cordination in Maoist China'. *China Quarterly* No. 121, pp. 36-60. March.

Lyons, Thomas P. (1991) 'Interprovincial Disparities in China: Output and Consumption: 1952-1987'. *Economic Development and Cultural Change*. Vol. 39, No. 3, pp. 471-506. April.

Lyons, Thomas P. (1992) 'Grain in Fujian: Intra-Provincial Patterns of Production and Trade, 1952-1988. *The China Quarterly*. Vol. 129, pp. 184-215. March.

Lyons, Thomas P. (1992) 'Market-Oriented Reform in China: Cautionary Tales'. Department of Economics, Cornell University, Mimeo. November.

Ma, Jun and Li, Yong (1992) 'China's Regional Economic Policy: Effects and Alternatives'. Mimeo. Georgetown University, Washington D.C. and Shandong Economics Research Center. September.

Ma, Jun (1992) 'China's Regional Policy and its Macroeconomic Implications'. Mimeo, IMF.

Manion, Melanie (1993) 'Corruption by Design: An Institutional Study of Political corruption in the People's Republic of China. Case 1: Enterprise Licensing in a period of Market Reform'. Department of Political Science. University of Rochester, NY. Mimeo.

Michalopoulos, Constantine and Tarr, David (1992) 'Trade and Payments Arrangements for the States of Former USSR'. Studies of Economies in Transition Paper No. 2. World Bank. Washington D.C.

McMillan, John and Naughton, Barry (1992) 'How to Reform a Planned Economy: Lessons from China'. *Oxford Review of Economic Policy*. Vol. 8, No. 1, pp. 130-143. Spring.

Ministry of Materials and Equipment, Government of China (1992) 'Reforms of the Materials and Equipment Planning System'. Background Paper 1. November

Ministry of Materials and Equipment, Government of China (1992) 'Reforms of Prices for Materials and Equipment'. Background Paper 2. November

Ministry of Materials and Equipment, Government of China (1992) 'Developemnt of Materials and Equipment Market'. Background Paper 3. November

Ministry of Materials and Equipment, Government of China (1992) 'Reform of Materials Enterprises'. Background Paper 4. November

Ministry of Materials and Equipment, Government of China (1992) 'Reform of the Administrative Departments for Materials Circulation'. Background Paper 5. November

Ministry of Materials and Equipment, Government of China (1992) 'Introduction to Materials and Equipment Circulation Facilities, P.R.C'. Background Paper 6. November

Murphy, Kevin M., Schleifer, Andrei and Vishny, Robert W. (1989a) 'Income Distribution, Market Size and Industrialization'. *Quarterly Journal of Economics*, Vol. 104, pp. 537-564. August.

Murphy, Kevin M., Schleifer, Andrei and Vishny, Robert W. (1989b) 'Industrialization and the Big Push' *Journal of Political Economy* Vol, 97 pp. 1003-26. October.

Naughton, Barry (1992) 'Implications of the State Monopoly Over Industry and its Relaxation'. *Modern China*. Vol. 18, No. 1 pp. 14-41. January.

Ody, Anthony (1991) China: Rural Enterprise, Rural Industry. World Bank, Washington DC.

OECD (Organization for Economic Cooperation and Development) (1991) Competition and Economic Development. Paris.

Oksenberg, Michael and Tong, James (1991) 'The Evolution of Central-Provincial fiscal Relations in China, 1971-1984: The Formal System. *The China Quarterly*. No. 25. March

Owen, Nicholas (1983) Economies of Scale, Competitiveness and Trade Patterns within the European Community. Oxford University Press. Oxford, New York.

Peck, M.J. (1989) 'Industrial Organization and the Gains from Europe 1992'. *Brookings Papers on Economic Activity*. Vol 2, pp. 277-99

Perotti, Enrico (1992) 'Financial Intermediation, Agency Theory and the Allocation of Control: An International Comparison'. Mimeo, Boston University School of Economics.

Pieters, Hans Jürgen (1992) Service. The New Focus in International Manufacturing and Trade. World Bank, Policy Research Working Papers WPS 950. August.

Pinder, John (1991) European Community: The Building of a Union. Oxford University Press. Oxford, New York.

Porter, Michael E. (1990) The Competitive Advantage of Nations. Basic Books. New York.

Putterman, Louis (1992) 'Institutional Boundaries, Structural Change and Economic Reform in China'. *Modern China*. Vol. 18, No. 1 pp. 3-13. January.

Qian, Yingyi and Stiglitz, Joseph (1993) 'A Report on the China Trip for the World Bank Project "Public Policy and the Asian Miracle". Department of Economics, Stanformd University. Mimeo.

Rajaram, Anand (1991) 'Reforming Prices. The Experience of China, Hungary and Poland'. World Bank Discussion Papers, China and Mongolia Department Series, No. 144. Washington D.C.

Rawski, Thomas G (1993) 'An Overvies of Chinese Industry in the 1980s'. Department of Economics, University of Pittsburgh. Mimeo. February.

Romer, Paul M. (1986) 'Increasing Returns and Long Run Growth.' *Journal of Political Economy*. Vol. 94, pp. 1002-1037.

Rutkowski, Mark (1991) 'China's Floating Population and the Labor Market Reforms'. World Bank, Draft.

Shen Liren and Dai Yuanchen (1992) 'Formation of Dukedom Economies and Their Causes and Defects', in *Chinese Economic Studies*, (eds.) Christine Wong and Dai Yuanchen. Vol. 25, Fall 1991-Summer 1992.

Solinger, Dorothy J. (1989a) 'Urban Reform and Relational contracting in Post-Mao China: An Interpretation of the Transition from Plan to Market'. Studies in Comparative Communism, Vol. XXII No 2/3. pp. 171-185. Summer/Autumn.

Solinger, Dorothy J. (1989b) 'City, Province and Region. The Case of Wuhan', in Bruce L. Reynolds and Ilpyong J. Kim (eds.) 'Chinese Economic Policy. Economic Reform at Midstream'. Paragon House, New York.

Solinger, Dorothy J. (1991) From Lathes to Looms: China's Industrial Policy in Comparative Perspective, 1979-1982. Stanford University Press, California.

Solinger, Dorothy J. (1992) 'The Floating Population in the Cities: Chances for Assimilation?' Paper presented at the conference on 'City Living, City Lives: The Potential for Community and Autonomy in Post-Mao China' Woodrow Wilson Center, Washington DC. May.

Solinger, Dorothy J. (1993) 'China's Transients and the State: A Form of Civil Society?'. *Politics and Society*. Vol. 21, No. 1, March.

State Commission for the Restructuring of the Economic System (SCRES), Government of China. (1990) 'New Progress Made in Enterprise Mergers During Economic Rectification'. China Economic Systems Reform Yearbook. pp 54-61.

Swann, Dennis (ed.) (1992) The Single European Market and Beyond. A Study of the Wider Implications of the Single European Act. Routledge, London and New York.

Swann, Dennis (1983) Competition and Industrial Policy in the European Community. Methuen, London.

Tidrick, Gene and Chen, Jiyuan (eds.) (1987) China's Industrial Reform. Oxford University Press for the World Bank. Washington D.C.

Tian Yuan and Qiao Gang (1991) 'China Price Reform Study'. Electronic Industry Press, Beijing.

Tinbergen, Jan (1965) 'International Economic Integration' 2nd revised edition. Elsevier Publishing Company. The Netherlands.

United States Government (1990) Staff Report No. 12: Highlights of Activity in the Property Motor Carrier Industry. Office of Transportation Analysis, Interstate Commerce Commission. January.

United States Government (1992) US Industrial Outloook. Transportation Services: pp 40-5. Department of Commerce. January.

United States Government (1992) The US Motor Carrier Industry Long After Deregulation. Interstate Commerce Commission. March

United States Government (1991) Overview of Consumer Protection Law in the United States. Mimeo prepared for officials in the Soviet Union, Federal Trade Commission.

Wall, David (1992) 'Special Economic Zones and Industrialization in China' in C. Kirkpatrick (ed) The Impact of Policy Reform on Trade and Industrial Performance in Developing Countries. Manchester University Press. pp. 198-212.

Wall, David (1993) 'Special Economic Zones in China: The Administrative and Regulatory Framework'. *The Journal of East Asian Affairs*, Vol. VII, No. 1, Winter/Spring. pp. 226-261.

Wall, David (1993) 'China's Reform and Opening Up Process: The Role of the Special Economic Zones'. *Development Policy Review*. September.

White, Gordon (1993) Riding the Tiger. The Politics of Economic Reform in Post-Mao China. The Macmillan Press, UK and Hong Kong.

Wiemer, Calla (1992) 'Price Reform and Structural Change: Distributional Impediments to Allocative Gains'. *Modern China*. Vol 18, No. 2, pp. 171-196. April.

Wang, Fang Yi and Mody, Ashoka (1993) 'Industrial Growth in Coastal China: Economic Reforms and What Else?'. Mimeo, World Bank, Washington DC. April.

Watson, Andrew, and Findlay, Christopher (1992) 'The "Wool War" in China' in Christopher findlay (ed.) Challenges of Economic Reform and Industrial Growth: China's Wool War. Allen and Unwin. Australia.

Winters, Alan L. and Venables, Anthony J. (1990) European Integration: Trade and Industry. Cambridge University Press.

Wong, Christine (1992) 'Fiscal Reform and Local Industrialization'. *Modern China*. Vol 18, No. 2, pp. 197-227. April.

Woo, Wing Thye (1993) 'The Art of Reforming Centrally-Planned Economies: comparing China, Poland and Russia'. Mimeo, University of California, Davis. May.

World Bank (1990a) China: Macroeconomic Stability and Industrial Growth under Decentralized Socialism. Washington DC. July.

World Bank (1990b) China: Country Economic Memorandum. Between Plan and Market. Report No. 8440-CHA. Washington DC. May

World Bank (1990c) China: Electronics Sector Report. Report No. 7962-CHA. June

World Bank (1990d) China: Reforming Social Security in a Socialist Economy. Report No. 8074-CHA. June

World Bank (1991) China: Government of Australia and People's Republic of China (1990e) Yangtze Economic Zone Study. Draft. December.

World Bank (1991) China: Industrial Organization and Efficiency Case Study: The Automotive Sector. Draft. June.

World Bank (1991) China: Urban Housing Reforms: Issues and Implementation Options. Report No. 9222-CHA. June.

World Bank (1991) China: Efficiency and Environmental Impact of Coal Use. Two Vols. Report No. 8915-CHA. Washington DC. March.

World Bank (1992) Payment Systems Project. Stocktaking Report. 31 January. Industry and Energy Division. Mimeo.

World Bank (1992) Telecommunications Sector Study. Report No. 9413-CHA. February.

World Bank (1992) China: Railway Investment Study. Report No. 10375-CHA. (3 volumes). February.

World Bank (1992) China's Railway Strategy. Report No. 10592. June.

World Bank (1992) China: Machine Tools Subsector Report. Report No. 10688. June.

World Bank (1992) China: Reforming the Urban Employment and Wage System. Report No. 10266-CHA. June.

World Bank (1992) Industrial Restructuring: A Tale of Three Cities. Report No 10479-CHA. July

World Bank (1992) China: Reform and the Role of the Plan in the 1990s. Washington D.C. September

World Bank (1992) China: Strategy for Reducing Poverty in the 1990s. October.

World Bank (1992) China: Budgetary Policy and Intergovernmental Relations. Report No. 11094-CHA. Draft. October.

World Bank (1992) China: Strategy for Road Freight Service. Initiating Memorandum. Draft.

World Bank (1992) China: The Achievements and Challenge of Price Reform. Country Study.

World Bank (1993) China: Strategies for the Reform and Restructuring of the Fertilizer Industry. February. Mimeo.

World Bank (1993) China: Financial Sector Reform Strategy. Industry and Energy Division. Mimeo, March.

World Bank (1993) China: Foreign Trade Reform: Meeting the Challenge of the 1990s. Report No. 11568-CHA.

Wu, Changqi (1990) 'Enterprise Groups in China's Industry'. *Asia Pacific Journal of Management*. Vol. 7 No. 2. pp. 123-136. October.

Wu Jinglian and Zhao Renwei (1987) 'The Dual Pricing System in China's Industry'. *Journal of Comparative Economics*. Vol. 11, No. 3 pp. 295-308. September.

Zhang Xiaohe, Weiguo, Lu, Keliang, Sun, Findlay, Christopher, and Watson, Andrew (1991) The 'Wool War' and 'Cotton Chaos'. Fibre Marketing in China. Chinese Economic Research Unit, University of Adelaide. No. 91/14.

Zhang, Xun-Hai (1992) Enterprise Reforms in a Centrally Planned Economy: The Case of the Chinese Bicycle Industry. Macmillans, U.K., and St. Martins Press, U.S.A.

Zou, Gang and Ma, Jun (1991-92) 'Promoting Overall Cooperation Between Chinese Coastal Areas and the East Asian Economies.' *Chinese Economic Studies*. Vol. 25, No. 2, pp. 67-83. Winter.

Zweig, David (1993) 'Trade and Investment on the China Coast: Understanding a 'Development Community' in rural China'. Fletcher School of Law and Diplomacy, Tufts University. Mimeo.

STATISTICAL APPENDIX

Table A1.1 Per Capita National Income by Province (1983-1991)
(Yuan)

	1983	1984	1985	1986	1987	1988	1989	1990	1991
All China	489	575	688	765	878	1075	1184	1248	1391
Beijing	1420	1661	2026	2113	2214	2785	3248	3379	3705
Tianjin	1354	1523	1868	2026	2234	2623	2738	2897	3098
Hebei	436	514	614	669	785	963	1074	1140	1274
Shanxi	474	585	656	678	696	847	999	1090	1135
Inner Mongolia	408	485	590	627	697	953	992	1079	1206
Liaoning	811	969	1155	1292	1500	1818	1989	1976	2180
Jilin	556	645	738	820	1015	1236	1268	1357	1424
Heilongjiang	707	804	851	994	1117	1286	1439	1592	1728
Shanghai	2470	2832	3367	3450	3789	4151	4599	4616	5201
Jiangsu	615	756	931	1059	1243	1505	1615	1682	1825
Zhejiang	549	693	908	1037	1235	1532	1660	1743	2037
Anhui	358	433	527	595	675	819	910	915	879
Fujian	406	481	607	668	806	1081	1243	1280	1493
Jiangxi	366	414	500	540	615	747	835	929	1011
Shandong	519	625	718	766	924	1135	1294	1347	1575
Henan	356	400	484	537	637	746	836	1412	954
Hubei	489	602	727	800	908	1067	1147	1079	1281
Hunan	398	446	535	600	692	840	899	965	1049
Guangdong	559	644	804	1034	1092	1509	1718	1784	2144
Guangxi	315	337	398	446	516	616	723	789	888
Hainan						989	1130	1161	1301
Sichuang	343	399	482	512	598	755	809	900	977
Guizhou	272	322	363	403	458	573	625	649	723
Yunnan	317	365	408	450	521	668	771	945	1009
Tibet	269	462	632	545	590	739	777	845	1148
Shaanxi	341	410	488	528	607	764	858	914	1021
Gansu	358	412	499	566	627	758	856	919	988
Qinghai	415	485	604	693	752	958	1048	1103	1165
Ningxia	384	450	538	610	657	836	970	1007	1081
Xinjiang	484	553	657	734	844	1083	1232	1340	1623
SD	447	509	611	630	682	752	832	831	934
Mean	577	680	816	889	1002	1213	1343	1428	1571
COV	0.77	0.75	0.75	0.71	0.68	0.62	0.62	0.58	0.59
GINI	0.300	0.294	0.295	0.291	0.285	0.272	0.271	0.255	0.264

Note: SD: Standard deviation; COV: coefficient of variation; GINI: Gini coefficient.
Source: China Statistical Yearbook (various issues).

Table A1.2 Per Capita Investment in Fixed Assets by Province (1983-1991)

	1983	1984	1985	1986	1987	1988	1989	1990	1991
All China	133.57	177.13	243.29	285.62	336.89	410.22	372.13	389.15	475.62
Beijing	542.61	726.82	984.58	1078.67	1313.50	1504.16	1410.22	1757.00	1861.52
Tianjin	502.15	609.01	828.47	879.61	935.62	1051.60	996.14	1000.90	1426.07
Hebei	117.84	157.32	203.88	238.61	312.54	413.01	364.38	295.70	396.62
Shanxi	174.03	257.50	337.11	357.06	385.02	383.99	377.16	415.49	494.05
Inner Mongolia	147.11	203.93	255.11	227.94	250.00	281.23	262.44	300.37	415.38
Liaoning	200.99	263.12	377.16	476.95	579.77	699.63	647.65	656.31	790.40
Jilin	132.86	184.33	273.72	273.95	334.70	393.30	334.21	376.60	454.32
Heilongjiang	209.68	257.75	333.80	369.54	409.75	452.11	448.92	459.78	530.63
Shanghai	636.60	767.72	975.84	1145.78	1482.24	1935.68	1913.71	1698.50	1927.61
Jiangsu	170.29	209.38	241.38	376.83	498.87	585.82	496.63	533.62	658.08
Zhejiang	110.98	162.51	261.64	319.85	450.50	551.99	505.51	618.76	773.37
Anhui	90.96	121.34	156.17	192.26	221.21	252.65	203.62	220.62	234.49
Fujian	99.51	128.61	202.69	218.30	278.10	322.92	303.45	357.39	430.30
Jiangxi	85.67	104.41	126.39	148.13	164.84	220.45	198.32	185.49	235.65
Shandong	124.39	182.36	251.36	286.87	374.16	458.78	412.55	394.20	513.56
Henan	79.92	113.69	164.53	200.45	204.13	254.76	228.02	388.97	292.61
Hubei	117.41	153.10	206.12	204.95	263.61	300.50	234.15	232.54	280.93
Hunan	88.46	105.79	143.69	165.68	205.28	241.14	185.95	196.39	251.88
Guangdong	155.95	221.83	314.39	365.73	429.95	679.49	633.99	640.89	786.78
Guangxi	59.17	74.01	108.62	139.96	160.10	189.38	160.83	160.92	207.33
Hainan						337.42	453.25	591.40	656.82
Sichuang	67.66	92.92	141.98	150.22	184.68	216.60	207.08	205.70	267.49
Guizhou	59.26	78.41	111.62	103.13	111.32	158.49	122.58	141.13	158.07
Yunnan	68.88	98.66	141.98	169.36	168.17	210.68	193.15	221.20	282.87
Tibet	104.66	253.81	356.28	225.12	331.25	366.51	325.16	431.98	651.33
Shaanxi	100.61	133.24	189.67	206.15	252.99	284.82	293.11	305.07	352.78
Gansu	88.53	117.61	159.77	180.59	209.74	252.35	212.50	249.40	285.16
Qinghai	263.36	318.66	396.31	427.43	502.57	612.90	460.04	480.36	527.31
Ningxia	136.43	200.25	301.45	374.06	425.75	408.09	379.89	437.45	531.25
Xinjiang	206.30	251.04	327.33	373.84	388.83	507.99	540.73	574.75	705.66
NRS									
SD	142.37	174.69	228.23	256.48	315.33	383.87	375.96	380.41	432.39
Mean	170.42	225.83	305.97	340.59	407.90	484.28	450.18	484.30	579.34
COV	0.84	0.77	0.75	0.75	0.77	0.79	0.84	0.79	0.75
GINI	0.360	0.342	0.330	0.333	0.341	0.346	0.364	0.352	0.348

Note: SD: Standard deviation; COV: coefficient of variation; GINI: Gini coefficient.
Source: China Statistical Yearbook (various issues).

Table A1.3 Per Capita Gross Value of Industrial Output by Province
(not including village enterprises) (1981-1990) (Y million)

	1981	1983	1984	1985	1986	1987	1988	1989	1990
All China	519.7	601.4	679.4	793.5	931.6	1094.5	1330.7	1571.5	1634.6
Beijing	2401.4	2683.1	2974.9	3277.8	3540.6	3740.3	4585.1	5811.6	5763.4
Tianjin	2614.5	2904.9	3147.6	3537.1	3896.5	4321.3	5114.4	5766.1	5933.6
Hebei	414.1	466.2	529.0	601.0	704.5	833.9	996.4	1200.3	1225.8
Shanxi	472.9	590.5	657.8	724.7	820.5	936.4	1145.6	1396.8	1462.4
Inner Mongolia	313.6	385.4	413.8	473.5	601.2	699.2	837.7	1035.0	1069.9
Liaoning	1276.8	1423.6	1580.5	1802.5	2124.1	2419.8	2828.0	3295.4	3281.3
Jilin	600.2	727.2	820.8	936.3	1149.0	1399.4	1679.0	1910.3	1926.1
Heilongjiang	773.7	872.7	959.6	1062.0	1362.4	1576.1	1807.0	2080.7	2199.6
Shanghai	5233.9	5683.2	6177.3	6838.7	7370.0	8071.0	8669.1	10763.9	11047.4
Jiangsu	774.9	928.2	1102.1	1389.9	1607.5	1987.0	2494.2	2894.6	3046.1
Zhejiang	552.0	676.5	836.1	1101.6	1311.0	1604.1	2040.4	2361.0	2514.1
Anhui	262.2	317.8	362.6	430.4	542.6	631.7	771.8	920.7	931.5
Fujian	319.9	362.9	432.4	518.9	613.9	757.7	1040.5	1268.9	1296.2
Jiangxi	277.5	313.8	354.3	435.3	540.7	647.4	808.8	908.8	900.6
Shandong	464.7	536.2	597.4	701.7	839.2	1038.2	1331.5	1680.4	1786.0
Henan	275.2	311.7	350.3	416.8	488.1	568.4	683.1	813.9	824.5
Hubei	520.2	646.7	736.9	858.6	987.2	1158.4	1340.2	1535.4	1529.3
Hunan	328.8	373.7	412.6	468.9	586.7	689.5	825.2	947.1	957.4
Guangdong	425.5	503.6	595.0	737.3	902.1	1184.2	1626.0	1999.5	2174.6
Guangxi	225.9	254.2	273.8	319.3	390.7	471.6	566.7	674.0	701.5
Hainan							391.4	494.1	544.3
Sichuang	277.4	337.4	386.7	445.8	524.7	617.6	743.6	873.0	907.6
Guizhou	155.0	214.5	250.2	281.7	328.0	374.4	458.0	546.7	583.1
Yunnan	219.9	268.6	312.2	354.1	406.8	488.7	601.9	742.8	825.4
Tibet	61.3	67.4	68.0	69.8	75.9	84.6	47.2	112.9	118.5
Shaanxi	367.5	441.7	487.4	564.2	629.2	719.5	889.6	1052.7	1084.4
Gansu	383.5	443.2	486.1	560.8	668.0	716.8	862.5	1030.2	1100.5
Qinghai	309.4	363.1	403.5	476.2	624.8	704.9	917.3	1149.4	1141.5
Ningxia	323.0	405.0	452.2	526.3	637.3	726.9	908.3	1141.2	1210.0
Xinjiang	315.9	405.8	445.5	535.9	686.4	788.8	860.7	1057.2	1139.6
SD	1029.70	1118.14	1215.07	1343.06	1441.62	1568.11	1719.05	2100.19	2141.32
Mean	722.10	824.45	917.46	1049.91	1205.50	1377.85	1595.71	1915.48	1974.20
COV	1.43	1.36	1.32	1.28	1.20	1.14	1.08	1.10	1.08
GINI	0.508	0.492	0.486	0.478	0.458	0.445	0.433	0.433	0.430

Note: SD: Standard deviation; COV: coefficient of variation; GINI: Gini coefficient.
Source: China Statistical Yearbook (various issues).

Table A1.4 Per Capita Gross Value of Industrial Output by Province
(including village enterprises) (1985-1991)

	1985	1986	1987	1988	1989	1990	1991
All China	885.4	1058.8	1278.1	1662.6	1980.1	2092.5	2438.9
Beijing	3504.6	3812.9	4095.4	2488.1	6836.7	6765.0	8051.1
Tianjin	3867.1	4287.3	4879.8	6214.2	7420.8	7691.5	8409.2
Hebei	740.3	901.2	1122.0	1451.5	1744.7	1820.5	2141.4
Shanxi	875.5	986.1	1119.9	1268.4	1746.0	1857.2	2044.4
Inner Mongolia	489.4	622.5	731.8	1106.2	1139.1	1199.6	1373.2
Liaoning	1949.2	2341.6	2764.7	3415.8	3989.8	4050.7	4663.1
Jilin	992.8	1220.2	1532.2	1033.5	2207.1	2224.7	2448.7
Heilongjiang	1098.1	1406.3	1646.8	1979.3	2292.8	2437.2	2751.7
Shanghai	7146.8	7729.0	8533.8	9514.5	11875.8	12213.5	14531.2
Jiangsu	1667.2	1970.0	2505.5	3344.1	3836.3	4084.7	4617.7
Zhejiang	1359.5	1655.0	2063.8	2736.3	3169.9	3437.0	4287.0
Anhui	492.4	621.7	745.2	963.7	1147.8	1181.2	1329.5
Fujian	609.4	743.9	946.9	1366.8	1688.4	1750.0	2139.9
Jiangxi	485.3	609.1	727.8	956.9	1099.2	1117.5	1288.3
Shandong	804.3	1005.4	1297.9	1805.3	2354.1	2592.1	3032.9
Henan	476.3	612.3	746.2	963.6	1158.5	1198.7	1395.3
Hubei	928.0	1074.2	1287.5	1610.4	1857.6	1888.3	2061.0
Hunan	515.8	647.6	785.4	987.9	1131.8	1163.0	1294.4
Guangdong	828.3	1022.3	1390.3	2224.9	2734.0	2997.5	3920.0
Guangxi	337.3	417.6	515.7	664.9	787.7	829.5	974.7
Hainan				497.6	609.3	668.5	841.1
Sichuang	484.5	580.0	693.6	911.6	1071.6	1131.9	1316.1
Guizhou	302.5	359.0	412.5	533.5	635.6	675.2	744.4
Yunnan	367.9	426.0	514.3	680.7	835.7	925.4	1040.8
Tibet	74.9	83.7	95.2	59.0	132.7	138.3	150.4
Shaanxi	625.2	720.5	836.6	1058.2	1274.4	1334.7	1513.0
Gansu	580.3	695.3	755.6	943.1	1143.1	1231.4	1375.8
Qinghai	497.1	650.2	731.3	979.5	1230.2	1233.0	1332.8
Ningxia	551.1	669.1	767.4	988.8	1285.5	1377.7	1522.9
Xinjiang	549.8	705.9	814.5	1045.5	1288.8	1438.4	1804.4
SD	1416.34	1526.75	1685.29	1851.74	2411.62	2466.02	2898.02
Mean	1144.86	1330.22	1553.78	1793.11	2324.17	2421.79	2813.21
COV	1.24	1.15	1.08	1.03	1.04	1.02	1.03
GINI	0.474	0.451	0.440	0.412	0.430	0.425	0.430

Note: SD: Standard deviation; COV: coefficient of variation;   GINI: Gini coefficient.
Source: China Statistical Yearbook (various issues).

Table A1.5 Number and Gross Output Value of Industrial Enterprises by Ownership
(1985-1991)

	Total			State Enterprises			Collectives			Individual		
	No. of firms 10,000	GOV/a Y 100m	Avg GOV Y 10,000	No. of firms 10,000	GOV/a Y 100m	Avg GOV Y 10,000	No. of firms 10,000	GOV/a Y 100m	Avg GOV Y 10,000	No. of firms 10,000	GOV/a Y100m	Avg GOV Y 10,000
1985	518.5	9716.5	18.7	9.4	6302.1	672.6	174.2	3117.2	17.9	334.8	179.8	0.5
1987	747.4	13388.7	17.9	9.8	7996.7	819.3	181.9	4634.8	25.5	555.3	487.0	0.9
1988	810.6	15425.0	19.0	9.9	8761.0	884.1	185.3	5575.4	30.1	614.8	669.0	1.1
1989	798.1	16741.9	21.0	10.2	9385.6	917.5	174.7	5975.3	34.2	612.4	804.3	1.3
1990	795.8	18041.1	22.7	10.4	9851.2	943.6	166.9	6426.9	38.5	617.6	973.0	1.6
1991	808.0	20660.7	25.6	10.5	10937.8	1044.7	157.7	7376.0	46.8	638.7	1176.9	1.8

/a Gross Output Value (GOV) deflated into 1985 constant prices.
The numbers of the three ownerships do not add up to the sum becasue of "other ownership."
Source: China Statistical Yearbook 1992.

Table A1.6 Number of Enterprises, Gross Output Value (GOV), and Number of Employees (1991)

	Coal Mining			Tobacco			Textiles		
	No. of firms	GOV Y100m	No. of persons 10,000	No. of firms	GOV Y100m	No. of persons 10,000	No. of firms	GOV Y100m	No. of persons 10,000
All China	9610	518.86	617.29	329	547.45	31.04	24596	2533.27	958.35
Beijing	51	3.68	6.65	2	4.43	0.16	300	46.52	13.74
Tianjin				1	4.47	0.41	373	53.28	20.96
Hebei	320	29.62	40.56	3	15.12	0.82	1474	130.27	48.64
Shanxi	1719	111.03	80.01	3	2.69	0.24	359	26.25	14.95
Inner Mongolia	362	17.66	22.77	2	4.88	0.27	231	22.61	9.95
Liaoning	255	37.79	43.50	5	4.99	0.61	860	91.91	47.46
Jilin	226	13.09	23.73	7	9.75	0.68	331	22.60	14.36
Heilongjiang	323	54.63	53.10	19	11.39	1.11	532	35.75	24.18
Shanghai	0	0.00	0.00	2	26.60	0.59	1011	219.40	60.78
Jiangsu	67	19.09	19.55	5	12.31	0.68	3898	482.73	151.76
Zhejiang	69	2.26	2.54	4	14.13	0.54	4275	317.79	92.31
Anhui	138	22.87	27.88	11	29.55	1.56	977	72.44	36.15
Fujian	134	3.95	4.60	18	15.28	0.60	442	26.96	11.79
Jiangxi	402	12.10	20.08	4	5.57	0.40	501	28.35	17.19
Shandong	338	46.71	51.51	15	30.43	2.05	2051	274.37	92.06
Henan	320	41.51	51.56	32	39.81	3.50	989	85.35	44.94
Hubei	362	3.46	6.47	20	31.00	2.42	1262	124.32	62.74
Hunan	812	16.49	27.40	17	44.66	2.47	574	40.03	26.16
Guangdong	145	5.52	7.74	39	35.66	1.31	1501	172.39	40.74
Guangxi	104	4.82	6.92	16	14.97	1.12	263	25.19	11.52
Hainan	1	0.05	0.06	1	1.71	0.10	25	1.78	0.81
Sichuan	1905	30.04	55.21	23	24.68	2.17	1112	101.53	57.74
Guizhou	432	7.80	12.52	16	33.84	2.14	97	5.89	4.17
Yunnan	257	6.15	8.57	20	101.87	2.68	113	12.72	6.11
Tibet	4	0.05	0.04	0	0.00	0.00	3	0.14	0.11
Shaanxi	380	9.68	18.68	16	19.75	1.84	459	53.75	22.59
Gansu	218	5.86	9.39	12	4.66	0.37	197	11.92	7.08
Qinghai	33	0.95	2.54	1	0.30	0.04	38	3.25	2.24
Ningxia	60	6.23	6.65	1	0.74	0.06	66	2.73	1.75
Xinjiang	245	5.76	6.86	14	2.21	0.13	282	41.02	13.35
SD	438	22.99	20.65	9.76	20.22	0.94	1008	108.57	33.56
Mean	334	17.89	21.28	11.34	18.88	1.07	848	87.35	33.05
COV	1.31	1.29	0.97	0.86	1.07	0.87	1.19	1.24	1.02

....contd./

Table A1.6 Number of Enterprises, Gross Output Value (GOV),
and Number of Employees (1991) (cont.)

	Chemicals			Building Materials			Ferrous Metals		
	No. of firms	GOV Y 100m	No. of persons 10,000	No. of firms	GOV Y 100m	No. of persons 10,000	No. of firms	GOV Y 100m	No. of persons 10,000
All China	19932	1625.07	445.38	52179	1055.40	718.14	3432	1538.50	323.03
Beijing	252	42.80	7.07	452	27.15	11.82	32	74.55	10.46
Tianjin	333	63.71	11.56	331	14.07	7.61	46	60.17	6.12
Hebei	1129	71.48	22.03	2824	62.39	39.81	260	97.27	23.04
Shanxi	640	40.87	19.82	1347	17.70	15.45	291	61.16	17.46
Inner Mongolia	255	12.37	6.36	1090	12.60	11.28	83	37.96	11.27
Liaoning	1142	114.14	35.29	2401	68.14	44.59	367	246.09	55.52
Jilin	614	62.84	15.52	1557	27.23	20.67	89	28.00	7.93
Heilongjiang	511	26.65	9.88	1799	28.45	23.89	92	24.27	7.74
Shanghai	506	125.67	15.92	465	36.52	14.29	96	221.46	18.93
Jiangsu	2309	236.43	50.68	5142	113.62	86.59	295	88.99	15.39
Zhejiang	1350	81.29	17.95	3563	63.80	42.22	133	26.07	4.85
Anhui	931	44.64	14.88	4388	40.12	43.5	83	40.71	11.61
Fujian	658	36.17	10.29	978	23.62	11.46	93	13.34	3.28
Jiangxi	562	23.58	9.44	1946	26.93	24.78	45	25.38	7.78
Shandong	1262	115.38	29.80	3532	94.98	50.39	151	56.30	11.42
Henan	932	63.16	23.39	2859	53.11	40.87	101	33.97	8.53
Hubei	1034	64.88	21.05	2793	47.18	38.06	152	107.56	22.44
Hunan	1117	61.37	20.38	3027	45.09	37.43	112	38.19	9.43
Guangdong	922	107.70	16.81	2045	102.62	34.66	117	33.69	6.11
Guangxi	441	30.12	8.36	1129	24.61	15.01	64	15.28	4.24
Hainan	49	1.41	0.47	80	2.06	1.35	3	0.33	0.11
Sichuan	1402	93.18	33.91	4009	54.40	47.54	320	123.41	30.48
Guizhou	235	14.34	5.62	513	9.82	7.87	91	15.84	5.94
Yunnan	253	27.04	8.57	562	11.62	8.14	97	19.48	6.23
Tibet	4	0.01	0.03	7	0.68	0.2			
Shaanxi	569	23.35	10.29	1640	19.19	17.23	86	13.61	4.52
Gansu	343	27.00	8.28	799	13.37	10.34	49	15.06	5.6
Qinghai	48	3.16	6.21	165	2.32	2.55	30	8.52	1.9
Ningxia	85	4.00	1.94	239	3.12	2.51	30	3.96	1.14
Xinjiang	144	6.35	3.61	497	8.88	6.02	24	7.84	3.58
SD	513	49.46	11.20	1399	29.80	19.49	94.22	58.55	10.93
Mean	668	54.17	14.85	1739	35.18	23.94	118.34	53.05	11.14
COV	0.77	0.91	0.75	0.80	0.85	0.81	0.80	1.10	0.98

....contd./

Table A1.6 Number of Enterprises, Gross Output Value (GOV),
and Number of Employees (1991)

	Machine Building			Electronics and Telecommunications		
	No. of firms	GOV Y 100m	No. of persons 10,000	No. of firms	GOV Y 100m	No. of persons 10,000
All China	42496	1995.40	990.96	4919	764.69	175.35
Beijing	684	68.52	25.60	162	45.69	8.86
Tianjin	750	56.90	25.10	133	28.97	6.53
Hebei	2245	80.37	44.41	127	9.51	3.11
Shanxi	1143	41.70	30.96	53	2.61	2.13
Inner Mongolia	564	21.10	14.81	31	4.05	0.93
Liaoning	3499	154.91	100.53	252	25.92	10.43
Jilin	1186	35.06	24.95	74	6.05	2.84
Heilongjiang	1497	63.19	45.61	64	4.05	1.88
Shanghai	1623	205.87	65.84	333	82.73	15.31
Jiangsu	4604	261.67	107.86	864	126.89	29.25
Zhejiang	5351	119.54	51.10	692	33.45	10.03
Anhui	1558	44.82	24.72	82	10.80	2.76
Fujian	916	27.55	13.01	236	37.57	4.49
Jiangxi	1197	29.07	20.77	72	10.10	3.80
Shandong	2314	160.91	65.06	161	23.68	5.61
Henan	1760	96.02	53.57	70	9.08	3.05
Hubei	1689	66.60	43.79	121	12.25	5.58
Hunan	1757	56.37	36.58	151	8.83	4.13
Guangdong	1762	117.00	32.47	868	174.51	27.78
Guangxi	636	29.23	12.45	42	4.98	1.87
Hainan	54	0.96	0.91	13	2.41	0.42
Sichuan	2971	129.50	70.79	158	39.94	11.70
Guizhou	289	17.56	10.26	30	5.25	2.64
Yunnan	330	21.38	12.25	19	3.80	0.65
Tibet	12	0.02	0.02	0	0.00	0.00
Shaanxi	1224	46.56	32.16	84	44.29	7.33
Gansu	400	18.97	12.50	16	5.74	1.74
Qinghai	119	5.61	3.74	3	0.28	0.19
Ningxia	134	8.79	4.16	4	0.16	0.14
Xinjiang	228	9.63	5.00	4	1.11	0.18
SD	1281	63.08	27.31	230	38.71	7.14
Mean	1417	66.51	33.03	170	26.37	6.05
COV	0.90	0.95	0.83	1.36	1.47	1.18

Source: China Industrial Statistical Yearbook 1992.

Table A1.7a Average Gross Output Value (GOV) Per Enterprise by Province and Industry (1990) (Y million)

	Coal Mining	Tobacco	Textiles	Chemicals	Building Materials	Ferrous Metals	Machine Building	Electronics & Telecomm
All China	4.76	161.51	9.32	7.72	1.68	38.30	3.95	12.60
Beijing	6.94	213.00	14.64	34.43	5.09	209.60	8.76	22.49
Tianjin		598.00	15.13	18.52	3.48	108.94	7.35	18.38
Hebei	9.30	465.67	7.69	5.70	1.86	31.90	3.06	5.93
Shanxi	5.60	85.67	6.75	6.14	1.08	17.48	3.40	4.98
Inner Mongolia	2.31	224.00	9.10	5.09	0.97	41.07	2.94	15.50
Liaoning	12.90	120.40	10.18	9.63	2.45	57.51	4.03	12.23
Jilin	4.77	136.86	6.66	9.57	1.50	28.33	2.59	8.81
Heilongjiang	12.88	57.32	6.26	4.40	1.37	23.01	3.58	5.39
Shanghai		1203.50	20.32	21.67	6.52	196.40	10.58	21.09
Jiangsu	23.47	256.40	11.82	9.39	1.89	27.04	4.64	12.52
Zhejiang	3.44	347.25	6.15	5.06	1.50	17.35	1.68	3.93
Anhui	14.70	271.45	6.74	5.10	0.82	43.29	2.37	10.70
Fujian	2.84	83.35	5.65	5.09	1.90	12.78	2.58	11.87
Jiangxi	2.78	183.00	5.42	4.02	1.18	67.56	2.07	12.99
Shandong	12.69	181.20	12.24	8.42	2.14	30.76	6.01	12.69
Henan	13.04	117.42	7.68	6.11	1.60	30.95	4.55	9.59
Hubei	1.04	160.59	8.63	5.78	1.49	62.31	3.45	10.58
Hunan	1.91	240.13	6.53	5.98	1.25	31.36	2.94	6.67
Guangdong	2.73	87.33	8.79	9.55	3.56	21.93	4.57	11.44
Guangxi	3.94	99.31	9.57	6.25	1.69	21.31	3.76	10.49
Hainan	4.00	147.00	6.15	2.31	1.73	11.00	1.43	31.13
Sichuan	1.35	97.83	8.62	6.12	1.08	32.65	3.55	23.66
Guizhou	1.55	217.13	6.89	5.18	1.65	16.81	5.77	19.57
Yunnan	2.23	488.37	10.63	10.08	1.64	16.09	5.58	18.06
Tibet	1.25	0.00	4.67	0.25	7.25	0.00	0.17	0.00
Shaanxi	2.32	119.00	11.03	3.82	0.85	14.62	3.29	37.46
Gansu	2.62	40.82	5.50	7.77	1.53	24.55	4.52	37.11
Qinghai	2.76	29.00	9.14	5.98	1.15	24.23	4.99	9.00
Ningxia	9.00	69.00	4.16	4.30	1.05	11.00	6.34	1.33
Xinjiang	1.91	15.77	10.98	4.09	1.38	34.89	3.07	34.50
SD	5.42	231.10	3.46	6.46	1.56	47.73	2.14	9.88
Mean	5.94	219.16	8.79	7.86	2.09	43.68	4.12	15.18
COV	0.91	1.05	0.39	0.82	0.75	1.09	0.52	0.65

Source: China Industrial Statistical Yearbook 1991.

Table A1.7b Average Gross Output Value (GOV) Per Enterprise by Province and Industry (1991)
(Y million)

	Coal Mining	Tobacco	Textiles	Chemicals	Building Materials	Ferrous Metals	Machine Building	Electronics & Telecomm
All China	5.40	166.40	10.30	8.15	2.02	44.83	4.70	15.55
Beijing	7.22	221.50	15.51	16.98	6.01	232.97	10.02	28.20
Tianjin		447.00	14.28	19.13	4.25	130.80	7.59	21.78
Hebei	9.26	504.00	8.84	6.33	2.21	37.41	3.58	7.49
Shanxi	6.46	89.67	7.31	6.39	1.31	21.02	3.65	4.92
Inner Mongolia	4.88	244.00	9.79	4.85	1.16	45.73	3.74	13.06
Liaoning	14.82	99.80	10.69	9.99	2.84	67.05	4.43	10.29
Jilin	5.79	139.29	6.83	10.23	1.75	31.46	2.96	8.18
Heilongjiang	16.91	59.95	6.72	5.22	1.58	26.38	4.22	6.33
Shanghai				24.84	7.85	230.69	12.68	24.84
Jiangsu	28.49	246.20	12.38	10.24	2.21	30.17	5.68	14.69
Zhejiang	3.28	353.25	7.43	6.02	1.79	19.60	2.23	4.83
Anhui	16.57	268.64	7.41	4.79	0.91	49.05	2.88	13.17
Fujian	2.95	84.89	6.10	5.50	2.42	14.34	3.01	15.92
Jiangxi	3.01	139.25	5.66	4.20	1.38	56.40	2.43	14.03
Shandong	13.82	202.87	13.38	9.14	2.69	37.28	6.95	14.71
Henan	1.08	124.41	8.63	6.78	1.86	33.63	5.46	12.97
Hubei	4.56	155.00	9.85	6.27	1.69	70.76	3.94	10.12
Hunan	0.68	262.71	6.97	5.49	1.49	34.10	3.21	5.85
Guangdong	3.32	91.44	11.49	11.68	5.02	28.79	6.64	20.10
Guangxi	4.63	93.56	9.58	6.83	2.18	23.88	4.60	11.86
Hainan	5.00	171.00	7.12	2.88	2.58	11.00	1.78	18.54
Sichuan	1.58	107.30	9.13	6.65	1.36	38.57	4.36	25.28
Guizhou	1.81	211.50	6.07	6.10	1.91	17.41	6.08	17.50
Yunnan	2.39	509.35	11.26	10.69	2.07	20.08	6.48	20.00
Tibet	1.25		4.67	0.25	9.71		0.17	
Shaanxi	1.54	123.44	11.71	4.10	1.17	15.83	3.80	52.73
Gansu	0.44	38.83	6.05	7.87	1.67	30.73	4.74	35.88
Qinghai	18.88	30.00	8.55	6.58	1.41	28.40	4.71	9.33
Ningxia	9.60	74.00	4.14	4.71	1.31	13.20	6.56	4.00
Xinjiang	0.00	15.79	14.55	4.41	1.79	32.67	4.22	27.75
SD	6.81	132.37	2.99	4.92	2.01	54.77	2.42	10.42
Mean	6.56	176.16	8.74	7.84	2.59	47.65	4.76	16.36
COV	1.04	0.75	0.34	0.63	0.78	1.15	0.51	0.64

Source: China Industrial Statistical Yearbook 1992.

Table A1.8a Average Number of Employees per Enterprise by Province (1990)
(persons)

	Coal Mining	Tobacco	Textiles	Chemicals	Building Materials	Ferrous Metals	Machine Building	Electronics & Telecomm
All China	628	934	378	221	132	938	227	349
Beijing	1246	750	460	422	243	4640	374	544
Tianjin		4200	566	359	216	1270	351	468
Hebei	1314	2667	317	191	134	902	192	256
Shanxi	450	767	403	325	114	567	267	338
Inner Mongolia	343	1300	410	256	99	1486	251	335
Liaoning	1703	1260	500	312	184	1508	283	431
Jilin	1006	1043	429	247	127	711	216	387
Heilongjiang	1559	500	456	183	133	815	300	292
Shanghai		2950	625	301	302	2102	398	454
Jiangsu	2678	1360	373	220	155	516	221	330
Zhejiang	349	1375	204	130	118	354	88	136
Anhui	1946	1436	433	173	98	1394	150	305
Fujian	343	335	268	149	113	339	150	193
Jiangxi	523	1200	335	166	124	2075	171	446
Shandong	1441	1367	427	235	130	731	272	333
Henan	1667	945	432	248	130	854	292	390
Hubei	177	1471	480	193	133	1540	257	454
Hunan	337	1388	430	186	118	863	201	289
Guangdong	589	336	283	185	157	502	189	275
Guangxi	662	738	436	196	128	687	191	513
Hainan	700	900	315	88	153	450	164	575
Sichuan	287	848	486	238	113	886	231	699
Guizhou	283	1320	442	215	142	731	365	946
Yunnan	326	1384	543	333	147	635	344	339
Tibet	100		367	100	338		17	
Shaanxi	485	1147	501	179	83	506	262	821
Gansu	443	309	387	258	128	1116	325	950
Qinghai	500	400	574	326	110	637	353	633
Ningxia	1125	600	263	220	97	370	288	200
Xinjiang	283	108	440	210	118	1795	194	450
SD	636	839	96	75	57	837	87	203
Mean	817	1186	420	228	146	1068	245	441
COV	0.78	0.71	0.23	0.33	0.39	0.78	0.35	0.46

Source: China Industrial Statistical Yearbook 1991.

Table A1.8b Average Number of Employees per Enterprise by Province (1991)
(persons)

	Coal Mining	Tobacco	Textiles	Chemicals	Building Materials	Ferrous Metals	Machine Building	Electronics & Telecomm
All China	642	943	390	223	138	941	233	356
Beijing	1304	800	458	281	262	3269	374	547
Tianjin		4100	562	347	230	1330	335	491
Hebei	1268	2733	330	195	141	886	198	245
Shanxi	465	800	416	310	115	600	271	402
Inner Mongolia	629	1350	431	249	103	1358	263	300
Liaoning	1706	1220	552	309	186	1513	287	414
Jilin	1050	971	434	253	133	891	210	384
Heilongjiang	1644	584	455	193	133	841	305	294
Shanghai		2950		315	307	1972	406	460
Jiangsu	2918	1360	389	219	168	522	234	339
Zhejiang	368	1350	85	133	118	365	95	145
Anhui	2020	1418	121	160	99	1399	159	337
Fujian	343	333	389	156	117	353	142	190
Jiangxi	500	1000	1838	168	127	1729	174	528
Shandong	1524	1367	219	236	143	756	281	348
Henan	1611	1094		251	143	845	304	436
Hubei	179	1210	207	204	136	1476	259	461
Hunan	337	1453	710	182	124	842	208	274
Guangdong	534	336	77	182	169	522	184	320
Guangxi	665	700		190	133	663	196	445
Hainan	600	1000	324	96	169	367	169	323
Sichuan	290	943	519	242	119	953	238	741
Guizhou	290	1338	430	239	153	653	355	880
Yunnan	333	1340	541	339	145	642	371	342
Tibet	100		367	75	286		17	
Shaanxi	492	1150	492	181	105	526	263	873
Gansu	431	308	359	241	129	1143	313	1088
Qinghai	770	400	589	1294	155	633	314	633
Ningxia	1108	600	265	228	105	380	310	350
Xinjiang	280	93	473	251	121	1492	219	450
SD	664	825	312	203	52	612	85	210
Mean	848.53	1182.82	401.04	257.30	152.47	997.18	248.47	449.56
COV	0.78	0.70	0.78	0.79	0.34	0.61	0.34	0.47

Source: China Industrial Statistical Yearbook, 1992.

Table A2.1 Price Controls: Reduction in Scope (1978-1991)

Year	Domestic Retail Goods			Farm Produce Sold by Farmers		
	Fixed price (%)	Guided prices (%)	Free prices (%)	Fixed price (%)	Guided prices (%)	Free prices (%)
1978	97.0	0.0	3.0	92.6	1.8	5.6
1985	47.0	19.0	34.0	37.0	23.0	40.0
1986	35.0	25.0	40.0	35.3	21.0	43.7
1987	33.7	28.0	38.3	29.4	16.8	53.8
1988	28.9	21.8	49.3	24.0	19.0	57.0
1989	31.3	23.2	45.5	35.3	24.3	40.4
1990	30.0	25.0	45.0	31.0	27.0	42.0
1991	20.9	10.3	68.8	22.2	20.0	57.8

Source: Data compiled by the CASS.

Table A2.2 Free Market Price Indices of Consumer Goods

Year	Free market Index (1950=100)	Free market Index (1979=100)	Free market Index (1984=100)	Free market Relative to State List
1962	354.8	151.0	130.5	270.0
1965	192.3	81.9	70.8	140.0
1970	197.7	84.2	72.7	142.0
1975	259.5	110.5	95.5	184.0
1978	246.0	104.7	90.5	169.0
1979	234.9	100.0	86.4	157.0
1980	239.6	102.0	88.2	148.0
1981	253.5	107.9	93.3	149.0
1982	261.9	111.5	96.4	148.0
1983	272.9	116.2	100.4	148.0
1984	271.8	115.7	100.0	143.0
1985	318.5	135.6	117.2	128.0
1986	344.3	146.6	126.7	117.0
1987	400.4	170.5	147.3	117.0
1988	521.7	222.1	191.9	117.0
1989	578.0	246.1	212.7	112.0
1990	545.1	232.1	200.6	107.7
1991	540.2	230.0	198.7	105.2

Source: China Statistical Yearbook (various issues).

Table A2.3 Free Market Prices Relative to State List Prices (1983-1991)
(List Price=100)

	1983	1984	1985	1986	1987	1988	1989	1990	1991
Overall Index	146.3	143.7	129.5	116.8	116.6	117.4	111.5	107.7	105.2
Consumer Goods	147.9	142.7	127.6	116.9	116.6	117.4	111.5	107.7	105.2
Grain	230.0	201.9	187.2	180.0	192.7	194.1	225.1	202.5	161.3
Edible Vegetable Oil	188.5	188.4	189.1	165.2	166.9	166.7	163.5	142.4	120.2
Fresh Vegetables	123.7	160.7	126.7	118.9	118.1	116.7	109.7	112.3	115.6
Dried Vegetables	132.2	131.3	127.8	120.3	115.4	116.2	104.0	103.8	101.3
Meat, Poultry and Eggs	186.8	130.2	119.8	105.5	107.0	121.6	111.6	109.9	106.6
Aquatic Products	141.7	165.2	133.5	119.9	128.5	121.7	109.8	105.1	103.8
Fresh Fruits	163.6	120.2	110.1	106.2	105.2	104.1	91.9	95.2	89.5
Dried Fruits	126.5	136.3	118.2	105.3	105.0	104.1	95.8	82.2	91.6
Daily Use Articles	115.1	112.1	112.5	101.6	107.2	117.3	125.8	94.7	102.6
Firewood and Grass	164.8	151.2	145.7	106.1	112.8	156.3	117.0	119.5	97.0
Other		128.4	120.4	125.6	116.6	146.1		107.7	98.9
Agricultural Producer Goods	140.1	145.5	158.7						
Fodder	218.6	178.4	194.8						
Small Farm Tools	119.3	147.2	130.1						
Young Poultry and Livestock	135.1	128.7	178.8						
Large Dometic Animal	154.3	149.5	189.0						
Bamboo and Timber	183.1	167.4	132.6						

Source: China Statistical Yearbook (various issues).

Table A2.4 Planned and Market Prices of Main Materials
(Y/ton)

	1986	1987	1988	1989	1990	1991
Steel products						
Controlled price (a)	1017	1047	1302	1616	1719	1780
Market price (b)	1501	1516	1900	2197	2092	1984
b/a (percent)	148	145	146	136	122	111
Cement						
Controlled price (a)	107	111	127	157	154	175
Market price (b)	131	133	161	212	184	194
b/a (percent)	122	120	127	135	119	111
Coal						
Controlled price (a)	44	45	52	65	75	83
Market price (b)	64	64	100	174	154	141
b/a (percent)	145	142	192	268	205	170
Copper						
Controlled price (a)	6051	6381	7824	10467	14825	14664
Market price (b)	6689	6944	14226	19653	17553	16582
b/a (percent)	111	109	182	188	118	113
Aluminium						
Controlled price (a)	3780	4483	6051	9014	9037	8436
Market price (b)	5389	6433	10912	15117	10831	9072
b/a (percent)	143	143	180	168	120	108
Lumber						
Controlled price (a)	247	310	378	418	430	441
Market price (b)	358	475	638	707	693	618
b/a percent)	145	153	169	169	161	140

Note: Unit for Lumber: Yuan per cubic meter.

Source: Ministry of Materials and Equipment.

Table A2.5   Planned and Market Prices of Main Materials (1987-1991)
(Y/ton)

	1987			1989			1991		
	Planned price (a)	Market price (b)	b/a (percent)	Planned price (a)	Market price (b)	b/a (percent)	Planned price (a)	Market price (b)	b/a (percent)
All China									
Steel products	1047	1516	145	1618	2197	136	1780	1984	111
Copper	6381	6944	109	10467	19653	188	14664	16582	113
Aluminium	4483	6433	143	9014	15117	168	8436	9072	108
Cement	111	133	120	157	212	135	175	194	111
Lumber	310	475	153	418	707	169	441	616	140
Coal	45	64	142	65	174	268	83	141	170
Chongqing City									
Steel products	1142	1471	129	1633	2326	142	1885	2435	129
Copper	6707	6700	100	10339	18914	183	16000	16563	104
Aluminium	4826	5600	116	8219	13907	169	8000	8750	109
Cement	102	129	126	111	176	159	142	143	101
Lumber	320	483	151	383	660	172	470	579	123
Coal									
Guangdong Province									
Steel products	1071	1456	136	1485	2057	139	1767	1958	111
Copper	6004	8671	144	12023	14066	117	15346	16007	104
Aluminium	4850	6759	139	9589	10671	111	8427	9001	107
Cement	145	190	131	216	223	103	213	234	110
Lumber		585			857			690	
Coal	71	85	120	114	178	156	144	167	116
Jiangsu Province									
Steel products	800	1500	188	950	2000	211	1704	2058	121
Copper	5650	7100	126	7700	19300	251	11275	16966	150
Aluminium	4000	6200	155	4800	14500	302	7758	9348	120
Cement	75	145	193	110	230	209	185	195	105
Lumber	195	410	210	300	700	233	517	741	143
Coal	70	100	143	95	220	232	113	147	130

.....contd./

	1987			1989			1991		
	Planned price (a)	Market price (b)	b/a (percent)	Planned price (a)	Market price (b)	b/a (percent)	Planned price (a)	Market price (b)	b/a (percent)
Zhejiang Province									
Steel products	1050	2000	190	1245	2260	182	1710	1930	113
Copper	5800	15700	271	8500	20400	240	12400	16500	133
Aluminium	2750	12000	436	6400	13000	203	8100	8990	111
Cement	130	195	150	165	250	152	170	220	129
Lumber									
Coal	70	140	200	85	240	282	120	150	125
Shanxi Province									
Steel products	760	1080	142	1463	1978	135	1768	2006	113
Copper	7300	13010	178	16485	17904	109	14013	17550	125
Aluminium	4500	8800	196	8722	12139	139	8508	8738	103
Cement	48	85	177	149	168	113	164	171	104
Lumber	280	460	164	453	748	165	439	563	128
Coal	35	50	143	56	76	136	85	107	126
Hebei Province									
Steel products	1079.3	1447.85	134	1516.53	2103.43	139	1718.45	1857.07	108
Copper	6335.84	6680.02	105	10595.13	17774.29	168	14814.53	15924.7	107
Aluminium	5223.13	6284.69	120	7665.78	13627.91	178	8239.27	10076.55	122
Cement	108.57	134.47	124	146.09	183.29	125	163.57	179.51	110
Lumber	320.37	418.13	131	514.84	718.42	140	431.23	555.47	129
Coal	35.72	40.82	114	62.49	96.73	155	61.98	87.33	141

Note: Unit for Lumber is yuan per square meter.
Source: Ministry of Materials and Equipment.

Table A2.6 Retail Prices of Major Commodities in 29 Provincial Capitals
(1986)

	Flour (Y/kg)	Rice (Y/kg)	Vegetable Oil (Y/kg)	Apples (Y/kg)	White Cotton cloth (Y/m)	Color TV 45 cm (Y)	Coal (resident use) (Y/100kg)	Kerosene (Y/kg)
Beijing	0.50	0.31	2.36	1.86	1.08	1330	3.10	0.73
Tianjin	0.50	0.30	2.21	1.89	1.11	1330	3.40	0.67
Shijiazhuang(Hebei)	0.50	0.40	2.29	1.78	1.18	1340	2.90	0.68
Taiyuan(Shanxi)	0.51	0.38	2.27	1.90	1.08	1382	2.80	
Huhehaote(Inner Mongolia)		0.40	2.07	2.07	1.11	1463	3.23	0.66
Shenyang(Liaoning)	0.55		1.68	1.52	1.38	1380	3.83	0.66
Changchun(Jilin)	0.54			2.41	1.12	1380	3.00	0.66
Harebin(Heilongjiang)	0.52	0.43		1.90	1.44	1380	3.50	0.66
Shanghai	0.44	0.30	2.43	2.36	1.45	1330	5.20	0.66
Nanjing(Jiangsu)	0.40	0.28	2.28	1.77	1.20	1360	4.60	0.66
Hangzhou(Zhejiang)	0.48	0.33	2.03	2.07	1.41	1330	4.20	0.66
Hefei(Anhui)	0.44	0.31	1.78	1.90	1.02	1377	3.20	
Fuzhou(Fujian)	0.54	0.33	2.29	1.98	1.07	1330	3.40	0.70
Nanchang(Jiangxi)	0.48	0.29	2.48	2.04	1.08	1370	3.40	0.70
Jinan(Shandong)	0.50	0.28		1.38	1.05	1390	3.20	
Zhenzhou(Henan)	0.50	0.34	2.50	1.77	1.24	1370	3.28	0.69
Wuhan(Hubei)	0.40	0.32	1.97	2.27	1.27	1390	3.70	0.70
Changsha(Hunan)	0.46	0.31	2.52	2.04	1.05	1383	3.40	0.72
Guangzhou(Guangdong)	0.64	0.34		2.65	1.28	1621	4.20	1.03
Nannin(Guangxi)	0.50	0.32	2.04	1.83	1.29	1452	4.00	0.75
Chongqing(Sichuan)		0.32	2.05	2.06	1.05	1377	3.33	0.76
Chendu(Sichunag)	0.46	0.29	2.00	2.34	1.20	1459	1.60	1.12
Guiyang(Guizhou)	0.50	0.36	1.65	2.07	1.50	1330		
Kunming(Yunnan)	0.51		1.76	1.75	1.13	1373	1.29	0.80
Xian(Shaanxi)	0.47	0.35	2.46	1.67	1.10	1360	3.90	0.68
Lanzhou(Gansu)	0.52	0.48	2.29	1.59	0.93	1390	4.10	0.85
Xining(Qinghai)		0.45	1.90	1.70	1.02	1390	4.00	0.68
Yinchuang(Ningxia)	0.50		2.68	1.43	1.23	1370	1.18	0.70
Yulumuqi(Xinjiang)	0.56	0.54	2.63	1.60	1.23	1386		0.58
SD	0.05	0.06	0.29	0.29	0.14	57.01	0.89	0.12
Mean	0.50	0.35	2.18	1.92	1.18	1384	3.37	0.73
COV	0.10	0.18	0.13	0.15	0.12	0.04	0.26	0.16

Source: China Price Statistical Yearbook 1987.

Table A2.7   Retail Prices of Major Commodities in 29 Provincial Capitals
(1989)

	Flour	Rice	Vegetable Oil	Apples	White Cotton Cloth	Color TV 45 cm	Coal (resident use)	Kerosene
	(Y/kg)	(Y/kg)	(Y/kg)	(Y/kg)	(Y/m)	(Y)	(Y/100kg)	(Y/kg)
Beijing	0.50	0.31	3.24	3.28	1.75	2735.00	3.10	0.76
Tianjin	0.50	0.30	2.77	3.30	2.58	2699.00	3.40	0.67
Shijiazhuang(Hebei)	0.50	1.05	2.17	3.22	1.63	2643.00	2.90	0.68
Taiyuan(Shanxi)	0.54	0.40	2.15	3.09	2.05	2833.00	2.80	
Huhehaote(Inner Mongolia)		0.36	3.30	3.88	2.16	2696.00	3.54	
Shenyang(Liaoning)	0.54			2.58		2611.00	4.40	0.66
Changchun(Jilin)	0.74			3.46	2.66	2750.00	3.00	0.66
Harebin(Heilongjiang)	0.52			3.03	2.37	2837.00	3.50	0.66
Shanghai	0.44	0.30	2.20	4.48	3.18	2675.00	5.20	0.66
Nanjing(Jiangsu)	0.40	0.30	3.04	2.87	2.23	2763.00	4.60	0.66
Hangzhou(Zhejiang)	0.53	0.32	3.00	3.09	2.05	2833.00	2.80	
Hefei(Anhui)	0.44	0.30	2.02	2.73	2.04	2508.00	3.20	
Fuzhou(Fujian)	0.46	0.67	4.26	3.28	2.34	2662.00	3.56	0.77
Nanchang(Jiangxi)	0.48	0.31	4.47	3.73	2.30	2860.00	3.40	0.70
Jinan(Shandong)	0.50			2.50	2.04	2817.00	3.20	0.66
Zhenzhou(Henan)	0.50	0.67	3.34	2.85	1.83	2688.00	3.28	0.69
Wuhan(Hubei)		0.34	2.51	3.95	2.47	2657.00	3.70	0.70
Changsha(Hunan)	0.47	0.33	2.35	3.34	2.09	2623.00	3.40	0.78
Guangzhou(Guangdon	1.02	0.69		5.59	2.64	2860.00	4.24	2.33
Nannin(Guangxi)	0.50	0.34	6.11	2.96	1.87	2773.00	4.00	1.61
Haikou(Hainan)	1.08	0.55		4.21	2.98	3912.00	8.24	0.78
Chendu(Sichuan)	0.46	0.32	2.73	4.43	2.09	2748.00	3.84	1.31
Guiyang(Guizhou)	0.50	0.38	2.14	2.91	2.41	2591.00		
Kunming(Yunnan)	0.52		2.47	3.56	3.86	2776.00	7.14	1.01
Xian(Shaanxi)	0.54	0.81	3.46	3.31	2.08	2754.00	3.86	0.68
Lanzhou(Gansu)	0.52	0.82	3.17	3.42	2.11	2655.00	7.15	1.18
Xining(Qinghai)		0.50	2.43	2.80	1.73	2733.00	4.00	0.68
Yinchuang(Ningxia)	0.50		1.78	2.53	1.82	2822.00	2.61	
Yulumuqi(Xinjiang)	0.56	0.63	3.22	2.43	1.55	2690.00		0.58
SD	0.16	0.21	0.95	0.69	0.49	233.05	1.38	0.40
Mean	0.55	0.48	2.97	3.34	2.25	2765.66	4.00	0.86
COV	0.28	0.44	0.32	0.21	0.22	0.08	0.34	0.46

Source: China Price Statistical Yearbook 1990.

Table A2.8   Retail Prices of Major Commodities in 29 Provincial Capitals
(1991)

	Flour (Y/kg)	Rice (Y/kg)	Vegetable Oil (Y/kg)	Apples (Y/kg)	White Cotton Cloth (Y/m)	Color TV 45 cm (Y)	Coal (resident use) (Y/100kg)	Kerosene (Y/kg)
Beijing	0.67	0.47	3.99	4.13	2.50	2145		1.35
Tianjin	0.67	0.45	4.36	4.21	2.95	1992		0.76
Shijiazhuang(Hebei)	0.67	0.62	2.81	3.86	2.46	2918		
Taiyuan(Shanxi)	0.61	0.48	3.45	4.14	2.20	2317	4.24	
Huhehaote(Inner Mongolia)		0.47	3.79	4.70	2.45	2150	5.04	
Shenyang(Liaoning)	0.75			3.20	2.44	2140	4.78	0.66
Changchun(Jilin)	0.86			4.83	3.37	2063	4.77	0.76
Harebin(Heilongjiang)	0.72			4.26	3.08	3185	5.57	
Shanghai	0.62	0.43	3.18	5.78	3.19	2208		0.95
Nanjing(Jiangsu)	0.60	0.51	3.50	3.84	2.88	2279		
Hangzhou(Zhejiang)	0.76	0.47	4.07	4.54	2.79	2300		0.66
Hefei(Anhui)	0.61	0.45	2.89	3.38	2.66	2316	6.60	
Fuzhou(Fujian)	1.13	0.87	4.48	3.99	2.47	2147		1.12
Nanchang(Jiangxi)	0.67	0.48	4.54	4.36	2.36	2092		0.83
Jinan(Shandong)	0.67	0.31	4.16	3.19	2.18	2435		0.66
Zhenzhou(Henan)	0.66	0.47	3.33	4.21	2.60	2043	4.53	0.79
Wuhan(Hubei)		0.45	3.93	4.64	3.04	2303		0.75
Changsha(Hunan)	0.70	0.48	4.19	4.07	2.47	2252	5.20	
Guangzhou(Guangdong)	1.12	0.91		6.59	2.70	1932		1.42
Nannin(Guangxi)	0.69	0.53		4.07	2.88	2374		1.84
Haikou(Hainan)	1.22	0.92		4.82	3.68	3080		0.88
Chendu(Sichuan)	0.65	0.42	3.71	4.95	2.59	2096	6.04	1.57
Guiyang(Guizhou)	0.70	0.54	3.42	3.21	2.52	1836		
Kunming(Yunnan)	0.69	0.45	3.86	3.86	3.91	2049	5.77	1.24
Xian(Shaanxi)	0.69	0.65	3.89	4.04	2.37	2001	6.64	0.79
Lanzhou(Gansu)	0.68	0.74	3.92	4.73	2.35	1925	9.95	0.96
Xining(Qinghai)		0.57	3.23	3.64	2.88	2475	4.25	0.69
Yinchuang(Ningxia)	0.63		2.50	3.52	2.34	2109	10.75	
Yulumuqi(Xinjiang)	0.72	0.66	3.98	3.27	2.85	2108	3.90	0.61
SD	0.16	0.16	0.53	0.75	0.41	315.34	1.94	0.34
Mean	0.74	0.55	3.70	4.21	2.73	2251	5.87	0.96
COV	0.22	0.28	0.14	0.18	0.15	0.14	0.33	0.35

Source: China Price Statistical Yearbook 1992.

Table A2.9 Average Price of Materials by Province (December 1990)
(Y/ton)

Location	Steel Sheet (16-20mm)	Copper	Coal	Cement (#425)	Timber
National Average	1856	16581	161	191	546
Beijing	1750	16000	141	214	578
Hebei(Shijiazhuang)		18000	85	185	500
Inner Mongolia (Hohhot)	2215	17200	75	190	
Liaoning(Shenyang))	1770		295	190	600
Jilin(Changchun)	2000		158		
Heilongjiang(Harbin)	1900	16200	131	186	930
Shanghai	1540	16700	175	210	350
Jiangsu(Nanjing)	1850	10900	125		400
Zhejiang(Hangzhou)	1700	16800	125	176	510
Anhui(Hefei)	2050	17500	170		500
Fujian(Fuzhou)	1800	17000		350	440
Jiangxi(Nanchang)	1930	17000	145	200	459
Shandong(Jinan)	1780	17361	146	160	560
Hubei(Huangshi)	1750	16000	124	177	470
Hunan(Xiangtan)	1940	16800	129	163	420
Guangdong(Guangzhou)	1750	16900	210	190	590
Guangxi(Guilin)					
Sichuang(Chengdu)	1700	16800	190	159	
Guizhou(Guiyang)	1750			156	750
Yunnan(Kunming)					
Shaanxi(Xi'an)	1900	16900	130	170	524
Ningxia(Yinchuan)					
Xinjiang(shihezi)					
Gansu(Lanzhou)	1950	16800	118	165	760
SD	148.55	1488.06	47.96	43.28	142.86
Mean	1941.09	18590.10	157.39	201.82	581.57
COV	.0765	.08	.347	.2145	.2456

Note: Average price is the average of planned and market prices weighted by their relative shares of quatity sold.
Source: China Price, 1991 (February).

Table A2.10 Average Price of Materials by Province (December 1991)
(Y/ton)

Location	Steel Sheet (16-20mm)	Copper	Coal	Cement (#425)	Timber
National Average	1842	16558	154	211	588
Beijing					500
Shanxi(Taiyuan)	1750				
Hebei(Shijiazhuang)					
Inner Mongolia (Hohhot)					
Liaoning(Shenyang))	1838	14253	143		530
Jilin(Changchun)		16650	158		850
Heilongjiang(Harbin)	1950	16400	134	205	940
Shanghai	1750	16600	170	220	500
Jiangsu(Nanjing)	1920	16800	180		561
Zhejiang(Hangzhou)	1900	16700	185	185	530
Anhui(Hefei)	1780	16000	142		550
Fujian(Fuzhou)	1820	17000	147	290	436
Jiangxi(Nanchang)	2100	17100	140	275	495
Shandong(Jinan)	1811	16750	172	178	510
Henan(Zhengzhou)	1800	16800	81		
Hubei(Huangshi)	1750	16700	204	207	530
Hunan(Xiangtan)					
Guangdong(Zhanjiang)	1820	16700	210	240	580
Guangxi(Guilin)					
Sichuang(Chengdu)	1651	16600	165		
Guizhou(Guiyang)		16500		160	770
Yunnan(Kunming)					
Shaanxi(Xi'an)	1850	16790	100	210	570
Ningxia(Yinchuan)	1850	16800	55	180	837
Xinjiang(shihezi)					
Gansu(Yinchuang)					
SD	101.93	632.49	33.78	39.20	139.42
Mean	1725.88	16537.82	149.12	213.60	605.56
COV	.0591	.0382	.2265	.1835	.2302

Note: Average price is the average of planned and market prices weighted by their relative shares sold.
Source: China Price, 1992 (February).

Table A2.11 Average Price of Materials by Province (June 1992)
(Y/ton)

Location	Steel Sheet (16-20mm)	Copper	Coal	Cement (#425)	Timber
National Average	1985	16721	151	212	565
Beijing					
Shanxi(Taiyuan)	1780		57		375
Hebei(Shijiazhuang)					
Inner Mongolia (Hohot)					
Liaoning(Shenyang)	1900	16547	165		410
Jilin(Changchun)	2000	17000	148		
Heilongjiang(Harbin)	1580	18000	147	205	950
Shanghai	1980	16700	176	205	530
Jiangsu(Nanjing)	2100	16800	190	228	550
Zhejiang(Hangzhou)	2200	16600	195		548
Anhui(Hefei)	1820				585
Fujian(Fuzhou)	2150	17000	207	258	460
Jiangxi(Nanchang)					
Shandong(Jinan)	2090	16750	174		
Henan(Zhengzhou)	1900	16750	80		476
Hubei(Huangshi)	2000	16500		220	670
Hunan(Changsha)	1909	16555	120	180	550
Guangdong(Guangzhou)					
Guangxi(Guilin)	2100	16700		185	380
Sichuang(Chengdu)	1850	16500	140	225	
Guizhou(Guiyang)					
Yunnan(Kunming)	1950	16500			
Shaanxi(Xi'an)	1860	16450			441
Gansu(Lanzhou)	2000	16400	116.9		
Qinghai(Xining)	1930	16500		160	427
Ninggxia(Yinchuan)	1980.00	16800.00	56.25	200.00	791.00
Xinjiang(Urumqi)	2000.00			245.00	
SD	135.57	353.60	47.53	27.56	153.42
Mean	1956.14	16725.11	140.87	210.09	542.87
COV	.0693	.0211	.3374	.1312	.2826

Note: Average price is the average of planned and market prices weighted by their relative shares of quatity sold.
Source: China Price, 1992 (August).

Table A2.12 Imports of Commodities from Other Provinces (1985-1992)
(Y million)

	1985	1988	1990	1991	1992
Beijing	7219.7	15927.2	16428.1	17246.5	20398.1
Tianjin	5304.7	3561.5	3731.4	3461.5	2952.5
Hebei	4732.7	8150.4	7414.2	8406.0	9021.3
Shanxi	3431.7	4426.6	4548.2	4427.5	4230.0
Inner Mongolia	2628.4	3601.5	3760.0	3423.3	3348.4
Liaoning	4968.7	8991.1	7805.5	10268.0	10552.2
Jilin	2930.3	3866.3	4150.6	3414.4	4168.4
Heilongjiang	3348.1	4635.2	4005.7	3506.7	3783.4
Shanghai	6616.9	10320.0	10571.0	13106.0	14417.0
Jiangsu	5593.4	9815.3	11280.0	14905.4	18329.3
Zhejiang	3987.6	n.a.	n.a.	9570.8	12547.8
Anhui	3192.0	3465.6	3511.0	4250.0	4301.0
Fujian	2551.4	3693.2	3490.4	4109.9	4722.5
Jiangxi	2664.4	3717.4	4124.2	5345.1	6637.7
Shandong	4461.3	5613.1	6273.0	7555.1	5855.9
Henan	4495.6	6269.4	5415.1	5986.7	5517.6
Hubei	4100.6	5599.0	6193.0	6128.0	5701.0
Hunan	3353.7	n.a.	n.a.	n.a.	n.a.
Guangdong	6529.4	10992.1	9230.8	11295.4	13337.6
Guangxi	2888.5	4235.3	3339.9	4378.6	4396.5
Hainan					
Sichuang	5239.4	11557.6	12479.4	14586.2	16902.5
Guizhou	1722.0	n.a.	n.a.	n.a.	n.a.
Yunnan	2290.0	3063.0	2484.9	2246.6	3187.1
Tibet	390.9	n.a.	n.a.	n.a.	n.a.
Shaanxi	2569.5	3025.9	3274.1	3306.6	3638.6
Gansu	2310.3	3355.8	3055.7	3336.1	3126.5
Qinghai	700.9	1011.8	972.1	917.3	n.a.
Ningxia	591.7	839.7	687.7	744.5	719.6
Xinjiang	1332.1	1693.9	1470.9	1864.8	1809.2
Total	132205.6	141427.9	139696.8	167786.9	183601.7

Note: "Total" refers to the sum of all provinces for which figures are available.
Source: State Statistical Bureau.

Table A2.13 Exports of Commodities to Other Provinces (1985-1992)
(Y million)

	1985	1988	1990	1991	1992
Beijing	4646.7	6885.8	6938.6	7757.1	9082.1
Tianjin	10547.6	5037.8	4060.6	3945.5	2872.4
Hebei	1985.9	4320.3	3989.7	5024.7	5934.2
Shanxi	1019.5	1694.5	1693.9	1664.7	1729.0
Inner Mongolia	963.4	1577.9	1674.2	2124.7	1769.0
Liaoning	5144.3	7465.1	6261.7	7899.5	7153.9
Jilin	1399.3	3107.0	2539.0	4674.5	4104.5
Heilongjiang	4870.4	5214.4	5453.5	3218.9	4414.7
Shanghai	16356.0	16254.0	15276.0	15330.0	16097.0
Jiangsu	5883.8	10962.3	14774.6	8535.6	9686.1
Zhejiang	2795.1	n.a.	n.a.	4825.6	6115.3
Anhui	2555.8	3709.8	3881.0	2731.0	329.2
Fujian	1612.4	1896.8	2707.4	2969.5	3236.3
Jiangxi	1299.1	2227.8	3628.2	4696.2	6129.5
Shandong	3018.8	6779.8	5613.4	6733.7	6513.8
Henan	5036.9	5783.9	5298.3	5983.3	5495.7
Hubei	2784.6	4799.0	4906.0	5712.0	8589.0
Hunan	2300.7	n.a.	n.a.	n.a.	n.a.
Guangdong	8512.1	15209.7	15292.1	16646.8	18129.0
Guangxi	1494.6	3403.8	3720.0	4107.3	3782.5
Hainan					
Sichuang	3919.4	11787.7	6336.6	8052.7	8833.8
Guizhou	811.4	n.a.	n.a.	n.a.	n.a.
Yunnan	1723.0	5089.0	8488.3	9562.9	12581.7
Tibet	58.4	n.a.	n.a.	n.a.	n.a.
Shaanxi	1221.6	1603.6	1825.0	2197.5	2658.2
Gansu	1928.4	2627.5	2285.2	2690.2	2551.0
Qinghai	149.0	428.8	213.5	346.5	356.3
Ningxia	234.7	377.4	345.2	427.5	391.5
Xinjiang	791.0	1607.2	2021.9	2587.3	2978.6
Total	95063.8	129850.8	129223.9	140445.2	151514.2

Note: "Total" refers to the sum of all provinces for which figures are available.

Source: State Statistical Bureau.

Table A2.14 Total Domestic Sales within Province (1985-1992)
(Y million)

	1985	1988	1990	1991	1992
Beijing	12922.1	25568.8	30947.4	35548.1	42461.7
Tianjin	8828.6	7723.4	8010.8	8889.6	9539.6
Hebei	17084.5	24996.2	26273.0	29272.0	33139.9
Shanxi	8815.3	13705.6	15963.6	14295.4	16528.0
Inner Mongolia	7075.0	11509.7	12604.2	11956.0	13261.3
Liaoning	19906.1	34143.5	22461.4	32231.6	38777.2
Jilin	9789.2	12566.9	14224.6	16381.2	17458.4
Heilongjiang	14382.6	18032.5	22274.6	20181.5	22262.2
Shanghai	21872.7	39820.0	44550.0	43771.8	n.a.
Jiangsu	28660.9	43011.2	50289.6	56443.7	70654.1
Zhejiang	17560.1	26248.9	29198.3	33038.0	41938.0
Anhui	12870.9	16132.0	17296.3	19033.0	21226.2
Fujian	8506.9	13222.4	13780.5	11970.4	13386.1
Jiangxi	7869.7	12574.5	13611.7	12140.4	13430.7
Shandong	24100.2	45443.2	50409.1	50251.2	57290.8
Henan	18867.3	29864.9	33522.4	30741.2	32541.9
Hubei	18100.1	28094.0	30271.0	31022.0	31860.0
Hunan	15070.6	n.a.	n.a.	n.a.	n.a.
Guangdong	28844.1	54461.2	54127.8	46386.3	52430.8
Guangxi	7702.6	14304.3	14796.9	14026.6	17275.8
Hainan					
Sichuang	24389.1	39074.8	41520.5	36559.8	40732.9
Guizhou	5227.5	n.a.	n.a.	n.a.	n.a.
Yunnan	8944.4	15172.9	15873.1	17041.2	19121.9
Tibet	634.7	n.a.	n.a.	n.a.	n.a.
Shaanxi	8103.1	12857.5	15116.7	12771.7	13765.4
Gansu	4896.3	8327.6	9035.5	8535.3	9384.1
Qinghai	1721.6	2551.0	2771.8	2402.2	n.a.
Ningxia	1338.5	1839.9	2110.1	2353.3	2572.8
Xinjiang	5725.0	9500.3	11167.4	31213.2	34938.5
Total	360923.6	524909.0	562113.4	589062.0	665978.0

Note: Figures are of state-owned commercial units and rural cooperatives.
"Total" refers to the sum of all provinces for which figures are available.
Source: State Statistical Bureau.

Table A2.15 Ratio of Interprovincial Exports to Total Domestic Sales (1985-1992)
(Y million)

	1985	1988	1990	1991	1992
Beijing	55.9	62.3	53.1	48.5	48.0
Tianjin	60.1	46.1	46.6	38.9	31.0
Hebei	27.7	32.6	28.2	28.7	27.2
Shanxi	38.9	32.3	28.5	31.0	25.6
Inner Mongolia	37.2	31.3	29.8	28.6	25.2
Liaoning	25.0	26.3	34.8	31.9	27.2
Jilin	29.9	30.8	29.2	20.8	23.9
Heilongjiang	23.3	25.7	18.0	17.4	17.0
Shanghai	30.3	25.9	23.7	29.9	n.a.
Jiangsu	19.5	22.8	22.4	26.4	25.9
Zhejiang	22.7	n.a.	n.a.	29.0	29.9
Anhui	24.8	21.5	20.3	22.3	20.3
Fujian	30.0	27.9	25.3	34.3	35.3
Jiangxi	33.9	29.6	30.3	44.0	49.4
Shandong	18.5	12.4	12.4	15.0	10.2
Henan	23.8	21.0	16.2	19.5	17.0
Hubei	22.7	19.9	20.5	19.8	17.9
Hunan	22.3	n.a.	n.a.	n.a.	n.a.
Guangdong	22.6	20.2	17.1	24.4	25.4
Guangxi	37.5	29.6	22.6	31.2	25.4
Hainan					
Sichuang	21.5	29.6	30.1	39.9	41.5
Guizhou	32.9	n.a.	n.a.	n.a.	n.a.
Yunnan	25.6	20.2	15.7	13.2	16.7
Tibet	61.6	n.a.	n.a.	n.a.	n.a.
Shaanxi	31.7	23.5	21.7	25.9	26.4
Gansu	47.2	40.3	33.8	39.1	33.3
Qinghai	40.7	39.7	35.1	38.2	n.a.
Ningxia	44.2	45.6	32.6	31.6	28.0
Xinjiang	23.3	17.8	13.2	6.0	5.2
Total	36.6	26.9	24.9	28.5	27.6

Note: "Total" refers to the sum of all provinces for which figures are available.
Source: State Statistical Bureau.

Table A2.16 Ratio of Inter-provincial Imports to Total Domestic Sales (1985-1992)
(Y million)

	1985	1988	1990	1991	1992
Beijing	36.0	26.9	22.4	21.8	21.4
Tianjin	119.5	65.2	50.7	44.4	30.1
Hebei	11.6	17.3	15.2	17.2	17.9
Shanxi	11.6	12.4	10.6	11.6	10.5
Inner Mongolia	13.6	13.7	13.3	17.8	13.3
Liaoning	25.8	21.9	27.9	24.5	18.4
Jilin	14.3	24.7	17.8	28.5	23.5
Heilongjiang	33.9	28.9	24.5	15.9	19.8
Shanghai	74.8	40.8	34.3	35.0	n.a.
Jiangsu	20.5	25.5	29.4	15.1	13.7
Zhejiang	15.9	n.a.	n.a.	14.6	14.6
Anhui	19.9	23.0	22.4	14.3	1.6
Fujian	19.0	14.3	19.6	24.8	24.2
Jiangxi	16.5	17.7	26.7	38.7	45.6
Shandong	12.5	14.9	11.1	13.4	11.4
Henan	26.7	19.4	15.8	19.5	16.9
Hubei	15.4	17.1	16.2	18.4	27.0
Hunan	15.3	n.a.	n.a.	n.a.	n.a.
Guangdong	29.5	27.9	28.3	35.9	34.6
Guangxi	19.4	23.8	25.1	29.3	21.9
Hainan					
Sichuang	16.1	30.2	15.3	22.0	21.7
Guizhou	15.5	n.a.	n.a.	n.a.	n.a.
Yunnan	19.3	33.5	53.5	56.1	65.8
Tibet	9.2	n.a.	n.a.	n.a.	n.a.
Shaanxi	15.1	12.5	12.1	17.2	19.3
Gansu	39.4	31.6	25.3	31.5	27.2
Qinghai	8.7	16.8	7.7	14.4	n.a.
Ningxia	17.5	20.5	16.4	18.2	15.2
Xinjiang	13.8	16.9	18.1	8.3	8.5
Total	26.3	24.7	23.0	23.8	22.8

Note: "Total" refers to the sum of all provinces for which figures are available.
Source: State Statistical Bureau.

Table A2.17 Ratio of Inter-provincial Trade to Total Domestic Sales (1985-1992)
(Y million)

	1985	1988	1990	1991	1992
Beijing	91.8	89.2	75.5	70.3	69.4
Tianjin	179.6	111.3	97.3	83.3	61.1
Hebei	39.3	49.9	43.4	45.9	45.1
Shanxi	50.5	44.7	39.1	42.6	36.1
Inner Mongolia	50.8	45.0	43.1	46.4	38.6
Liaoning	50.8	48.2	62.6	56.4	45.7
Jilin	44.2	55.5	47.0	49.4	47.4
Heilongjiang	57.1	54.6	42.5	33.3	36.8
Shanghai	105.0	66.7	58.0	65.0	n.a.
Jiangsu	40.0	48.3	51.8	41.5	39.7
Zhejiang	38.6	n.a.	n.a.	43.6	44.5
Anhui	44.7	44.5	42.7	36.7	21.8
Fujian	48.9	42.3	45.0	59.1	59.5
Jiangxi	50.4	47.3	57.0	82.7	95.1
Shandong	31.0	27.3	23.6	28.4	21.6
Henan	50.5	40.4	32.0	38.9	33.8
Hubei	38.0	37.0	36.7	38.2	44.9
Hunan	37.5	n.a.	n.a.	n.a.	n.a.
Guangdong	52.1	48.1	45.3	60.2	60.0
Guangxi	56.9	53.4	47.7	60.5	47.3
Hainan					
Sichuang	37.6	59.7	45.3	61.9	63.2
Guizhou	48.5	n.a.	n.a.	n.a.	n.a.
Yunnan	44.9	53.7	69.1	69.3	82.5
Tibet	70.8	n.a.	n.a.	n.a.	n.a.
Shaanxi	46.8	36.0	33.7	43.1	45.7
Gansu	86.6	71.8	59.1	70.6	60.5
Qinghai	49.4	56.5	42.8	52.6	n.a.
Ningxia	61.7	66.2	49.0	49.8	43.2
Xinjiang	37.1	34.7	31.3	14.3	13.7
Total	63.0	51.7	47.8	52.3	50.3

Note: "Inter-provincial trade" refers to imports from other provinces and exports to other provinces. "Total" refers to the sum of all provincial figures that are available.

Source: State Statistical Bureau (Calculations in Appendix Tables A2.12 to A2.16).

Table A2.18 Interprovincial and Foreign Trade (RMB Y billion and %)

	Retail Sales, GDP/a	Total Foreign Trade	Foreign Trade Ratio/a	Interprovincial Trade	Interprovincial Trade Ratio/a
1. Guangdong					
1992	221.18	149.11	67.4%	40.68	18.4%
1991	178.056	117.26	65.9%	33.76	19.0%
1990	147.184	77.624	52.7%	29.62	20.1%
1985	55.385	15.489	28.0%	18.19	32.8%
1980	24.571	3.865	15.7%	10.18	41.4%
2. Shaanxi					
1992	23.727	6.17	12.2%	10.70	45.1%
1991	20.337	4.33	21.3%	9.67	47.5%
1990	18.443	2.76	15.0%	8.42	45.6%
1985	9.19	0.31	3.3%	5.16	56.1%
1980	5.125	0.01	0.3%	3.40	66.4%
3. Sichuan					
1992	71.93	13.78	19.2%	29.71	41.3%
1991	62.18	9.12	14.7%	26.62	42.8%
1990	54.53	6.52	12.0%	21.78	39.9%
1985	27.43	1.42	5.2%	9.15	33.4%
1980	15.19	1.20	7.9%	7.04	46.3%
4. Shanghai					
1992	47.9	53.5	111.7%		
1991	40.2	42.8	106.5%	31.1	77.4%
1990	35.3	35.5	100.7%	28.2	79.9%
1985	18.3	15.18	83.0%	22.9	125.1%
1980	8.8	6.8	76.8%	19.5	221.6%
5. Liaoning					
1992	58.9			26.6	45.2%
1991	51.1	36.2	70.8%	24.6	48.1%
1990	46.0	30.1	65.5%	20.6	44.8%
1985	23.2	16.2	69.6%	8.2	35.3%
1980	12.0	5.9	49.6%	6	50.0%

/a Ratio to retail sales, except for Guangdong, where the ratio to GDP is given.
Source: CASS Survey.

Table A2.19 China and Other Regional Trading Areas: Interregional Trade

	Imports	Exports	GDP/a	Imports/ GDP %	Exports/ GDP %	Total Trade/GDP %
Guangdong(1991)	11295.4	16646.8	178056.0	6.3	9.3	15.7
Jiangxi(1989)	4244.7	2930.3	36347.0	11.7	8.1	19.7
Sichuan(1989)	14594.7	7531.1	99849.0	14.6	7.5	22.2
Guizhou(1989)	2522.8	2440.1	23554.0	10.7	10.4	21.1
Beijing(1990)	16428.1	6938.6	50072.0	32.8	13.9	46.7
Subtotal	49085.8	36486.8	387878.0	12.7	9.4	22.1
Economic Community (1989): (ECU million)						
Belgium/Luxemburg	64.1	71.1	145.4	44.1	48.9	93.0
Denmark	12.9	13.2	95.1	13.6	13.9	27.5
Germany	130.6	165.3	1079.9	12.1	15.3	27.4
Greece	9.1	5.1	49.2	18.6	10.4	29.0
Spain	35.0	25.7	345.2	10.1	7.4	17.6
France	118.9	100.0	870.3	13.7	11.5	25.1
Ireland	11.0	13.5	30.8	35.6	43.7	79.3
Italy	78.8	71.4	786.5	10.0	9.1	19.1
Netherlands	61.1	84.9	203.2	30.1	41.8	71.9
Portugal	11.6	8.4	41.1	28.3	20.4	48.7
United Kingdom	91.3	65.9	760.3	12.0	8.7	20.7
EC Total	624.5	624.5	4406.9	14.2	14.2	28.3
Former Soviet Union (1990): (Ruble million)						
Russia	56583	86449	1288577	4.4	6.7	11.1
Ukraine	42468	35968	329563	12.9	10.9	23.8
Belarus	17259	16043	81224	21.2	19.8	41.0
Uzbekistan	10993	6889	70125	15.7	9.8	25.5
Kazakhstan	14570	8450	110673	13.2	7.6	20.8
Georgia	4464	2852	29500	15.1	9.7	24.8
Arzabaijan	4308	4576	29812	14.5	15.3	29.8
Lithuania	7169	4155	27755	25.8	15.0	40.8
Moldova	4947	2704	26474	18.7	10.2	28.9
Latvia	4873	3939	24011	20.3	16.4	36.7
Kyrghyzstan	2910	1954	17560	16.6	11.1	27.7
Tadjikstan	3082	1643	15242	20.2	10.8	31.0
Armenia	3155	1989	20094	15.7	9.9	25.6
Turkmenistan	2438	2773	15791	15.4	17.6	33.0
Estonia	3116	1951	16778	18.6	11.6	30.2
Subtotal (Excluding Russia)	125752	95886	814602	15.4	11.8	27.2
Subtotal (all FSU countries)	182335	182335	2103179	8.7	8.7	17.3

/a The Chinese figures for the GDP column are GNP.
Sources: Basic Statistics of the Community, 1990, 28th edition; Guangdong Statistical Yearbook 1989 and 1991, Jiangxi Statistical Yearbook 1999 and 1990, Sichuan Statistical Yearbook 1990, Guizhou Statistical Yeabook 1990 and 1991, China Statistical Yearbook 1991, Michalopoulos and Tarr (1992).

Table A2.20 Interprovincial and Foreign Investment in Selected Provinces
(1985-1992)

	1992	1991	1990	1989	1988	1985
National Investment (RMB Y billion)		551.1	444.9	413.8	449.7	
Investment, 6 provinces		165.3	136.2	124.4	133.0	
% of National, 6 provinces		30.0%	30.6%	30.1%	29.6%	
1. Guangdong (RMB Y billion)						
Total Investment	84.5	47.8	36.2	34.7	35.4	
Inv. from outside provinces	1.4	1.1				
% from outside provinces	1.7%	2.3%				
Foreign investment	26.8	13.8	9.6	9.0		
%Foreign Investment	31.7%	28.8%	26.6%	25.9%		
Total inv. to outside provinces	2.1					
2. Shaanxi (RMB Y million)						
Total Investment	15200	12493	10372	9518	9472	5799
Inv. from other provinces	370	431	380	315	349	430
% Inv. from other provs.	2.4%	3.4%	3.7%	3.3%	3.7%	7.4%
provincial govts	20	21	20	20	20	20
local govts.	10	10	10	10	10	10
enterprises	340	400	350	285	319	400
o/w SOEs	310	370	330	270	300	380
%SOEs in outside Inv.	83.8%	85.8%	86.8%	85.7%	86.0%	88.4%
Foreign Investment/a	340	235	224	456	346	
% Foreign Investment	2.2%	1.9%	2.2%	4.8%	3.7%	
Outward Investment of Shaanxi		350	300	250	300	200
% total investment		2.8%	2.9%	2.6%	3.2%	3.4
3. Sichuan (RMB Y million)						
Total Investment	36390	28252	20390	21219	14488	8047
Inv. from other provinces	80	70	35	15	3	1
% Inv. from other provs.	0.22%	0.25%	0.17%	0.07%	0.02%	0.01%
provincial govts	10	8	2	2		
local govts.	2	2				
enterprises	68	60	33	13	3	1
o/w SOEs	57	50	30	12	3	1
%SOEs in outside Inv.	71.3%	71.4%	85.7%	80.0%	100.0%	100.0%
Foreign Investment/b	1950		301	960	750	
% Foreign Investment	5.4%		1.5%	4.5%	5.2%	
Outward Investment of Sichuan	1620	1350	1150	600		
% total investment	4.45%	4.78%	5.64%	2.83%		

....contd/

	1992	1991	1990	1989	1988	1985
4. Beijing (RMB Y billion)						
Total Investment/c	19.38	19.19	17.92	13.95	16.3	
Inv. from other provinces	0.031	0.027		0.064	0.071	0.05
% Inv. from other provs.	0.16%	0.14%		0.46%	0.44%	
Foreign Investment			1.88	1.80		
% Foreign Investment			10.46%	12.87%		
5. Shanghai (RMB Y billion)						
Total Investment	32.5	25.8	22.7	21.5	24.5	11.7
Inv. from other provinces/d	10.69	7.9		6.1		
% Inv. from other provs.	32.9%	30.6%		28.4%		
Foreign Investment/e	4.35	0.93	1.54	1.59	0.364	0.062
% Foreign Investment	13.4%	3.6%	6.8%	7.4%	1.5%	0.5%
6. Liaoning (RMB Y billion)						
Total Investment		31.8	26.29	24.32	26.13	
Inv. from other provinces/f		0.79	0.19	0.17	0.34	
% Inv. from other provs.		2.48%	0.72%	0.70%	1.30%	
Foreign Investment			3.48	1.46	0.388	
% Foreign Investment			13.23%	6.01%		
Outward Investment of Liaoning/f		0.24	0.22	0.1	0.14	
% total investment		0.75%	0.84%	0.41%	0.54%	

/a Shaanxi: There were only 18 foreign or foreign joint venture enterprises(1991)
/b Sichuan: The total for 1988 to 1992 was 6.6 billion RMB Y
/c Beijing: Total investment for 1992 is an estimate
/d Shanghai: In 4550 enterprises, including the Pudong Zone
/e Shanghai: Joint Venture investment statistics
/f Liaoning: Figures for inward and outward investment in the context of 'horizontal integration'
Source: Provincial Yearbooks, provincial Departments of Cooperation and CASS Survey.

Table A2.21 Effective Tax Rates by Province (1986)
(percent)

	No. of Observations	Total Effective Tax Rates	Commodity Tax Rates	Profit Rate		
				Profit-maker	Loss-maker	Average
Total	562	82.91	15.46	66.96	-95.98	66.62
Beijing	22	62.43	10.36	49.29	-88.34	48.08
Qinghai	21	73.54	10.99	36.80	-100.00	21.81
Sichuan	24	78.51	9.87	57.04	-88.67	54.60
Gansu	22	79.19	9.33	66.09	-105.49	57.66
Heilongjiang	15	80.41	8.53	60.30		60.30
Tianjin	30	81.37	11.64	69.51		69.51
Hubei	47	81.97	17.67	62.83	-100.00	62.78
Jiangsu	35	83.23	7.35	74.14		74.14
Shanghai	46	85.86	13.10	75.24	-100.00	75.24
Shanxi	18	85.96	4.52	74.72	-100.00	72.34
Guangdong	42	87.30	22.08	67.20	-100.00	66.96
Hebei	16	87.92	17.08	67.18		67.18
Liaoning	62	88.38	14.55	79.34	-110.71	79.37
Hunan	26	88.82	22.49	66.49	-112.42	65.71
Jiangxi	18	88.97	22.35	63.84	-100.00	63.53
Jilin	18	89.05	8.61	75.43		75.43
Henan	32	90.55	25.17	63.36	-300.22	62.23
Zhejiang	18	91.65	26.06	75.11		75.11
Anhui	23	91.66	35.63	61.66		61.66
Shandong	27	93.34	40.98	71.34		71.34
SD		7.14	9.45	9.76	55.62	12.41
Mean		84.51	16.92	65.85	-70.29	64.25
COV		0.085	0.559	0.148	0.791	0.193

Note: Total effective tax rate is defined as (commodity taxes + profit tax)/(commodity taxes + profit tax + retained profits)
Commodity tax rate is defined as commodity taxes/sales revenue;
Profit tax rate is defined as profit taxes/(sales revenue - material costs - depreciation).
Source: Calculated from the CESRRI Database, STICERD, London School of Economics.

- 216 -

Table A2.22 Effective Tax Rates by Province (1987)
(percent)

Total	No. of Observations	Total Effective Tax Rates	Commodity Tax Rates	Profit Rate		
				Profit-maker	Loss-maker	Average
	562	82.07	14.41	65.54	-109.61	65.02
Beijing	22	60.96	9.93	48.04	-115.59	46.24
Qinghai	21	80.50	10.80	46.77	-100.00	38.01
Sichuan	24	79.49	9.78	55.14	-100.47	51.41
Gansu	22	82.58	8.69	71.10	-95.82	64.68
Heilongjiang	15	86.77	7.61	72.99	-100.00	72.14
Tianjin	30	81.34	10.55	69.08		69.08
Hubei	47	80.71	16.97	59.64	-100.00	59.59
Jiangsu	35	78.82	5.57	69.81		69.81
Shanghai	46	85.70	12.46	74.50	-100.00	74.49
Shanxi	18	81.75	4.32	69.90		69.90
Guangdong	42	84.77	19.45	61.65	-100.00	61.64
Hebei	16	86.07	16.48	67.38		67.38
Liaoning	62	88.13	12.99	79.05	-203.88	78.94
Hunan	26	91.87	23.69	74.23	-180.04	73.69
Jiangxi	18	87.14	18.34	62.26	-100.00	60.89
Jilin	18	86.49	7.90	70.16		70.16
Henan	32	89.93	21.71	67.33	-137.56	64.04
Zhejiang	18	89.40	24.92	68.52		68.52
Anhui	23	92.39	31.30	64.02		64.02
Shandong	27	93.40	38.23	75.31		75.37
SD		6.88	8.67	8.44	34.56	9.88
Mean		84.41	15.58	66.34	-71.67	65.00
COV		0.081	0.556	0.127	0.482	0.152

Note: Total effective tax rate is defined as (commodity taxes + profit tax)/(commodity taxes + profit tax + retained profits);
Commodity tax rate is defined as commodity taxes/sales revenue;
Profit tax rate is defined as profit taxes/(sales revenue - material costs - depreciation).
Source: Calculated from the CESRRI Database, STICERD, London School of Economics.

Table A2.23 Effective Tax Rates by Province (1988)
(percent)

	No. of Observations	Total Effective Tax Rates	Commodity Tax Rates	Profit Rate		
				Profit-maker	Loss-maker	Average
Total	562	81.87	14.08	63.79	-107.45	63.03
Beijing	22	57.24	9.30	43.52	-113.18	41.21
Qinghai	21	83.30	11.44	55.63	-109.62	46.92
Sichuan	24	75.78	10.11	49.18	-100.55	43.73
Gansu	22	79.83	8.47	66.13	-101.96	52.41
Heilongjiang	15	88.22	7.38	77.00	-100.00	76.23
Tianjin	30	88.31	10.57	78.85	-100.00	78.81
Hubei	47	78.94	17.23	55.74	-100.00	55.68
Jiangsu	35	77.28	5.03	65.86		65.86
Shanghai	46	84.96	11.82	72.04	-100.00	72.02
Shanxi	18	82.31	3.90	71.85		71.85
Guangdong	42	90.39	20.07	71.24		71.24
Hebei	16	87.91	15.03	71.38		71.38
Liaoning	62	89.31	12.79	79.77	-118.95	79.66
Hunan	26	91.05	24.64	69.89	-162.27	69.24
Jiangxi	18	89.72	16.92	69.70	-100.00	69.44
Jilin	18	85.58	8.14	67.32		67.32
Henan	32	90.24	16.96	70.72	-100.00	66.30
Zhejiang	18	91.43	26.13	71.30		71.30
Anhui	23	95.90	31.10	78.37		78.37
Shandong	27	95.06	33.98	79.81	-100.00	79.75
SD		8.41	8.21	9.81	16.72	11.70
Mean		85.14	15.05	68.27	-70.33	66.44
COV		0.099	0.546	0.144	0.238	0.176

Note: Total effective tax rate is defined as (commodity taxes + profit tax)/(commodity taxes + profit tax + retained profits); Commodity tax rate is defined as commodity taxes/sales revenue; Profit tax rate is defined as profit taxes/(sales revenue - material costs - depreciation).
Source: Calculated from the CESRRI Database, STICERD, London School of Economics.

Table A2.24 Effective Tax Rates by Province (1989)
(percent)

	No. of Observations	Total Effective Tax Rates	Commodity Tax Rates	Profit Rate		
				Profit-maker	Loss-maker	Average
Total	562	81.71	14.42	59.04	-105.52	56.85
Beijing	22	55.90	11.37	38.68	-112.15	35.81
Qinghai	21	85.75	11.51	56.27	-169.75	41.68
Sichuan	24	75.22	10.59	50.01	-100.00	32.63
Gansu	22	86.26	8.77	72.75	-100.00	47.19
Heilongjiang	15	89.07	7.63	74.93	-78.87	74.68
Tianjin	30	90.46	10.72	80.90	-133.33	80.83
Hubei	47	78.52	16.93	51.49	-100.00	51.32
Jiangsu	35	82.96	4.19	73.64		73.64
Shanghai	46	86.31	11.61	70.07	-100.00	70.03
Shanxi	18	80.70	3.77	67.42	-103.06	-2.22
Guangdong	42	91.88	22.99	68.99		68.99
Hebei	16	87.98	16.13	67.75	-100.00	66.32
Liaoning	62	93.24	12.70	83.12	-112.67	81.35
Hunan	26	89.03	29.13	58.47	-112.49	57.01
Jiangxi	18	92.89	18.59	70.97	-73.40	70.90
Jilin	18	88.29	8.31	69.93	-100.00	69.54
Henan	32	86.07	16.05	61.17	-100.00	44.98
Zhejiang	18	88.89	25.03	56.45		56.45
Anhui	23	96.77	34.06	72.70		72.70
Shandong	27	94.26	29.62	72.68	-100.00	71.94
SD		8.63	8.41	10.81	20.96	19.99
Mean		86.02	15.49	65.92	-84.79	58.29
COV		0.100	0.543	0.164	0.247	0.343

Note: Total effective tax rate is defined as (commodity taxes + profit tax)/(commodity taxes + profit tax + retained profits);
Commodity tax rate is defined as commodity taxes/sales revenue;
Profit tax rate is defined as profit taxes/(sales revenue - material costs - depreciation).
Source: Calculated from the CESRRI Database, STICERD, London School of Economics.

Table A2.25 Effective Tax Rates by Province (1990)
(percent)

	No. of Observation	Total Effective Tax Rates	CommodityTax Rates	Profit Rate		
				Profit-maker	Loss-maker	Average/a
Total	562	82.73	14.64	56.67	-99.75	51.58
Beijing	22	55.88	11.88	35.35	-100.07	30.46
Qinghai	21	90.67	13.30	54.61	-107.50/0a	-441.86
Sichuan	24	79.62	10.42	57.77	-100.14	3.28
Gansu	22	97.86	8.51	95.06	-100.00/0a	-212.30
Heilongjiang	15	90.12	6.80	75.06	-97.84	50.47
Tianjin	30	90.47	10.69	77.22		77.22
Hubei	47	79.17	16.72	50.61	-100.00	48.50
Jiangsu	35	88.22	3.87	77.90	-100.00	77.76
Shanghai	46	87.60	11.80	66.02	-111.88	64.49
Shanxi	18	90.61	3.40	83.78	-100.00	79.94
Guangdong	42	94.39	27.87	73.04	-89.90	70.70
Hebei	16	92.36	16.16	76.92	-100.00	75.62
Liaoning	62	93.93	12.31	81.34	-96.90	80.13
Hunan	26	93.03	29.86	64.24	-100.00	60.73
Jiangxi	18	94.62	19.73	69.69	-92.88	9.05
Jilin	18	94.53	7.91	80.31	-100.00	74.05
Henan	32	93.50	16.18	81.30	-100.00	9.38
Zhejiang	18	94.87	27.07	72.47	-100.00	70.37
Anhui	23	98.67	35.82	72.28	-100.00/0a	-146.02
Shandong	27	95.45	31.74	81.53	-100.00	80.63
SD		9.20	9.32	13.23	4.38/36.45a	127.80/31.61a
Mean		89.78	16.10	71.33	-94.86/-79.48/a	8.13/48.14a
COV		0.102	0.579	0.185	0.046/0.459/a	15.719/0.657a

/a Due to the high average negative values for Qinghai, Gansu and Anhui in this year, the standard deviation is also very high. Adjusting for this by putting the averages for these three provinces equal to zero, we obtain the second set of values.

Note: Total effective tax rate is defined as (commodity taxes + profit tax)/(commodity taxes + profit tax + retained profits); Commodity tax rate is defined as commodity taxes/sales revenue; Profit tax rate is defined as profit taxes/(sales revenue - material costs - depreciation).

Source: Calculated from the CESRRI Database, STICERD, London School of Economics.

Table A3.1 Supply by Government Contracts (1983-1991)
(10,000 ton)

	1983	1984	1985	1986	1987	1988	1989	1990	1991
Coal	365.31	383.07	400.25	405.85	402.58	407.98	426.66	455.19	456.6
Coke	3.56	4.2	3.9	4.02	3.94	3.65	3.41	4	3.61
Pig Iron	5.82	6.75	6.43	6.24	5.75	4.96	3.94	3.94	4.22
Steel Products	17.85	18.85	18.81	19.41	18.96	0.74	16.56	15.8	16.31
Caustic Soda	1.4	1.42	1.41	1.37	1.39	1.33	1.03	1.01	0.98
Soda Ash	1.56	1.54	1.53	1.52	0.93	1.32	1.28	1.62	1.44
Sulphuric Acid	3.11	3.03	2.61	2.39	2.91	2.81	2.16	1.85	1.86
Concentrated Nitrc Acid	0.21	0.22	0.21	0.18	0.21	0.19	0.16	0.16	0.17
Cement	23.83	25.27	24.2	24.1	23.56	2.38	21.22	21.25	20.04
Timber	35.12	39.73	18.81	18.53	16.5	13.74	14.34	14.25	11.28

Source: China Statistical Yearbook (various issues).

Table A3.2 Production of Main Products (1983-1991)
(10,000 tons)

	1983	1984	1985	1986	1987	1988	1989	1990	1991
Coal	714.53	789.23	872.28	894.04	928.08	979.88	1054.14	1079.88	1087.41
Coke	42.2	45.57	48.02	52.76	57.95	61.08	66.24	73.28	73.52
Pig Iron	37.38	40.01	43.84	50.64	55.03	57.04	58.2	62.38	67.65
Steel Products	30.72	33.72	36.93	40.58	43.86	46.89	48.59	51.53	56.38
Caustic Soda	2.12	2.22	2.35	2.52	2.74	3.01	3.21	3.35	3.54
Soda Ash	1.79	1.88	2.01	2.15	2.36	2.61	3.04	3.8	3.94
Sulphuric Acid	8.7	8.17	6.76	7.63	9.83	11.11	11.53	11.97	13.33
Concentrated Nitrc Acid	0.26	0.26	0.27	0.28	0.29	0.3	0.33	0.32	0.34
Cement	108.25	123.03	145.95	166.06	186.25	210.14	210.29	209.71	252.61
Timber	52.32	63.85	63.23	65.02	64.08	62.18	58.02	51.09	58.07

Source: China Statistical Yearbook (various issues).

Table A3.3 Distribution of Retail Sales in Quantity and Value (1985-1991) (Y 100 million)

| | Total Retail Sales | | | | Retail Sales by Agricultural to Non Agricultural Residents | | | |
| | 1985 | | 1991 | | 1985 | | 1991 | |
	Quantity	Value	Quantity	Value	Quantity	Value	Quantity	Value
Total		3801.40		8245.70		291.00		909.80
Food		2003.54		4537.48		269.00		866.94
Grain(10000 tn)	9011.60	372.81	9242.60	603.41	550.00	28.08	710.10	58.23
Veg. oil(10000 tn))	349.10	83.78	467.20	188.27	22.50	7.24	62.40	29.75
Hogs(10000 heads)	15324.60	272.17	21035.20	687.51	3631.00	65.10	5864.10	202.68
Beef cattle(10 th heads)	376.20	12.39	666.90	35.93	175.00	4.14	353.30	19.97
Sheep(10 th heads)	2664.80	8.84	3602.60	22.82	1280.00	4.24	2041.00	13.28
Fowls(10 th)	59430.00	25.85	89025.30	82.35	39980.00	14.99	63049.00	63.68
Eggs(10 th tn))	192.70	52.51	336.90	143.31	90.00	26.82	161.50	84.56
Fish (10 th tn)	268.40	70.81	427.70	249.10	119.00	38.08	220.20	129.25
Dried, fresh veg.(100 mil Y)		109.40		222.50	0.00	46.50		163.36
Dried, fresh fruit.(100 mil Y)		59.40		139.83	0.00	22.00		95.97
Apples(10 th tn)					81.00	7.94	130.60	24.96
Citrus and Oranges(10 th tn)					45.00	5.67	106.30	25.09
Tea(10 th tn)	25.30	25.85	31.80	56.29	1.00	1.10	2.70	4.24
Honey(10 th tn)					0.20	0.06	0.50	0.25
Sugar cane(10 th tn)					50.00	0.80	57.80	2.22

Source: China Statistical Yearbook 1992.

Table A3.4 Total Value of Retail Sales by Ownership (1960-1991)
(Y 100 million)

Year	Retail Sales By Ownership					Sales of Agr. to Non-Agricultural Residents
	Total Value of Sales	State-Owned Units	Collective Owned Units	Jointly Owned Units	Indivudually Owned Units	
1960	67.45	58.50	6.70		1.45	0.80
1965	67.03	35.55	28.93		1.25	1.30
1975	127.11	70.83	53.60		0.18	2.50
1978	158.97	85.10	67.44	0.21	3.11	3.11
1980	214.00	110.07	95.49	0.04	1.50	6.90
1983	284.94	133.88	118.95	0.36	18.45	13.30
1985	430.50	174.00	160.03	1.27	66.10	29.10
1986	495.00	195.10	180.40	1.52	80.48	37.50
1987	582.00	224.90	207.96	1.88	101.16	46.10
1988	744.00	293.59	255.79	2.72	132.40	59.50
1989	810.14	316.78	268.97	3.63	150.96	69.80
1990	830.01	328.59	263.10	4.03	156.96	77.33
1991	941.56	378.37	282.62	5.15	184.44	90.98

Source: China Statistical Yearbook (various issues).

Table A3.5 Composition of Total Retail Sales Value by Ownership (1960-1991)
(Y 100 million and percent)

Year	Retail Sales By Ownership					Sales of Agricultural to Non- Agr. Residents (%)
	Total Value of Sales (Y 100m)	State-Owned Units %	Collective Units %	Jointly Owned Units %	Individual Units %	
1960	67.45	86.7	9.9	0.0	2.1	1.2
1965	67.03	53.0	43.2	0.0	1.9	1.9
1975	127.11	55.7	42.2	0.0	0.1	2.0
1978	158.97	53.5	42.4	0.1	2.0	2.0
1980	214	51.4	44.6	0.0	0.7	3.2
1983	284.94	47.0	41.7	0.1	6.5	4.7
1985	430.5	40.4	37.2	0.3	15.4	6.8
1986	495	39.4	36.4	0.3	16.3	7.6
1987	582	38.6	35.7	0.3	17.4	7.9
1988	744	39.5	34.4	0.4	17.8	8.0
1989	810.14	39.1	33.2	0.4	18.6	8.6
1990	830.01	39.6	31.7	0.5	18.9	9.3
1991	941.56	40.2	30.0	0.5	19.6	9.7

Source: China Statistical Yearbook, various issues.

Table A3.6 Number of Domestic Trade Units by Ownership and Region (1985-1991)

	1985				1991			
	Total	State Owned Units	Collective Units	Individually Owned Units	Total	State Owned Units	Collective Units	Individually Owned Units
All China	8250472	429424	1578953	6238600	9797708	534145	1443617	7817454
Beijing	53228	7023	11934	34238	91254	8060	12338	70794
Tianjin	62313	4355	7630	50316	74717	5459	10173	59035
Hebei	456142	16416	64938	374697	512356	18338	52400	441598
Shanxi	193394	12077	44799	136350	210699	13257	39515	157922
Inner Mongolia	137050	8927	26415	101694	148699	11004	29789	107906
Liaoning	288492	15107	41250	232124	378816	18100	43692	317005
Jilin	185872	9740	30438	145647	212764	10814	28690	173256
Heilongjiang	215901	12637	38032	165232	249522	13789	37062	198667
Shanghai	74665	9320	20922	44324	92306	10472	24249	56939
Jiangsu	541287	24702	117483	399050	592401	23090	111292	457981
Zhejiang	398058	13309	71691	312973	580679	16606	63936	500086
Anhui	383423	19952	71540	291579	407930	22828	70672	314265
Fujian	223208	12738	50807	159292	276733	14766	42041	219656
Jiangxi	195910	11581	41448	142806	282051	17233	42799	221985
Shandong	611274	18650	118231	474216	850530	27094	96542	726862
Henan	534490	27069	139890	367431	524490	32028	90122	402339
Hubei	432829	25480	83552	323735	413634	37915	73275	302443
Hunan	474618	21301	93139	360102	505321	26958	74844	403514
Guangdong	605389	37816	94815	471755	809962	47471	99459	662188
Guangxi	327006	13058	38325	275552	409806	16228	37436	356102
Hainan					79713	4460	7324	67894
Sichuang	930661	44577	215736	670205	1076726	59778	211694	805220
Guizhou	188027	12173	29964	145890	206684	15315	22214	169137
Yunnan	261043	16706	34630	209649	247310	19887	34601	192821
Tibet	22827	419	954	21375	23786	1595	947	21237
Shaanxi	192386	12401	47955	131797	215442	15032	42634	157679
Gansu	107936	8625	19197	80063	137472	11060	22212	104200
Qinghai	26270	2103	3099	21068	29622	2528	3021	24065
Ningxia	21823	1782	3891	16145	31860	2497	3859	25504
Xinjiang	104714	9380	16212	79095	124423	10483	14776	99054

Note: The sum of state-, colletive- and individual-owned units is less than the total because the total also includes joint-owned units.

Source: China Statistical Yearbook, 1986 and 1992.

Table A3.7 Composition of Domestic Trade Units by Ownership and Region (1985-1991)
(percent)

	1985			1991			Difference in percentage 1985-91		
	State Units	Collect. Units	Individ. Units	State Units	Collect. Units	Individual Units	State Units	Collective Units	Individual Units
All China	5.2	19.1	75.6	5.5	14.7	79.8	0.2	-4.4	4.2
Beijing	13.2	22.4	64.3	8.8	13.5	77.6	-4.4	-8.9	13.3
Tianjin	7.0	12.2	80.7	7.3	13.6	79.0	0.3	1.4	-1.7
Hebei	3.6	14.2	82.1	3.6	10.2	86.2	0.0	-4.0	4.0
Shanxi	6.2	23.2	70.5	6.3	18.8	75.0	0.0	-4.4	4.4
Inner Mongolia	6.5	19.3	74.2	7.4	20.0	72.6	0.9	0.8	-1.6
Liaoning	5.2	14.3	80.5	4.8	11.5	83.7	-0.5	-2.8	3.2
Jilin	5.2	16.4	78.4	5.1	13.5	81.4	-0.2	-2.9	3.1
Heilongjiang	5.9	17.6	76.5	5.5	14.9	79.6	-0.3	-2.8	3.1
Shanghai	12.5	28.0	59.4	11.3	26.3	61.7	-1.1	-1.8	2.3
Jiangsu	4.6	21.7	73.7	3.9	18.8	77.3	-0.7	-2.9	3.6
Zhejiang	3.3	18.0	78.6	2.9	11.0	86.1	-0.5	-7.0	7.5
Anhui	5.2	18.7	76.0	5.6	17.3	77.0	0.4	-1.3	1.0
Fujian	5.7	22.8	71.4	5.3	15.2	79.4	-0.4	-7.6	8.0
Jiangxi	5.9	21.2	72.9	6.1	15.2	78.7	0.2	-6.0	5.8
Shandong	3.1	19.3	77.6	3.2	11.4	85.5	0.1	-8.0	7.9
Henan	5.1	26.2	68.7	6.1	17.2	76.7	1.0	-9.0	8.0
Hubei	5.9	19.3	74.8	9.2	17.7	73.1	3.3	-1.6	-1.7
Hunan	4.5	19.6	75.9	5.3	14.8	79.9	0.8	-4.8	4.0
Guangdong	6.2	15.7	77.9	5.9	12.3	81.8	-0.4	-3.4	3.8
Guangxi	4.0	11.7	84.3	4.0	9.1	86.9	0.0	-2.6	2.6
Hainan				5.6	9.2	85.2	5.6	9.2	85.2
Sichuan	4.8	23.2	72.0	5.6	19.7	74.8	0.8	-3.5	2.8
Guizhou	6.5	15.9	77.6	7.4	10.7	81.8	0.9	-5.2	4.2
Yunnan	6.4	13.3	80.3	8.0	14.0	78.0	1.6	0.7	-2.3
Tibet	1.8	4.2	93.6	6.7	4.0	89.3	4.9	-0.2	-4.4
Shaanxi	6.4	24.9	68.5	7.0	19.8	73.2	0.5	-5.1	4.7
Gansu	8.0	17.8	74.2	8.0	16.2	75.8	0.1	-1.6	1.6
Qinghai	8.0	11.8	80.2	8.5	10.2	81.2	0.5	-1.6	1.0
Ningxia	8.2	17.8	74.0	7.8	12.1	80.1	-0.3	-5.7	6.1
Xinjiang	9.0	15.5	75.5	8.4	11.9	79.6	-0.5	-3.6	4.1

Note: The sum of state-, collective- and individual-owned units is less than the total because the total also includes joint-owned units.

Source: China Statistical Yearbook, 1986 and 1992.

Table A3.8 Staff and Outlets of Materials Circulation System (1985-1991)

	Staff and Workers (1000)				Outlets			
	1985	1989	1990	1991	1985	1989	1990	1991
National Total	843.3	1049.7	1105.4	1160.9	32466	41564	44297	51165
Local MME	814.5	1004.3	1059.7	1115.5	32370	41468	44201	49138
Beijing	14.7	16.0	15.7	15.7	213	407	433	454
Tianjin	32.9	29.8	29.7	29.2	647	731	678	715
Hebei	43.9	58.6	61.2	65.4	1890	2807	2909	3141
Shanxi	17.4	19.2	25.5	28.4	914	995	1167	1264
Inner Mongolia	21.8	34.0	35.7	37.8	907	1091	1239	1489
Liaoning	92.4	103.4	106.3	111.1	2593	3167	3380	3398
Jilin	41.7	51.2	53.2	54.9	1091	1569	1617	1760
Heilongjiang	67.0	83.7	87.3	91.3	2128	2453	2563	2662
Shanghai	34.5	35.3	35.4	35.3	2140	2167	2156	2177
Jiangsu	83.8	100.3	102.8	107.0	3807	3890	4060	4260
Zhejiang	28.5	38.5	45.9	49.4	1455	2131	2073	2439
Anhui	20.8	30.2	34.1	37.0	1202	1470	1624	1911
Fujian	10.5	11.1	12.2	12.7	439	529	550	609
Jiangxi	9.6	13.5	14.3	15.8	407	606	645	825
Shandong	49.3	71.4	75.7	81.6	3008	3562	3989	4395
Henan	53.0	72.4	77.9	82.3	1285	2626	2715	3052
Hubei	37.7	49.9	52.3	54.8	1616	1644	1932	2185
Hunan	19.4	25.6	26.9	28.6	731	1171	1314	1606
Guangdong	32.9	33.2	34.4	36.4	1292	1592	1715	1877
Guangxi	11.2	11.4	13.0	11.0	558	691	768	1120
Hainan		3.0	3.1	3.2		213	204	193
Sichuang	27.3	34.7	36.2	38.4	1357	1941	2225	2797
Guizhou	7.1	10.0	11.1	10.9	386	665	708	845
Yunnan	9.0	10.3	10.6	11.5	494	538	588	646
Tibet	0.8	0.8	0.9	0.9			20	20
Shaanxi	24.5	30.2	30.4	32.9	847	1032	1437	1671
Gansu	10.4	11.7	12.6	15.6	444	812	787	837
Qinghai	3.6	4.2	4.3	4.4	80	100	105	134
Ningxia	3.2	3.7	4.0	4.3	150	207	231	257
Xinjiang	5.6	7.0	7.0	7.7	289	391	369	399
Agencies under MME	28.8	45.4	45.7	45.4	96	96	96	2027

Source: China Statistical Yearbook (various issues).

Table A3.9 Number of Units and Personnel in Domestic Trade by Ownership (1985-1991)
(10,000)

	1985		1991		Annual Average Growth Rate (1985-91)	
	Units	Personnel	Units	Personnel	Units	Personnel
National Total	825.1	2398.4	979.8	2944.9	2.9	3.5
Administrative Units	11.2	222.4	13.3	245.1	2.9	1.6
State-ownership	5.2	135.5	6.4	151.5	3.5	1.9
Collective-ownership	7.5	95.5	9.1	107.1	3.3	1.9
Supply and Marketing Cooperatives	4.5	78.3	4.7	80.1	0.7	0.4
Business Units	811.7	2113.6	936.9	2624.8	2.4	3.7
(1) State ownership	36.5	499.9	45.5	663.7	3.7	4.8
Purchasing farm and sideline products	9.6	118.3	10.2	139.8	1.0	2.8
Wholesale industrial products	2.8	70.5	4.6	102.2	8.6	6.3
Retail outlets	22.9	290.7	29.0	388.3	4.0	4.9
owned by state, run by collectives			2.7	42.1		
leased and run by individuals			0.9	10.3		
Other Units	1.2	20.3	1.8	33.6	7.0	8.8
(2) Collective ownership	151.0	767.9	136.4	816.3	-1.7	1.0
Supply and Marketing cooperatives	59.0	276.6	63.0	325.4	1.1	2.7
Purchasing farm and sideline products	6.6	41.0	6.3	45.7	-0.8	1.8
Wholesale industrial products	2.3	19.2	3.9	35.6	9.2	10.8
Retail outlets	46.7	191.6	48.6	213.6	0.7	1.8
Other units	3.4	24.8	4.2	30.5	3.6	3.5
Other collective ownership units	92.0	491.3	73.4	490.8	-3.7	0.0
Retail Outlets	89.5	473.8	68.9	488.9	-4.3	0.6
Transformed from state to collective-owned			0.1	1.9		
Purchase and sales agents in rural areas	28.3	34.7	14.6	18.2	-10.4	-10.2
(3) Joint ownerhsip	0.3	3.6	0.3	4.9	0.0	5.3
Joint China-Foreign country ownership	0.0	0.3	0.0	1.2	20.1	26.0
Retail Sales Unit	0.3	2.9	0.2	3.6	-6.5	3.7
Licensed Individual Merchants	623.9	842.2	781.7	1139.8	3.8	5.2
Storage and transport units	2.2	62.4	2.6	74.9	2.8	3.1
State ownership	1.2	51.1	1.5	62.4	3.8	3.4
Collective ownership	1.1	13.4	1.2	15.6	1.5	2.6
Supply and Marketing Cooperatives	0.9	9.2	1.0	9.3	1.8	0.2

Source: China Statistical Yearbook, varous issues.

Table A3.10 Sales of Machinery and Electrical Trading Companies under MME (1991)
(Y 10 thousand)

Rank	Name	Total Sales
1	China National Mechanical and Electrical Equipment Corporation	386852
2	Shanghai Mechanical and Electrical Equipment Supply Company	249755
3	Zhejiang Machinery and Electrical Company	82229
4	Tianjin Machinery and Electrical Company	72227
5	Guangdong Mechanical and Electrical Company	60945
6	Wuxi Mechanical and Electrical Company, Jiangsu	55888
7	Hubei Machinery and Electrical Company	52432
8	Guangxi Machinery and Electrical Company	51100
9	Tangshan Mechanical and Electrical Equipment General Company, Hebei	50584
10	Yunnan Machinery and Electrical Company	50010
11	Liaoning Machinery and Electrical Company	45060
12	Shanxi Machinery and Electrical Company	42907
13	Zhengzhou Machinery and Electrical Company, Henan	40407
14	Heilongjiang Mechanical and Electrical Equipment General Company	37578
15	Henan Machinery and Electrical Company	37036
16	Xinjiang Machinery and Electrical Company	36369
17	Shenyang Mechanical and Electrical Equipment General Company	36075
18	Nanjiang Machinery and Electrical Company, Jiangsu	34262
19	Chongqing Machinery and Electrical Equipment Company, Sichuan	33970
20	Hangzhou Machinery and Electrical Company, Zhejiang	33375

Source: Ministry of Materials and Equipment.

Table A3.11 Sales of Metal Materials Trading Companies under MME (1991)
(Y 10 thousand)

Rank	Name	Total Sales
1	Shanghai Metals Company	504522
2	China National Ferrous Materials Corporation	484115
3	China National Non-ferrous Materials Corporation	320755
4	Zhejiang Metal Materials Company	115690
5	Beijing Metal Materials Company	106754
6	Liaoning Metal Materials Company	103059
7	Wuxi Metal Materials Company, Jiangsu	85338
8	Guangdong Metal Materials Company	82452
9	Hunan Metal Materials General Company	78680
10	Tianjin Metals Company	78416
11	Guangdong Metals Company	76915
12	Hubei Metals Company	65691
13	Wuhan Ferrous Meterials Company	65559
14	Guangxu Metals Company	58379
15	Qingdao Metals Company	58054
16	County of Wuxi Metals Company, Jiangsu	57113
17	Nanjing Metals Company, Jiangsu	55465
18	Henan Metal Materials Company	51300
19	Chongqing Metal Materials Company	49347
20	Sichuan Metals Company	48720

Source: Ministry of Materials and Equipment.

Table A3.12 Sales of Fuel Trading Companies under MME (1991)
(Y 10 thousand)

Rank	Name	Total Sales
1	Shanghai Fuel Company	171935
2	Zhejiang Fuel Company	91582
3	Tianjin Fuel and Construction Company	74720
4	Jiiangsu Fuel Company	68343
5	Guangdong Fuel Company	61573
6	Nantong Fuel Company, Jiangsu	46468
7	Liaoning Fuel Company	44454
8	Shenyang Fuel General Company	43411
9	Xuzhou Fuel Company, Jiangsu	37490
10	Suzhou Fuel Company, Jiangsu	34400
11	Wuxi Fuel Company, Jiangsu	33730
12	Dalian Fuel Compnay, Liaoning	31191
13	Zhenjiang Fuel Company, Jiangsu	30066
14	Nanjing Fuel Company, Jiangsu	28369
15	Heilongjiang Fuel General Company	27526
16	Harbin Fuel Compnay	26160
17	Hubei Fuel Compnay	26089
18	Jinan Fuel Company, Shandong	25659
19	Shantou No.2 Fuel Company, Guangdong	25643
20	Qingdao Fuel Company, Shangdong	25358

Source: Ministry of Materials and Equipment.

Table A3.13 Sales of Comprehensive Trading Center under MME (1991)
(Y 10 thousand)

Rank	Name	Total Sales
1	Suzhou Goods and Materials Trading Center, Jiangsu	103091
2	Shanghai Goods and Materials Trading Center	91874
3	Liaoning Goods and Materials Group Company	81020
4	Shanghai Materials of Production General Company	75141
5	Sichuan Goods and Materials Trading Center	65535
6	Chengdu Goods and Materials Trading Center, Sichuan	50294
7	Wujin Goods and Materials Trading Center, Jiangsu	45772
8	Zhejiang Economic Cooperation Company	31046
9	Zhejiang Materials of Production Company	28279
10	Cangzhou Goods and Materials Comprehensive Trading Center, Hebei	25413
11	Tianjin Goods and Materials Comprehensive Trading Cnter	23344
12	Shanghai Goods and Materials Cooperation and Development Company	23226
13	Zhenjiang Materials of Production Company, Jiangsu	20122
14	Chongqing Goods and MAterials Trading Center	19308
15	Hubei Goods and Materials Trading Center	17924
16	Kunshan Materials of Production Service Company, Jiangsu	17772
17	Yixing Goods and Materials Company, Jiangsu	17765
18	County of Wuxi Goods and Materials Trading Center, Jiangsu	17380
19	Shiyan Goods and Materials Trading Center, Hubei	17111
20	Changzhou Materials of Production Service Company, Jiangsu	11595

Source: Ministry of Materials and Equipment.

Table A3.14 Purchase, Sales and Inventory of Commercial Units (1962-1991)
(Y 100 million)

Year	Total Purchase	Total Sales	Total Inventory	Inventory/Sales (%)
1962	49.72	63.76	38.36	60.16
1963	53.59	64.81	41.81	64.51
1964	62.71	72.78	42.60	58.53
1965	71.05	79.01	45.83	58.01
1966	81.15	86.40	51.82	59.98
1967	76.90	87.30	50.20	57.50
1968	72.70	85.00	54.20	63.76
1969	82.10	90.50	56.20	62.10
1970	93.30	99.70	63.20	63.39
1971	95.79	110.26	70.57	64.00
1972	104.70	121.33	73.08	60.23
1973	122.35	131.34	83.44	63.53
1974	124.51	138.09	88.05	63.76
1975	139.74	150.56	94.88	63.02
1976	137.86	157.02	93.20	59.36
1977	156.63	170.54	104.56	61.31
1978	173.97	187.22	118.31	63.19
1979	199.24	208.93	132.06	63.21
1980	226.30	235.10	144.17	61.32
1981	246.90	250.14	159.68	63.84
1982	262.25	266.15	172.44	64.79
1983	287.57	288.35	181.16	62.83
1984	310.33	324.69	178.90	55.10
1985	353.25	369.21	189.24	51.26
1986	403.34	408.05	208.84	51.18
1987	530.52	562.68	170.92	30.38
1988	686.13	734.28	319.82	43.56
1989	760.60	813.62	367.40	45.16
1990	822.12	835.81	408.76	48.91
1991	934.79	919.40	423.79	46.09

Note: 1952-1986 figures include to state-owned units and supply and marketing cooperatives only.
Source: China Statistical Yearbook (various issues).

Table A3.15 Coal Industry: Inventory and Working Capital Requirements in Sample Enterprises
(1986-1991) (Y million)

	1986	1987	1988	1989	1990	1991
Inventory Requirements						
Seven prodution enterprises						
Total turnover (a)	3293.1	3693.1	4737.2	5838.9	5433.8	6372.3
Total inventory (b)	626.4	637.7	722.3	936.5	1099.1	1157
a/b (percent)	19.02	17.27	15.25	16.04	20.23	18.16
Seven distribution enterprises						
Total turnover (a)	1777.4	1937.5	2222.3	3031.6	3358.7	3042
Total inventory (b)	276.9	365.5	403.2	442.6	514.4	603
a/b (percent)	15.58	18.86	18.14	14.60	15.32	19.82
Working Capital Requirements						
Seven prodution enterprises						
Total turnover (a)	3293.1	3693.1	4737.2	5838.9	5433.8	6372.3
Total working capital (b)	490	575.5	502.4	499	679.1	796
a/b (percent)	14.88	15.58	10.61	8.55	12.50	12.49
Seven distribution enterprises						
Total turnover (a)	1777.4	1937.5	2222.3	3031.6	3358.7	3042
Total working capital (b)	108	116.2	129.2	137.4	147.2	161.7
a/b (percent)	6.08	6.00	5.81	4.53	4.38	5.32

Note: Inventory refers to Yearnend Balance of Imprest Working Capital. The numbersare larger than "raw materials + work in process + finished products."

Working Capital is the summation of State Current Fund, Enterprise Current Fund and Working Capital Loan.

The seven prodution enterprises in the survey are: Ping Dingshang Mining Bureau, Yunshou Mining Bureau, Huinan Mining Bureau, Jincheng Mining Bureau, Lu An Mining Bureau, Yanquan Mining Bureau and Huibei Mining Bureau.

The seven disribution enterprises are: Guangzhou Municipal Coal Company, Wuhan Municipal Coal Company, Dalian Municipal Fuel Company, Shenyang Municipal Fuel Company, Shanghai Municipal Fuel Company, Tianjin Municipal Coal Company (Headquarter), Beijing Municipal Coal Company (Headquarter).

Source: MME enterprise survey data.

Table A3.16 Cement Industry: Inventory and Working Capital Requirements in Sample Enterprises
(1986-1991) (Y million)

	1986	1987	1988	1989	1990	1991
Inventory Requirements						
Seven prodution enterprises						
Total turnover (a)	476.1	547.7	613.1	762.7	895.4	
Total inventory (b)	98.9	93.9	182.9	192.1	192	
a/b (percent)	20.77	17.14	29.83	25.19	21.44	
Seven user enterprises						
Total turnover (a)	223.38	240.99	267.44	274.13	292.51	312.3
Total inventory (b)	67.33	78.26	81.3	121.42	110.51	125.13
a/b (percent)	30.14	32.47	30.40	44.29	37.78	40.07
Working Capital Requirements						
Seven prodution enterprises						
Total turnover (a)	476.1	547.7	613.1	762.7	895.4	
Average working capital (b)	125.8	190.6	202.6	275.3	374.2	
a/b (percent)	26.42	34.80	33.05	36.10	41.79	
Seven user enterprises						
Total turnover (a)	223.38	240.99	267.44	274.13	292.51	312.3
Average working capital (b)	66.85	71.26	77.99	96.05	128.5	172.91
a/b (percent)	29.93	29.57	29.16	35.04	43.93	55.37

Note: Inventory refers to Yearnend Balance of Imprest Working Capital. The numbers are larger than "raw materials + work in process + finished products."
Average Balance of Working Capital refers to the average of year- beginning and year-end working capital average.
The seven prodution enterprises in the survey are: Jidong Cement Factory, Taiyuan Cement Factory, Mudanjiang Cement Factory, Shanghai Cement Factory, Ninguo Cement Factory, Luoyang Cement Factory and Liuzhou Cement Factory.
The seven user enterprises are factories under the Ministry of Railway.
Source: MME enterprise survey data.

Table A3.17 Steel Industry: Inventory and Working Capital Requirements in Sample Enterprises
(1986-1991) (Y million)

	1986	1987	1988	1989	1990	1991
Inventory Requirements						
Seven prodution enterprises						
Total turnover (a)	12294.2	15303.1	18478	21379.1	24627.2	33298.9
Total inventory (b)	3801.4	3934.7	17096.2	5935.3	7637.7	8188.4
a/b (percent)	30.92	25.71	92.52	27.76	31.01	24.59
Seven distribution enterprises						
Total turnover (a)	6610.4	7682.9	8794.8	10740.9	10005.5	10586.2
Total inventory (b)	1323.1	1592.2	1947.5	2460.1	2295.2	1986.6
a/b (percent)	20.02	20.72	22.14	22.90	22.94	18.77
Seven user enterprises						
Total turnover (a)	268.1	288.7	387.3	383.6	351.5	435.9
Total inventory (b)	167.2	183.7	228.4	273.3	284.8	352.7
a/b (percent)	62.36	63.63	58.97	71.25	81.02	80.91
Working Capital Requirements						
Seven prodution enterprises						
Total turnover (a)	12294.2	15303.1	18478	21379.1	24627.2	33298.9
Total working capital (b)	4013.9	4302.4	4827.4	6385.3	8580.7	9954.4
a/b (percent)	32.65	28.11	26.13	29.87	34.84	29.89
Seven distribution enterprises						
Total turnover (a)	6610.4	7682.9	8794.8	10740.9	10005.5	10586.2
Total inventory (b)	1326.7	1679	2233.7	2723	3037.4	2432.9
a/b (percent)	20.07	21.85	25.40	25.35	30.36	22.98
Seven user enterprises						
Total turnover (a)	268.1	288.7	387.3	383.6	351.5	435.9
Total working capital (b)	148.2	160.5	184.8	214.4	273.3	326
a/b (percent)	55.28	55.59	47.71	55.89	77.75	74.79

Note: Inventory refers to Yearnend Balance of Imprest Working Capital. The numbers are larger than "raw materials + work in process + finished products."

Average Balance of Working Capital refers to the average of year- beginning and year-end working capital average.

The seven prodution enterprises in the survey are: Anshang Steel and Iron Company, Capital Steel and Iron Company, Shanghai Baoshan Steel and Iron Company (Headquarter), Qingdao Steel and Iron Company (Headquarter), Jinan Steel and Iron Company (Headquarter), Taiyuan Steel and Iron Company, and Dalian Steel Factory.

The seven distribution enterprises are: Shanghai Metal Material Company (Headquarter), Liaoning Province Metal Material Company, Zhejiang Metal Material Company, Hubei Province Metal Material Company, Guangdong Province Metal Material Company, Beijing Municipal Metal Material Company, and Tianjin Municipal Metal Material Company.

The seven user enterprises are: Jinan Bearing Factory, Qingdao Tractor Factory, Hangzhou Bearing Factory, Hangzhou Fork Truck Factory, Nanjin Steam Turbine Factory, Shanghai Jinshan Agricultural Machinery Factory, and Shenyang No.3 Machine Tool Factory.

Source: MME enterprise survey data.

Table A3.18 Length of Transportation Routes by Province (1983-1991)
(kilometer)

	1983			1991			Annual Growth Rate 1983-91 (%)		
	Railways	Water-ways	Highways	Railways	Water-ways	Highways	Railways	Water-ways	Highways
All China	51603.9	108904	915079	53414.8	109703	1041136	0.43	0.09	1.63
Beijing	859.9		8058	1011.4		10259	2.05		3.06
Tianjin	398.3	458	3722	470.4	89	4068	2.10	-18.52	1.12
Hebei	2589.8	48	40187	2977.2	75	45464	1.76	5.74	1.55
Shanxi	2176.7	170	27887	2332	170	31040	0.87	0.00	1.35
Inner Mongolia	4796.8	602	36727	5081.5	602	43396	0.72	0.00	2.11
Liaoning	3533.4	508	29878	3562.6	508	40195	0.10	0.00	3.78
Jilin	3480.9	737	24114	3472.7	1114	27110	-0.03	5.30	1.47
Heilongjiang	5088.2		45295	4997.2		47188	-0.23		0.51
Shanghai	244.7	2474	2109	259	2100	3156	0.71	-2.03	5.17
Jiangsu	713.4	23528	21313	748.4	23670	24929	0.60	0.08	1.98
Zhejiang	830.9	10620	21399	871.3	10617	29218	0.60	0.00	3.97
Anhui	1543.0	5490	25934	1544.5	5528	30448	0.01	0.09	2.03
Fujian	1027.6	3875	34445	1015.2	3888	41745	-0.15	0.04	2.43
Jiangxi	1433.1	4937	30687	1581.6	4937	33222	1.24	0.00	1.00
Shandong	1671.8	1859	35722	2042.1	1861	41937	2.53	0.01	2.03
Henan	1973.2	1110	37196	2084.9	1110	44199	0.69	0.00	2.18
Hubei	1597.2	7859	44985	1690.1	7907	47661	0.71	0.08	0.72
Hunan	2300.5	10164	55483	2271.3	10110	57693	-0.16	-0.07	0.49
Guangdong	846.0	11090	63360	684.4	10857	55307	-2.61	-0.27	-1.68
Guangxi	1659.9	4519	32529	1665.8	4521	36660	0.04	0.01	1.51
Hainan				219	264	12922			
Sichuang	2875.6	8192	84624	2876.6	7904	98122	0.00	-0.45	1.87
Guizhou	1395.8	1661	27675	1419.4	1773	31588	0.21	0.82	1.67
Yunnan	1620.5	1010	46230	1625.2	1130	58123	0.04	1.41	2.90
Tibet			21551			21842			0.17
Shaanxi	1857.2	688	36832	1826.1	843	38193	-0.21	2.57	0.45
Gansu	2221.5	121	32365	2219.4	219	34776	-0.01	7.70	0.90
Qinghai	1097.5		15692	1094.7		16769	-0.03		0.83
Ningxia	428.4		6867	428.5	397	8200	0.00		2.24
Xinjiang	1342.1		22213	1342.5		25697	0.00		1.84
Non-regional Specific				7509					

Source: China Statistical Yearbook (various issues).

Table A3.19 Per Capita Length of Transportation Routes by Province (1983-1991)
(kilometer)

	1983			1991			Annual Growth Rate 1983-91 (%)		
	Railways	Water-ways	Highways	Railways	Water-ways	Highways	Railways	Water-ways	Highways
All China	50.3	106.3	892.8	46.1	94.7	898.9	-1.09	-1.43	0.09
Beijing	92.1	0.0	862.7	92.4	0.0	937.8	0.05		1.05
Tianjin	50.5	58.0	471.7	51.7	9.8	447.5	0.31	-19.95	-0.66
Hebei	47.8	0.9	741.5	47.9	1.2	730.9	0.02	3.93	-0.18
Shanxi	84.6	6.6	1084.3	79.3	5.8	1055.1	-0.82	-1.67	-0.34
Inner Mongolia	245.4	30.8	1878.6	232.7	27.6	1987.0	-0.66	-1.38	0.70
Liaoning	97.4	14.0	823.3	89.3	12.7	1007.4	-1.08	-1.18	2.55
Jilin	153.3	32.5	1062.3	138.4	44.4	1080.5	-1.27	3.99	0.21
Heilongjiang	153.9	0.0	1370.1	139.8	0.0	1319.9	-1.20		-0.46
Shanghai	20.5	207.2	176.6	19.3	156.7	235.5	-0.73	-3.43	3.66
Jiangsu	11.6	383.5	347.4	10.9	345.9	364.2	-0.77	-1.28	0.59
Zhejiang	21.0	268.0	540.0	20.7	252.7	695.3	-0.14	-0.73	3.21
Anhui	30.5	108.6	512.9	26.8	96.0	528.5	-1.61	-1.53	0.37
Fujian	38.9	146.8	1304.7	33.0	126.3	1355.8	-2.05	-1.86	0.48
Jiangxi	42.3	145.9	906.8	40.9	127.7	859.6	-0.43	-1.65	-0.67
Shandong	22.1	24.6	472.3	23.8	21.7	489.3	0.94	-1.54	0.45
Henan	26.0	14.6	490.0	23.8	12.7	504.4	-1.10	-1.78	0.36
Hubei	33.0	162.5	930.4	30.7	143.5	864.7	-0.93	-1.55	-0.91
Hunan	41.8	184.5	1007.1	36.6	162.8	929.2	-1.64	-1.55	-1.00
Guangdong	13.9	182.6	1043.0	10.6	168.6	858.9	-3.32	-0.99	-2.40
Guangxi	44.5	121.1	871.4	38.5	104.6	847.8	-1.78	-1.81	-0.34
Hainan				32.5	39.2	1917.2			
Sichuang	28.5	81.3	839.9	26.4	72.5	900.4	-0.97	-1.42	0.87
Guizhou	48.1	57.3	954.0	42.8	53.5	952.9	-1.45	-0.85	-0.01
Yunnan	48.8	30.4	1392.9	43.0	29.9	1536.8	-1.58	-0.23	1.24
Tibet	0.0	0.0	11166.3	0.0	0.0	9664.6			-1.79
Shaanxi	63.4	23.5	1256.6	54.3	25.1	1135.7	-1.91	0.82	-1.26
Gansu	111.7	6.1	1628.0	97.1	9.6	1521.9	-1.74	5.84	-0.84
Qinghai	279.3	0.0	3992.9	241.1	0.0	3693.6	-1.82		-0.97
Ningxia	107.6	0.0	1725.4	89.3	82.7	1708.3	-2.31		-0.12
Xinjiang	101.8	0.0	1685.4	86.3	0.0	1652.5	-2.04		-0.25
SD	64.48	93.53	1935.13	57.18	81.64	1644.04	-1.49	-1.69	-2.02
Mean	72.78	82.67	1463.15	64.87	74.25	1422.75	-1.43	-1.33	-0.35
COV	0.89	1.13	1.32	0.88	1.10	1.16	-0.06	-0.36	-1.67

Source: China Statistical Yearbook (various issues).

Table A3.20 Average Shipping Distance of Freight (1962-1991)
(kilometer)

Year	Railways	Highways	Waterways	Civil Aviation
1962	488	19	259	836
1965	549	19	291	924
1970	513	24	366	954
1976	478	28	736	1292
1978	485	32	873	1521
1979	500	20	1056	1539
1980	514	20	1184	1573
1981	530	21	1241	1809
1982	539	25	1236	1961
1983	559	19	1285	1983
1984	584	22	1351	2074
1985	636	31	1216	2128
1986	646	34	1042	2143
1987	673	37	1174	2183
1988	681	44	1128	2226
1989	686	46	1281	2226
1990	705	46	1447	2218
1991	718	46	1554	2234
Growth Rate/a	1.34	3.10	6.37	3.45

/a Annual average percentage, 1962-1971.
Source: China Statistical Yearbook (various issues).

Table A4.1 China's Foreign Trade in Non-Ferrous Metals (000 tonnes)

		1988	1989	1990	1991	1992
Copper						
	Imports					
Concentrates		173	178	242	310	340
Metal		84.3	70	42	114	379
	Exports					
Metal		93	28	43	42	55
Aluminum						
	Imports					
Alumina		159.5	298	582	686	800
Metal		75.4	175.5	71.7	43.7	230
	Exports					
Bauxite		364	575	680	542	860
Metal		159	20	83	96	88
Lead						
	Imports					
Metal		N/A	N/A	N/A	N/A	N/A
	Exports					
Metal		N/A	N/A	N/A	N/A	N/A
Zinc						
	Imports					
Metal		N/A	N/A	N/A	N/A	N/A
	Exports					
Metal		14	20	17	6	85
Tin						
	Imports					
Metal		N/A	N/A	N/A	N/A	N/A
	Exports					
Metal		11	10	10	15	30
Nickel						
	Imports					
Metal		N/A	N/A	N/A	N/A	N/A
	Exports					
Metal		N/A	N/A	N/A	N/A	N/A
Pig Iron						
	Imports					
Ore		10540	12592	14342	18549	25220
Metal		870	690	1310	360	150
	Exports					
Metal		2330	530	380	680	620

Note: N/A means that the data were not available from the Ministry of Materials and Equipment.
Source: Ministry of Materials and Equipment, Beijing.

Table A4.2 Trading Volume on the Shenzhen Metal Exchange
A. 1st - 20th January, 1993

Contract	Average Price (RMB/ton)	Volume (tons)	Value of Turnover (Mn RMB)	Number of Transactions
Copper	21,369	12,940	276.51	66
Aluminum	12,318	39,900	491.49	150
Lead	0	0	0.00	0
Zinc	7,650	200	1.53	1
Tin	45,000	60	2.70	1
Nickel	56,012	400	22.40	7
Manganese	18,700	40	0.75	1
Antimony	0	0	0.00	0
TOTAL			795.38	226

B. 1st - 28th February, 1993

Contract	Average Price (RMB/ton)	Volume (tons)	Value of Turnover (Mn RMB)	Number of Transactions
Copper	21,193	10,300	218.29	51
Aluminum	12,542	62,400	782.62	271
Lead	0	0	0.00	0
Zinc	8,300	200	1.66	1
Tin	48,142	140	6.74	3
Nickel	56,591	240	13.58	5
Manganese	0	0	0.00	0
Antimony	0	0	0.00	0
TOTAL			1,022.89	331

Source: Shenzhen Metal Exchange.

Table A4.3 Trading Volume on the Shanghai Metal Exchange
10th March 1993

Contract	Average Price (RMB/ton)	Volume (tonnes)	Value of Turnover (Million RMB)
No. 1 Copper	20,590	70,920	1,460.24
Other Copper	0	0	0.00
High Grade Aluminum	12,010	37,300	447.97
Other Aluminum	11,600	200	2.32
No. 1 Zinc	0	0	0.00
Other Zinc	0	0	0.00
No. 1 Tin	49,500	20	0.99
Other Tin	0	0	0.00
Lead	0	0	0.00
Nickel	55,560	1,700	94.45
Pig Iron	0	0	0.00
TOTAL			2,005.97

Source: Shanghai Metal Exchange.

Table A5.1a Size Distribution of Industry by Number of Employees and Number of Firms (1991)

	Number of Firms (Nos)										Percentage of Firms				
	Total	Above 10000	5000-10000	3000-5000	1000-3000	500-1000	100-500	50-100	10-50	below 10	Total	Above 3000	1000-3000	100-1000	Below 100
Total	418,869	356	697	1,144	9,186	16,675	110,795	76,113	161,488	42,406	100.0	0.5	2.2	30.4	66.8
Timber Processing	10,782	3	12	23	68	129	1,318	1,300	5,680	2,249	100.0	0.4	0.6	13.4	85.6
Food	39,319	0	3	24	306	704	7,397	6,422	16,796	7,667	100.0	0.1	0.8	20.6	78.5
Tobacoo	329	0	2	15	91	64	81	32	42	2	100.0	5.2	27.7	44.1	23.1
Textile	24,596	15	163	254	1,699	2,503	9,546	4,370	5,379	667	100.0	1.8	6.9	49.0	42.3
Clothing	17,499	0	3	10	152	603	5,897	3,673	5,900	2,261	100.0	0.1	0.9	37.1	67.6
Leather	8,308	0	1	5	80	301	2,459	1,664	3,262	536	100.0	0.1	1.0	33.2	65.7
Building Materials	52,179	5	18	48	705	1,548	16,965	10,736	19,060	3,094	100.0	0.1	1.4	35.5	63.0
Paper Making	10,875	0	11	23	165	428	3,021	2,578	4,151	498	100.0	0.3	1.5	31.7	66.5
Chemical Industry	19,932	15	29	78	645	1,482	4,730	3,441	8,136	1,376	100.0	0.6	3.2	31.2	65.0
Pharmaceuticals	3,305	0	5	15	133	310	1,457	610	657	119	100.0	0.6	4.0	53.5	41.9
Chemical Fibres	616	4	10	12	71	96	196	76	137	14	100.0	4.2	11.5	47.4	36.9
Rubber	3,818	0	8	15	188	223	1,211	738	1,268	167	100.0	0.6	4.9	37.6	56.9
Plastic	14,554	0	2	6	89	305	3,514	3,032	6,585	1,021	100.0	0.1	0.6	26.2	73.1
Ferrous Metals	1,449	7	9	8	59	49	252	131	356	578	100.0	1.7	4.1	20.8	73.5
Machine Building/a	42,496	29	122	190	1,493	2,225	12,845	7,430	14,398	0	100.0	0.8	3.5	35.5	51.4
Transport Equipment	11,203	27	59	64	385	579	3,008	2,219	4,216	646	100.0	1.3	3.4	32.0	63.2
Electric Machinery	14,763	4	23	34	397	725	4,398	2,820	5,503	859	100.0	0.4	2.7	34.7	62.2
Electronics&Telecom	4,919	5	16	35	327	513	1,881	852	1,127	163	100.0	1.1	6.6	48.7	43.5

/a   Percentage data do not add up to 100 for this sector.
Note: Data in the table are of independent accounting enterprises at and above township level.
Source: China Industrial Statistical Yearbook 1992.

Table A5.1b Size Distribution of Industry by Number of Employees and Persons Employed (1991)

	Number of Persons Employed (in 10 thousand)										Percentage of Persons Employed				
	Total	Above 10000	5000-10000	3000-5000	1000-3000	500-1000	100-500	50-100	10-50	Below 10	Total	Above 3000	1000-3000	100-1000	Below 100
Total	7,798	961	476	428	1,442	1,144	2,374	536	413	24	100.0	23.9	18.5	45.1	12.5
Timber Processing	88	4	8	8	11	9	25	9	13	1	100.0	22.5	12.3	38.8	26.3
Food	342	0	2	8	47	48	148	45	40	4	100.0	2.9	13.7	57.1	26.2
Tobacco	30	0	1	6	16	5	2	0	0	0	100.0	22.7	53.7	22.4	1.2
Textile	938	19	111	95	268	174	224	31	15	0	100.0	24.0	28.5	42.5	5.0
Clothing	236	0	2	4	22	39	127	26	16	1	100.0	2.3	9.2	70.4	18.1
Leather	107	1	2	12	20	53	12	9	0	88	100.0	13.3	18.7	59.8	90.5
Building Materials	717	7	12	18	109	106	340	76	48	2	100.0	5.1	15.2	62.1	17.7
Paper Making	164	0	8	8	24	29	65	18	12	0	100.0	9.8	14.7	57.1	18.4
Chemical Industry	433	31	20	28	97	103	108	24	21	1	100.0	18.5	22.5	48.5	10.5
Pharmaceuticals	93	0	4	5	21	22	35	4	2	0	100.0	10.2	22.3	60.6	6.9
Chemical Fibres	45	11	6	4	11	6	5	1	0	0	100.0	47.2	25.2	25.4	2.1
Rubber	93	0	5	5	31	16	27	5	3	0	100.0	11.0	33.6	46.0	9.4
Plastic	148	0	1	2	12	20	73	21	17	1	100.0	2.4	8.3	62.8	26.5
Ferrous Metals	317	185	21	20	37	18	29	5	2	0	100.0	71.2	11.7	15.0	2.2
Machine Building	973	45	85	72	239	154	286	53	37	0	100.0	20.7	24.6	45.2	9.3
Transport Equipment	315	54	40	25	63	40	66	16	11	0	100.0	37.7	20.0	33.6	8.7
Electric Machinery	276	5	15	13	62	49	97	20	14	1	100.0	12.0	22.4	53.1	12.6
Electronics&Telecom	173	6	11	13	52	36	45	6	3	0	100.0	17.5	30.1	47.0	5.4

Note: Data in the table are of independent accounting enterprises at and above township level.

Source: China Industrial Statistical Yearbook 1992.

Table A5.1c Size Distribution of Industry by Number of Employees and Gross Output Value (1991)

	Total Output Value (100 million Y)										Total Output Value (in percentage)				
	Total	Above 10000	5000-10000	3000-5000	1000-3000	500-1000	100-500	50-100	10-50	Below 10	Total	Above 3000	1000-3000	100-1000	Below 100
Total	22,089	3,206	1,562	1,504	4,822	3,238	5,676	1,146	823	112	100.0	28.4	21.8	40.4	9.4
Timber Processing	122	1	3	7	17	17	41	13	20	3	100.0	8.9	14.0	47.4	29.7
Food	1,473	0	7	38	216	201	695	174	130	12	100.0	3.1	14.7	60.8	21.5
Tobacoo	547	0	44	168	275	41	17	2	0	0	100.0	38.7	50.3	10.6	0.3
Textile	2,533	40	282	242	733	446	651	94	41	3	100.0	22.3	28.9	43.3	5.5
Clothing	523	0	3	13	66	111	260	42	24	3	100.0	3.1	12.6	71.0	13.3
Leather	253	0	1	4	32	53	126	21	15	1	100.0	2.1	12.7	70.7	14.6
Building Materials	1,055	13	23	35	213	188	430	85	65	4	100.0	6.8	20.2	58.5	14.6
Paper Making	423	0	35	27	73	86	148	34	20	1	100.0	14.6	17.3	55.1	13.0
Chemical Industry	1,625	163	81	136	380	353	366	78	59	3	100.0	23.3	23.4	44.3	8.6
Pharmaceuticals	454	0	25	23	109	124	149	17	6	1	100.0	10.7	24.1	60.0	5.1
Chemical Fibres	325	101	39	20	76	56	29	3	2	0	100.0	49.0	23.4	26.1	1.5
Rubber	317	0	37	29	127	49	60	9	6	0	100.0	20.7	40.1	34.4	4.8
Plastic	439	0	0	4	37	79	222	56	39	3	100.0	1.1	8.3	68.4	22.2
Ferrous Metals	1,539	961	114	89	172	74	107	16	7	0	100.0	75.6	11.2	11.7	1.5
Machine Building	1,995	107	213	157	522	307	528	92	64	0	100.0	23.9	26.2	41.8	7.8
Transport Equipment	976	219	140	75	257	104	133	27	19	1	100.0	44.5	26.3	24.3	4.9
Electric Machinery	917	18	46	46	281	178	264	50	33	2	100.0	12.0	30.6	48.1	9.2
Electronics&Telecom	765	28	77	98	264	127	140	21	10	1	100.0	26.5	34.5	34.9	4.1

Note: Data in the table are of independent accounting enterprises at and above township level.
Source: China Industrial Statistical Yearbook 1992.

Table A5.2a Size Distribution of Industry by Gross Value of Industrial Output and Number of Firms (1991)

	Number of Firms (Nos)										Number of Firms (in percentage)				
	Total	Above Y100m	Y50m - Y100m	Y30m - Y50m	Y10m - Y30m	Y5m - Y10m	Y1m - Y5m	Y0.5m - Y1m	Y500,000 - Y100,000	Below 100,000	Total	Above Y30m	Y10m - Y30m	Y1m - Y10m	Below Y1m
Total	418,869	2,648	3,526	5,187	24,308	27,064	106,750	62,577	124,225	62,584	100.0	2.7	5.8	31.9	9.5
Timber Processing	10,782	6	24	26	126	235	1,482	1,467	4,530	2,886	100.0	0.5	1.2	15.9	82.4
Food	39,319	94	284	503	2,609	2,791	9,333	5,271	11,025	7,409	100.0	2.2	6.6	30.8	60.3
Tobacoo	329	110	36	15	35	27	44	25	31	6	100.0	48.9	10.6	21.6	18.8
Textile	24,596	446	598	872	601	3,100	7,695	2,848	3,925	1,511	100.0	7.8	2.4	43.9	33.7
Clothing	17,499	20	67	144	977	1,254	4,825	2,597	5,058	2,557	100.0	1.3	5.6	34.7	58.4
Leather	8,308	8	45	82	470	519	2,226	1,292	2,722	944	100.0	1.6	5.7	33.0	59.7
Building Materials	52,179	59	117	242	1,545	2,189	12,519	10,563	18,224	6,721	100.0	0.8	3.0	28.2	68.1
Paper Making	10,875	38	62	132	631	740	3,297	1,901	3,005	1,069	100.0	2.1	5.8	37.1	54.9
Chemical Industry	19,932	233	298	474	2,132	1,770	5,493	2,757	4,879	1,896	100.0	5.0	10.7	36.4	47.8
Pharmaceuticals	3,306	64	140	174	581	524	992	288	388	155	100.0	11.4	17.6	45.9	25.1
Chemical Fibres	616	70	67	40	101	71	136	45	70	16	100.0	28.7	16.4	33.6	21.3
Rubber	3,818	51	83	75	316	299	1,163	559	956	316	100.0	5.5	8.3	38.3	48.0
Plastic	14,554	17	76	132	744	958	4,146	2,337	4,492	1,652	100.0	1.5	5.1	35.1	58.3
Ferrous Metals	3,432	186	104	137	497	420	1,178	342	390	178	100.0	12.4	14.5	46.6	26.5
Machine Building	42,496	239	338	549	2,774	3,302	12,660	6,350	11,148	5,136	100.0	2.6	6.5	37.6	53.3
Transport Equipment	11,203	128	152	169	710	690	3,128	1,882	3,289	1,053	100.0	4.0	6.3	34.1	55.6
Electric Machinery	14,763	137	192	244	1,090	1,272	4,621	2,181	3,798	1,228	100.0	3.9	7.4	39.9	48.8
Electronics&Telecom	4,919	134	131	171	584	563	1,565	632	873	266	100.0	8.9	11.9	43.3	36.0

Note: Data in the table are of independent accounting enterprises at and above township level.
Source: China Industrial Statistical Yearbook 1992.

Table A5.2b Size Distribution of Industry by Gross Value of Industrial Output and Number of Employees (1992)

	Number of Employees (in 10 thousand)										Number of Employees (in percentage)				
	Total	Above Y100m	Y50m-Y100m	30m-Y50m	Y10m-Y30m	Y5m-Y10m	Y1m-Y5m	Y0.5m-Y1m	Y100,000-Y500,000	Below 100,000	Total	Above Y30m	Y10m-Y30m	Y1m-Y10m	Below Y1m
Total	7,798	1,605	625	576	1,442	893	1,635	448	461	112	100.0	36.0	18.5	32.4	13.1
Timber Processing	88	2	4	6	16	11	24	9	13	4	100.0	13.0	17.5	39.6	29.8
Food	342	19	27	30	78	47	82	23	27	8	100.0	22.4	22.7	37.8	17.1
Tobacoo	30	22	3	1	2	1	1	0	0	0	100.0	87.7	5.1	6.0	1.2
Textile	938	188	115	101	233	115	139	24	20	5	100.0	43.0	24.9	27.1	5.1
Clothing	236	6	7	11	47	37	78	22	23	5	100.0	10.1	19.9	49.0	21.0
Leather	107	2	5	5	22	16	34	9	11	2	100.0	11.9	20.3	47.1	20.6
Building Materials	717	26	23	33	112	89	235	100	85	13	100.0	11.4	15.6	45.3	27.7
Paper Making	164	14	9	13	35	23	44	12	12	2	100.0	21.7	21.5	41.0	15.8
Chemical Industry	433	87	44	42	119	48	60	14	14	4	100.0	39.9	27.5	25.0	7.6
Pharmaceuticals	93	15	15	12	24	12	12	2	1	0	100.0	45.1	25.8	25.3	3.8
Chemical Fibres	45	27	7	3	4	2	2	0	0	0	100.0	82.8	9.0	7.1	1.1
Rubber	93	16	13	8	20	10	18	4	3	1	100.0	40.2	21.6	29.7	8.5
Plastic	148	2	6	9	27	24	48	14	15	3	100.0	11.9	18.0	48.9	21.3
Ferrous Metals	317	230	16	16	25	11	15	2	2	1	100.0	82.5	7.8	8.2	1.5
Machine Building	973	134	89	88	211	134	215	45	39	7	100.0	32.0	21.7	35.9	9.4
Transport Equipment	315	97	35	25	54	28	50	13	12	2	100.0	49.8	17.0	24.7	8.4
Electric Machinery	276	39	27	22	59	37	64	14	13	2	100.0	31.6	21.4	36.4	10.5
Electronics&Telecom	173	35	19	16	37	22	32	6	4	1	100.0	40.8	21.5	31.7	6.1

Note: Data in the table are of independent accounting enterprises at and above township level.
Source: China Industrial Statistical Yearbook 1992.

Table A5.2c Size Distribution of Industry by Gross Value of Industrial Output and Output Value (1992)

	Total Output Value (100 million Y)										Total Output Value (in percentage)				
	Total	above Y100m	Y50m - Y100m	Y30m - Y50m	Y10m - Y30m	Y5m - Y10m	Y1m - Y5m	Y0.5m - Y1m	Y100,000 - Y500,000	Below 100,000	Total	Above Y30m	Y10m - Y30m	Y1m - Y10m	Below Y1m
Total	22,089	8,530	2,418	1,981	4,040	1,897	2,426	444	324	29	100.0	58.5	18.3	19.6	3.6
Timber Processing	122	8	15	10	19	16	31	10	11	1	100.0	27.0	15.8	38.8	18.4
Food	1,473	163	193	193	439	197	220	37	28	3	100.0	37.3	29.8	28.3	4.7
Tobacoo	547	508	24	6	6	2	1	0	0	0	100.0	98.2	1.2	0.6	0.0
Textile	2,533	733	410	335	613	221	190	21	11	1	100.0	58.3	24.2	16.2	1.3
Clothing	523	34	45	54	159	88	110	19	14	1	100.0	25.4	30.5	37.8	6.3
Leather	253	11	31	31	77	36	51	9	7	0	100.0	28.7	30.4	34.4	6.5
Building Materials	1,055	97	78	91	248	153	262	75	49	3	100.0	25.1	23.5	39.3	12.1
Paper Making	423	78	44	50	105	51	74	14	8	0	100.0	40.4	24.7	29.6	5.3
Chemical Industry	1,625	593	202	179	363	126	128	20	13	1	100.0	59.9	22.3	15.7	2.1
Pharmaceuticals	454	124	99	67	97	38	25	2	1	0	100.0	64.0	21.4	13.9	0.7
Chemical Fibres	325	235	47	16	19	5	3	0	0	0	100.0	91.5	5.8	2.6	0.2
Rubber	317	121	57	30	55	21	26	4	3	0	100.0	65.7	17.3	14.9	2.1
Plastic	439	26	51	51	120	67	95	17	12	1	100.0	29.0	27.3	37.0	6.7
Ferrous Metals	1,539	1,267	70	53	85	29	31	2	1	0	100.0	90.3	5.5	3.9	0.2
Machine Building	1,995	508	232	209	449	229	291	45	30	2	100.0	47.6	22.5	26.1	3.9
Transport Equipment	976	542	107	65	120	48	70	13	9	1	100.0	73.2	12.3	12.1	2.3
Electric Machinery	917	288	134	92	181	90	106	15	10	1	100.0	56.1	19.8	21.3	2.9
Electronics&Telecom	765	423	91	66	99	40	39	5	2	0	100.0	75.8	12.9	10.3	0.9

Note: Data in the table are of independent accounting enterprises at and above township level.
Source: China Industrial Statistical Yearbook 1992.

Distributors of World Bank Publications

ARGENTINA
Carlos Hirsch, SRL
Galeria Guemes
Florida 165, 4th Floor-Ofc. 453/465
1333 Buenos Aires

Oficina del Libro Internacional
Alberti 40
1082 Buenos Aires

**AUSTRALIA, PAPUA NEW GUINEA,
FIJI, SOLOMON ISLANDS,
VANUATU, AND WESTERN SAMOA**
D.A. Information Services
648 Whitehorse Road
Mitcham 3132
Victoria

AUSTRIA
Gerold and Co.
Graben 31
A-1011 Wien

BANGLADESH
Micro Industries Development
   Assistance Society (MIDAS)
House 5, Road 16
Dhanmondi R/Area
Dhaka 1209

BELGIUM
Jean De Lannoy
Av. du Roi 202
1060 Brussels

BRAZIL
Publicacoes Tecnicas Internacionais Ltda.
Rua Peixoto Gomide, 209
01409 Sao Paulo, SP

CANADA
Le Diffuseur
151A Boul. de Mortagne
Boucherville, Québec
J4B 5E6

Renouf Publishing Co.
1294 Algoma Road
Ottawa, Ontario
K1B 3W8

CHINA
China Financial & Economic
   Publishing House
8, Da Fo Si Dong Jie
Beijing

COLOMBIA
Infoenlace Ltda.
Apartado Aereo 34270
Bogota D.E.

COTE D'IVOIRE
Centre d'Edition et de Diffusion
   Africaines (CEDA)
04 B.P. 541
Abidjan 04 Plateau

CYPRUS
Center of Applied Research
Cyprus College
6, Diogenes Street, Engomi
P.O. Box 2006
Nicosia

DENMARK
SamfundsLitteratur
Rosenoerns Allé 11
DK-1970 Frederiksberg C

DOMINICAN REPUBLIC
Editora Taller, C. por A.
Restauración e Isabel la Católica 309
Apartado de Correos 2190 Z-1
Santo Domingo

EGYPT, ARAB REPUBLIC OF
Al Ahram
Al Galaa Street
Cairo

The Middle East Observer
41, Sherif Street
Cairo

FINLAND
Akateeminen Kirjakauppa
P.O. Box 128
SF-00101 Helsinki 10

FRANCE
World Bank Publications
66, avenue d'Iéna
75116 Paris

GERMANY
UNO-Verlag
Poppelsdorfer Allee 55
53115 Bonn

GREECE
Papasotiriou S.A.
35, Stournara Str.
106 82 Athens

HONG KONG, MACAO
Asia 2000 Ltd.
46-48 Wyndham Street
Winning Centre
7th Floor
Central Hong Kong

HUNGARY
Foundation for Market Economy
Dombovari Ut 17-19
H-1117 Budapest

INDIA
Allied Publishers Private Ltd.
751 Mount Road
Madras - 600 002

INDONESIA
Pt. Indira Limited
Jalan Borobudur 20
P.O. Box 181
Jakarta 10320

IRAN
Kowkab Publishers
P.O. Box 19575-511
Tehran

IRELAND
Government Supplies Agency
4-5 Harcourt Road
Dublin 2

ISRAEL
Yozmot Literature Ltd.
P.O. Box 56055
Tel Aviv 61560

ITALY
Licosa Commissionaria Sansoni SPA
Via Duca Di Calabria, 1/1
Casella Postale 552
50125 Firenze

JAMAICA
Ian Randle Publishers Ltd.
206 Old Hope Road
Kingston 6

JAPAN
Eastern Book Service
Hongo 3-Chome, Bunkyo-ku 113
Tokyo

KENYA
Africa Book Service (E.A.) Ltd.
Quaran House, Mfangano Street
P.O. Box 45245
Nairobi

KOREA, REPUBLIC OF
Pan Korea Book Corporation
P.O. Box 101, Kwangwhamun
Seoul

Korean Stock Book Centre
P.O. Box 34
Yeoeido
Seoul

MALAYSIA
University of Malaya Cooperative
   Bookshop, Limited
P.O. Box 1127, Jalan Pantai Baru
59700 Kuala Lumpur

MEXICO
INFOTEC
Apartado Postal 22-860
14060 Tlalpan, Mexico D.F.

NETHERLANDS
De Lindeboom/InOr-Publikaties
P.O. Box 202
7480 AE Haaksbergen

NEW ZEALAND
EBSCO NZ Ltd.
Private Mail Bag 99914
New Market
Auckland

NIGERIA
University Press Limited
Three Crowns Building Jericho
Private Mail Bag 5095
Ibadan

NORWAY
Narvesen Information Center
Book Department
P.O. Box 6125 Etterstad
N-0602 Oslo 6

PAKISTAN
Mirza Book Agency
65, Shahrah-e-Quaid-e-Azam
P.O. Box No. 729
Lahore 54000

PERU
Editorial Desarrollo SA
Apartado 3824
Lima 1

PHILIPPINES
International Book Center
Suite 1703, Cityland 10
Condominium Tower 1
Ayala Avenue, H.V. dela
   Costa Extension
Makati, Metro Manila

POLAND
International Publishing Service
Ul. Piekna 31/37
00-677 Warszawa

For subscription orders:
IPS Journals
Ul. Okrezna 3
02-916 Warszawa

PORTUGAL
Livraria Portugal
Rua Do Carmo 70-74
1200 Lisbon

SAUDI ARABIA, QATAR
Jarir Book Store
P.O. Box 3196
Riyadh 11471

**SINGAPORE, TAIWAN,
MYANMAR,BRUNEI**
Gower Asia Pacific Pte Ltd.
Golden Wheel Building
41, Kallang Pudding, #04-03
Singapore 1334

SOUTH AFRICA, BOTSWANA
For single titles:
Oxford University Press
   Southern Africa
P.O. Box 1141
Cape Town 8000

For subscription orders:
International Subscription Service
P.O. Box 41095
Craighall
Johannesburg 2024

SPAIN
Mundi-Prensa Libros, S.A.
Castello 37
28001 Madrid

Librería Internacional AEDOS
Consell de Cent, 391
08009 Barcelona

SRI LANKA AND THE MALDIVES
Lake House Bookshop
P.O. Box 244
100, Sir Chittampalam A.
   Gardiner Mawatha
Colombo 2

SWEDEN
For single titles:
Fritzes Fackboksforetaget
Regeringsgatan 12, Box 16356
S-103 27 Stockholm

For subscription orders:
Wennergren-Williams AB
P. O. Box 1305
S-171 25 Solna

SWITZERLAND
For single titles:
Librairie Payot
Case postale 3212
CH 1002 Lausanne

For subscription orders:
Librairie Payot
Service des Abonnements
Case postale 3312
CH 1002 Lausanne

THAILAND
Central Department Store
306 Silom Road
Bangkok

TRINIDAD & TOBAGO
Systematics Studies Unit
#9 Watts Street
Curepe
Trinidad, West Indies

UNITED KINGDOM
Microinfo Ltd.
P.O. Box 3
Alton, Hampshire GU34 2PG
England

ZIMBABWE
Longman Zimbabwe (Pvt.) Ltd.
Tourle Road, Ardbennie
P.O. Box ST 125
Southerton
Harare

R